DOCTORS IN HOSPITALS

DOCTORS IN HOSPITALS

Medical Staff Organization and Hospital Performance

MILTON I. ROEMER
AND
JAY W. FRIEDMAN

THE JOHNS HOPKINS PRESS

BALTIMORE AND LONDON

The Johns Hopkins Press, Baltimore, Maryland 21218
The Johns Hopkins Press Ltd., London

Library of Congress Catalog Card Number 79-109096

International Standard Book Number 0–8018–1239–9

CONTENTS

v

PREFACE

THE ISSUE EXPLORED in this book is the relationship of the pattern of medical staff organization in general hospitals to the performance of those hospitals. The relevance of this question to the larger problems of health service organization in society has become increasingly evident. In 1965 the American Hospital Association commented in its official journal that during recent decades "the general hospital has made many contributions to health care, but perhaps the most significant has been the formulation of the concept of the self-disciplining organized medical staff."[1]

The degree of that "self-disciplining" in different hospitals, however, is highly variable. In their simplest classification, medical staffs have long been described as "open" or "closed,"[2] but the realities are much more complex. The relationships of the staffing style to the hospital's program of service are marked by still greater complexities and subtleties.

A half century ago Doctor Winford H. Smith, who was later identified with the origins of the hospital accreditation movement, wrote of "hospital efficiency" and the factors responsible for it. Among other things, he said:

The (medical) staff organization is no mean factor in hospital efficiency, and much can be said on the subject. First, I wish to say that no member of the staff should be eligible to the office of trustee. With regard to appointments to the staff, it cannot be too strongly emphasized that such appointments should be made on merit alone—the merit of achievement, of recognized ability, the best man for the place. Appointment should not depend on local residence, political influence, social standing, or length of service, which may have been and often is a service

[1] Editorial Notes, *Hospitals* (1 April 1965): 37.
[2] Malcom T. MacEachern, *Hospital Organization and Management* (Revised third edition; Berwyn, Illinois: Physicians' Record Company, 1962), pp. 169–70.

of questionable merit. One thing more—the staff member who fails to recognize the necessity of co-operation, of teamwork, who has an eye only to self-advancement, is a stumbling block, no matter what his ability as an individual performer.[3]

In this research we speak of "hospital performance" rather than "efficiency," and we attempt to explore, with empirical observations, the influence on it of medical staff organization, which Doctor Smith and others since have considered to be "no mean factor." In more recent days it has become popular to speak of "hospital effectiveness," including in that concept "the accessibility of health services of all kinds, the suitability of services to needs, the quality of the services, and the economy with which the services are delivered to the population."[4] While one can distinguish differences in meaning between "efficiency," "effectiveness," and our use of "performance," the common element is concern for what the hospital as a social organization *does.*

We hypothesize in this study that, in general, higher levels of hospital efficiency, effectiveness, or performance are achieved in conjunction with more firmly disciplined medical staff organization. Exploration of this hypothesis required analysis of both "performance" and "medical staff organization" into their many components. As in any scientific investigation, we made every effort to see that our hypothesis did not bias our observations. It is not easy to achieve complete objectivity in social science research, and we hope we have succeeded.

Preliminary work on this study began in 1959, while one of us (MIR) was at Cornell University, so that the effort spans a decade. It started with some pilot observations in eight general hospitals of upstate New York, and the first findings were published in 1960.[5] In June 1961 a research grant was received from the United States Public Health Service to support the investigation more systematically, and this grant was transferred to the University of California (where the senior author moved) in February 1962. In April 1964 a second research grant was received to proceed with the work until 1967. From July of that year to mid-1968, support was received from a third Public Health Service research grant, designed to facilitate comparative studies in a variety of "patterns of medical care organization."

[3] Winford H. Smith, "What Is Meant by Hospital Efficiency and Some of the Factors Which Are Often Responsible for Lack of Efficiency," *Medical Record*, 89:874–76 (13 May 1916).

[4] Secretary's Advisory Committee on Hospital Effectiveness, *Report* (Washington: U.S. Department of Health, Education, and Welfare, 1968), p. 35.

[5] Milton I. Roemer and Max Shain, "Contractual Physicians in General Hospitals: A Pilot Study," *Hospitals* (1 May 1960): 38–43.

Over these years it was inevitable that some of our conceptions of the problem in this research and our methodology for approaching it should change. As new observations were accumulated, fresh insights were gained on previous observations. Early drafts, therefore, had to be rewritten, and the text presented here has been produced mainly in 1969.

The actual findings, of course, apply to the time they were collected. This means that much of the data, especially quantitative information, is now out of date. The disadvantages of this time lapse are reduced by the fact that we are not attempting to define the current scene with accuracy, but rather to explore a set of relationships and principles. We believe that organizational dynamics in hospital affairs, found to apply ten or eight or four years ago, are probably still generally valid today.

The limitations of place may be more serious than those of time. The greater part of the research was conducted in California, where hospitals —like anything else—cannot be assumed to be typical of the whole nation. On the other hand, much data were also collected from a nationwide sample of hospitals, observations were made in European and other countries, and a great deal of information was gathered from the general literature, which reports on research made everywhere. More important, the concepts applied and the kinds of relationship explored are on a level sufficiently generalized, we trust, to be applicable anywhere in the United States. California, being one of the newest states in the nation, free-wheeling and rapid in its social development, may have attributes that give a glimpse of the future for older sections. Observers from other countries can tell best if the principles found here have wider relevance.

The names of hospitals in the "case-study" central core of this research are all fictitious. Our aim was to collect the data in confidence and to underscore the point that our interest was not in criticizing any particular institution. We hope the camouflage has been successful, but if not we trust that any unintended disclosure of the identity of any hospital or person will cause no harm. We hope that the lessons to be learned will be worth the price of any public revelation of a hospital's inner workings.

The detailed methodology of the study is explained in the Appendix. In relation to the hypothesis offered above, the reader may be struck with its many inadequacies. To explore the influence of medical staff organization on hospital performance, one can speculate on an ideal research design. One would select several sets of hospitals which were identical in all respects, except for their patterns of medical staff organization. In size, in sponsorship, in patient-composition, in social environment, in all attributes these sets of hospitals would be perfectly matched—differing only in their style of medical staffing. Then, to determine their performance one would collect information on the end-results of the care their patients received—their rates of recovery, reduction of disability, or mortality. This would apply to both in-patients and out-patients. Equivalent measurements would be applied to the final outcomes of other hospital functions—test-scores of learning to evaluate the educational programs, new discoveries for research evaluation, and so on.

Unfortunately, as we will see, reality did not permit so simple and elegant a research design. The constraints of money, the circumstances of our social laboratory, and our own personal limitations compelled us to make many compromises. Despite these deficiencies we hope that our conclusions have sufficient merit to induce other investigators to take up where we left off and to do better. We are sure that others can and will do better.

Our findings in this research are presented in eleven chapters. Chapter I sets the stage of current issues in medical care, with consideration of the controversies between doctors and hospitals; the many social determinants of hospital programs, aside from medical staff organization, are discussed, to clarify our view of medical staffing as an intervening variable—one of many forces at play. We step back in chapter II to examine the history of the physician's role in hospitals, in Europe and elsewhere, leading up to current American developments. Following the time dimension, we explore the space axis in chapter III, and review medical staff patterns in the hospitals of other nations.

Chapter IV takes a nationwide view in the United States, presenting the findings of a statistical survey of "contractual physicians" in hospitals and the relationship of their level of engagement to several indicators of hospital performance. In chapter V we offer a general typology for analyzing medical staff organization (MSO), along with a scoring system to measure the degree of structuring. In chapter VI we apply this typology to a hospital at the mid-point of the range of medical staff structuring. This case study of Pebble City Community Hospital is relatively complete, describing also the program of in-patient care, the various hospital functions constituting a wider community role, and then discussing the apparent relationships between the medical staff organization of the hospital and its over-all program of services.

Similar case-studies were made of nine other general hospitals along the full range of medical staff structuring. In chapter VII, capsule sketches are presented of four of these at the less-structured end of the range and one at about the same point as the Pebble City Hospital. Then, for the four more highly structured hospitals, relatively detailed accounts are given of their medical staff patterns, with only brief comments on their relationships to the hospital programs.

Chapter VIII analyzes "horizontally" across the series of ten hospitals the range of detailed characteristics of the different types of medical staff. The same sort of horizontal analysis is offered in chapter IX on the many features of in-patient care, considering how each feature tends to be related to the MSO pattern. Chapter X explores corresponding relationships between MSO patterns and the diverse activities by which hospitals fulfill a wider community role. In the final chapter, we summarize the book, consider the implications of our findings with respect to several current issues in the medical care world, and make estimates—with some recommendations—about trends and future prospects.

Collection of the information on which this study was based depended on the assistance and co-operation of many persons. Our first appreciation goes to the administrators and staffs of the ten California hospitals whose co-operation, despite many pressures, made possible the "anthropological" case-studies that constitute the central pillar of this research. We are grateful also to the 48 state hospital associations and over 2,400 general hospitals throughout the United States that co-operated in our survey of contractual physicians. The American Hospital Association was most helpful in furnishing us with abundant supplementary data on all these hospitals.

Research assistance in the initial collection of data from the case-study hospitals was provided by Roland C. Bower and Lynn Stegmaier. In the pilot study of contractual physicians in New York State, Max Shain was an invaluable colleague. On coding, editing, and analyzing the nationwide data on contractual physicians, assistance was rendered by Judith Aronson, Sandra Hudson, and Patricia Bennett. Computer programming for analyzing these data was done by John E. Roemer, and assistance on certain tabulations was given by Joel Kovner. Major assistance in the final preparation of research instruments and the collection of data from the ten study hospitals was provided by Tess Weiner. From Beatrice Dinerman, assistance was received in the "horizontal" analyses of these data, as well as in the assemblage of much of the historical material; the latter was supplemented by painstaking search of early twentieth-century sources by Shirley Rich. To Ruth Roemer goes our appreciation for valiant assistance in the task of editorial revision. For tireless typing and re-typing we are grateful to Marge Peppers and Annette Lefcourt. To our colleagues in the Division of Medical Care Organization of the University of California, Los Angeles, School of Public Health go our thanks for various criticisms and suggestions made at research conferences along the way.

As noted earlier, this research was supported by grants from the U.S.

Public Health Service—initially grant number CH 00046 (01 to 05) and later by grant number CH 00102. For part of the international hospital study, support, in the form of a consultation appointment, was received from the World Health Organization.

Finally, for fallacies of fact or judgment the authors must take responsibility. If any credit is deserved, it is not for conducting this study and reporting it—which has drawn upon the efforts of so many people— but for anticipating ten years ago that the subject was worth exploring. Over the decade in which this work was done, questions on the organization of health services have become all the more pressing. With rising demands for medical care, rising costs, rising quality expectations, the concern of people for finding improved methods of organization has become more insistent. A great part of this concern is focused on hospitals.

The old battle cries about "socialized medicine" and preservation of the doctor–patient relationship from "third-party interference" have acquired a hollow ring. While personal freedom is guarded as jealously as ever, more and more people have come to appreciate that its maintenance depends not on abdication but on strengthening of group responsibility.[6] Organization has become the keynote to assurance of sound health service for every individual. The meaning of this concept—and its many shadings in the world of doctor–hospital relations—is the question that we seek to clarify in the pages that follow.

M. I. R. and J. W. F.

[6] American Academy of Political and Social Science, "Medicine and Society" (John A. Clausen and Robert Straus, editors), *Annals,* vol. 346 (March 1963).

I

DOCTOR–HOSPITAL RELATIONS AND THE CURRENT AMERICAN HOSPITAL SCENE

THE IMPORTANCE OF the general hospital in the constellation of modern medical care is recognized by everyone. No longer simply a place for the bed-bound patient, the hospital today is conceived also as a center for all technical services for the ambulatory patient, as a place for basic and postgraduate training of personnel, as a laboratory for medical research, and even as a center for preventive services and health promotion among the general population.[1]

Yet this idealized broad scope of functions, while often articulated, is far from fully achieved in practice. The large medical centers, attached to medical schools, come closest to the ideal, but even in these the activities in certain sectors may be quite limited.[2] In most general hospitals of the United States, the overwhelming bulk of energies still go to the bed care of the sick and very little to the other medical or social functions. Within the sphere of in-patient care, moreover, the range of services offered by hospitals to meet the physical and mental needs of patients may be highly variable.

BROADENING HOSPITAL FUNCTIONS AND MEDICAL STAFF ISSUES

More specifically, the full range of hospital functions in the modern world consists of five main types. First, there are diagnostic and treatment services to in-patients. Within this broad function are many subdivisions of medical, surgical, obstetrical, pediatric, and other special forms of care. Psychiatric service and rehabilitation may be included. Involved

[1] John H. Knowles, *Hospitals, Doctors, and the Public Interest* (Cambridge: Harvard University Press, 1965).
[2] Raoul Tunley, "A Jury of Experts Picks America's 10 Best Hospitals," *Ladies Home Journal* (February 1967): 34 ff.

1

in all these in-patient services are various modalities, including nursing, dietetics, pharmaceutical skills, laboratory and x-ray services, and various refinements of diagnosis and therapy. Second, there are services to out-patients, with an equally wide range of specialties and technical modal-ities. A third hospital function concerns professional and technical educa-tion, for many classes of health personnel must work in hospitals and thereby receive training. A fourth function is medical research, since the accumulation of patients in hospitals provides the basis for scientific in-vestigation into the causes, diagnosis, and treatment of disease. A fifth function concerns prevention of disease or health promotion in the sur-rounding population; there are many ways that hospitals, as centers of technical skill, can offer services to people before they are sick or can protect patients from the hazards of disease beyond that for which they have come to the hospital.

One of the principal features of hospital organization contributing to the hospital's range of functions is the manner in which physicians do their work. For many reasons, to be explored later, there are different patterns of medical staff organization (MSO) in various types of hospi-tals, and the MSO pattern in all hospitals is undergoing changes due to many external influences. Some of these influences tend to adjust the MSO pattern to a wider range of hospital functions, while others work in the opposite direction. In a sense, the modern general hospital in America is a battleground for two opposing philosophies of health service —one regarding health service mainly as a social responsibility and the other mainly as a private, individual concern.

This conflict of philosophies has been expressed within the dynamics of medical staff organization for many years. It has been manifested in a score of contentions about specific innovations in the organizational ar-rangements through which doctors work. Since 1949 the American Medi-cal Association has been issuing a series of policy statements on physician hospital relations, counselling generally on the maintenance of physician independence, professionally and economically.[3] The many social forces impinging on hospitals and modifying their functions will be examined later. The response of a hospital to these pressures, however, invariably affects the method of organization of its medical staff, and it is the latter topic which this book aims to explore. The basic question is: How does the pattern of organization of doctors in hospitals influence the hos-pital's ability to carry out the functions which society demands?

When we speak of "the hospital," of course, it is a great over-simpli-cation. There are many different types of hospitals in America, varying in their sponsorship, the scope of diseases they treat, their size, and other

---

[3] American Medical Association, Council on Medical Service, "Physician-Hos-pital Relations," *J.A.M.A.*, 190:74–79 (5 October 1964).

dimensions.[4] Corresponding to these differences are variations in their patterns of medical staff organization. Even within the type of hospital that is most numerous in the United States—the general hospital for short-term illness, under the sponsorship of a voluntary nonprofit association—there is a wide range of variations in the characteristics of the medical staff organization.

It is this pluralism and variation that makes possible the research that this book will report. Since hospitals may be identified with many different forms or styles of medical staff organization, it is feasible to make comparisons among them. It is then possible to examine the relationships between the pattern of medical staff organization (MSO) and the functions performed by the hospital. It is possible to determine whether one form of medical staff organization is more conducive than another to achieving the range of functions that society has come to expect of hospitals.

Carrying out any or all of these functions effectively requires the organization of doctors, as well as other personnel in hospitals, but the manner and degree of organization are subject to many alternative choices. As an approach to analyzing the relationship between the MSO pattern and the effectiveness of a hospital's performance of the five functions sketched above, it was necessary to develop a scheme of classifying these patterns. This was done by conceptualizing medical staffs along an organizational range from loosely structured or "permissive" to highly structured or "rigorous." The details of this scheme of analysis will be reviewed in chapter V.

It is quite evident that the trend in recent decades has been toward the highly structured end of this range.[5] In order to perform their socially expected functions better, almost all hospitals have taken steps to tighten the organization of their medical staffs. Many external forces, both governmental and voluntary, have pushed hospitals in this direction. Along the way, however, there have inevitably been controversies, as physicians—accustomed to a tradition of private, independent medical practice—have resisted the pressures to constrain them in an organizational framework when they work within the hospital.

In the early 1950's these controversies reached a high point, involving a sort of confrontation between the national organizations of doctors—the American Medical Association and several specialty societies—and the American Hospital Association. The focal issue involved the increasing tendency of general hospitals to engage doctors on a full-time salary

[4] James A. Hamilton, *Patterns of Hospital Ownership and Control* (Minneapolis: University of Minnesota Press, 1961).

[5] C. Wesley Eisele (editor), *The Medical Staff in the Modern Hospital* (New York: McGraw Hill, 1967).

or by some other contractual arrangement under which the physician's economic liaison is with the hospital administration rather than the individual patient. Hospitals were accused by doctors of "profiteering" at their expense and of promoting "socialized medicine." While this issue of "contractual physicians" in hospitals was clearly only a part of the larger issue of the over-all tightening of medical staff organization, it will be helpful to examine the background of the controversy. We wrote of this in a paper published in 1960.[6]

BACKGROUND OF DOCTOR–HOSPITAL CONFLICTS

Since colonial days the predominant pattern of American medical practice has been individualistic and private. Most physicians have been and still are in practice by themselves and are remunerated on a private fee basis. Even the steady growth of health insurance plans has not greatly modified the pattern of private, solo medical practice; as in Europe before America, it has even tended to fortify the pattern.

During the last hundred years, however, there has occurred in the United States a growth in various forms of collective financing of medical service (through insurance, tax funds, industry, etc.). The extent of changed professional relationships in the practice of medicine has also increased. Industrial corporations and trade unions have engaged physicians on salary to care for workers.[7] Medical schools have greatly enlarged their faculties of full-time professors.[8] Hospitals everywhere have engaged radiologists and pathologists in various contractual relationships, and here and there a voluntary general hospital has developed an entire staff of salaried physicians.[9] In larger hospitals, salaried directors of medical education have been appointed, as well as full-time chiefs of certain clinical services.[10]

New specialties, such as physical medicine, have furthered the trend toward hospital-based contractual practice. Consumer-sponsored prepayment plans of many types have extended support for group-practice medical clinics. Finally, specialized hospitals for mental illness, for

---

[6] Milton I. Roemer and Max Shain, "Contractual Physicians in General Hospitals: A Pilot Study," *Hospitals* (1 May 1960): 38–43.

[7] U.S. Coal Mines Administration, *Medical Survey of the Bituminous Coal Industry* (Washington: Government Printing Office, 1947).

[8] Commission on Medical Education, *Final Report* (New York: Office of the Director of Study [Willard C. Rappleye], 1932).

[9] George Bugbee, "The Physician in the Hospital Organization," *New Eng. J. Med.*, 261:896–901 (29 October 1959).

[10] Charles F. Wilinsky, "Even the Medium-sized Hospital Should Have a Full-time Chief of Staff," *Hospitals*, 20:47 (November 1947).

veterans, or for nonspecific long-term illness—hospitals long associated with full-time medical staffs—have continued to grow.[11]

With these developments in the organization of medical service in hospitals, it can be no surprise that a growing percentage of American physicians came to be working on full-time salaries. Based on analysis of the *American Medical Directory* (published by the American Medical Association), the 14 per cent of physicians so engaged in 1930 had risen to 35 per cent in 1949. This did not include physicians with some part-time salaried employment, but it did include interns and residents, and physicians in the armed forces. Even if the latter groups are excluded, and one considers only civilian physicians who had completed their training, there were in 1949 more than 22 per cent of American physicians employed on full-time salaries.[12]

Only part of this segment of the medical profession, of course, was composed of physicians engaged on a full-time salary in hospitals. The *American Medical Directory* for 1958, however, discloses that of 228,300 doctors of medicine in the United States, there were 13,600 employed full-time in hospitals as specialists or administrators. Additional thousands were engaged in "government agencies" (14,800) and "health plans" (7,200); many of these worked in hospitals.[13] If one excludes from consideration retired physicians (11,200), as well as those still in hospital training periods (24,400), and if one estimates that about two-thirds of government and health plan physicians are essentially in hospital service, it is found that about 15 per cent of American practicing physicians in 1958 were in some form of full-time hospital employment.

Such continual modification of the traditional relationship of physicians to hospitals was bound to cause certain frictions. The medical profession has long guarded its independence. Since about 1920 in the United States—earlier in Europe—the growth of various forms of organized medical service inevitably led to many bitter controversies. In the 1930's and 1940's this controversy was in large measure associated with the expanding role of government in medical care and the growth of health insurance plans under varied auspices.[14]

For many years, organized private physicians in America were haunted by the threat of a national compulsory health insurance law. With the high level of economic prosperity and the change to a conservative national administration in the 1950's, the atmosphere changed.

[11] G. E. Armstrong, "The Medical Program of the Veterans Administration," *J.A.M.A.*, 171:540 (3 October 1959).

[12] Michael M. Davis, *Medical Care for Tomorrow* (New York: Harper, 1955), p. 53.

[13] "What 228,295 Doctors of Medicine Do," *Med. Economics* (11 May 1959): 136.

[14] New York Academy of Medicine, *Medicine in the Changing Order* (New York: Commonwealth Fund, 1947).

The likelihood of federal legislation on the financing of medical care for the general population receded greatly. Other streams of social change, all the while flowing quietly along, now began to attract attention. Among these was the increasing engagement of physicians by hospitals on a salary.[15]

The principal articulate objections to the practice came from radiologists in a number of localities. Pathologists followed suit. The professional societies of these specialties became increasingly concerned and passed resolutions declaring it undesirable for physicians to sell their services to hospitals (or other organizations) for a flat salary. It was argued that this meant "exploitation" of the physician, since the revenue collected by the hospital for the services of the x-ray and laboratory departments might be applied in part to the support of other hospital departments.[16]

Nonprofit hospitals were accused of making a "profit" on the work of the radiologist or pathologist. Since surgeons, internists, and other attending physicians were paid on a fee-for-service basis, why not radiologists? It is hard to know which was most vexing to the radiologists and pathologists: the amount of their salaries, the status-connotations of being a salaried employee (hence less independent than a fee-for-service physician), anxieties about domination by laymen, or fears about future reductions in salary. Arguments were brought forward that salaried employment was associated with poor quality medical care, that diagnostic departments under salaried physicians did not grow and develop, that these men lost their incentive for doing good work.[17]

Whatever may have been the causes, the issue became so contentious that it led to litigation in the courts of Iowa and then in South Carolina.[18] These cases were based on the grounds that hospitals were corporations and that state laws prohibited the "corporate practice of medicine." The engagement of physicians on salary, or other arrangements permitting the hospital to bill for physicians' services, meant that the hospital was breaking the law. (Similar arguments had previously been used to combat nonprofit consumer-sponsored prepayment plans for medical care.)

Court decisions, in general, tended to reject this argument and to hold that the common hospital practice of engaging pathologists and

---

[15] J. S. Kenney, "Are Hospitals Increasingly Encroaching on the Private Practice of Medicine?" *Connecticut State Med.J.* (March 1957).

[16] "AMA Acts on Hospital-Physician Relations," *Hospitals* (16 December 1959): 17–19.

[17] Dwight H. Murray, "Hospital-Professional Relations: The Physician," *Hospitals* (1 January 1957): 31 ff.

[18] "Iowa Hospital-Doctor Law in Effect" (editorial), *J.A.M.A.*, 166:374–75 (25 January 1958).

radiologists on salary was reasonable and legal.[19] Nevertheless, the state attorneys general in Colorado, Florida, Idaho, Iowa, New Mexico, Ohio, Virginia, and West Virginia, as well as a district court in Iowa, advised that hospitals, being corporations, were indeed not permitted to engage salaried physicians. Contrary rulings were made in several other states. The legislatures of Iowa, Virginia, and Wisconsin undertook to deal specifically with this problem through changes in the medical practice acts.

As Willcox stated in his comprehensive monograph on the problem, it was palpably unsound and opposed to the public interest to allow a legal fiction, like the prohibition of "corporate medical practice," to obstruct policies that were found in actual practice to be good for hospitals, patients, and physicians. What is "good" for everyone, however, is subject to debate, and much debate continued to occur, quite aside from litigations.[20]

The argument started with the implication of various systems of paying physicians who provide diagnostic laboratory and other supportive services in hospitals, but it inevitably extended far beyond this.[21] In brief, physicians tended to see the issue as an encroachment of hospitals on private medical practice, while the hospital administrators saw the issue in the 1950's, as they do now, as a problem in integrated hospital operation.[22]

It was this issue surrounding engagement of contractual physicians by hospitals that led us to undertake the exploration of the larger question of medical staff organization and its relationship to hospital performance of socially expected functions, which this book reports. With the debate in the 1960's over the provisions of the Medicare Law— the Social Security Act Amendments of 1965—the issue took on another practical meaning. Since Medicare has separate administrative and fiscal provisions for hospital services and physician services, the question arose as to whether the services of a hospital-based specialist were to be reimbursed under the first mechanism or the second.[23] Amidst many

[19] Alanson W. Willcox, Selma Levine, and Morton Namrow, *Hospitals and the Corporate Practice of Medicine* (Chicago: American Hospital Association [Hospital Monograph Series No. 1], 1957).

[20] Albert W. Snoke, "The Future of Hospitals in Medical Care," *Amer. J. Public Health*, 48:468 (April 1958).

[21] American Hospital Association, *Statement on Hospital and Physician Relationships in Anaesthesiology, Pathology, Physical Medicine, and Radiology* (Chicago: The Association, 1960).

[22] H. D. Pritzkes, D. C. MacNeill, and G. H. Agnew, "Provision and Payment of Diagnostic Services: A Symposium," *Canadian J. Public Health*, 48:413 (October 1957).

[23] John Carlova, "Medicare and the Captive Specialist," *Med. Economics* (20 September 1965).

other contentious issues on this national health insurance law, this issue was decided essentially in favor of medical individualism. The decision of the law was to regard the services of contractual physicians in hospitals as "medical" rather than "hospital" for reimbursement purposes. Thus, despite the probable long-term influence of Medicare toward systematizing the whole pattern of American health services, this provision operated to put a brake, probably temporary, on the trend toward tightening the MSO framework in hospitals.[24]

Most of the discussion of medical staff organization in hospitals has been exhortative. Arguments are offered in defense of one or another pattern of MSO, based on abstract logic or perhaps the experience of an acknowledged expert in his own hospital. Often arguments are based on observation of past trends, sometimes distorted, with apprehension about future possibilities. The attempt in this book, however, is to offer the findings of systematic and empirical observation of a variety of MSO patterns in a number of different hospital situations. It is to explore relationships, as objectively as possible, between the MSO pattern in a hospital and its performance of various hospital functions.

In posing the question this way, we do not and must not imply that the pattern of medical staff organization is the only determinant of a hospital's performance. Obviously there are many forces influencing what a hospital is and what it does. In order to clear the air of this question of cause-and-effect, therefore, we must pause to examine the multiple determinants of hospital programs today and something of the main hospital trends.

The MSO pattern may be viewed essentially as an intervening factor that mediates between certain social forces and the final features of hospital activity. Thus social influences—in the broad sense, including economic, scientific, and other phenomena—contribute ultimately to the nature of the functional output of hospitals, and also to the patterns by which doctors work in them, thereby making possible that output.

GENERAL SOCIAL INFLUENCES ON HOSPITALS

In the next chapter, on historical developments, we will consider some of the broad social movements—religious, humanitarian, governmental—that gave rise to hospitals centuries ago. Here we will examine developments in the recent decades which have exerted particular force on the scope of hospital activities in the United States today.

Changes in the Population and Disease. From the viewpoint of health services, one of the central facts of recent decades is the rising

---

[24] Herman M. Somers and Anne R. Somers, *Medicare and the Hospitals: Issues and Prospects* (Washington: Brookings Institution, 1967).

proportion of aged persons and, with this, the enlargement of the problem of chronic disease. With the reduction in communicable diseases and in infant and childhood mortality, people live on to the age period when chronic illness almost inevitably occurs.[25] We need not review all the developments in public health work and the rise in our whole standard of living that account for this, to recognize the many changes that these demographic trends have induced in hospital affairs. Although short-stay cases constitute the overwhelming majority of admissions, the small fraction who are chronic patients use a high proportion of the available bed-days in general hospitals. Thus, only about 5 per cent of patients admitted may become "long-stay cases," remaining for over thirty days, but they account for 25 to 33 per cent of the bed-days of care in many hospitals.[26]

To facilitate care of these long-term cases, general hospitals have been induced to make many adjustments. Special wards or wings have been developed for "intermediate" or "advanced" care.[27] While some physicians and hospital administrators argue that the chronic patient should not be relegated to a separate section where he may be neglected, the possibility of developing in such a section a more home-like atmosphere and assigning personnel who are skillful and sympathetic with geriatric patients is a strong countervailing argument. Thus, the proportion of general hospitals with special provisions for the long-term patient is increasing.

Related to this is the concept of "progressive patient care," in which nursing units and certain associated features in a general hospital are classified as intensive, intermediate, self-care, and long-term care levels.[28] Whether this pattern of organization reduces net costs or not, which is far from clear, it has obvious administrative advantages and seems to make possible a more sophisticated quality of care for patients at all stages.

Another response of hospitals to the rising problem of chronic illness has been the development of hospital-based "home care" programs.[29] Through an organized team of personnel, the hospital takes responsibility for service to the patient in his own home, thereby releasing a bed for another admission, while at the same time giving the patient the benefits of a return to his family. There are questions about the net

[25] Commission on Chronic Illness, *Care of the Long-Term Patient* (Cambridge, Massachusetts: Harvard University Press, 1956).

[26] L. S. Rosenfeld, F. Goldman, and L. A. Kaprio, "Reason for Prolonged Hospital Stay: Study of Need for Hospital Care," *J. Chronic Dis.*, 6:141–51 (1957).

[27] American Hospital Association, *The Extended Care Unit in a General Hospital* (Chicago: The Association, 1966).

[28] U.S. Public Health Service, *Elements of Progressive Patient Care*, PHS pub. No. 930-C-1 (Washington: Government Printing Office, 1962).

[29] David Littauer, I. J. Flance, and A. Wessen, *Home Care* (Chicago: American Hospital Association [Monograph No. 9], 1961).

economies achieved—since the over-all volume of service by the hospital is usually expanded—and also about the relative advantages of different forms of administrative base (for example, a Health Department or Visiting Nurse Association, as against a hospital), but the home-care idea has obviously widened the scope of hospital functions. Its implications go beyond the chronic disease field, because it represents an approach to systematic surveillance of out-of-hospital care, just as medical staff organization tends to systematize the quality of care within the hospital walls.

The expansion of rehabilitation and physical medicine services in hospitals is another development due in part to the rising burden of chronic illness.[30] From small units with one or two physical therapists, there have been developed in many hospitals large multi-disciplinary departments of rehabilitation, under the direction of full-time specialists in physical medicine. Through these departments, the hospital becomes more concerned in the full restoration of the patient to social useful-ness after recovery from the acute phase of his illness.

To bridge the gap between institutional and community life, hospitals have also developed social service departments of wider scope.[31] Such departments have many functions, of course, outside of the chronic ill-ness problem, but as "means testing" of applicants for charitable care has declined in importance, social workers have become able to devote increasing attention to meeting this type of need. The social worker helps to establish liaison between the hospital and numerous other vol-untary or governmental agencies that may help the patient on discharge.

General hospitals alone could not absorb the whole rising volume of chronic patients, and as a result other types of long-term care institutions have proliferated. There are many full-fledged hospitals for long-term care, but the most numerous type of institution is the nursing home or "extended care facility" as it is called under the 1965 Medicare Law.[32] Many custodial homes for the aged have also added medical sections. Most nursing homes are proprietary and quite deficient in the quality of medical care and rehabilitation offered, but public demand has led to numerous steps for their improvement. Among these is the move-ment for closer liaison with general hospitals; the requirement in the Medicare Law of "transfer agreements" between extended care facilities and general hospitals has, of course, fortified such relationships. From

---

[30] American Hospital Association, *Rehabilitation Services in Hospitals and Related Facilities* (Chicago: The Association, 1966).

[31] U.S. Public Health Service, *Social Work in Hospitals*, PHS pub. no. 519 (Washington: Government Printing Office, 1957).

[32] J. Solon, D. W. Roberts, D. E. Kruger, and A. M. Baney, *Nursing Homes: Their Patients and Their Care*, PHS pub. no. 503 (Washington: Government Printing Office, 1957).

the viewpoint of the hospital, this constitutes a further widening of community responsibilities.

A special type of long-term illness—mental disease—is coming to occupy the increasing attention of general hospitals. Many factors doubtless contribute to this—e.g., the improvements in methods of psychiatric therapy and the extension of insurance coverage, to be discussed below—but the net effect has been for over 10 per cent of general hospitals to make systematic provision for treatment of patients with mental disorders.[33] Likewise, increasing ties are developing between mental hospitals, previously quite isolated, and community general hospitals—further widening the latter's role.

The decline in infectious disease has led to the virtual disappearance of the separate isolation hospital, and with this certain general hospitals are expected to provide facilities for the occasional communicable disease case. A similar evolution seems to be affecting tuberculosis sanatoria, which are being closed down or converted to other purposes with the decline of this disease. Thus, to handle the residual problem, tuberculosis sections are being established in certain general hospitals under governmental auspices.

Advancements in Science and Technology. The effects of the endless stream of advancements in medical science on the organization and the output of hospitals are so obvious as to require little comment. Specialization in medicine leads inevitably to specialization in the departments of hospitals and in the structuring of medical staffs. The whole army of auxiliary personnel, required for modern diagnosis and treatment, demands an organizational umbrella for their effective use; this has been provided in the modern hospital and accounts for the increasing importance of hospital services in the panorama of medical care.

Within hospitals, the co-ordination of the various specialties of medicine and the allied fields of nursing, pharmacy, physical therapy, dietetics, laboratory and x-ray technology, social work, etc., requires increasingly sophisticated administration. The demands for specialized skills have led to increasing engagement of contractual physicians, particularly in fields like pathology and radiology, necessary to back up the primary physician in the care of a large proportion of all patients. The influence of contractual physician policies on the over-all functioning of medical staffs will be discussed throughout subsequent chapters. Their quantitative characteristics are the subject of chapter IV.

The increasing dependence of the doctor on elaborate technology

---

[33] Joint Commission on Mental Illness and Health, *Action for Mental Health* (New York: Basic Books, 1961), p. 265.

which can be provided only in hospitals has brought more doctors into more frequent contact with hospitals. These connections are stronger in America than in other countries, as we shall see in chapter III, but they are growing everywhere. Increasingly, private doctors are establishing their offices close to hospitals and sometimes in buildings actually owned by hospitals.[34] Outside of hospitals the demands of specialization have led to a steady growth of private group practice clinics.[35] While the growth of these clinics may to some extent reduce the demands on hospitals for various technical services, it also means that physicians gain greater experience in working together, and this teamwork concept doubtless influences their behavior within hospitals as well.

The advancements of science create an expanding need for professional education and further research, and this puts additional important pressures on hospitals. For several hundred years, hospitals—with their concentration of seriously sick patients—have been centers of basic medical education. Most of the European medical schools were developed in and around large hospitals. But today the hospital is expected to be a center for postgraduate medical education as well, and also for the training of nurses and a wide variety of other health personnel. Much research, requiring large numbers of patients with specific diagnoses, can only be done in hospitals. These demands associated with scientific advancements have obvious influence on the scope of functions of hospitals.

Scientific advancements and specialization influence also the nature of out-patient services offered by hospitals. No longer a place exclusively for the poor, the hospital out-patient department (OPD) becomes a facility for any patient requiring diagnostic tests or treatment procedures that cannot be done in a private medical office. Out-patient clinics that are organized for the indigent and medically indigent are increasingly complicated places, with various specialized subdivisions. As an "emergency" resource, the hospital OPD is increasingly used by all sorts of patients who are unable or unwilling to see a private doctor for all sorts of ailments.[36]

The concentration of numerous medical and surgical specialties in the hospital has inevitably led to greater concern for maintenance of

[34] C. Rufus Rorem, *Physicians' Private Offices at Hospitals* (Chicago: American Hospital Association [Monograph No. 5], 1959).

[35] U.S. Public Health Service, *Promoting the Group Practice of Medicine*, Report of the National Conference on Group Practice, October 19–21, 1967 (Washington: Government Printing Office, 1967).

[36] E. R. Weinerman, "Out-patient Clinic Services in the Teaching Hospital," in *Medical Care: Social and Organizational Aspects*, L. J. DeGroot, editor (Springfield, Illinois: Charles C Thomas, 1966), pp. 161–81.

scientific standards. If only to protect their professional position, specialists must guard against the claims and actions of poorly qualified practitioners. Various measures of professional group discipline and quality review have evolved—medical audits, tissue committees, and other activities of medical staffs. Thus, the advancement of science and the resultant specialization have expanded the mechanisms of quality surveillance in hospitals.[37] At the same time, specialization has created certain impersonalities in patient care and, to compensate, the nurse or nursing team is being called upon for more "tender loving care." Administrative measures are necessary to integrate the impact of so many different skills on the individual patient.

All these technical advancements cost money. They would hardly be possible without an increase in the general economic productivity of society and in the financial resources available for health service. To mobilize these resources there have developed over the last century increasingly collective arrangements for supporting the costs of medical care, especially that given in hospitals. These constitute a third general set of influences on the current character of hospital programs.

Extended Social Financing of Health Service. The widening social base of health service financing has led to great strengthening of the resources of hospitals and the services they render. The community and nation, rather than the sick individual, are becoming increasingly responsible for the costs of health care. Two principal mechanisms are involved: governmental revenues and voluntary health insurance. In 1929 some 14 per cent of total health expenditures in the United States came from government and a negligible percentage came through the mechanism of insurance. By 1950 the proportion from government had risen to 23 per cent and from voluntary insurance to 9 per cent. In 1967 the governmental share was over 32 per cent, and the insurance share was 22 per cent. Over these years the proportion of health care expenditures from philanthropy declined slightly from approximately 3 to 2 per cent. Thus, in 1967, of all health care costs, 56 per cent were derived from social sources and only 44 per cent from out-of-pocket private spending.[38]

Over the last forty years, furthermore, the gross amounts spent on medical care have risen both absolutely and as a percentage of national income. From under 4 per cent in 1930, the proportion of national income allocated to health purposes has risen to over 6 per cent in 1967.

[37] Karl S. Klicka, "Control of Quality of Medical Care," in *The Medical Staff in the Modern Hospital*, C. Wesley Eisele, editor (New York: McGraw-Hill, 1967), pp. 55–63.

[38] Dorothy P. Rice and Barbara S. Cooper, "National Health Expenditures 1950–67," *Social Security Bulletin* (January 1969): 3–20.

Parallel with this 50 per cent proportionate increase has been an enlarging share of total health expenditures going to hospital care; in 1967 over $50,000,000,000 was spent on health purposes in the United States, and 35 per cent of this ($89 per capita) went to hospitals. There can be little doubt that the over-all rise in moneys spent for health is due in part to the increasingly collectivized financing which, in effect, reserves money for health purposes before it is spent on other things. Hospital care, moreover, is more heavily collectivized in its support— through both governmental revenues and insurance—than any other sector of personal health service.

The implications of these economic trends for hospital operations are very great. The increase in financial support, of course, has meant that hospitals could be greatly expanded, their construction standards and equipment improved, and their staffing enlarged. Strengthened support has meant strengthened services and services of a wider range. The elaborate programs of in-patient care, out-patient service, education, and research to be reviewed in this book would not have been possible without the abundant financial support of recent decades.

At the same time, the social origin of most of these funds has promoted in the general population an increasing concern about hospital affairs. When the whole community, and not the individual patient, is paying the costs of hospital care, it has a natural interest in how the money is spent. Hence, increasing external influences have been brought to bear on hospitals to assure their efficient management. Governmental and other outside bodies have become more concerned about the maintenance of quality standards.[39]

A fundamental form of public concern applies to the initial construction of hospitals or the expansion of existing ones. The size and location of facilities and the net bed-population ratio in an area determines in large part the aggregate volume of hospital service that will be provided.[40] Increasing interest has been shown, therefore, in area-wide planning of hospital facilities. Various types of governmental and voluntary councils exert an influence on the decisions of hospitals to expand their physical plants. These decisions obviously affect the extent and scope of services that hospitals will be able to offer.[41]

Another feature of the tide of social financing of health services

[39] U.S. Department of Health, Education, and Welfare, *Report of the Secretary's Advisory Committee on Hospital Effectiveness* (Washington: Government Printing Office, 1968).

[40] Milton I. Roemer, "Controlling Hospital Use through Limiting Hospital Bed Supply," in *Where Is Hospital Use Headed* (Chicago: University of Chicago, Graduate Program in Hospital Administration, 1963), pp. 69–72.

[41] National Advisory Commission on Health Facilities, *A Report to the President* (Washington: Government Printing Office, 1968).

has been the extension of the insurance principle to wider sectors of medical care. Hospitalization is still the major sector to which insurance is applied, but through various types of insurance plans, a great proportion of the costs of physician's services is also coming under insurance protection.[42] This leads to more frequent access of people to doctors and the detection of more illness. Insurance of out-of-hospital costs may reduce some unnecessary hospital admissions, but under conditions of free choice and fee-for-service medical practice, it appears to lead to an increased rather than a decreased rate of admission to hospitals.[43] (The reduction in hospital admission rates, associated with comprehensive ambulatory care insurance, has involved group practice and salaried physicians—important deviations from the prevailing free choice and fee-for-service pattern.)

As for hospital insurance, including the Medicare Law for the aged, its extension has undoubtedly led to a democratization of patient-care policies in hospitals. The patient with insurance for both hospital and physician's care is a private patient; without insurance, if he were of low income, he might be treated in a large public ward rather than a private room. Thus, the extension of insurance coverage has contributed to a blurring of the distinction between hospital care of the rich and that of the poor. There is still a great deal of segregated ward service for the poor, of course, but the proportion is declining and the trend is toward a single standard. The Intensive Care Unit in general hospitals, for example, is an administrative mechanism for providing to patients of any income the level of nursing care that in former years would only have been within the means of families who could afford private-duty nurses.

The Medicare and Medicaid programs have had an especially great impact on hospitals, not only because of their support of increasing rates of utilization by the aged and by low income groups but also because of the governmentally enforced standards of hospital operation associated with these programs.[44]

Urbanization and General Cultural Developments. The whole urbanization of our society and, with it, rising levels of public education and communication have heightened the use of hospitals beyond the influence of the other forces reviewed. In cities, people see doctors more frequently and go to hospitals more often. With more knowledge

[42] H. M. and A. R. Somers, *Doctors, Patients, and Health Insurance* (Washington: Brookings Institution, 1961).

[43] Milton I. Roemer, "The Influence of Prepaid Physicians' Service on Hospital Utilization," *Hospitals* (16 October 1958): 48–52.

[44] H. M. and A. R. Somers, *Medicare and the Hospitals: Issues and Prospects* (Washington: Brookings Institution, 1967).

and higher general standards of living they acquire higher expectations in all spheres, including medical care. The rise in use of hospital emergency rooms is doubtless due in part to the sophistication of people, who are determined to get care in the face of a relative inaccessibility of doctors in private offices.[45]

At the same time, the advances feasible in the cities have raised the sights of those who live in rural areas. The concept of hospital regionalization arose originally from the social desire to assure rural people the level of medical care available in the larger cities.[46] Similar problems affect people in the slums of the cities or those served by small suburban hospitals. Regionalization has gradually acquired other meanings and purposes, but at the root its implementation depends on democratic demands for equality in the application of medical science to all persons, wherever they may live.

Democratization is also affecting the composition of the governing boards of hospitals and, with this, their policies. Representatives of labor unions, racial minorities, and various consumer groups on boards of directors can speak with a voice somewhat different from that of upper class philanthropists. Such representation is still somewhat limited on voluntary hospital boards, but its effect is bound to broaden the hospital's role, especially with respect to service for lower income groups. Extension of the hospital's scope in the sphere of disease prevention and general community relations is perhaps due in part to such democratic influences.

It is evident that many forces at play in our society are shaping the program of services provided by modern hospitals and the patterns of medical staff organization required to provide those services effectively. Along with these influences there have developed many specific social mechanisms to assure or at least encourage compliance with standards deemed necessary to carry out those functions. As the importance of hospitals has become increasingly appreciated they have become more and more endowed, as the lawyers put it, with a "public interest." Consideration of these external sanctions will provide further background for understanding the influences, discussed in later chapters, of medical staff organization per se.[47]

[45] Henry F. Vaughan and C. E. Gamesber, "Why Patients Use Hospital Emergency Departments," *Hospitals* (1 October 1966).

[46] Milton I. Roemer, "Hospital Regionalization in Perspective," *Public Health Reports*, 74:916–22 (October 1959).

[47] Max Shain and Milton I. Roemer, "Hospitals and the Public Interest," *Public Health Reports*, 76:401–10 (May 1961).

EXTERNAL CONTROLS ON HOSPITAL PERFORMANCE

The justification of external social controls over hospital activities springs from many sources. Fundamentally it lies in the right and obligation of a society to protect the health of its members. Controls are exercised through both voluntary and governmental actions which may be reviewed after we first examine the basis of the "public interest" in hospitals.

The Foundations of a "Public Interest." Through a long tradition of political experience and legal precedent, a deep-rooted basis for governmental concern about hospitals is embodied in constitutions. The United States Constitution may not spell out "hospitals" or even "health" as subjects of governmental concern, but the "general welfare" clause has been interpreted again and again to include within it the power to safeguard the public health. Except for foreign or interstate activities, however, power in health affairs rests essentially with the state governments. The New York State constitution, for example, says that "the promotion and protection of the health of the inhabitants of the State are matters of public concern."

The states are amply endowed legally to support this public concern. They possess what is called juridically "police power," permitting state governments to protect the health, welfare, safety, and morals of their citizens. The rational foundation of this power may be the need to protect individuals from the harmful acts of others or even from personal imprudence. Hence, the state exercises its police power over the sale of drugs or the wages and hours of working people. It may require vaccination against smallpox and quarantine of persons exposed to diphtheria. Likewise, it may regulate hospitals since these institutions may intimately affect the life and well-being of the people.

Beyond these philosophical and legal foundations for a public interest in their operation, hospitals derive from government certain special privileges. At the same time, government imposes certain obligations on them.

Generally, hospitals (whether nonprofit or proprietary) are incorporated bodies, chartered by the state like other corporations. Directors are substantially relieved of individual responsibility for the wrongdoing of the corporation; instead, the legally created corporate "person" is responsible and liable only to the extent of its collective assets. Considering the possibilities of negligence, harmful acts, and malpractice suits in a hospital, this limited liability is obviously of great importance. As corporations, hospitals have the capacity for perpetual existence, without the necessity of complex transfers of title on the death of individual founders. The responsibilities of corporations are defined by law and are subject to a charter granted usually by the secretary of state in each state.[48]

Because of their usually charitable and nonprofit character, except for the relatively small number of proprietary institutions, hospitals enjoy tax exemptions of many sorts. They are exempt from federal income taxes and from many excise taxes levied on other enterprises. They are also exempt from local property taxes, and often from local sales taxes on their purchases. Moreover, hospitals may receive gifts from donors who thereby enjoy reductions of their net incomes for tax purposes; hospitals thus receive funds which would otherwise be payable in large part to the government as private income taxes.

Hospitals may receive substantial grants of public money for construction purposes. The extent, of course, differs with the hospital's sponsorship. About one-third of the hospitals in the United States are fully owned by units of government, predominantly state and local, and were built entirely with governmental tax funds. Even excluding special hospitals for tuberculosis and mental disorders, all federal facilities, and all long-term facilities, and counting only short-term general hospitals serving local communities, there were in 1967 more than 1,500 such institutions which had been built substantially from public funds. Beyond this, voluntary hospitals have long received governmental construction grants. Such support has been given since the earliest days of the Republic, when the Pennsylvania Hospital in Philadelphia and the Massachusetts General Hospital in Boston received grants from state legislatures and municipal governments. State governments have in more recent years given such grants to help hospitals in rural communities. Since 1946 the Hill-Burton program has provided substantial federal money to assist voluntary and public hospital construction on a nationwide scale. Such contributions of public funds have entailed public responsibility for overseeing how the construction money is spent.[49]

Governmental units purchase services from hospitals on behalf of certain legal beneficiaries. The largest share of these are indigent persons receiving public assistance from federal, state, or local governments; that is, recipients of categorical or general assistance. In addition, many states and localities assume responsibility for hospital services to selected persons who are "medically indigent"; that is, unable to pay hospital bills, although not on the relief rolls for their general living needs. The Medicaid Law of 1965 greatly enlarged these entitle-

---

[48] E. Hayt and L. R. Hayt, *Legal Guide for American Hospitals* (New York: Hospital Textbook Company, 1940), p. 30.

[49] G. A. Harrison, *Government Controls and the Voluntary Non-profit Hospital* (Chicago: American Hospital Association, 1961).

ments. Then there are a variety of other beneficiaries of governmental programs, such as those for workmen's compensation, vocational rehabilitation, or crippled children, who are ordinarily treated in community hospitals. Finally, there are beneficiaries of the federal government, ordinarily served in special federal hospitals, who may receive care in local general hospitals on occasion; these include veterans, uniformed service dependents, American Indians, and others. The scope and quality of care given to all these beneficiaries is a matter of public concern. In some states, indeed, it is the principal legal foundation for the whole facility licensure program, with responsibility being assigned to the welfare department because of its authority for overseeing care of the indigent.

Another reason for public interest in hospitals is their provision of a locale for the work of several licensed health professions.[50] Physicians, nurses, physical therapists, technicians, and others who work in hospitals derive their individual rights to practice from special examinations and licensing procedures. But the very concentration of these personnel under one roof places a special responsibility on government regarding the technical standards of the environment under that roof. Surveillance over the management of hospitals provides a channel for some continued assurance of proper performance by these personnel after the initial licensure.

The hospital is also an educational institution, most conspicuously for nurses but also for other occupations. Laboratory technicians, rehabilitation therapists, social workers, dieticians, and pharmacists may receive substantial parts of their basic training in hospitals. Physicians are educated in hospitals throughout their professional lives, not to mention their periods of service as interns and residents and their training years as medical students. In so far as supervision of education is widely considered a public responsibility in our society, the hospital is, in a sense a school requiring such supervision.

The hospital, furthermore, is an employer of men and women, subject accordingly to the laws of the land controlling the conditions of labor.[51] Exemptions may be made regarding certain wage, hour, and collective bargaining provisions, because of the hospital's usually nonprofit character, but such exemptions are a matter of legislative decision rather than constitutional right. The exemptions could be withdrawn, and there have been legislative winds blowing this way. In any event, conditions

---

[50] Edward H. Forgotson and Ruth Roemer, "Government Licensure and Voluntary Standards for Health Personnel and Facilities," *Med. Care*, 6:345–54 (September–October 1968).

[51] J. V. Terenzio, "What Every Administrator Should Know and Do about Labor Relations," in *Readings in Hospital Law* (Chicago: American Hospital Association, 1965), pp. 113–17.

of work in hospitals are obviously matters of public interest, when over 1,500,000 persons are employed in them on a full-time basis.

Finally, there is the question of hospital operating costs, which have obvious importance for the general public. In recent years social concern about this has become an overriding issue. Not only has there been widespread popular reaction to the sharp rises in hospital costs, but the channel of expression of this reaction has been widened through a separate but closely related social movement: hospital insurance. The Blue Cross plans inevitably reflect hospital costs in their premium charges to subscribers. Being insurance organizations, though nonprofit, they come under the supervision of State Insurance Commissioners, and these officials must be responsive to public attitudes.[52] Thus, the insurance financing of a major share of hospital costs in recent years—in other words, support by the mass of people rather than solely by the sick—has heightened public interest in hospital costs. If there is inefficiency or extravagance, the people have a proper concern in seeing it eliminated.

Perhaps it epitomizes the situation to say that hospitals have essentially become public utilities. They are so important to the survival of the community that they have been granted many special immunities and statutory rights. At the same time, their actions may lead to serious consequences for the people. For both reasons, citizens and organizations outside the walls of the hospital have assumed a variety of responsibilities for looking in on them and exerting various pressures to assure proper performance.

Voluntary Social Influences. The board of directors of the nongovernmental hospital is, in a sense, intended to represent the general community interest and thereby to exercise controls over both hospital employees and attending doctors. In practice, we know that this representation may be poor and the surveillance over the "public interest" may be weak, but the mechanism nevertheless is important. It places over internal hospital affairs the supervision of citizens who have an interest in achieving for the institution a reputaton of sound public service.

There are other boards of citizens at the local level that may examine aspects of hospital operation from time to time. Community chests or councils may look into how funds they have granted are spent. Blue Cross boards may indirectly call for economies. Other agencies buying services for various beneficiaries may demand that certain standards be met, but the focus of each of these groups tends to be narrow and their impact is limited.

---

[52] F. R. Smith, *Adjudication in the Matter of the Filing of the Associated Hospital Service in Philadephia (Blue Cross)* (Harrisburg: Insurance Commissioner of the Commonwealth of Pennsylvania, 1958).

To provide more general surveillance over hospitals, a number of national nongovernmental associations have taken action. The first such body of wide impact was the American College of Surgeons which, shortly after World War I, developed a nationwide system for approval of hospitals meeting certain standards of organization and practice (see chapter II). Meanwhile, the American Hospital Association established limited standards for membership and "listing" in its annual roster. The American Medical Association developed a system of approval of hospitals for internships, residencies, and postgraduate education. Special approval programs for such services as tumor clinics, blood banks, and schools for x-ray and laboratory technicians were organized by other professional societies or voluntary agencies. These specialized approvals, on the whole, continue, but in 1952 there was organized an over-all system of hospital approval by the Joint Commission on Accreditation of Hospitals (see chapter II). This commission undertakes inspections throughout the nation and has doubtless had a major effect in upgrading hospital performance.

Despite the notable achievements of these voluntary bodies, their shortcomings must be recognized.[53] First, they are voluntary, and no hospital need even apply for their approval; indeed, some of the marginal institutions in greatest need of improvement avoid the whole process. Even if an institution seeks approval and fails to get it, there is no penalty except nonapproval. In a one-hospital community, without "competition" for patients, this moral penalty may have little effect. Second, the Joint Commission on Accreditation makes a policy of examining only hospitals of twenty-five beds or more. Yet 500 hospitals in the United States in 1967 were smaller than this, and these institutions often present the thorniest problems. Third, these professional societies and commissions are, of course, independent and responsibile only to themselves. While their integrity may be beyond question, they cannot unfailingly reflect the public interest. Their viewpoint, indeed, is sometimes parochial; they avoid inspection and accreditation of osteopathic hospitals, for example, despite the fact that these institutions give care to thousands of patients.

In the light of these shortcomings of voluntary mechanisms for protection of the public interest in hospital operations and in spite of their great positive achievements, there remains in a democratic society an overriding need for public supervision of hospitals. Only through governmental authorities, responsible ultimately to the whole people, can their supervision be fully and effectively exercised. Diligence in doing so has been increasingly fortified by merit systems for appointment of officials, especially in technical fields. Government agencies may solicit and re-

---

[53] G. Binder, "How Regulation Differs from Accreditation," *Modern Hospital*, 94:113 (May 1960).

ceive expert advice from many sources, but the final policy decisions rest with the agencies. They are ultimately accountable to the citizenry, who can vote the top policymakers out of office if dissatisfied. Governments have, in summary, not only the power but also the obligation to protect the public interest.

Government Controls. The principal means by which governmental agencies have come to protect the public interest in the operation of hospitals is through licensing by state authorities. The Federal Hospital Survey and Construction Act of 1946 required that every state receiving federal grants for aiding in hospital construction should have a law governing minimum standards of maintenance and operation for at least the subsidized facilities. In time, every state passed such a law, and in all but two states, Delaware and Louisiana, it has come to be applied to all hospitals in the state.[54]

In these state laws, the legislature usually declares that every hospital must have a license granted by a particular state agency, typically the Health Department. This department is authorized to issue regulations to carry out the legislative intent, which is usually broadly defined. The Missouri statute, for example, declares it tc be the legislative purpose to "provide for the development, establishment, and enforcement of standards (a) for the care and treatment of individuals in hospitals and (b) for the construction, maintenance, and operation of hospitals, which, in the light of advancing knowledge, will promote safe and adequate treatment of such individuals in hospitals," and authorizes the Missouri Department of Public Health and Welfare to adopt, amend, promulgate, and enforce rules to accomplish the purposes of the law.[55]

The adoption of such a statute represents a forceful exercise of the police power of the state. It grants to the public authority the power to determine the precise conditions under which a hospital shall be operated. If anyone sets out to operate a hospital without meeting these standards, he is subject to prosecution. While these powers are seldom invoked, their existence strengthens the effectiveness of suggestions for improvements made by state agencies.

The older state hospital regulations tended to define public authority narrowly. Their attention was concentrated on protection of the safety of patients; they were explicit about details of the physical plant, including such items as fireproof construction, number and location of exits, the maintenance of buildings, and so on. Details of water supply and

---

[54] L. M. Abbe and A. M. Baney, *The Nation's Health Facilities: Ten Years of the Hill-Burton Hospital and Medical Facilities Program 1946–56*, PHS pub. No. 616 (Washington: Government Printing Office, 1958).

[55] "Hospital Licensing Law," Missouri: Senate Bill No. 422, 67th General Assembly, 1953.

sewage disposal were spelled out, in the older public health tradition. Public concern for mothers and babies was also expressed in special requirements for hospital maternity departments.

The newer state hospital regulations are concerned with much broader aspects of hospital organization. There are requirements on the functions of a governing board and administrator, on the medical staff organization (bylaws, selection of physicians, restrictions, and so on), on detailed clinical records, on the laboratory and x-ray departments, on the nursing service, dietary management, and so on. A few state agencies ventured into the ticklish problem of requiring admission-discharge control committees, some years before "utilization review" procedures became required under the Medicare Law. There are still, of course, requirements on physical plant and sanitation. In short, the scope of the hospital licensure regulations in most states today is broad enough to determine whether the hospital is built, organized, equipped, and staffed in a manner adequate to do the job expected in modern society.[56]

Nevertheless, many state hospital licensure programs are less effective in practice than they would appear by studying the language of the written regulations. The responsible state agencies tend to be meagerly financed and staffed. The qualifications of licensure personnel are often modest.[57] Many states seem to rely heavily on registered nurses or sanitarians whose competence outside nursing or sanitation is often limited. At bottom, perhaps, there is a certain hesitation on the part of state governments to pry too closely into the affairs of voluntary institutions associated with a tradition so prestigious as that of the community hospital.

Beyond the basic hospital licensure laws, governmental influences are exerted in relation to other hospital functions reviewed earlier. For each of the specified beneficiaries of public medical care (the indigent, crippled children, etc.), there are standards as a condition for hospital participation.[58] Likewise, the educational functions of hospitals are subject to review by state educational authorities, as are labor relations by labor or industrial authorities. Narcotics and alcohol used in hospitals come under the control of special federal agencies.

Thus, many explicit governmental authorities are exercised over hospitals and, along with the operation of numerous voluntary programs, they shape the scope and quality of hospital performance. Because of the broad social changes affecting hospitals and reviewed in the previous sec-

[56] Keith O. Taylor and D. M. Donald, *A Comparative Study of Hospital Licensure Regulations* (Berkeley: University of California, 1957).

[57] Hilary G. Fry, *The Operation of State Hospital Planning and Licensing Programs* (Chicago: American Hospital Association [Monograph No. 15], 1965).

[58] Milton I. Roemer, and M. H. McClanahan, "Impact of Governmental Programs on Voluntary Hospitals," *Public Health Reports*, 75:537–44 (June 1960).

tion, however, the range of governmental influences that should be authorized is under continual debate. With the pervasive "public interest" in the hospitals, pressures are continually being applied to widen the impact of official surveillance. The deep public concern with rising costs has led to proposals that the rate of hospital utilization be more carefully controlled. Since the supply of beds sets limits on the utilization rate, it has been advocated that all new hospital construction be subject to governmental review and franchise—not simply to assure compliance with construction standards but to determine whether the new beds are justified at all.[59] One state, New York, has enacted legislation requiring that "public need" be demonstrated before the state health commissioner authorizes construction of any additional hospital facilities. The hospital "utilization review" committees required under the Medicare Law are a further instance of governmental intervention in this sphere.

Other public interventions concern the freedom of a hospital board of directors to deny appointment of a qualified physician to the medical staff, the right of a pharmacist to substitute a generically equivalent drug for a brand-name product prescribed by the physician, and the general obligations of a hospital board with regard to responsibilities for patient care.[60] The right of labor unions to bargain collectively with hospital management has also been subject to governmental protection.[61] A very large body of law, along with court decisions, governs the obligations of the hospital to protect the personal safety of the patient, and to award damages if harm has been done due to negligence or other avoidable causes. These laws put permanent pressure on hospitals to observe caution and to maintain reasonable standards of service.

These governmental and voluntary "social controls" have been discussed as a general influence on the entire universe of hospitals, shaping the nature of their programs. There are great differences, however, in the affect of these forces on specific hospitals. Within the individual hospital, the range and type of activities depend also on certain other attributes that should now be discussed briefly.

DETERMINANTS WITHIN SPECIFIC HOSPITALS

Beyond the broad social forces and the defined external controls over hospital performance, several intrinsic attributes influence what a hospital does. These include principally its legal sponsorship, its size, and its local community setting. The hospital's type of patient—that is, general

[59] Ray E. Brown, "Let the Public Control Utilization through Planning," *Hospitals* (1 December 1959).

[60] John F. Horty, "Survey of Hospital Law," *Public Health Reports*, 79:723–34 (August 1964).

[61] W. L. Daykin, "How Labor Legislation May Affect Hospitals," *Modern Hospital* (July 1960).

diagnosis, mental illness, tuberculosis, etc.—is also obviously important, but our focus here is entirely on general hospitals.

Sponsorship. The sponsorship of a general hospital inevitably affects the scope of its program. The government hospital is ordinarily established to serve defined beneficiaries—indigent persons, military personnel, veterans, merchant seamen, etc.—so that its range of services is set accordingly. Support from tax revenues creates pressures for economies which are reflected in personnel–patient ratios, in the layout of wards, in the type of food and supplies provided, etc.[62] Orientation to the poor leads to a heavy emphasis on out-patient services. To give medical service to the poor, moreover, at relatively low cost, government hospitals usually make heavy use of young doctors-in-training; the intern and the resident benefit from the learning opportunity, and the hospital becomes a "teaching institution." The programs of government hospitals are also influenced by the competing demands of other agencies of government—local, state, or federal—which must be financed from finite revenues.[63]

Sponsorship by a voluntary nonprofit association has different implications for hospital programs. The predilections of its board of directors —usually upper class or middle class business and professional men— are bound to be important, and also the wishes of its medical staff, ordinarily composed mainly of private practitioners.[64] Achievement of excellence in patient care is likely to be a motivating goal, especially for private patients, but teaching and research objectives do not ordinarily figure prominently. Yet the tradition of social service, characterizing hospitals since the Middle Ages, may be felt by the voluntary sponsoring body and provisions made for some degree of service to the poor. In hospitals under religious sponsorship, sensitivity to this tradition is likely to be greater. Religious principles may also affect the type of food served in a hospital or the performance of certain procedures (e.g., therapeutic abortions). Voluntary nonprofit hospitals may receive bequests and hold endowments which enable them to offer charitable services. The dynamic and often turbulent relationships among the three loci of power—the board, the administration, and the medical staff—set conditions for relatively rapid movement in the programs of voluntary hospitals.[65]

Certain types of voluntary hospitals are sponsored by bodies exerting

[62] J. Masur, "Government and Hospitals," in *Hospitals, Doctors, and the Public Interest*, John H. Knowles, editor (Cambridge, Massachusetts: Harvard University Press, 1965), pp. 125–46.

[63] Thomas B. McKneely and W. C. Jansen, "Purchase of Hospital Care: The State Welfare Department's Point of View," *Welfare in Review* (June 1964): 1–7.

[64] Arthur B. Moss, W. G. Broehl, R. H. Guest, and J. H. Hennessey, *Hospital Policy Decisions: Process and Action* (New York; G. P. Putnam, 1966).

[65] Temple Burling, E. M. Lentz, and R. N. Wilson, *The Give and Take in Hospitals* (New York: G. P. Putnam, 1956).

other special influences on hospital programs. The university as a sponsor, of course, creates a hospital with a heavy commitment to medical student teaching and research; this, in turn, will influence the type of patient accepted, preference being usually given to the "interesting case" of teaching value.[66] Sponsorship by a private industrial company or even by a consumer organization means that the patient population is restricted, and the range of services may be limited accordingly. If a health insurance plan or a "group practice" of doctors (with or without insurance) is involved in the establishment of a hospital, the nature of the hospital program will obviously be affected.

Sponsorship of a hospital by private individuals for profit sets other probable limits on the range of functions. Proprietary hospitals have little motivation to serve the poor, to provide education, do research, or maintain relationships with other community agencies. With profit as a motive, the objective becomes to maximize services that yield income and minimize those that do not. The wishes of the private doctor, whose goodwill brings in the patients, have top priority; hence hospital activities that might be construed as "competing" with private practice (such as out-patient x-rays for private patients) are avoided.

Each of the forms of hospital sponsorship has influence also on the pattern of medical staff organization, as we shall see in later chapters. The more highly structured patterns of government and certain types of voluntary hospital are an outgrowth of the social missions and economic constraints of those institutions. The loosely structured patterns of most voluntary and proprietary hospitals are associated with the dominance of private practice values in them.

Hospital Size. The size of a hospital is another basic determinant of its scope of services. Quite aside from their sponsorship, large hospitals are usually more capable of offering a wide range of technical services as well as educational and research functions. While the point is debated, the evidence suggests that there are certain economies of scale with increasing bed capacity; the fact that per diem costs are usually higher rather than lower in large hospitals is due essentially to their offering a richer mixture of services, while the cost per specific unit of service is usually lower.[67] The administrative tasks are usually greater and more complex in large hospitals, and management policies usually must differ from those in small hospitals. With a greater number of specialized personnel per patient, there is need for more systematic procedures in large

[66] E. T. Neumann, "The Nature of a Teaching Hospital and Its Relation to Changes in the Community," in *Hospitals, Doctors, and the Public Interest,* op. cit., pp. 47–63.

[67] Ralph E. Berry, "Returns to Scale in the Production of Hospital Services," *Health Services Research,* 2:123–39 (Summer 1967).

hospitals, resulting in certain impersonalities in patient care; bigness may even cause delays and errors in the medical care process.[68] Yet, only with a large enough complement of patients can the full range of scientific techniques be mobilized in a hospital, so that with advances in science the average size of hospitals nationally is gradually increasing.

A hospital's size also affects the complexity of its medical staff organization. The need for departmentalization, control committees, formal rules and regulations, etc. increases with greater numbers of beds and larger numbers of doctors. In the chapters that follow, it is quite evident that more highly structured medical staffs tend to develop in larger hospitals, although size is obviously not the only determinant. The pattern of staff organization then serves to implement the programs of patient service, education, research, etc. Small hospitals can theoretically adjust for their handicaps by establishing relationships with other hospitals and agencies in an area, but in practice this seldom occurs.[69] The "natural history" of general hospitals is one of physical growth over the years, with periodic increments of beds and equipment to keep pace with scientific advancements and public expectations.

Setting and Age of Hospital. Beyond sponsorship and size, a third determinant of a hospital's program is its immediate environment—urban or rural, affluent or depressed—and the nature of other hospitals nearby. If a hospital is the only one for miles around, it will be induced to offer a wider range of services to patients. On the other hand, even in a densely populated city there may be several hospitals in a small area, with unnecessarily duplicated equipment and services.[70] In a large city, nevertheless, the availability of a highly organized out-patient service at a municipal hospital, for example, reduces the pressure on nearby voluntary hospitals to develop such programs. Similarly, a strong educational program for interns and residents in one hospital limits the potential of another hospital to attract the limited output of young doctors into such training activities. The location and number of hospitals in an area also influences the affiliations and travel time of physicians; hence the commitment of doctors to any one hospital and their working efficiency are affected.[71]

The very age of a hospital will also influence the nature of its program. Aside from the tendency of hospitals to grow in bed-capacity over

[68] David B. Starkweather, *Organizational Performance of Different Sized Hospitals*, (Doctoral dissertation, University of California, Los Angeles, 1968).

[69] Mark S. Blumberg, "The Effects of Size and Specialism on Utilization of Urban Hospitals," *Hospitals* (16 May 1965): 43–47.

[70] U.S. Public Health Service, *Area-wide Planning for Hospitals and Related Health Facilities*, PHS pub. No. 855 (Washington: Government Printing Office, 1961).

[71] Jerome W. Lubin, I. M. Reed, G. L. Worstell, and D. L. Drosness, "How Distance Affects Physician Activity," *Modern Hospital* (July 1966): 80–82.

the years, the community involvements of an institution are bound to increase with time. Long existence usually yields prestige, and with this a sense of community responsibility develops. Respected citizens and outstanding doctors seek to be identified with the more prestigious hospitals in an area. To enhance their personal reputations, perhaps in the ancient spirit of *noblesse oblige*, such leaders strive continuously for hospital excellence—for more advanced features of hospital service, education, and research. On the other hand, the new hospitals may "try harder" and be motivated by a competitive desire to outshine the older institutions.

Thus, one can identify a vast complex of environmental and internal factors that exert influence on the shape of hospital programs and also on the patterns of medical staff organization. These influences range from the broad movements in population demography and medical science to the operation of formal governmental and voluntary measures of social discipline and the intrinsic attributes of a hospital's sponsorship or size.

The implementation of many features of the hospital program depends on the manner of organization of the medical staff. The latter therefore, while largely a result of social influences, becomes an intervening factor, a link in the chain of causes contributing to the scope and content of hospital performance. By focusing, as we do in this book, on the dynamics of medical staff organization (MSO) we are not thereby ignoring the operation of all the forces reviewed in this chapter. Rather, we are exploring how this particular aspect of hospital organization contributes to the capacity of the hospital to respond to all the demands made by a rapidly changing society.

Before proceeding to the central, empirical core of this study—the description and analysis of current MSO patterns in America and their relationship to hospital performance—it will be helpful to examine medical staff organization along two other dimensions—those of time and space. First, we will examine medical staff organization historically and try to discover how current American patterns evolved. Then, we will examine MSO patterns in hospitals of other nations, so that the attributes we may take for granted in the United States are seen in balanced perspective.

II

HISTORIC DEVELOPMENT OF MEDICAL STAFF ORGANIZATION IN HOSPITALS

THE HISTORY OF hospitals has been told many times,[1] but in this chapter we will focus on the way that doctors have worked in hospitals. Current patterns of medical staff organization in the United States are an outcome partly of heritages from Europe and partly from developments uniquely American.[2]

The evolution of the hospital from an ancient custodial institution for the sick poor to a modern facility for scientific as well as humanistic service to persons of all social classes was associated with different forms of relationship to doctors. Even today the relationship of the doctor to the hospital is still generally different when the object of his work is a private patient, as compared with an indigent patient; this differentiation may be seen not only in various hospitals but in different wards in the same facility. As hospitals have become increasingly important for everyone, various external social controls have come to be applied to regulate or influence the relationships and obligations of doctors to hospitals, so that the welfare of patients may be protected.

THE EARLY ROLE OF DOCTORS IN HOSPITALS

Throughout most of recorded history the hospital was developed by units of government or organized religion for the care of special population groups—the military forces, the poor, slaves, or others. Doctors were appointed by the relevant authorities to give care to these patients. In the earliest times doctors were evidently paid for this work, but in the later Christian era service to the poor in hospitals was expected without

---

[1] Charles Letourneau, "A History of Hospitals," parts I–IV, *Hospital Management*, vol. 87 (March–June 1959).

[2] E. H. L. Corwin, *American Hospital* (New York: Commonwealth Fund, 1946).

remuneration; the physician was rewarded in nonmonetary ways which
we will discuss below.

As early as the eleventh century B.C., in ancient Egypt, there were,
according to Pliny, physicians serving as paid officers of the state to treat
the poor. When the patient was severely ill he was presumably cared for
in "official houses."[3] In imperial Rome there were hospitals attached to
the army and served by military surgeons. There were also rudimentary
hospitals maintained by large landowners for their slaves; since slaves
were valuable property, their recovery from illness meant the protection
of investments. The doctors treating slaves were attached to the estate of
the landowners, presumably on a salary, while other doctors were practicing as craftsmen in the town, paid by private fees. A few doctors in each
city were also salaried by the state to provide care to the poor who were
freemen.

The beginnings of the modern hospital, however, are usually traced
to the advent of Christianity. With Emperor Constantine's recognition of
Christianity in 325 A.D. came his direction to the bishops of the realm
to establish a hospital for the poor in every cathedral city. In this early
Christian period there were no physicians in these charitable hospitals,
but clerics who had learned something about medicine were in charge.
These early institutions were really houses of hospitality or "xeno-
dochia" for the destitute and the pilgrim as well as the sick, so that medical care was not an important feature of their work. In the eleventh and
twelfth centuries, during the crusades to the east, similar custodial hospitals were established by the church leaders along the main routes. The
monasteries also had infirmaries in which care was given to sick brothers
as well as to destitute travellers who came for help.

With the growth of cities and the emergence of a medical profession
in the later Middle Ages, the place of doctors in hospitals changed. Most
doctors were either medical craftsmen or surgeons (including barber-
surgeons) with shops in the towns, treating people on their premises or
in the patient's home. In the larger cities, however, these doctors were
gradually called upon by the religious hospital authorities to come and
treat the sick poor. This was regarded as a Christian duty and not as a
source of livelihood. In Constantinople, for example, there was a large
hospital attached to a monastery in the year 1112, with a rotating staff
of physicians.[4] These doctors from the city were expected to visit patients
at least once a day, and there were two doctors for each ward of about

[3] Henry C. Burdett, *Hospitals—History and Administration* (London: Scientific
Press, 1893).

[4] George Rosen, "The Hospital: Historical Sociology of a Community Institution,"
in *The Hospital in Modern Society*, Elliot Friedson, editor (New York: Free Press of
Glencoe, 1963).

ten beds. The entire medical staff was divided into two groups, rotating their periods on duty each month. The pattern of charitable hospital service by doctors was not exclusively Christian, for in Moslem cities, such as Baghdad and Cairo, there were also hospitals visited by doctors from the town, according to a regular schedule but presumably without remuneration.

From the thirteenth century onward, a great many hospitals were established throughout Europe, initially by the Christian church but then often transferred to municipal authorities. With their gradual secularization, some of the medical service in hospitals was given by municipally appointed and salaried physicians. Sometimes the municipal doctor also had duties as a sanitary officer in the city, and sometimes he served as a professor in the medical school. From the twelfth century medical faculties were developed in the universities, and their teaching of medical students increasingly took place on the wards of the large municipal or church-supported hospitals for the poor.[5]

With the Renaissance and the beginnings of medical science, hospitals became more medical and less custodial in character. The doctors serving in them were either donating their service as a religiously inspired *noblesse oblige* or were salaried municipal physicians. But, in either case, private patients within hospital wards were virtually unknown. Only for medical care outside a hospital would the doctor be paid by the patient.

As industrialization developed and a working class took shape in the cities, various organized arrangements evolved to pay for medical care.[6] In the sixteenth century the guilds organized mutual benefit plans to help members in distress, and these included payment of doctors for medical services. These "insurance" plans led to the "friendly societies" of England or the "Kranken Kassen" of Germany in the eighteenth and nineteenth centuries. The Elizabethan Poor Laws of the early seventeenth century established local public responsibility for the destitute, including some provision for their medical care. In so far as doctors were paid by any of these programs, however, it was for services in the home of the patient or the doctor's office, but not within the hospital. Hospitals and the services of doctors in them remained charitable or tax-supported.

By the late eighteenth and early nineteenth centuries, however, another form of hospital took shape, especially in England. This was the "voluntary" institution formed by a group of leading citizens on a charitable

---

[5] Henry E. Sigerist, "An Outline of the Development of the Hospital," in *Sigerist on the Sociology of Medicine*, Milton I. Roemer, editor (New York: M.D. Publications, 1960), pp. 319–26.

[6] René Sand, *The Advance to Social Medicine* (London: Staples Press, 1952).

basis but not directly tied to the church or local government. These places were intended mainly for acute or short-stay cases, while chronic and long-stay patients still went to government hospitals. In these voluntary hospitals, while most beds were for the poor, a small number were reserved for well-to-do patients who could pay their personal doctor for his service. Thus, the doctors on the medical staff of the hospital took care of the poor on the large wards without remuneration, and they also served in out-patient departments limited to the poor. (In the mid-nineteenth century, nursing in these hospitals was greatly improved through formal programs of training.) In return for this charitable service, doctors were permitted to use the hospital for treatment of their private patients.

A further boost to this use of hospitals for nonindigent or self-supporting patients came in the later nineteenth century with the enactment of social insurance legislation providing medical care, beginning in Germany in 1883. Insured workers were not indigent and they did not wish to be treated as paupers if they required hospitalization. In this same period the technology of medicine made enormous strides, with the recognition of the bacterial origin of much disease and the development of antisepsis.[7] Anesthesia, after 1850, made surgery far more feasible for a wide variety of pathological conditions. The hospital, therefore, became a far safer place, and health or sickness insurance funds made arrangements for their members to be served in special sections of government or voluntary hospitals. The doctors serving these patients were sometimes paid by the insurance funds.

As hospitals in the later nineteenth century became more highly developed centers of medical science, demanding more time from doctors, it was no longer reasonable to expect them to provide services without monetary reward. In the government hospitals of European cities and also in the church-supported hospitals devoted to the poor, doctors came to be appointed on full-time salaries. Hospitals also became the principal centers for education of medical and nursing students. Only the most highly qualified physicians were appointed to these hospital posts; as the number of doctors rapidly increased, the great majority of them worked solely in their offices and had no connection of any sort with hospitals. Thus, there evolved the European "closed-staff" hospital and the growth of medical and surgical specialization among hospital doctors. The general practitioner in the town, who constituted the great majority of the profession, had to refer any patient requiring hospitalization to a hospital-based specialist.

Within hospitals, over 300 or 400 years, there gradually developed a

[7] Richard H. Shryock, *The Development of Modern Medicine* (Philadelphia: University of Pennsylvania Press, 1936).

spirit of discipline and organization affecting both the doctors and other hospital personnel. When nursing became professionalized—through formal regimes of education—and as antiseptic techniques became better understood and more widely applied, these disciplinary influences over medical behavior were naturally accelerated. Outside the hospital the social control over physicians was much more limited. It was offered chiefly through the medical licensure laws, which had originated around the twelfth century in Europe.[8] The first licensure, designed to clarify for the general public the background of a healing craftsman, was entrusted to the medical faculties of the universities; from the thirteenth century, however, it became a function of the state, where it remains today. As the hospital has extended its role, however, in the whole social institution of medicine, it has come to supplement the medical licensure laws in influencing the quality of medical practice even outside the hospital walls. This influence has been especially prominent in the United States for reasons to be explored below.

THE HOSPITAL DOCTOR IN AMERICA
AND THE STANDARDIZATION MOVEMENT

In its early years the British colony that was to become the United States adopted the pattern of hospital organization which then prevailed in England. The first American hospitals evolved from almshouses for the poor in New York City (Bellevue Hospital) in 1658 and in Philadelphia (Philadelphia Hospital) in 1713. While originally intended for the aged and the insane as well as the sick poor, these institutions evolved into municipal hospitals for the poor. They were served by doctors who received small stipends from the city governments.

The Pennsylvania Hospital was founded in 1752 as a voluntary hospital, intended from the beginning to serve the patients of private doctors as well as the poor. Physicians served the poor in large public wards without pay, while they attended their own patients in private rooms; these patients made payments to both the hospital and the doctor, according to the pattern that was to become prevalent in America. As the country grew and the western territories were opened up, both voluntary and government hospitals were established in all the main cities. Typically, the government hospitals were restricted to the care of the poor, and physicians were appointed to serve in them for small public salaries. The voluntary hospitals also had wards for the poor, but by the mid-nineteenth century the majority of their patients were private. Doctors

---

[8] Henry E. Sigerist, "The History of Medical Licensure," in *Sigerist on the Sociology of Medicine*, Milton I. Roemer, editor, op. cit., pp. 308–18.

received fees only from their private patients and they treated the poor without remuneration.

With steady immigration from Europe and the westward movement of the frontier, the number of doctors in America rapidly increased.[9] Standards were lax and many physicians had learned their skills only by apprenticeship. In 1775 it has been estimated that of about 3,500 doctors in the country, only 400 held medical degrees. Medical schools were organized everywhere, mostly on a commercial basis with no ties to universities; in the mid-nineteenth century there were estimated to be 400 such schools that soon earned the epithet "diploma mills." It was the medical profession itself that responded to this need by organization of the American Medical Association in 1847 and an attempt to establish standards for "ethical practice" through local medical societies. Beginning in 1873 in Texas, state boards of medical examiners were established to examine candidates as a basis for medical licensure by the states.

There were no real constraints, however, on the development of voluntary hospitals and the pattern of medical activity in them. While certain physicians were designated to treat the poor in charity wards, the private rooms were open to the patients of almost any private physician. Thus, the typical American voluntary hospital in the late nineteenth and early twentieth centuries came to be known as having an "open staff." The disruption of the Civil War did not help, and many small hospitals were simply set up by private physicians for their own patients and those of any other doctor, so long as the costs of room and board could be paid. There was no systematic policy in voluntary hospitals toward exercise of controls over the work of private physicians.

Toward the end of the nineteenth century the organized medical profession sought to improve the situation by directing its main attention to the improvement of medical education. These efforts, supported by private philanthropic foundations, led to the nationwide survey of medical schools by Abraham Flexner and publication of his monumental report in 1910. The state licensure laws and the rough-and-tumble of competition had already led to the reduction of medical schools to 148 by this date, and the system of "grading" schools led to their further reduction by 1930 to 76 reasonably satisfactory training institutions. It was only after the Flexner Report, as we will see, that the medical profession turned its attention to improvement of standards in hospitals.

In the late nineteenth century certain frictions developed between private doctors and hospitals that forecast problems still with us today. The public and voluntary hospitals in the larger American cities, as in Europe, had developed out-patient departments for the poor. So long

---

[9] Henry E. Sigerist, *American Medicine* (New York: W. W. Norton, 1934).

as the country had relatively few doctors these clinics were readily accepted by the profession, but as the number of doctors increased the dispensaries came to be viewed as competitive. The medical literature from about 1870 onward is full of discussions of the "abuse of medical charity" in hospital clinics by patients who could afford private medical care.[10] In subsequent years it was doctors who launched the idea of hospital social workers—ladies who would not only assist the poor but also make certain that the nonindigent did not seek OPD care. In New York State, the concern about "abuse" of dispensaries was so great that a law was enacted in 1899 placing all clinics under the supervision of the state board of charities and providing penalties for persons who falsely claimed to be indigent.

The post-Flexner reduction in medical schools led not only to an improvement in medical education but to a reduction in the output of doctors. This reduced professional competition, and with the rising economic prosperity of the country it allayed the hostility of doctors toward hospital clinics. In these years also, enormous strides were made in medical science, so that the conscientious physician became increasingly dependent on the diagnostic and therapeutic facilities which only a hospital could provide. It was in this period that the first organized steps were taken in the United States to improve and systematize the way that physicians worked in hospitals. And, just as the Flexner Report was motivated by an objective of improving the quality and reducing the quantitative output of medical schools, the hospital movement was also motivated by a combination of professional and entrepreneurial purposes. The surgeons—specialists in surgery—wanted to improve the standards of postgraduate surgical training and simultaneously to restrict entrance into specialty ranks to those who were properly qualified. These efforts came to be known as the "hospital standardization" movement, and they were led by a private association of American and Canadian surgeons.

The American College of Surgeons (ACS) was founded in 1913, three years after the Flexner Report. In order to establish a basis of merit for membership in this private professional society, the College required that each candidate submit 100 complete medical records of patients on whom he had operated, demonstrating thereby his technical ability and judgment.[11] It was soon discovered, however, that few applicants could comply with this requirement. Outside of the large public and sometimes

[10] George Rosen, "The Impact of the Hospital on the Physician, the Patient and the Community," *Hospital Administration*, 9:15–33 (Fall 1964).

[11] American College of Surgeons, "History, Development, and Progress of Hospital Standardization," in *Manual of Hospital Standardization* (Chicago, 1946), pp. 5–10.

voluntary hospitals connected with university-affiliated medical schools, it was found that few hospitals maintained proper patient records. Many of the voluntary and proprietary hospitals that had mushroomed since the 1890's lacked adequate laboratory and x-ray facilities to permit proper preoperative diagnosis. Most important, it was recognized that the physicians of "open-staff" hospitals were not organized into medical staffs which might provide some self-discipline over the appointment and activities of all doctors. All this was documented in a survey of 2,700 hospitals throughout the country conducted during the years 1916–18. (It is of interest that in 1913 the ACS had petitioned the U.S. Public Health Service to conduct a national survey of hospitals to provide background data for developing a standardization program, but the federal government declined with the reply that this was a task for private initiative.) [12]

To correct these deficiencies, the American College of Surgeons proceeded to establish a national program for "standardization" of hospitals which was to have far-reaching results. It promoted standards of organization of hospital facilities, and especially of medical staffs, that eventually came to be emulated throughout the nation. In 1919 a "Minimum Standard for Hospitals" was adopted by the House of Delegates of the College. It contained five main provisions, with various specific points under each, as follows: (1) Physicians and surgeons privileged to practice in the hospital must be organized as a "definite medical staff," whether the hospital was "open" or "closed." This staff might include subgroups of "active," "associate," and "courtesy" members. (2) Medical staff membership must be restricted to doctors competent in their fields and worthy in character; in the latter connection, fee-splitting must be prohibited. (3) There must be formal rules and regulations governing professional work in the hospital, and these must include provision for monthly staff meetings and reviews of clinical experience in various departments (such as medicine, surgery, and obstetrics). (4) To facilitate these reviews, accurate and complete medical records must be written and maintained for all patients. (The detailed contents of the medical record were specified in the Minimum Standard.) (5) Clinical laboratory and x-ray facilities must be available under the charge of trained technicians.

Over the next 30 years, numerous small changes were made in the Minimum Standard, but it is evident that in this 1919 formulation there are the foundations of most (though not all) of the features of medical staff organization found in accredited hospitals today. The leaders of the American College of Surgeons (ACS) included the Mayo brothers, Harvey Cushing, George Crile, Ernest Codman, and other distinguished surgeons associated with university teaching hospitals and various institu-

---

[12] John A. Hornsby, "Standardization of Hospitals—Introduction and Classification," *Modern Hospital*, 8:256 (1917).

tions with "closed staffs" of full-time doctors. Thus, even though the problems which induced the standardization movement arose principally from "open-staff" community hospitals, the proposed criteria for reform were obviously influenced by practices in the more rigorously organized "closed-staff" institutions. The spirit of national purpose associated with World War I also probably had an influence; in a wartime atmosphere, an organized rather than *laissez faire* approach to problems seemed appropriate and necessary.

It is of interest that this national movement to promote uniform standards for medical staff organization in hospitals should have developed first in America, rather than in Europe where the history of hospitals was much older. As we have noted, however, in Europe the hospitals were staffed mainly by small groups of highly selected doctors; the patients, being mainly public beneficiaries, were the responsibility of the hospital rather than of private physicians. It was the free-wheeling, "open-staff" voluntary hospital in the rapidly expanding American environment that presented the problems and induced the reforms. The abuses of private practice, in a medical marketplace characterized by large numbers of poorly trained doctors competing for patients, were an important feature of the setting. Thus, in the medical literature of the period 1912–20 there were endless discussions of fee-splitting and its evils. Also prominent in the literature of the period were appeals that medical staff appointments in hospitals be based on some objective determination of merit, rather than the doctor's social or political connections or no standards at all.[13] It was these problems that explain the several components of the ACS Minimum Standard for Hospitals.

The standardization program exerted a rapidly expanding influence on medical staff organization. The first three surveys were conducted among 692 hospitals in 1918–20, and the percentage found to meet the standards rose from 13 per cent in the first year to 59 per cent in the third year. The rapid improvement was attributed by the Executive Secretary of the American Hospital Association, at least partly, to the influence of the postwar return to civilian life of many physicians who had served in highly organized military hospitals.[14] After 1920 the hospitals surveyed increased in number each year as well as in the percentage found to be approvable. By 1945 there were 3,938 hospitals surveyed and 81 per cent of these were approved.

Over these years the ACS, despite its obvious success, met resistance from many doctors and they had to emphasize that standardiza-

[13] Warren L. Babcock, "The Open Hospital—A Factor in Preventive Medicine," *Modern Hospital*, 7:411 (1916).

[14] A. R. Warner, "Development and Progress in the Field of Hospital Administration," *Modern Hospital*, 14:176 (1920).

tion did not mean reducing all hospitals and medical staffs to a deadly uniformity, nor discouragement of individual creativity in doctors, nor abandonment of humanistic patient care in favor of a purely "technical" approach. The American Medical Association, which in its early years was more representative of the general practitioner than the specialist, was "distinctly hostile"—according to one of the ACS leaders, Dr. Franklin Martin—and, as the standardization movement grew, gave it only passive support.[15] The American Hospital Association and the Catholic Hospital Association gave the movement active support from the beginning.

The focus of the ACS program was, of course, mainly on the requirements of surgery, but inevitably the requirements for all types of medical care were influenced. Technological advances were occurring in internal medicine, obstetrics, pediatrics, and all the subspecialties, and their application called for more systematic organization within hospitals. With the growth of specialization and its formalizing through the various specialty boards after 1920, an increasing basis was laid for departmentalization of medical staffs, even in small hospitals. Large hospitals with public wards for the poor had long found such departmentalization an administrative necessity. Once a medical department or an obstetrical department was organized with a medical staff, its members could readily be induced to emulate the self-disciplinary features being applied in the surgical department.

Through the 1920's, while the standardization program was having its impact, new hospitals were being rapidly constructed and old ones enlarged all over the United States. The rate of hospital utilization by the population was steadily rising, as technical developments outstripped the capacity of home or office care, as childbirth came to be considered a matter for hospitalization, and as economic prosperity enabled an increasing proportion of people to pay for private service. With the economic depression of 1930–39, the utilization of private hospital care fell off, but patients in government institutions and in the public wards of voluntary hospitals continued to increase. It was in these settings that systematic organization of medical staffs was more readily achieved. Also, the vast growth of internships, as a virtual requirement after medical school graduation, had further implications for the development of American hospitals.[16]

Almost coincident with the start of the hospital standardization program, the Council on Medical Education of the American Medical As-

15 Loyal Davis, *Fellowship of Surgeons* (Springfield, Illinois: Charles C Thomas, 1960), p. 217.

16 J. A. Curran, "Internships and Residencies: Historical Backgrounds and Current Trends," *J. Med. Education*, 34:873–84 (September 1959).

sociation (concerned mainly with the grading of medical schools) enlarged its scope to include postgraduate medical education in hospitals. In 1914 it published its first list of hospitals offering internship training, but this was not very selective. By 1919, however, standards had been formulated with the issuance of "Essentials of an Approved Internship," and the next year the Council changed its name to Council on Medical Education and Hospitals.[17] After 1920 this Council gave increasing attention to hospital residencies for specialty training, and the "Essentials of Approved Residencies" was issued in 1928. The Advisory Board for Medical Specialties was established by the American Medical Association in 1933, developing a link between the specialty boards, which were rapidly increasing, and the setting of standards for various hospital residencies. All these normative bodies in the field of postgraduate medical education obviously put further pressures on hospitals to tighten up their patterns of medical staff organization.

THE JOINT COMMISSION ON ACCREDITATION OF HOSPITALS

The war years 1939–45 ended the economic depression and created new pressures on American hospitals by boosting the demand for hospital care at a time when new hospital construction had to be halted.[18] The demand for beds, the reduction in civilian doctors, and the general temper of national emergency stimulated further need for improved hospital organization. Formal training for hospital administration in university courses was producing a new professional class of administrators who were knowledgeable about national developments and the recommended organizational patterns. "Postwar planning" was popular in every field, to help define the purpose for which World War II was being fought. This planning inevitably meant a greater role for government in the health services, including hospitals.

One of the first postwar legislative enactments was the Hospital Survey and Construction (Hill–Burton) Act of 1946. While intended mainly to subsidize, with federal funds, hospital construction in areas with deficient bed supply, this law also required that every state receiving funds must have a hospital licensure law. When the act was passed only ten of the forty-eight states had such laws, and these were usually quite limited in scope—applying, for example, only to the care

[17] John C. Nunemaker, "Mechanisms for the Approval of Internships and Residencies," in *The Medical Staff in the Modern Hospital*, C. Wesley Eisele, editor (New York: McGraw-Hill, 1967), pp. 405–18.
[18] Commission on Hospital Care, *Hospital Care in the United States* (Washington, 1947).

of indigent patients or to operation of maternity services. Promptly after 1946 all the states enacted hospital licensure laws.

The federal government distributed literature on a "model statute" for hospital approval, and since the ACS standardization program had been operating for over a quarter century by then, its provisions naturally influenced the federal recommendations. As a result, the hospital licensure statutes enacted by most of the states closely resembled the requirements of ACS standardization. Most of the state laws called for an organized medical staff, the adoption of formal medical staff bylaws, a procedure for appointment of doctors according to professional qualifications, the designation of different classes of staff membership (active, associate, courtesy, etc.), departmentalization, election of a staff chief, periodic meetings to review clinical work, and even such details as the recording of minutes of staff meetings.[19] The statutes also contained extensive provisions on the physical plant, laboratory, nursing service, pharmacy, and other features of hospital operation.

Thus, the influence of a voluntary body of surgeons on medical staff organization became crystallized into state law in most jurisdictions, although there were many variations in the details. Implementation and enforcement of these laws, however, has been weak, as noted in chapter I. Nevertheless, the embodiment of ACS standards into law, even if weakly enforced, raised the issue of moving still further ahead with a voluntary program in the field. A wider organizational base was sought, and this was achieved in 1952 by the formation of the Joint Commission on Accreditation of Hospitals (JCAH), composed of the ACS along with the American College of Physicians, the American Medical Association, the American Hospital Association, and the Canadian Medical Association (the latter agency later withdrew to form a separate Canadian body with the same function).[20] The JCAH rapidly became an even more influential force than the ACS had been. At the outset it adopted the same standards as the ACS, but it elaborated on certain details and provided a larger staff for visits of inspection. By 1952 the ACS standards had become more highly developed than those incorporated in the five original requirements cited earlier.

Over its first thirty years (1920–50), the ACS standards had come to embody nearly all the features by which we analyze medical staff organization in this research. The composition of the staff into classes of active, associate, courtesy, consulting, and honorary members was specified. Appointment procedures, with formal applications were required

[19] Keith O. Taylor and Donna M. Donald, *A Comparative Study of Hospital Licensure Regulations* (Berkeley: University of California, School of Public Health, 1957).

[20] American Hospital Association, *Hospital Accreditation References* (Chicago: The Association, 1965).

to assure objectivity and proper qualifications. Departmentalization of the various specialties was required—at least to a minimum duality of medicine and surgery. Model bylaws, rules, and regulations on meetings, election of officers, ethical behavior, etc. were promulgated.

In one respect, however, the JCAH made a significant addition to the ACS standards. The latter had stipulated that "the medical staff review and analyze at regular intervals their clinical experience" on the basis of study of written patient records. Suggestions were even offered on "professional service accounting" methods, which one would now define as "medical audits." There was no administrative provision in ACS standards, however, for actual implementation of such a review process. The JCAH filled this gap by specifying two medical staff mechanisms as a condition for accreditation: a medical records committee and a tissue committee. Regarding the latter, the JCAH standards state: "The Tissue Committee shall review and evaluate all surgery performed in the hospital on the basis of agreement or disagreement among the preoperative, post-operative and pathological diagnoses; and on the acceptability of the procedure undertaken. The Committee shall meet at least once a month and submit a report in writing to the Executive Committee."[21] The principle embodied in this was applied later for still other facets of medical performance, e.g., drug use (pharmacy committee) or sterile techniques (infections committee). This concept provides the basis for the inclusion in our analysis of medical staff organization of "control committees."

The historic background of the "control committee" concept, however, is much older than the JCAH. In 1916 Dr. E. A. Codman, who had been an active surgeon at the Massachusetts General Hospital in Boston, published *A Study in Hospital Efficiency: The First Five Years*, which outlined a system for judging the "efficiency" of hospitals by detailed examination of patient records and classification of the end-results as favorable or unfavorable.[22] Codman had, indeed, attempted to get his "end-result" approach incorporated in the original procedures of the ACS standardization program, but he was ahead of his time and his views were rejected as too likely to induce opposition from doctors. Neither ACS nor JCAH standards, therefore, demanded hard quantitative data on the outcome of physician performance, but the stipulation of professional control committees at least lays a foundation for collection of such data.

Careful medical audits of samples of patient records, with judgment

[21] Joint Commission on Accreditation of Hospitals, *Standards for Hospital Accreditation* (Chicago: January 1964), p. 8.
[22] Paul A. Lembcke, "Evolution of the Medical Audit," *J.A.M.A.*, 199:543–50 (20 February 1967).

of the adequacy and quality of care rendered, have been done only as specific research projects or as special investigations to settle some medical staff crisis in a hospital. Paul A. Lembcke did important work in this field beginning with the Council of Rochester Regional Hospitals in 1946, and in the 1950's contributions were made by Eisele, Rosenfeld, Trussell, Makover, and others. The Commission on Professional and Hospital Activities was established in 1956 for developing a massive computerized system for analyzing basic data on all medical records in participating hospitals.[23] The whole field of methodology on medical audits or schemes for evaluating the ultimate quality of medical care in hospitals is still very much in ferment (see chapter VIII). Research over the last several decades and still going on, however, has clearly been influencing the standards being applied by the JCAH and may be expected to have continuing impact on the whole character of medical staff organization in hospitals.

Beyond the Joint Commission on Accreditation of Hospitals and the state hospital licensure laws, other forces have shaped the patterns of medical staff organization seen in hospitals today. The influences of standard-setting in postgraduate medical education (internships and residencies) and of specialization (the specialty boards) have already been mentioned. Judicial decisions in litigated cases have also played a significant role. Until the mid-1950's the state courts made a sharp distinction between government and voluntary hospitals, with respect to the "rights" of a physician to be appointed to the medical staff. Previously the courts had held that voluntary and proprietary hospitals might deny staff privileges to qualified physicians, so long as their own bylaws had been followed—but not government hospitals. More recently the courts have decided that both government and private hospitals are vested with a "public interest" and, therefore, medical staff bylaws must not be unreasonably restrictive. It is for this reason that membership in a local medical society is no longer defensible as a condition for appointment to a medical staff—the courts having found this unconstitutional or contrary to sound public policy.[24]

After World War II, the whole level of hospital utilization in America continued to rise, not only because of technological developments in medicine but also because of the great expansion of hospitalization insurance. With the growth of population, new construction barely kept pace, and the bed-population ratio changed little, but a higher rate of admissions occurred along with a reduction in the average length

[23] R. S. Myers, V. N. Slee, and R. G. Hoffman, "Medical Audit," *Modern Hospital*, 85:77–83 (September 1955).

[24] Gladys A. Harrison, *Control of Medical Staff Appointments in Voluntary Non-profit Hospitals* (Chicago: American Hospital Association, 1963).

of stay. This meant that more persons were served in hospitals during a year, hospital costs per day rose sharply, and the general population became increasingly interested in hospital affairs. As noted in the previous chapter, pressures came from many sources to improve skills and economy in internal hospital management. Consumer organizations, labor unions, health insurance plans, government agencies paying for certain beneficiaries made demands on the governing boards of hospitals to eliminate waste and increase efficiency. The effect of all these pressures has been felt also in the approach to organization of medical staffs, pushing them toward greater self-discipline.

CURRENT PATTERNS OF MEDICAL STAFF ORGANIZATION IN AMERICAN HOSPITALS

With these historical developments one can better understand the patterns of medical staff organization that characterize most American hospitals today. The basic forces at play sprang from the whole development of medical science, the rapid population growth and economic expansion of the country, the rise in public expectations and demands for medical care. In reaction to a century or more of free-wheeling, *laissez faire* hospital growth, reactions set in to achieve more careful controls over the whole operation of hospitals, and especially over how physicians should work in them. The resultant reforms were mediated through specific professional organizations—the American College of Surgeons and the Joint Commission on Accreditation of Hospitals—as well as through state laws and judicial decisions.

Later in this book, the current structure and function of medical staffs in hospitals are analyzed according to seven features: (1) staff composition; (2) appointment procedures; (3) departmentalization; (4) control committees; (5) commitment of doctors; (6) documentation; and (7) informal dynamics. In over-all interpretation of the historical developments, we may consider briefly the forces in back of each of these organizational features.

The composition or structure of medical staffs into categories of active, associate, courtesy members, and so on, was the compromise solution in the American scene to the problems generated by the completely "open-staff" hospital. Relatively firm standards could be applied to attainment of membership on the "active staff," and to these physicians would be entrusted duties for which the hospital was legally responsible, such as service to indigent patients or various functions in administration or teaching. Courtesy staff members, on the other hand, were not expected to meet such high standards, and the scope of their work in the hospital was limited to attendance of individual private patients.

These distinctions—the standards for which, of course, have changed over the years—allowed hospitals to continue receiving the patronage of the private patients of many local doctors, while gradually upgrading the qualifications and responsibilities of the basic "active" medical staff.

The development of systematized and objective appointment procedures was intended to enable hospitals to exclude physicians who were inadequately trained or believed to be unethical. With the large number of physicians trained at substandard medical schools and engaged in practice in the early twentieth century, some method of discrimination was necessary. It was important to consider the medical school from which a doctor had graduated and to rule out favoritism.[25] Exclusion of fee-splitting could be made a condition of appointment, especially since it was believed that the less-competent surgeon was the most inclined to split his fee with a referring general practitioner. Later, delineation of "privileges," on the basis of specialty qualifications, could be added to the appointment procedures. As a double-check on the objectivity of medical staff judgment, as well as being an affirmation of legal responsibility, the governing board of the hospital was expected to finalize all appointments to the medical staff.

Departmentalization of medical staffs came about principally as a result of the specialization of medicine. Through grouping of persons in the same specialty, more effective discipline could be expected. As specialization rapidly increased, after about 1915, medical staff departmentalization developed. Size-of-hospital was also obviously a factor, and the enlargement of urban hospitals, with population growth, naturally brought greater pressure for departmental organization of the patient-care units; medical staff departmentalization accompanied this. The large government hospitals affiliated with medical schools were departmentalized before 1900, and their practices set a model for the medical staffs in other hospitals. Through a departmental structure it was possible to appoint in each specialized field a "chief of service," who would supervise all the medical activities of attending physicians in his department. *The Modern Hospital* magazine recommended this in 1917, before the ACS program was underway.[26]

The concept of "commitment" in a medical staff involves a judgment of the degree to which doctors are involved in or committed to the hospital, as compared with other components of their professional lives —especially private practice. On the American scene, its historic development is bound up with the policies of different hospitals in engaging certain physicians on full-time salary. As noted below, certain types of

---

25 R. L. Dickinson, "The Practicability of Ratings in Appointment and Promotion of Members of the Visiting Staff," *Medical Record*, 89:872 (1916).

26 Editorial: "Open-door Hospitals," *Modern Hospital*, 9:419 (1917).

hospitals for designated beneficiaries or special diseases have long had full-time salaried physicians as the mainstay of their medical staffs. In the predominant type of American hospital, however—the general hospital under voluntary auspices, serving mainly paying patients—the level of physician commitment has been relatively weak. It was the rising importance of pathology and radiology in the early twentieth century that led to the appointment of contractual physicians in these fields. In 1916 it was evidently still innovative for Dr. Charles Mayo to recommend such salaried diagnostic specialists for the average hospital.[27] Gradually more types of full-time physicians have been appointed in voluntary general hospitals, including salaried chiefs of clinical departments in some hospitals where the great majority of staff members are still private practitioners. Along with this trend, the total staff complement of doctors has been spending an increasing proportion of its time in the institution, as the general importance of the hospital in over-all medical care has become more obvious. This means greater professional commitment, which has been fortified by various obligations imposed on the physician through the medical staff organization.

The place of professional control committees in medical staff organization came somewhat later, as discussed in the previous section. The emphasis on accurate patient records, that gave birth to the whole ACS standardization program in 1919, laid the groundwork for the "medical audit," and the tissue committee came later. Periodic conferences of the entire medical staff or of departmental staffs had as their major purpose the self-critical review of medical performance. In 1916 surgical staff conferences were being held in a large New York teaching hospital to review deaths, infections, postoperative complications, and unsatisfactory postoperative results.[28] It was thirty or forty years, however, before this type of case review was systematically carried out through tissue committees or other types of control committees in the majority of hospitals. Impetus was given to this important instrument of medical staff discipline by the rise in recent years of malpractice suits by patients against both doctors and hospitals.

Documented rules and regulations were very rare in medical staffs before the ACS standardization program. In 1918 the Editor of *The Modern Hospital* could still recommend a flexible word-of-mouth procedure for achieving medical staff discipline in small hospitals; only in the large departmentalized hospital were written policies advocated.[29]

[27] Charles Mayo, "Nature, Value, and Necessity of Team-work in a Hospital," *Modern Hospital*, 7:1 (1916).

[28] Frank E. Adair, "The Surgical Staff Conference," *N. Y. Med. J.*, 54:21 (1916).

[29] Editorial: "Written Versus Oral Instructions for the Hospital Staff," *Modern Hospital*, 11:221 (1918).

As the number of physicians on the average medical staff increased and the complexity of staff organization became greater, the necessity for formal documentation became more widely appreciated. Likewise, accountability to the governing board of the hospital called for some system of written reports by the medical staff. Written medical staff bylaws were also stimulated by the litigations of doctors who had been denied staff appointment; the courts insisted on formal appointment procedures, the faithful application of which could be assessed through study of the written word.

As for the "informal dynamics" of medical staffs, one can hardly trace this feature historically, except to suggest that it has doubtless always been with us. In earlier days, when medical staffs as a whole were less structured, informal relationships within the staffs, the hospital administration, and the governing board, were more decisive than formal policies. At the turn of the twentieth century, the general "efficiency movement" in industry, associated with Frederick Taylor, had its impact on the hospital field. Greater concern for systematic management in over-all hospital affairs (including nursing, record-keeping, feeding, laundry, etc.) naturally influenced medical staff practices as well. But as medical staff structuring has increased, informal relationships have obviously not disappeared; they may have even increased, in absolute terms, simply because more doctors are now involved more of the time in hospital affairs. To keep the formal staff structure viable, an intricate pattern of informal dynamics has inevitably developed in every medical staff organization—as we will see in later chapters.

This review of the historic development of current features of medical staff organization in American hospitals has focused on voluntary institutions served mainly by physicians committed primarily to private practice. As mentioned above, however, outside this medical "mainstream" are several other types of hospitals, in which the objective is limited to the care of certain defined populations or diseases. These include government hospitals—usually at the municipal or county level—for the care of the poor. They include federal hospitals for military personnel or for veterans. They include hospitals, mostly under state governments, for mental illness, tuberculosis, and sometimes other long-term disorders. They also include nongovernmental hospitals operated in certain industries (such as railroads or mining enterprises) and hospitals associated with special health insurance plans.

In these types of hospitals, the evolution and current structure of medical staff organization has been quite different from the "mainstream" model. Especially in the sphere of "commitment" there are important differences, since the full-time salaried physician has always played a far greater role in these hospitals. Because of this basic difference, the characteristics of other medical staff features, such as departmentalization or control committees, also vary considerably from the national norm for general hospitals. The general hospital standardization movement of the 1920's exerted an influence on these hospitals, too, even though that movement had been stimulated by the problems of the "open-staff" hospital. The effect was mainly to elevate standards for initial appointment to the staffs of these special institutions. By 1928 all the hospitals of the U.S. Veterans Bureau had been approved by the American College of Surgeons. In municipal hospitals more systematic Civil Service procedures were developed for appointment of doctors. The general structure and function of these medical staffs, however, evolved quite differently from patterns in the average voluntary hospital. These differences, in fact, provide the basis for the methodology of comparative analysis, which this research will employ, as explained in later chapters.

In all types of hospitals in America, nevertheless, the evolution of medical staff organization has clearly been in the direction of greater structuring. As the hospital has become more important for both patient and doctor, the pressures have mounted from many sources to achieve greater supervision or discipline over the doctor's work. Traditions of private medical practice and individual freedom have inevitably led to various conflicts, as reviewed in the previous chapter, but the medical profession expects increasing services from the hospital, both in the way of efficient diagnostic and treatment procedures and in postgraduate professional education. Likewise, the general public expects and demands more from hospitals—more sensitive patient care, education of paramedical personnel, medical research, and even preventive services. The hospital is looked upon also as a place for ambulatory care, not only for needy persons in out-patient departments but for patients of any social status in "emergency rooms." It is also expected to be a locale from which organized "home care" can be offered.[30]

These pressures on the hospital to extend its role from a place for bed care of the seriously sick to a wide-ranging "community health center" have inevitably demanded a more rigorous organization of the medical staff. The degree of response, of course, varies greatly among individual hospitals. In hospitals which interpret their social role broadly, the medical staff organization tends to become tighter; likewise, in medical staff organizations of higher self-discipline, there is greater capacity to

[30] John Knowles, *Hospitals, Doctors, and the Public Interest* (Cambridge: Harvard University Press, 1965).

respond to the social demands made on the hospital. In the most highly structured medical staffs, the doctors became integrated into the hospital organization, sharing its goals.

Even in the most permissive medical staff, however, there is some surveillance over physician performance that at least goes beyond the span of the basic medical licensure laws. The medical staff of a hospital is a social group of doctors, and the mere presence of one another must have an influence on the behavior of each. Historical developments in Europe and America have operated to increase this group consciousness. As the hospital evolved from a custodial to a medical institution, from a refuge for the poor to a preferred locale for services to all social classes, external social controls have increasingly come to be exerted upon both hospital managements and the doctors associated with them. The evolution is obviously still in process, and there are many parallel streams in the larger flow of health services.

III

THE WORLD SCENE IN DOCTOR–HOSPITAL RELATIONS

JUST AS HISTORIC developments give us perspective on doctor–hospital relationships today, so does examination of the contemporary scene in nations outside the United States. The features of medical staff organization that we have come to take for granted in America are by no means universal. In fact, the predominant features of the American hospital scene are quite atypical in the worldwide view; the patterns of high structuring that characterize only a minority of general hospitals in this country are the prevailing ones in most other nations of the world.

ECONOMIC DEVELOPMENT, AUTHORITY PATTERNS, AND HOSPITALS

Through the auspices of the World Health Organization, we studied in 1966 and 1968 the general organization of hospitals in a series of countries, chosen to represent different types in a simple conceptual typology.[1] This involved two dimensions: (a) the country's economic development and (b) the degree of centralized authority over its hospital system.

Economic development has obvious influences on hospitals. It affects the resources of personnel and equipment available which, in turn, tend to influence the scheme of organization by which those resources are deployed. Economic development also affects the educational level of the people and their use of and expectations about hospital care.

Within a hospital system, its authority pattern is a fundamental characteristic. Examining a nationwide hospital system as a whole, what

[1] Milton I. Roemer, "Hospital Systems in Different Nations" (Geneva: World Health Organization [unpublished] 1967); bibliographic references are cited in this report, and further references are cited in an expanded version of this study scheduled for publication by the World Health Organization in 1971.

is the degree of centralized authority over the operation of local units? Is there autonomy in each hospital or is it part of a national framework subject to control from the top? Between these two extremes, there may be various gradations. Moreover, certain hospitals in a country may be quite independent, while others are part of a hierarchical network.

These two theoretical dimensions permit us to draw a typology into which any country may be placed. By dividing each dimension into a three-level scale, we derive a conceptual matrix with nine cells, as shown below. Placement of a country and its hospital system within any cell involves some oversimplification, but it enables us to consider many features of hospital organization in relation to the broad social environment. Thirteen countries were studied, and they fall into the proposed typology as shown in the table below.

National economic development	Hospital authority pattern		
	Localized	Partially centralized	Highly centralized
Weak	Peru	Philippines	Togo Malaysia
Moderate	Israel	Iran Chile	USSR Bulgaria
Strong	United States	France Sweden	England

Many elements of hospital organization will be influenced by a country's place in this matrix. Policies of hospital construction, financial support of services, external legal controls or standards, regional relationships, etc. are all affected. Here we will consider, however, only the basic policies of internal hospital administration, including the patterns of medical staff organization.

There are great variations in policies of internal hospital administration, depending on a country's place in the two conceptual dimensions. Hospital management is related at the same time to the over-all system of health service organization and financing in a country. The relative strength of public versus private economic sectors in support of medical care has substantial influence on how hospitals are organized and how doctors work within them.

Countries with a large sector of private medical practice, such as the United States, Canada or Australia, tend also to be those with relatively weak central governmental authority over hospitals. In those countries there is usually much autonomy in the work of physicians. General hospitals of the United States are typically characterized by two lines of internal authority: the medical and the administrative. While theoretically the medical staff comes under the supervision of the hospital board of directors, its latitude for decisions tends to be very wide. Since most general hospital patients are under the private care of an individual physician, he has the greatest legal and moral responsibility for patient care. Limitations and restrictions on his behavior are imposed by an organization of the medical staff itself, and only indirectly by the board of directors. There are usually rather strict limitations to the responsibility of the hospital administrator—who is nearly always a nonmedical man—despite his being the agent of the board of directors.

This American pattern, however, is quite exceptional in the world scene. In the less economically developed countries with localized authority patterns (Peru and Israel), the internal management of hospitals is not split between medical and administrative lines. The top executive of the hospital is typically a physician, who is assisted by a business manager or administrative officer. The medical staff members are usually on full-time or part-time salaries and work according to some type of hierarchical framework. Appointments of doctors and other personnel are usually made, however, by local boards rather than a centralized ministry.

In the countries with moderately centralized authority patterns, the internal administration of hospitals is quite variable. The hospitals of the Ministry of Health in Iran, the Philippines, and Chile have no boards of trustees, but they have a bureaucratic structure leading from the medical director of each facility up to a provincial or district health officer and thence to the central ministry. The medical staff consists of salaried civil servants. The numerous voluntary hospitals in those countries, however, usually have a local board of directors, with a more flexible medical staff receiving individual fees from private patients, as well as some salary for the care of indigent patients. Among more economically developed countries, for instance, in France, the composition of the board of directors of public hospitals (with the great majority of total beds) is determined by national law and includes various government officials or those to whom they designate authority; daily administration is entrusted to a nonmedical administrator. Sweden, on the other hand, allows each local county council to designate the hospital board of directors. The daily management is assigned to a medical superintendent who is appointed by the central government from a short list of nominees submitted by the county council. Under him is an administrative hospital secretary who is appointed directly by the county council. In both France and Sweden all personnel in nongovernment hospitals are appointed simply by their boards of directors.

In the countries of highly centralized pattern, those of weaker economic development (Togo and Malaysia) vest appointment powers at the top in the central ministry of health—not only for the hospital director, who is always a physician, but for the entire professional staff. The doctors are typically a small corps of full-time salaried civil servants. In Malaysian hospitals there are boards of visitors, but they are solely advisory. An exception is made in the national capital of both Togo and Malaysia for a single large teaching and research hospital, in which a board of trustees functions (but still under the minister of health). Throughout these countries, however, the public hospitals providing 90 per cent of the patient care are administered essentially as outposts of the central government.

In the more economically advanced countries of the centralized authority pattern, the internal hospital arrangements in England illustrate one policy and in the USSR another. The English regional hospital boards appoint the hospital management committees, which take direct charge of each hospital; they also appoint the senior medical staff and the hospital secretary who, in turn, appoints subordinate personnel. Under the hospital management committee the daily operations are carried out through tripartite administration by the hospital secretary, the chief of the medical staff, and the matron. Only if an issue cannot be settled by these officials is it brought to the management committee for decision.

The Soviet hospitals do not have boards of directors, but rather chief physicians who are appointed by the echelon above them—that is, a "rayon" hospital chief is appointed by the "oblast" hospital chief physician, and he in turn by the "oblast" health department. All other hospital personnel are appointed by the chief physician. He is assisted by various deputies for economic matters, for out-patient services, etc., as well as by advisory committees composed of other hospital personnel; final decisions, however, are his, subject to review by his superiors in the hierarchy.

In all these patterns except the North American, physicians are usually employees of the hospitals, full-time or part-time. They may have some private practice outside the hospital, but in so far as they work in the hospital it is as medical employees. They are legally responsible to the hospital's governing body or chief physician, rather than to the individual patient—except for the relatively small number of patients whom they may serve privately. Because of this close identification of hospital physicians with the administrative authority of the hospital, appointments to the medical staff are typically quite selective. In the more highly developed countries appointments are usually limited to specialists or consultants, while general practitioners may only work in offices or health centers outside of hospitals. The principal exception is in North America, where the general hospitals (not the special ones for mental diseases or tuberculosis) are typically "open-staff"—that is, permitting most licensed physicians to join the staff and admit private patients. In Soviet hospitals there is also a policy of assigning general physicians or pediatricians to certain limited responsibilities on the hospital wards, though they are primarily attached to polyclinics. In English hospitals, general practitioners may have some access to laboratory or x-ray services through the hospital out-patient clinic, but may not attend in-patients.

On a world level one can detect a certain movement toward a more balanced relationship between physicians inside and outside the hospital. Since the hospital is increasingly recognized as a center of postgraduate medical education and research, there is a recent tendency in Europe (both Western and Eastern) to let down the barriers and permit access of extra-mural practitioners to the stimulating internal environment of the hospital. On the other hand, in North America where such interchange has traditionally been very great, the movement is in the other direction and the medical staff organization is becoming more rigorous.

As for the scope of hospital services, everywhere it is becoming wider. From its original focus on the bed care of the seriously sick, the hospital in nearly all countries has been giving proportionately more attention to out-patient services and also to professional education and medical research. This is quite aside from the widening range of diagnostic and treatment services offered to in-patients. In the economically developing countries the range of health services emanating from hospitals tends to be very wide, including out-patient and preventive work as well as all aspects of therapy.

Another important determinant of the range of hospital services anywhere is, of course, the size of the institution; generally a large hospital can offer a wider range of services than a small one. For any given size of institution, however, the diversity of internal programs tends naturally to be greater in countries with more localized authority than in those with highly centralized hospital systems. Many interesting innovations have originated in the general hospitals of the United States—for example, organized "home care" programs or "progressive patient care"—but they have not necessarily been widely applied. (Most American hospitals, in fact, do not offer such programs.) On the other hand, in the countries with more centralized authority, a specific practice which has been found by the ministry of health to be effective is more likely to be applied across the land.

In a few countries the broad concept of the hospital as a center for all health services in a specific area has taken on special significance. This is the philosophy of the Chilean National Health Service and also of the Soviet and Bulgarian health systems. Administratively, the hospital director in these countries is theoretically responsible for all health activities in the geographic area served by that hospital, including the ambulatory and the preventive services. In many developing countries the main hospital in a rural region is made responsible also for smaller ambulatory service health centers surrounding it. In England the concept of the "general, general hospital"—with acute, chronic, mental, and other special patients being served flexibly under one administration—has been advanced, but only rarely applied.

Considering the totality of health services there is no question that everywhere the hospital is playing a larger proportionate part. Its share of total health expenditures over the last several decades has gradually been rising, not because of price inflation which applies to out-of-hospital services as well, but because many services formerly offered outside of hospitals or not offered at all are now part of the normal hospital program. Many health leaders are concerned about the need for greater strengthening of out-of-hospital services, which are generally less expensive and more preventively oriented. Nevertheless, the widening scope of health services coming under the wing of hospitals—for either in-patients or out-patients—has an important hidden advantage: namely, the placement of services within an administrative framework, through which they may be more readily integrated in the interests of economy and quality.

DOCTOR–HOSPITAL RELATIONS IN EUROPE

More specifically relevant to the United States hospital scene than this global view is a consideration of hospital policies in Europe. In 1960 and 1961, as part of this general research on medical staff organization, field studies were made in several European countries, including Great Britain, Norway, France, Italy, Switzerland, Yugoslavia, and the Soviet Union.[2] In each of these countries visits were made to two or three hospitals, estimated as typical by the ministry of health, and information was gathered on the patterns of medical staff structuring and the general features of the hospital program. There are obviously great differences among these countries, and yet compared with American conditions a few general observations can be cautiously offered.

For one thing, general hospitals in Europe are obviously older institutions. Many currently important hospitals, like St. Bartholomew's in London or the Hotel Dieu in Paris, were founded in the Middle Ages. This

[2] Milton I. Roemer, "General Hospitals in Europe," in *Modern Concepts of Hospital Administration*. J. K. Owen, editor (Philadelphia: W. B. Saunders, 1962), pp. 17–37. Bibliographic references are cited in the article.

has important influences on their operating policies, which can be traced more readily to their medieval origins than policies in institutions founded yesterday. Thus, the beginnings of the European hospital as a refuge for the sick poor have left their mark strongly on contemporary European hospitals. The large public ward of thirty beds is seen more often than in America. The conception of charity and even *noblesse oblige* is more prominent. The great majority of patients are treated by hospital physicians, in whose choice they have no part. The relationship of patient to doctor is not a private one, fortified by a personal financial transaction, but rather a social one in which the institution takes responsibility for providing the needed medical service. Nurses are more often nuns, even in non-Catholic hospitals, recalling their origin as medieval sisters of mercy. In Great Britain the head nurse on a hospital ward is always called the "sister." In Italy the insurance organizations, unlike some American plans, make no earmarked payment for the donated services of religious nurses. It is assumed that the hospital, as a social agency, has a charitable role to play.

In Europe, more than in America, the hospital is the center for advanced medical science in its community. The physicians attached to it are, in general, a class apart from other physicians. They are the specialists and the professors, the physicians of the highest technical skill. Elaborate resources for diagnosis and therapy are more heavily concentrated in the hospitals; those in the community physician's office are meager by comparison. For the European patient, the hospital must be a more awesome place. He is admitted less frequently than in the United States, and when he is the occasion tends to be more serious.

The European hospital, compared with the American, is more of a public place. It is much more often under government auspices of some type. When ownership is by a voluntary agency, it is nevertheless subjected to greater supervision and control by public authorities. The decisions of its administrators are more subject to review by third parties; they are more fully defined by rules and regulations. As a result, there tends to be greater uniformity than on the American scene, though much diversity still remains. Despite these broad differences, the basic goals of European hospitals are the same as those of American hospitals. The mission is humanitarian; the method is scientific.

More fundamental perhaps than any other difference between European and American hospitals is their pattern of medical staff organization. In Europe the conception of the doctor's relation to the hospital is quite different from the American "open-staff" pattern. Medical services in hospitals are generally regarded as the responsibility of a relatively small proportion of the physicians in each community or region—those who are highly qualified as specialists. A hospital staff appointment is a mark of great prestige, held only by this élite minority. The majority of physicians practice outside the hospital, in private offices or, sometimes, ambulatory-care clinics. When a patient requires hospitalization, he is sent to the general hospital and turned over to the care of the hospital doctor, just as is conventional in America for patients requiring institutional care for tuberculosis or mental disease. In Geneva, Switzerland, for example, there were in 1960 about 400 physicians practicing medicine. Of these, only 64, or 16 per cent, were attached in any way to the hospital; patients of the other 84 per cent of physicians must be referred to the hospital staff if they require hospital care. That is, the physician–bed ratio in an average American general hospital is much higher than in Europe. In our study of 10 hospitals, reported later in this book there was an average of about 60 active staff doctors per 100 beds (plus additional "courtesy staff" members); in Europe the ratio would be about 10 or 20 per 100 beds.

This does not mean that all hospital physicians in Europe work exclusively or full-time in the hospital. There is a wide range of customs with regard to their time allotments. While a generalization is difficult to make, because of great variations between countries and also within countries, it appears that European hospital physicians tend to range in the proportion of time devoted to hospital work from about 50 to 100 per cent. It is extremely rare to find instances of the American pattern where a physician spends, say, 10 per cent of his time in the hospital and 90 per cent in an outside office. So widely accepted is the concept of the full-time staff in general hospitals that an official of the British National Health Service could write in 1958: "The general hospital with no locally resident specialist staff is an anachronism."[3]

With its carefully selected corps of full-time or major-time physicians, the medical staff of the European hospital tends to work in a highly structured framework. At the head of each clinical department is a consultant or specialist with great authority. Whether or not it is a teaching hospital, he tends to command the respect associated with the "distinguished professor" of the old European universities. Under this chief of service is a network of other physicians working according to specified responsibilities. In Great Britain these include senior registrars, registrars, and house officers in descending order. (These are equivalent to residents, assistant residents, and interns in the larger American general hospital.) In some British hospitals there is a fifth class of resident doctor, the senior medical house officer, a physician who is not working for

³ G. E. Godber, "Health Services, Past, Present, and Future," *Lancet* (5 July 1958): 1–6.

advancement to consultant status but who has some specified duty under the consultant's direction. The role of the entire junior staff in patient care is much greater than its equivalent in a typical American hospital. These young physicians attend nearly all patients (not just ward cases) and they actually carry out the measures for diagnosis and treatment. The consultant's role is to supervise and to take direct responsibility only for selected cases. The economic relationship of the doctor to the patient, it must be recalled, is essentially the same for the junior staff as for the senior staff; unlike the American setting, both are on salary and neither depends on a private fee from the patient.

This hierarchy, of course, is most highly developed in the large teaching hospitals associated with British universities, but in essence it is found almost everywhere. In the nonteaching hospitals, large or small, there are always consultants as chiefs of service, but the senior registrars may be few or lacking, and the bulk of patient care is given by registrars and house officers. There are also a number of small "general practitioner" hospitals with no resident staff—whose aggregate bed capacity is only a trivial percentage of the total—for simple maternity cases or minor medical or surgical procedures. These are regarded, however, as somewhat outside the mainstream of British hospital service. In the usual general hospital, appointments to consultant posts are widely advertised and subject to keen competition. Such a position is coveted and, once achieved, usually is held for life.

The hospital physicians in Great Britain are paid a salary by the regional hospital board. For all men below the consultant, this is regarded as 100 per cent full-time; no work outside the hospital is permitted. The consultant is often full-time also, but he is permitted, if he wishes, to spend two or three half-days a week in a private office. Anyone consulting him there for ambulatory care must pay for it privately; if they wish to see the same consultant under the National Health Service (i.e., without personal cost), they may see him at the hospital outpatient department on referral by their general family physician.

In Norway full-time, salaried medical staffs are also the prevailing pattern in general hospitals. The hierarchy of junior staff members is somewhat different, but, as in Britain, the chief of service has great authority. There is an elaborate system for advertising openings and making selections of candidates for all hospital posts. The national director-general of health services is involved, appointing the selection committees. These committees prepare a "short list" of three applicants, from which the hospital board of directors makes the final selection. Medical staff members below the chief of service are ordinarily 100 per cent full-time in the hospital. The chiefs are permitted to spend a few periods each week seeing private patients, for which they get extra remuneration, but, unlike the British system, this is ordinarily done at their hospital offices; for this use of public facilities in private practice, the physician pays a rental charge to the hospital.

In the Eastern European countries hospital physicians are even more fully engaged within the institution. While they serve ambulatory patients in out-patient clinics, private practice is not allowed. In Yugoslavia the prohibition of private practice was effected in 1957; it was pointed out that permitting private practice created seriously divided loyalties for the physician, with his private patients benefiting at the expense of his more numerous public patients. The real problem was to remunerate the hospital physician at a rate high enough to eliminate the temptation to supplement his earnings with fees from private cases. In Soviet Russia, where medical care has long been fully public, there is a rotation between posts in the hospitals and the polyclinics; in this way, both types of physician acquire an appreciation of the problems of one another.

The effects of a relatively low rate of remuneration of hospital physicians are seen in Italy. Here the medical staff in most general hospitals is ostensibly full-time. The doctors are expected to work an approximately eight-hour day, for which they are paid a supposedly satisfactory salary. In fact, the salaries tend to be so low that private practice outside the hospital, for supplemental earnings, tends to be the general rule—not just for chiefs of service but for all hospital physicians. This external income is derived in large part from insurance funds, for service to insured patients, but it is paid to the physician directly.

In France and Switzerland a full-time medical staff in hospitals is less prevalent than in the northern and eastern European countries. Not that hospitals are "open-staffed" as in America (for only a minority of physicians have hospital appointments), but the general rule is for nearly all hospital physicians past their initial years of hospital training to have separate offices for private specialty practice, because hospital payments to senior physicians have been little more than token honoraria—in the ancient tradition of hospital service as a charitable function. The specialist, therefore, like the general practitioner, must earn his living essentially from the care of private patients. This was, indeed, the prevailing pattern in Great Britain before the National Health Service. Interestingly enough, there has been a movement underway in France to increase greatly full-time hospital appointments, with adequate salaries to be paid. This is being done first in the teaching hospitals and the large nonteaching centers. Even in these institutions, however, some 5 per cent of the beds are reserved for the private patients of chiefs of clinical services and 3 per cent of beds for assistant physicians. (Such small concessions to private medical interests are common in Western Europe.)

Despite this wide range of full-time to part-time status in European hospital appointments, there is no question that the whole organization of medical services is more tightly structured than in American hospitals of comparable size and function. (Smaller hospitals in Europe, as in the United States, are, of course, less rigidly organized.) The chief of service exercises wide discretion in shaping policies on medical care and the management of cases, but almost all others work under some form of supervision. At the Drammen hospital in Norway, for example, ward rounds are made daily by the team of physicians on each service. The status of each patient, including a consideration of all x-ray and laboratory reports, is reviewed by the whole team. The therapy and progress of each case is followed and the appropriate time for discharge is discussed. Of course, the immediate responsibility for patients is held by the physician in charge of each hospital ward, but his judgment is exercised in a teamwork setting. The autonomy of the American private physician treating his private patient is rare indeed in the European hospital.

EUROPEAN AND AMERICAN CONTRASTS

Because of this intrinsic structuring of the European hospital staff, there are some paradoxical differences in medical staff procedures on the two continents. Meetings of the entire medical staff at monthly or more frequent intervals, for example, are regarded as a key measure for maintaining quality performance in the American general hospital. Yet, in Europe such total staff meetings are rare; instead there are departmental meetings almost daily. In American hospitals there are "tissue committees" to provide some surveillance over surgical operations, by studying the pathological reports on tissues removed and calling for explanations of normal specimens. In Europe there is no such procedure. Likewise, one seldom finds "credentials committees" or "record committees" or other such devices designed to maintain a high level of performance among the large numbers of independent doctors in open-staff American hospitals.

These paradoxes are easily explained by the built-in group discipline of the European hospital staff. Observation of one's medical colleagues is part and parcel of all professional work in the European general hospital. Surveillance is applicable to all cases at all times. By contrast, it is really the relatively loose and *laissez faire* character of medical practice in American hospitals that has stimulated the various meetings and committees, and made the establishment of such committees a requirement of the Joint Commission on Accreditation of Hospitals.

With this relatively rigid medical staff structure in hospitals, it is no surprise that one of the major problems facing European medicine is the level of performance of the general practitioner working in an office or "surgery" (Great Britain) or health center (Eastern Europe) outside the hospital. Studies in England have corroborated the impressions of American observers that the quality of general practice is often very poor and that the family doctor in town suffers seriously from his isolation from the hospital.[4] To cope with this problem, hospitals throughout Europe are doing several things. The general practitioner is invited to visit his hospitalized patients and to discuss cases with the hospital staff; reports are sent to him on the patient's discharge, advising what has been done and what follow-up is advisable. Then, there are clinical case conferences held in many hospitals, to which local community doctors are invited. Refresher courses of many sorts are spreading throughout the continent. In the Eastern European countries attendance at formal postgraduate courses given in hospitals is periodically required. Sometimes there are specific duties, usually in an out-patient department, which may be assigned to community doctors. In British hospitals, here and there, a laboratory and x-ray service is directly accessible to the general practitioner. Thus, European medical and hospital leaders have become very conscious of the problem and are exploring various methods of adding scientific stimulation to the professional life of the nonhospital doctor.

Finally, it must be realized that all general hospitals in each of the European countries are not cut of one mold. The characteristics of hospitals in a specific country tend to belong to the larger institutions. In the small hospitals, policies are less uniform in medical staffing as well as in over-all administration. There are many small "cottage hospitals" in the more rural sections of England, Germany, Greece, France, and elsewhere that are indistinguishable from small rural hospitals in the United States. On the other hand, a moment's consideration shows the great diversity of hospital patterns in America. While the open-staff, loosely structured, and nongovernmental general hospital is certainly the predominant type, there are university teaching hospitals and government facilities here with a distinctly European organizational flavor. One must be cautious, therefore, about generalizations which go beyond a statement of the "predominant" hospital patterns in a country.

To epitomize the entire pattern of European hospitals, compared with American, one may say that, being obviously older, the European hospital is a more crystallized system. Among all the health services in Europe, hospitals are of greater importance and have greater stability.

[4] J. S. Collings, "General Practice in England Today," *Lancet* (25 March 1950): 555 ff.

Ownership is more often by the government, and financing comes from large social insurance or public funds. Planning of construction and operation is more centralized. The number of beds is usually greater, but they are used each year by a smaller proportion of the population for longer average stays. Services for the ambulatory patient, both in out-patient polyclinics and in individual physician's offices, are relatively more numerous, so that the hospital tends to be reserved for the more serious cases. Hospital personnel have longer tenures and are paid less, so that hospital costs are relatively lower.[5] Medical services in hospitals are provided by a highly select corps of specialists, quite distinct from those doctors serving patients living at home. The whole hospital system is subject to national and regional planning that attempts deliberately to integrate the hospital into an over-all system of medical care.

It does not take much imagination to see that the American hospital system is moving in the same general direction as the European. As hospital finance here becomes more collective, through both insurance and public support, the exercise of "third-party" surveillance over how the consumer's money is spent is becoming greater. There is more state and regional planning. Hospital employees are becoming unionized and hospital employment will probably thereby become more stable. Medical staff organization is becoming more structured. The state hospital licensure laws are being strengthened and better enforced, while, at the same time, voluntary accreditation bodies are widening their impact. The general role of the American hospital in its community is obviously expanding and the "medical center" idea—bringing together the general hospital with the special units for mental disorders, long-term illnesses, research, and education—is taking root in almost all large cities. American affluence has accounted for many of the differences in hospitals and medical care on the continents, but rising hospital costs are driving administrators toward European patterns. Yet, in such features as clinical departmentalization and relations with community doctors, the American pattern will probably continue to differ from the European, being adjusted to the newer American society.

[5] Paul A. Lembcke, "Hospital Efficiency: A Lesson from Sweden," *Hospitals* (1 April 1959).

IV

CONTRACTUAL PHYSICIANS AND THEIR INFLUENCE

THE SIGNIFICANCE OF contractual physicians in general hospitals of the United States and the controversies surrounding their work have been reviewed in earlier chapters. In the Appendix, we have presented the methodology used for examining both the prevalence of contractual physicians of various types and their relationship to indicators of hospital performance. Here we will review the findings of this research.

PREVALENCE AND TYPES OF CONTRACTUAL PHYSICIANS IN THE UNITED STATES

Our data on this statistical survey approach to medical staff organization applies to the year 1959. As we saw in the historical review, there was undoubtedly an increase in the rate of appointment of contractual physicians in general hospitals before this year, and since then the trend has certainly continued. Hospital emergency rooms requiring medical coverage have expanded, medical education and research programs in hospitals have increased, and hospitals have widened their general community role over the last decade. The Medicare Law of 1965 has led to certain changes in the methods of medical remuneration, but the forces impelling hospitals to appoint physicians to accept formal responsibilities in an organized framework have obviously continued to operate.

Since our primary objective is to explore the *relationship* between the contractual physician—as a barometer of the structure of the medical staff—and the characteristics of the hospital's program of service, the age of this statistical information is not a serious handicap. It must be kept in mind, nevertheless, that the number of doctors of various specialties and their variety, reported here, apply to the hospital scene of 1959.[1]

---

[1] Two preliminary reports of partial findings from this study were published: Milton I. Roemer, "Contractual Physicians in General Hospitals: A National Survey," *Amer. J. Public Health*, 52:1453–64 (September 1962). Also: Milton I. Roemer "The Growth of Salaried Physicians," *Hospital Progress* (September 1964): 79–83 ff.

TABLE 1. General Hospitals with Contractual Physicians: Percentages of general hospitals (of 50 beds or more) having designated specialists under contract, by time-status, among 2,434 institutions in the continental United States, 1959

Specialty	Percentages of hospitals having:			
	Full-time only	Part-time only	Both full-time and part-time	All types
Radiology	48.3	39.1	8.4	95.9
Pathology	44.8	39.6	6.5	90.9
Anesthesiology	21.6	8.1	2.5	32.1
Internal medicine	4.9	10.6	4.8	20.3
Physical medicine	6.0	8.0	1.4	15.4
EKG, BMR readings, etc.	1.4	12.2	0.1	13.7
Medical education	4.2	8.7	0.4	13.3
Medical administration	9.9	1.7	0.8	12.4
Surgery	4.1	3.1	4.6	11.8
"Other fields"	2.4	6.0	1.9	10.3
Psychiatry	2.7	3.9	3.0	9.6
Pediatrics	2.5	2.9	1.2	6.7
Obstetrics & gynecology	2.1	3.0	0.6	5.7
Medical research	2.7	1.1	1.2	4.9
Any specialty	—	—	—	98.1

In that year, we set out to determine the extent of engagement of contractual physicians of various specialties by general hospitals throughout the United States, and to examine various correlates of such practices. A mail questionnaire was sent to every general hospital of fifty beds or more in the country and responses were received from 84 per cent. The ultimate tabulation and analysis was based on 2,434 general hospitals under voluntary nonprofit or governmental (but nonmilitary) sponsorship.

Distribution of Contractual Specialists. In Table 1 the principal findings of this survey are reported, in descending order of frequency for all types of medical contract—either full-time or part-time. The importance of radiology, pathology, and anesthesia are no surprise, but the 20 per cent of general hospitals with contractual physicians in internal medicine may be startling. Most of the hospitals with such appointees, it may be noted, use the internists on a part-time basis, and a good proportion of these doctors are probably involved in employee health services, emergency room duties, or possibly EKG readings (though not specifically reported as such). The 15 per cent of hospitals with physical medicine specialists on contract and the 13 per cent with doctors devoted to medical education are significant, even though most of these appointments are also part-time.

In a word, nearly all general hospitals in the nation (98.1 per cent) have at least one contractual physician on their staffs. The numbers among different specialties, of course, are very different. While radiology and pathology are most frequent in the hospital universe, and the clini-

TABLE 2. Contractual Physicians by Specialty in General Hospitals: Number of such physicians,* by specialty (per 100 hospitals), and number per hospital having any given type of specialist, among 2,434 general hospitals in the continental United States, 1959

Specialty	Number per 100 hospitals	Number per hospital having any such specialist
Radiology	121.4	1.3
Pathology	108.2	1.2
Anesthesiology	57.4	1.8
Internal medicine	109.9	5.4
Physical medicine	14.4	0.9
EKG, EEG, BMR readings, etc.	11.8	3.4
Medical education	8.9	0.7
Medical administration	17.7	1.4
Surgery	78.0	6.6
"Other fields"	35.5	0.9
Psychiatry	32.6	3.4
Pediatrics	16.7	2.5
Obstetrics & gynecology	9.6	1.7
Medical research	18.7	3.8
Any specialty	640.8	2.5

* Expressed in full-time equivalents, with "part-time" assumed to equal 0.3 of full-time.

cal specialties have contractual physicians in only a minority of institutions, the latter hospitals actually have a relatively large total number of those doctors. These figures are shown in Table 2. Thus, while only 20 per cent of all hospitals have a specialist in internal medicine under contract, those hospitals that do, have an average of 5.4 internists each. Thus, there are 109.9 internists per 100 hospitals in the nation as a whole, a number actually exceeding the number of pathologists per 100 hospitals. Similar clustering of surgery and other specialties may be observed in Table 2.

Without commenting on the implications of each specialty presented in these tables, we should note of a few of the new developments reflected in these findings. The larger community hospitals are increasingly trying to emulate teaching institutions by appointing directors of medical education, to increase the effectiveness of their training programs for interns and residents, as well as for continuing education of practicing physicians. A small but growing number of predominantly open-staff hospitals are also appointing full-time chiefs of clinical services, with functions not only in house-staff education but also in the direct supervision of patient care on public wards, in consultations, and in medical research. Some of these appointees are doubtless included under the designations of "medical administration" or "medical research" in the table. Physicians with assigned responsibilities for the hospital emergency room are also probably included under other categories in the table; the rapidly increasing utilization of emergency rooms in recent years is a testimony to the growing public confidence in hospitals and, perhaps, to the declining accessibility of private medical practitioners. Another pattern, still small on the horizon but undoubtedly destined to grow, is the appointment of contractual physicians to supervise organized home-care programs which are now reported to be operating in 7.5 per cent of hospitals in the country. The appointment of a hospital based specialist in preventive or social medicine is still another innovation, rare but significant.

Methods of Remuneration. Findings on the methods of remuneration under physician–hospital contracts are presented in Table 3. Considering the aggregate of all fourteen specialties listed in these tables, the commonest scheme of payment is simply by straight salary. Nearly 50 per cent of all contractual physicians are paid by this method, another 7 per cent by salary plus other methods, and 43 per cent by various other schemes. Radiology—the specialty most frequently under contract —however, is remunerated in 70 per cent of the hospitals by a sharing of departmental income (gross or net) through diverse formulas. This is the commonest method also for pathology—that is, in 45 per cent of the contracts. Anesthesiology is most frequently remunerated on a fee-for-service basis (43 per cent of the contracts). EKG, BMR readings, and the like are duties also paid for most often by an income-sharing scheme.

TABLE 3. REMUNERATION OF CONTRACTUAL PHYSICIANS: PERCENTAGES OF PHYSICIAN–HOSPITAL CONTRACTS FOR DESIGNATED SPECIALTIES, BY METHOD OF REMUNERATION, AMONG 2,434 INSTITUTIONS IN THE CONTINENTAL UNITED STATES, 1959

Specialty	Method of remuneration by hospital:				
	Salary	Salary plus other method	Share of departmental income	Fee-for-service	Two or more methods
Radiology	16.7	5.5	69.8	5.0	3.0
Pathology	28.7	8.7	45.0	13.8	3.8
Anesthesiology	31.6	8.4	13.8	43.0	3.2
Internal medicine	54.7	5.7	18.8	16.0	4.8
Physical medicine	60.2	9.9	21.7	6.1	2.1
EKG, BMR readings, etc.	10.2	1.2	49.4	36.8	2.4
Medical education	93.5	6.2	—	0.3	—
Medical administration	94.0	4.7	—	0.3	1.0
Surgery	81.6	6.6	1.7	5.2	4.9
"Other fields"	74.5	5.2	6.8	7.2	6.4
Psychiatry	78.2	8.5	2.1	6.0	5.1
Pediatrics	79.6	10.5	1.2	5.6	3.1
Obstetrics & gynecology	81.3	10.1	0.7	5.8	2.2
Medical research	95.8	2.5	—	0.8	0.8
Any specialty	49.8	6.8	27.4	12.3	3.8

The other ten special fields, while occuring in a much smaller proportion of hospitals, are all remunerated most often by salary, full-time or part-time.

The administrative and professional implications of each of these methods of contractual payment are different. In the hospital setting, the argument is waged most frequently over salaries and it is usually posed in terms of incentives. The specialist will do more and better work, it is contended, if he is paid on a fee basis or by a share of the departmental income (which has, in turn, been derived from patient fees). Those who favor salaries argue that incentives can operate through inducing pride in professional performance, gaining the respect of one's peers, and providing all the inducements or "controls" of an organizational structure, independent of financial rewards. Salaries, moreover, avoid creation of incentives for superfluous service, and they permit the hospital administration to plan its budget more carefully in advance. If the level of salary is satisfactory, the doctor's performance in a word becomes motivated by professional rather than pecuniary objectives. This whole question has been explored by one of us elsewhere, and it may be helpful to quote sections of this discussion, especially as it concerns payment of doctors by the salary method.[2]

The salaried physician has no financial incentive for either a large or small volume of service, but in an organized professional framework he has other incentives toward optimal performance. He wishes to win the respect of his colleagues and his superiors, both for economic advancement and professional prestige. It is the judgment of other doctors, more than of patients, that counts. Nearly all salary systems base the level of remuneration on such factors as training, experience, and demonstrated skills, with increments being awarded for seniority and scope of responsibility. These qualifications are judged by other physicians or, at least, experts in personnel affairs and are theoretically based on rational criteria. Of course, there may be errors in judgment or even prejudices interfering with the reasonable operation of the system, and it is such factors that make many physicians apprehensive about salaries and in favor of taking their chances with the buy-and-sell market of fee-for-service practice.[3]

In a salaried medical organization with reasonable teamwork, the physician has every reason to consult with colleagues in other specialties on the handling of a case. Such a pattern also permits the physician to undertake postgraduate studies periodically, as well as to enjoy a rest or

[2] Milton I. Roemer, "On Paying the Doctor and the Implications of Different Methods," *J. Health and Human Behavior*, 3:4–14 (Spring 1962).

[3] William Glaser," "Doctors and Politics," *Amer. J. Sociology*, 66:230–45 (November 1960).

vacation without loss of income. When a young physician starts work in a salaried framework, he can apply himself to full capacity at the outset, without many half-idle months or years waiting to "build up a practice" in a private office. At the same time, his work can be supervised by more experienced colleagues and adjusted to the level of his capacities. All these factors undoubtedly contribute to advancing the quality of medical care.

In one respect, the quality of medical care under salaried arrangements is believed by many to suffer. This is in the level of sensitivity of the physician to the personal feelings of his patient. Undoubtedly, many physicians of apathetic personality and little ambition accept salaried employment because they cannot thrive in the competitive medical market or they crave a secure job and an eight-hour day. Such physicians may well be insensitive to patients, as they probably would also be in private practice, but there is no objective evidence that in the over-all American scene salaried physicians are less sensitive to patient needs than physicians paid by the other methods. There are certainly enough complaints about callous or unsympathetic doctors in ordinary private practice.[4] In Europe, where salaried physicians are responsible for nearly all hospital-based medical care, the connotations of a salary are just as humane as those of other forms of medical remuneration. Even in the Soviet Union, where all physicians are on government salary, American observers report professional attitudes toward patients to be warm and considerate.[5]

Considering the criterion of costs, there is no doubt that the salary pattern tends to be less expensive for the consumer than any other method. Everything depends, of course, on the amount of the salary. The bargaining power of an organization hiring medical talent, however, tends to be greater than that of the individual doctor, so that his net earnings are bound to be lower than they would be if he levied a fee for each service rendered a patient. Despite this, as health services have become increasingly organized the proportion of American physicians in full-time salaried employment has risen steadily.

As the demand for salaried physicians in hospitals, public agencies, medical schools, and other organizations has increased, medical salaries have risen. The average income of physicians in research or public health work is still below that of private practitioners, but the earnings of salaried physicians in most clinical specialties have come to exceed, on

[4] Selig Greenberg, "The Decline of the Healing Art," *Harper's Magazine* (October 1960): 132–37.

[5] U.S. Public Health Service, *Report of the United States Public Health Mission to the Union of Soviet Socialist Republics* (Washington: Government Printing Office, 1959).

the average, earnings from independent practice. This can be seen in the relatively high earnings of salaried physicians in group practice clinics, compared with income from solo practice.[6] Remarkably high salaries are paid also to specialists employed in community general hospitals (mental hospital medical salaries are still relatively low), particularly radiologists and pathologists. A survey in 1960 found the average net earnings of radiologists from hospital work to be $30,680 and of pathologists $28,000.[7]

Yet it has been shown that a given volume of services remunerated on a fee basis would cost the consumers of medical care even more.[8] The fact is that the extension of salaried medicine has gone hand-in-hand with a rise in the per capita volume of medical services received by the United States population. Therefore, the salary system has enabled the average American patient to receive an expanding volume of services at a somewhat lower cost than he would pay (directly or indirectly through taxes, philanthropy and so on) if fee-for-service were the exclusive method of medical remuneration.

As for its administrative implications, the salary system is manifestly simpler than any other. The paper work for both physician and paying agency is much less. Neither units of service nor units of patients have to be accounted for, but only units of time, such as hours, months or years. There are, of course, other phases of administration involved in a salary system, but they are incident to the process of organization, supervision, and co-ordination of the medical service, rather than the mechanism of paying the doctor.

Finally, the political implications of the salary system must be considered, and there is no question that this pattern is more beset with controversy than any other. This is by no means true of all countries, for in Europe, as noted earlier, salaried positions in hospitals are more prestigious than any others. In the United States, however, the majority of physicians are clearly opposed to salaries as an exclusive scheme of payment. The reasons are complex, but they doubtless combine economic and professional factors. Economically, physicians oppose salaries because they believe, whether rightly or wrongly, that they mean lower income. Moreover, the opportunity for exceptionally high incomes—possible in private practice—is virtually eliminated. Professionally, doctors oppose salaries because the organization of services associated with them means a restriction of their independence. An ellipsis between method of payment and method of medical care organization is readily made, and

[6] Arthur Owens, "Net Earnings Hit an All-time High," *Med. Economics* (11 December 1967): 70–75.

[7] Anon., "Specialist Arrangements Not Changing," *Modern Hospital* (March 1960): 67–71.

[8] United Mine Workers of America, Welfare Retirement Fund, unpublished data from the medical care program, Washington, D.C., 1955.

the physician—usually a staunch individualist—bridles at the thought of working under someone else's supervision. While he has, of course, done this throughout his years of training, the doctor embarking on clinical practice expects to be free and unfettered.[9]

The bitterness which many physicians feel about salaried employment has led to endless controversies about "socialized medicine" over the last forty or fifty years. Even health insurance plans paying physicians on a fee basis have been opposed or viewed suspiciously for fear that they might ultimately lead to salaried arrangements.[10] The most recent battles have been pitched in hospitals, where radiologists and pathologists have launched campaigns against salaries, as reviewed in earlier chapters. A more detailed examination of the findings of the national study of contractual physicians, with respect to methods of payment of one type of specialist—the radiologist—has been reported elsewhere.[11] Now, we may proceed to discussion of the relationship of a hospital's use of contractual physicians to its professional performance.

RELATIONSHIP TO HOSPITAL PERFORMANCE

The methodology applied to express a hospital's aggregate contractual physician practices, as a numerical score, is explained in the Appendix. In connection with the above discussion on the deviation of the salary method from the usual norms in American medical life, it will be noted that computation of the "contractual physician score" took these dynamics into account. Thus, a higher weighting was assigned to a hospital's use of salaries for any given specialty than for other methods of remuneration that are more individualistic and traditional in their implications.

Using the method of ranked quartiles of "contractual physician scores" in relation to the various features of hospital performance, as explained later, the over-all findings in the full series of 2,434 hospitals are presented in Table 4. For the great majority of the twenty-six features, a higher record of achievement tends to be positively associated with hospitals in the higher quartiles, compared with the lower quartiles, of contractual physician score. For some features, the gradient is clear and consistent through all four quartiles, while in a few the relationship is negative or irregular, but the general pattern of relationships is such as to suggest that a higher contractual physician score

[9] Mary E. W. Goss, "Influence and Authority among Physicians in an Out-Patient Clinic," in *Medical Care: Readings in the Sociology of Medical Institutions*, W. R. Scott and E. H. Volkart, editors (New York: John Wiley and Sons, 1966), pp. 420–37.

[10] Richard Carter, *The Doctor Business* (New York: Doubleday and Company, 1958).

[11] Milton I. Roemer, "Radiologists and Hospitals—Survey Reflects Trends," *Your Radiologist* (Winter, 1965): 5–10.

TABLE 4. CONTRACTUAL PHYSICIANS AND SELECTED HOSPITAL CHARACTERISTICS: PERCENTAGES (AND OTHER DESIGNATED RATES) OF GENERAL HOSPITALS WITH SPECIFIED CHARACTERISTICS IN QUARTILE GROUPS, RANKED ACCORDING TO THEIR TOTAL "CONTRACTUAL PHYSICIAN SCORE," AMONG 2,434 GENERAL HOSPITALS, UNITED STATES, 1959

Hospital characteristic	Total contractual physician score quartile groups of hospitals			
	Lowest N = 609	Second N = 609	Third N = 608	Highest N = 608
Over-all performance				
General accreditation	75.2	88.5	91.6	91.6
Approved cancer program	10.3	14.4	25.3	39.3
Autopsy percentage[a]	23.4	29.2	32.8	36.7
Amplitude of staffing[b]				
Total personnel	2.1	2.2	2.3	2.0
Professional nurses	30.1	34.1	37.2	34.6
Technical personnel	23.8	26.0	28.7	30.8
Diagnostic procedures offered				
Electroencephalography	10.7	18.1	23.8	41.6
Radioactive isotopes	19.5	30.9	38.7	46.7
Surgical facilities				
Blood bank	60.6	69.0	70.7	69.6
Postoperative recovery room	61.9	67.2	72.4	70.7
Intensive care unit	3.8	8.0	9.5	17.3
Other significant therapies				
Therapeutic x-ray	48.1	59.6	67.3	63.8
Physical therapy	39.2	50.6	57.7	71.9
Dental department	23.0	28.1	39.0	60.2
Premature infant nursery	71.8	71.9	76.5	59.9
Psychiatric beds	4.2	5.6	7.0	22.1
Educational functions				
Internships	13.6	33.0	35.9	40.5
Residencies	12.8	21.7	34.9	51.0
Medical school affiliation	2.5	2.3	4.9	18.3
Professional nursing school	24.8	31.5	35.4	28.0
Affiliation with nursing school	1.3	.5	1.5	3.6
Preventive and community service				
Hospital bed occupancy[a]	69.8	72.6	75.0	78.4
Routine chest x-rays	34.0	43.2	44.6	57.4
Out-patient visits[c]	63.2	68.2	83.3	131.1
Long-term beds	2.7	2.4	1.9	7.0
Social service department	8.4	11.8	25.7	54.3

[a] Average percentage for quartile group.
[b] Average personnel per 100 beds for quartile group.
[c] Average visits per bed per year for quartile group.

is usually associated with various specific hospital services, approvals, or features reflecting higher levels of performance. To interpret the meaning of these relationships it is necessary to take a closer look at the findings for each of the hospital performance features explored.

Over-all Hospital Performance. Three variables are examined as measures of over-all hospital performance—approval by the Joint Commission on Accreditation of Hospitals, a cancer program approved by the American College of Surgeons, and the hospital's autopsy percentage. For all three, the relationships to contractual physician score are positive and consistent.

The most all-inclusive system of review of hospital functions is undoubtedly the program of the Joint Commission. This inspection of all general hospitals that wish to participate (so long as they are at least of twenty-five-bed capacity) examines every aspect of a hospital's service, but puts greatest stress on medical staff practices believed to affect the quality of patient care. As discussed in earlier chapters, much stress is put on proper medical records, staff meetings, and the activities of various professional control committees. While a substantial majority of the hospitals in all four quartiles are found to be accredited, the greater percentages in the upper two quartiles are an especially important finding.

Approval of a hospital's "cancer program" by the American College of Surgeons requires a satisfactory level of performance in several departments: surgery, pathological laboratory, records, out-patient department, and so on. The relationships for this feature show a striking correspondence to the contractual physician (C.P.) score, the highest quartile having almost four times the percentage of approved programs as the lowest.

The autopsy percentage of a hospital (the percentage of decedents autopsied in a year) has long been regarded as a useful index of its quality. It reflects, of course, not simply the hospital's ability to have post-mortem examinations carried out but also the over-all diligence of its medical staff in practicing thoughtful and scientific medicine. The conscientious physician will be eager to learn the final pathological findings in a patient who has died, and will extend himself to overcome the usual family resistance to granting permission for autopsy; the less diligent physician may behave in the opposite way. It is quite significant, therefore, that the autopsy percentage is consistently higher in hospitals of higher C.P. score.

Amplitude of Staffing. Indirect reflection of a hospital's capacity to carry out its wide range of functions is found in its supply of personnel of various types. Our data permitted three measurements under this heading, each involving number of personnel per 100 beds.

As for total personnel, the relationships are inconclusive. The highest C.P. quartile of hospitals do, indeed, have a greater ratio of personnel per 100 beds than the lowest, but the gradient is not consistent. The same applies to the ratio of professional nurses (that is, excluding vocational nurses, nurse aides, etc.). Perhaps these two measures are not very good indicators of hospital performance, since they are quite crude, lumping together personnel of a wide variety of functions.

The third measure, on "technical personnel" per 100 beds, refers to engagement by a hospital of laboratory and x-ray technicians, dieticians, physiotherapists, pharmacists—types of staff associated with the more advanced elements of diagnosis and therapy. It is significant that for this category the amplitude of staffing is positively and consistently related to the C.P. score of the hospitals.

Diagnostic Procedures. The modern hospital is a center for complex diagnostic procedures, so that its capacities in this field ought surely be important marks of quality. Although data were available on such elementary diagnostic facilities as clinical laboratories or diagnostic x-rays, these are so generally provided that their presence would not serve to discriminate between hospitals. The two techniques selected for study—electroencephalography and radioactive isotopes—may be taken as reflective of the more progressive and enterprising institutions, in which the presence of personnel capable of handling these techniques may be assumed. Keeping in mind that the hospital C.P. scores have been already adjusted for size of institution, the positive relationships of these diagnostic measures are consistent and striking.

Surgical Facilities. Of all therapies in the healing arts, that which belongs most clearly in a hospital, as against the home or the physician's office, is surgery. The availability of an operating room may be virtually taken for granted in American general hospitals, so that our explorations were applied to more refined indices of surgical service: blood banks, postoperative recovery rooms, and intensive care units. The latter, while relatively uncommon, are used also for nonsurgical cases, and they have an additional attribute: they reduce the need for private-duty nurses, who are relatively expensive, and hence imply a kind of democratization of hospital care.

For blood banks there is a lower record in the lowest C.P. quartile of hospitals, but the upper three quartiles are almost the same, at about 70 per cent. These figures do not reveal any differences in the technical adequacy of blood banks, which might well be more sophisticated in the higher scoring hospitals. The relationships for postoperative recovery rooms and especially for intensive care units are clearly in the positive direction. Of these two indicators, the intensive care unit has become particularly important in recent years, as the facility in which all sorts of highly advanced equipment and specially trained staff are mobilized for life-saving purposes. The gradient for this measure is impressive, with the highest C.P. quartile having four times the percentage found for the lowest quartile.

Other Significant Therapies. Five types of therapy beyond surgery were examined. While surgery is part and parcel of almost every general hospital, there are other forms of therapy provided only in institutions at a relatively advanced stage of technical development. Therapeutic x-ray service is one such activity, reflecting a major investment in technology for patients with serious disorders, especially cancer. For this the relationship of percentages to the C.P. score is generally positive, in spite of a slight reduction at the highest quartile.

Physical therapy, provided through an organized department, may be taken to reflect a hospital's orientation toward the emerging field of rehabilitation, with its various social implications, as well as toward a specific form of treatment. The positive relationship to C.P. score for this measure is consistent.

Dental care is commonplace enough as an out-patient health service, but is far from fully accepted as an intramural hospital function. Hospitals with formal dental departments are probably, to this extent, oriented toward widening the scope of their services to the community. For this indicator again, the relationship is positive and consistent, with an especially large differential in the highest C.P. quartile of institutions.

The existence of a special hospital nursery for premature infants would tend to reflect an institution's sensitivity to tackling difficult problems, but its presence would depend on the operation of a maternity service in the first place. Many hospitals with highly developed programs in other clinical fields, however, do not admit maternity cases. This may explain the quite irregular relationship of this performance indicator to the C.P. score.

The provision of psychiatric beds is a fifth type of special therapy associated with modern conceptions of the general hospital. Whether psychiatric patients are kept in a separate department or are placed amidst other cases, their admission to a general hospital reflects a willingness to broaden hospital functions beyond the traditional care of acute physical disorders, and to alter the deleterious isolation of mental patients in special institutions. The relationship of this indicator to C.P. score is consistently positive, and in the highest quartile the jump is large. Undoubtedly, many of the hospitals accounting for the 22 per cent figure in this column have full-time psychiatrists among their contractual physicians.

Educational Functions. Beyond patient care, the modern hospital has many functions in the education of health personnel. Aside from providing continuous postgraduate training for the doctor in his day-to-day work, a variety of formal courses of instruction may be offered. It is generally agreed that such educational programs can exert positive influences on the quality of patient care, beyond their contribution to the production and improvement of health manpower.

The provision of internships is one such educational function, and residencies are a second. It may be noted that approval of both these forms of postgraduate medical training is carried out by the American Medical Association, an organization long championing quality, in contrast to quantity, in the provision of medical care. For both of these indicators of performance, the relationship to C.P. score is positive and consistent—almost linear in the gradient from lowest to highest quartiles.

Medical school affiliation is another indicator of a hospital's educational functions, involving the teaching of medical students, as distinguished from programs for graduate physicians. While this is infrequent, the relationship to C.P. score is clearly positive, with a sizable jump in the highest quartile group.

Operation of a school of nursing by a hospital has another type of relationship to the C.P. score. A nursing school, of course, educates young women to become nurses, but it also serves as a production unit for nursing manpower to staff the hospital. Thus, some hospitals doubtless operate such schools largely for the purpose of maintaining their own supply of nurses. Other hospitals of high quality may not operate nursing schools, simply because they can easily attract nurses from the open market, and they prefer to direct their educational efforts along other lines. This may explain the relationship shown to C.P. score in Table 4, in which there is a rise in the percentages along the first three quartiles, but a decline for the hospitals in the highest quartile.

A fifth educational function may be a hospital's secondary affiliation with a nursing school that is based in another institution. For example, a pediatric nursing course might be offered to nursing students from a hospital that lacked a children's ward; since the primary nursing school exercises a choice of such an affiliated hospital, quality standards would presumably influence the selection. It is accordingly of interest that by this indicator the hospitals in the highest C.P. quartile do indeed have the highest percentage of such affiliations.

Preventive and Community Service. A final set of criteria of hospital performance, on which data were available, concerns the hospital's role as a community health facility—a place oriented to prevention, to service for patients outside its walls, to social problems in the community. Such activities are not easy to isolate quantitatively, but five specific indicators, that perhaps reflect larger policies, are available.

The simple rate of hospital bed occupancy is one such indicator. For a given bed capacity, the hospital that is more fully occupied is rendering a relatively greater volume of service to patients. While the range of variation is small, it is evident from the table that the relationship of occupancy rates to the C.P. quartiles is positive and consistent.

The performance of routine chest x-rays on all admissions may be taken as an indicator of a hospital's preventive orientation. Over the last thirty years, this procedure has become widely adopted in the United States as a measure for detecting tuberculosis, cardiac abnormalities, and other diseases of the chest. (Even though some caution has been exercised in recent years because of the danger of excessive radiation and the decline of tuberculosis, in 1959 when these data were gathered, such restraint was not prominent.) By this measure, the relationship of preventive policies in a hospital to its C.P. score is positive and the gradient is consistent.

The rate of out-patient visits is a measure of a hospital's attention to patients outside its walls, especially involving the indigent. The variable here is more sensitive than that used for other services, since it is not simply the percentage of hospitals with an out-patient department, but rather the rate of out-patient visits expressed as number of visits per year for each bed on the hospital's wards. Examining the average of such rates in each of the quartiles, we see a clear rising gradient in relation to C.P. score, with a substantial jump in the highest quartile. The rate of out-patient services in that quartile is over twice that in the lowest quartile.

Another reflection of a social orientation is the maintenance of special beds for long-term patients in a hospital. Only a very small proportion of hospitals evidently operate such extended care units, and the relationship in the first three quartiles is irregular, but the highest C.P. quartile seems to have an appreciably higher percentage of hospitals with long-term beds available.

Finally, one may examine the operation of a social service department in a hospital as a reflection of its orientation to solving the family and social problems of patients during hospitalization and after discharge. By this indicator, the relationship to C.P. score is strongly positive, and the gradient in the two highest quarters is steep. It would seem that hospitals with relatively greater use of contractual physicians are far more likely to have social service programs than those with lesser use of such physicians; the highest quartile of hospitals has such programs at more than six times the frequency found in the lowest quartile.

This examination of the relationships of twenty-six separate hospital features to the institution's total score for appointment of contractual physicians warrants the general conclusion that a greater use of contractual physicians is impressively associated with a higher rate of hospital characteristics that imply good quality performance. For the few hospital characteristics on which the relationship is inconclusive, like the maintenance of premature infant nurseries or the operation of schools of nursing, it is likely that artifacts in the data are responsible or that the finding does not really reflect quality of performance. For all seven main sets of measures of hospital performance, the preponderant relationships to the contractual physicians' score are clearly in a positive direction.

These statistical explorations have all been based on what was described earlier as the "total contractual physician score." For a sample of the hospitals from eleven states, two other subscores on contractual physicians were also computed: one, based solely on physicians receiving a salary (as distinguished from other methods of remuneration), and the other, based solely on the "supportive specialties" (pathology, radiology, etc. as distinguished from the clinical specialties). When C.P. quartile groups of hospitals were formed on the basis of these two subscores, the relationships to the twenty-six features of hospital performance were nearly the same. In fact, with the "salaried physician" subscore, the relationships for many features become even more strikingly positive. We believe it soundest, however, to use the total C.P. score as the best measure of the hospital's policies with respect to contractual physicians— keeping always in mind that this is regarded as a reflection of the general degree of structuring in its medical staff (see chapter V).

ADJUSTMENTS FOR TYPE OF GENERAL HOSPITAL

The relationships explored above are all based on the universe of 2,434 general hospitals in the continental United States. Several questions may be raised, however, about the intervention of other hospital characteristics. What influence is exerted by hospital size, as distinguished from the medical staff organization with its C.P. score as barometer? What is the influence of hospital sponsorship? What are the findings in different regions of the country? It is possible to consider these questions by examining the findings within various subgroups of hospitals, in which size, sponsorship, or region is held constant.

Hospital Size. It will be recalled that the "contractual physician score" has been originally computed in a way intended to adjust for hospital size. Thus, the weighted sum of figures on contractual physicians in each hospital was divided by the number of beds, so that the final C.P. score represents a measure of such physicians per hospital bed.

It is true that the hospitals in the higher C.P. score quartiles tend to be of larger size. A tabulation done on the hospitals in a sample of 11 states, with 757 out of 2,434 hospitals in the full series, showed the following average sizes: lowest quartile—154 beds, second quartile—169 beds, third quartile—185 beds, and highest quartile—336 beds. It may well be that larger size enables a hospital to offer a wider range of services—and there is plenty of evidence of this, but this does not nullify the finding that these offerings are, indeed, associated with a greater use of contractual physicians per 100 beds. The use of contractual physicians remains a relevant factor associated with the 26 hospital characteristics reviewed above.

Moreover, the size correction built into the C.P. score was made in a simple linear manner—that is, in direct proportion to the number of beds. Analysis done subsequently in this over-all study suggested that this was probably an "over-correction" for hospital size. In chapter V, the reasoning involved in size-adjustments necessary for studying organizational structure is discussed, and we conclude that an exponential correction (square root or logarithmic) is probably sounder than a linear one. Without recapitulating this reasoning here, the effect of an exponential correction on the C.P. scores, as applied in this chapter, would render the high scores relatively higher and the low scores relatively lower. The probable effect of this form of size-correction in computing C.P. scores would have been to heighten the degree of positive relationships to the various features of hospital performance. Thus, the relationships between C.P. score and the 26 features of hospital performance shown in Table 4 are in all probability an understatement and not an exaggeration of the true dynamics.

In spite of all this, it is still possible to examine our findings on the 26 hospital features in relation to C.P. score quartiles, within defined size-groups of hospital. It would be tedious to review these findings for 26 hospital characteristics, along four quartiles of C.P. scores, in each of five size-groups of hospitals, but the main thrust of the relationships may be summarized.

For the entire series of hospitals, it will be recalled, the C.P. score was found to be positively related to the great majority of the 26 hospital characteristics reflecting performance. The relationships were consistently positive, or nearly so, as C.P. quartile increased, for 22 of the 26 characteristics (the exceptions being: total staffing, professional nurses, premature infant nursery, and nursing school). If we streamline the examination and compare just the two poles of the C.P. score range—that is, the lowest quartile and the highest quartile—then, in 25 of the 26 characteristics the relationship is positive; only for premature infant nurseries is the proportion of hospitals in the top C.P. quartile not higher than in the bottom quartile. Applying this streamlined type of statistical analysis, we may seek the main thrust of the findings for different hospital size-groups.

Thus, for hospitals in the 50–99 bed size-group (805 facilities), the data show a positive relationship between C.P. quartile and hospital performance features in 23 out of the 26 items. For all but three features, the highest C.P. quartile of hospitals had a stronger record than the lowest quartile. In the 100–199 bed size-group (791 hospitals), the positive relationship prevailed also for 23 of the 26 features. In the 200–299 bed size-group (412 hospitals), the relationship was positive for 18 out of the 26 features or 70 per cent of them. The same proportion of positive relationships applied to the 300–499 bed size-group (302 hospitals). In the largest size-group, however, of 500 beds or over (124 hospitals), the positive relationship fell to 14 out of the 26 features.

This decline in the apparent extent of positive association between C.P. score and the features of hospital performance, as the size-group increases, probably reflects certain artifacts in our data and in our method of analysis. As for the data, comments on the special significance of nursing schools and premature infant nurseries have been made earlier, suggesting that these may not be reliable indicators of hospital performance. As for our method of analysis, it must be kept in mind that in most of the hospitals of the larger size-groups, especially 500 beds and over, the C.P. scores are relatively high—even in the lower quartiles of those groups. The nature of our computation of the C.P. score (the system of weightings and the simple linear size-correction) and our calculations by ranked quartiles are not so precise as to distinguish reliably among a series of C.P. scores, all of which are relatively high. The differentiation, in other words, between high and low C.P. scores would not be so reliable, when—as in the 500-bed-and-over hospital size-group—the whole series of scores is relatively high and the number of cases is relatively small. (For example, the differential between scores of 1.0 and 10.0 in a long series is great, while the differential between 100 and 200 in a short series would be less.)

Keeping in mind these qualifications in our methodology, the data suggest that even when hospital size is held constant the C.P. score is positively related to hospital performance for the great majority of indicators in all hospital size-groups except the very largest. Moreover, it must be repeated that C.P. score itself was inherently size-adjusted in its initial calculation, with the adjustment being made in a conservative linear manner.

Hospital Sponsorship. When the hospitals in our full series are analyzed by the principal sponsorship groups, the generally positive relationship of C.P. score to the 26 features of hospital performance still prevails. It will be recalled that proprietary hospitals were omitted in the final analysis because of numerous reporting errors, but findings are available for the other sponsorship categories.

The commonest type of general hospital in the United States is the voluntary nonprofit and nonsectarian institution. Under this form of sponsorship, our series contained 1,118 hospitals. Comparing the lowest and the highest C.P. quartiles among these hospitals, a positive relationship was found for 25 out of the 26 performance features; the presence of premature infant nurseries was the only exception.

Likewise, for the 730 hospitals sponsored by nonprofit but church-related bodies, the positive relationship prevailed for twenty-five out of the twenty-six features. The only exception in this series applied to the provision of long-term beds, for which the highest C.P. quartile had a slightly smaller percentage than the lowest quartile.

A third sponsorship category is government at jurisdictions below the federal level. There were 480 nonfederal—that is, principally municipal, county, or state—general hospitals in our series. In this category all 26 of the hospital performance features were found to be positively related to the C.P. score when the highest and lowest quartiles are compared.

It is only for the final sponsorship category that a positive relationship of C.P. score to hospital performance features does not prevail in our data. Our series contained 106 general hospitals sponsored by the federal government. It will be recalled that military hospitals were excluded, but the category doubtless contains a high proportion of hospitals under the Veterans Administration and the U.S. Public Health Service. These are mainly very large hospitals, they seldom have maternity services or schools of nursing, and their patient populations differ markedly from those of the local community hospitals that constitute the great bulk of our series. Moreover, they tend to have generally high C.P. scores, with large numbers of full-time salaried doctors, so that the statistical problems discussed above in connection with hospital size would also apply to them. It should be no surprise, therefore, that for only 11 of the 26 performance features was there found to be a positive relationship to the C.P. score. In the light of the special circumstances, however, this finding would not seem to invalidate our general conclusion that performance features are positively related to C.P. score when hospital sponsorship is held constant.

In order to refine the analysis further, we examined the twenty-six hospital features and C.P. scores in a series of tabulations classifying hospitals by both sponsorship and size. By summating all voluntary general hospitals—both nonsectarian and religious—we derived a series of 1,848 hospitals, which could be examined under five size-groups.

In the smallest voluntary hospital size-group of 50–99 beds (588 hospitals) a positive relationship between C.P. quartile and hospital features characterized 22 out of the 26 items. In the 100–199 bed size-group (631 hospitals), the relationship was positive for 23 out of the 26 features. In the 200–299 bed size-group (342 hospitals), it was positive for 20 of the 26 features. In the 300–499 bed size-group (237 hospitals), it was positive for 19 of the 26 features. And once again, in the largest size-group of 500 beds and over (50 hospitals), the positive relationships decline to 14 out of the 26 features. It would appear that the statistical artifacts associated with large hospital size and generally high C.P. scores, discussed earlier, probably distort the findings for voluntary hospitals as well as for those sponsored by the federal government. In general, however, except for the largest size-group (containing only 50 hospitals), the relationships of C.P. score to the various features of hospital performance, within a single sponsorship type, were strongly positive.

Geographic Region. Analysis of the data separately by geographic regions of the United States also confirmed the general findings reported above. When the forty-eight states in the continental mainland are divided among nine regions, the positive relationship of the C.P. score to the great majority of hospital performance features holds for each region.

Among the nine multi-state regions, the lowest proportion of positive relationships was found in the region of the Mountain States, where the relationships were still positive for 19 out of the 26 features. These are thinly settled states (Montana, Idaho, Wyoming, Colorado, New Mexico, Arizona, Utah, and Nevada), with predominantly small hospitals. The highest proportion of positive relationships occurred in the east south central states (Kentucky, Tennessee, Alabama, and Mississippi), where the C.P. score was positively related to hospital performance for all 26 of the features studied.

CONCLUSIONS

This statistical survey of the universe of general hospitals of over fifty beds throughout the United States in 1959 permits only limited general conclusions, but the findings are certainly suggestive. The data present relatively superficial variables both on the independent and the dependent side. The hospital policies with respect to contractual physicians have been quantified by a scoring system in which certain speculative weightings are incorporated. The indicators of hospital performance are, of course, rather indirect; the presence or absence of certain approvals, facilities or services (as reported by the hospital in an annual questionnaire sent to the American Hospital Association) is regarded as reflecting larger characteristics of the hospital's total range of activities. In spite of these limitations, the findings point in a certain direction and add evidence on one aspect of the medical staff organization in general hospitals and its relationship to the hospital's program of services. This evidence gains greater strength when it is considered in conjunction with separate evidence from other studies, reported in later chapters of this book.

From the survey we have found that a wide range of medical specialists are now working in general hospitals, under both voluntary and governmental auspices, and according to various methods of remuneration. While radiologists and pathologists are the most frequent specialties under contract, the aggregate of other specialties greatly exceeds that for these laboratory fields. Moreover, counting all specialties, 98 per cent of hospitals have contractual arrangements with physicians of some type. As for methods of remuneration, the commonest over-all pattern is payment of straight salaries, either full-time or part-time, and this method predominates for every specialty except radiology, pathology, and anesthesiology (in which sharing of departmental income or fee-for-service is commonest).

Exploration of the relationships between a hospital's over-all policies on engagement of contractual physicians and independent measures of its performance suggests that these policies are positively associated with approvals, facilities, and functions reflecting better quality service. These positive relationships prevail for the great majority of twenty-six characteristics examined in seven spheres of hospital service by which performance may be analyzed. For certain features, like premature infant nurseries, in which a positive relationship is not found, it appears that artifacts in the survey approach are responsible. The "contractual physician score," on which the entire study rests, embodies a correction for hospital size, but when the relationships are further explored under five hospital size-groups separately, the positive relationships still predominate. Only for hospitals of 500 beds and over is the relationship weak, and this is probably explained more by a peculiarity of the statistics than by the objective facts. Likewise, the positive relationships prevail within separate types of hospitals sponsorship and in separate geographic regions of the country.

Taken alone, of course, findings of this sort cannot establish a simple cause-and-effect relationship. The forces doubtless act in both directions; that is, hospital performance features lead to the engagement of contractual physicians as much as the latter lead to certain types of performance. The point is that contractual physicians enable a hospital to carry out certain functions expected in modern medicine, and probably to perform those functions more effectively.[12] In the light of the contro-

[12] American Hospital Association, *Relationships: Hospitals and Hospital-Based Specialists* (Chicago: The Association, 1966).

versies over the entire question of medical staff patterns, moreover, one can conclude with assurance that this study provides no evidence for the contention of some that a policy of institutional appointment of specialists on salary or other forms of contract is associated with a deterioration in the quality of hospital care. All the evidence suggests that such physician–hospital contracts are positively associated—regardless of which is cause and which is effect—with a higher record of those hospital performance traits that are generally regarded as desirable, traits reflecting better patient care, education, and community health service. A deeper probing of these associations will be reported in later chapters.

V

MEDICAL STAFF ORGANIZATION:
A TYPOLOGY FOR ANALYSIS

IN THIS CHAPTER, we will take a much closer look at the anatomy and physiology—the structure and functioning—of medical staffs in general hospitals.[1] The statistical survey of a relatively large number of hospitals (reported in the previous chapter) focused on a limited feature of medical staff organization—the engagement of contractual physicians. Here we will try to take a more comprehensive view of all the features of medical staff organization and consider how they may be conceptualized for the purpose of quantification. We will also explore how the specific policies of a hospital regarding contractual physicians appear to relate to the over-all structuring of medical staffs. This will lay the groundwork for probing in greater depth, in a small sample of hospitals, the association between medical staff organization and hospital performance.

INTRODUCTION

In medicine, as in other human affairs, complex phenomena are often classified in dichotomies. We speak of the sick and the well, prevention and treatment, private medicine and "socialized medicine." Yet, more careful observation usually reveals a range of values, with many subtle variations along the way.

In describing the organization of medical staffs in hospitals, it has long been conventional to speak of it as "open" or "closed." The implication has been that the "open-staff" hospital permitted any private physician to admit patients, while the "closed-staff" institution had a restricted corps of salaried physicians who controlled all hospital activities. Arguments were long waged on the merits and defects of these polar

---

[1] A preliminary version of this chapter was published as: Milton I. Roemer and Jay W. Friedman, "Medical Staff Organization in Hospitals—A New Typology," *Hospital Management* (April 1968): 58–61; (May 1968): 41–44; (June 1968): 56–59.

models.[2] This simple classification of the relationship of doctors to hospitals may have had its value in an earlier day, but the enormous growth and diversification of hospitals in America now demands a better typology. This chapter will attempt to offer one based upon our research.

Among various features of hospital organization and administration on which research has been conducted, the structure or function of medical staffs has seldom been investigated in depth. The nursing staff and services, the administrator, the board of trustees, the kitchen, the laundry —almost every supportive aspect of hospital service has been subjected to study.[3] But the way doctors work in hospitals has been a sensitive issue; social researchers have shied away from it. Yet there is probably nothing more basic to patient care.

In order to examine this problem it is necessary to view the full landscape of American hospitals. Even within the limitation of *general* hospitals (i.e., excluding those for mental disorders or other special diseases), there has often been a tendency to confine observations to institutions of certain sponsorship—typically the voluntary, nonprofit association facility. Many studies are restricted to this type of hospital.[4] Although the most common variety of general hospital in the nation, it is by no means the only type, and some of the most significant developments in medical staff organization are occurring in institutions of other sponsorship like the federal government, state and local governments, health insurance plans, or universities.

When one looks at all types (that is, sponsorship, size, and administrative model) of general hospitals, one finds a wide range of medical staff patterns. Despite the somewhat idealized model presented by the best-known books in the field—MacEachern,[5] Ponton,[6] and LeTourneau[7]— the actuality is much more diverse. This is not to gainsay the progress in medical staff organization that has come about from promotion of a sound model for the voluntary, general hospital, with a staff of visiting physicians whose principal locales are in private offices. The Joint Commission on Accreditation of Hospitals, as we have noted in earlier chap-

---

[2] J. S. Goldwater, *On Hospitals* (New York: Macmillan Company, 1951).

[3] See Eliot Freidson (editor), *The Hospital in Modern Society* (New York: Macmillan, 1963). See also: U.S. Public Health Service, *Hospital Administrative Research*, PHS pub. No. 930–C.-8 (Washington: June 1964).

[4] For example: Temple Burling, Edith Lentz, and Robert N. Wilson, *The Give and take in Hospitals* (New York; Putnam, 1956). Also: B. S. Geogopoulos and F. C. Mann, *The Community General Hospital* (New York: Macmillan, 1962).

[5] M. T. MacEachern, *Hospital Organization and Management* (Chicago: Physicians Record Company, 1962).

[6] T. R. Ponton, *The Medical Staff in the Hospital* (Chicago: Physicians Record Company, 1953).

[7] Charles U. LeTourneau, *The Hospital Medical Staff* (Chicago: Starling, 1964).

ters, has done much to strengthen the self-discipline for quality surveillance in this prevailing type of medical staff in America.

Developments in the larger medical care scene in the United States, however, have led to a growing diversity of patterns in internal hospital organization for both medical and paramedical services. As the scope of the hospital functions has widened, the necessity for more elaborate organization has increased, especially as applied to the mode of work of doctors. Intramural medical staff organization, in turn, has had an increasing impact on the extramural world of medicine. As the leadership of the American Hospital Association has said, "The hospital medical staff is becoming increasingly the organizational center of the professional activities of the whole medical care system in a community."[8]

An understanding of the influence of medical staff patterns on the over-all operations of the medical care system, both inside hospitals and outside, demands a scheme of analysis. If greater or lesser degrees of organizational structure have differential effects on this system, we must find a method of definition and measurement of this structure. We can then determine if different scope and qualities of over-all performance are associated with diverse patterns of medical staff organization.

APPROACH TO A TYPOLOGY OF
MEDICAL STAFF ORGANIZATION

Organization has been defined as "a set of stable social relations deliberately created, with the explicit intention of continuously accomplishing some specific goals or purpose."[9] An organization thus requires a structure of *social controls* over the behavior of individuals in order to effectively unite their efforts in the pursuit of the stated goals. The degree to which individual behavior is influenced and regulated by the group or social controls defines its effective level of organization. It is evident that the level of organization of the medical staff will be heavily influenced by the basic goals of the hospitals. At the same time, the anatomy of this organization determines, in part, how well the goals will be reached or if they will be reached at all.

The designing of an efficient system of social controls in medical staffs is also influenced by the prevailing social concepts in medicine.[10] Since in the United States private medical practice is the predominant

---

[8] American Hospital Association, "Statement on the Changing Hospital and the American Hospital Association," *Hospitals*, 39:35–36, 104 (July 1964).

[9] Arthur L. Stinchcombe, "Social Structure and Organizations," in James G. March (editor), *Handbook of Organizations* (Chicago: Rand McNally, 1965), pp. 142–93.

[10] A. W. Snoke, "The Future Role of Hospitals in Medical Care," *Amer. J. Public Health*, 46:468–76 (April 1958).

form, it is natural that the American hospital should be widely regarded as the "doctor's workshop." The implications of this concept—which puts the private doctor at the center of the hospital stage—are quite different from those associated with the concept of the hospital as a "community health center." In a word, it has been the growth of the latter concept, associated with the many factors discussed in chapter I, which has been largely responsible for the increasing levels of medical staff organization. This trend has been manifest in hospitals of all sizes and sponsorships. In large hospitals and in those under government control, the trend has been most prominent for obvious reasons. Large size demands effective co-ordination for efficient performance. Accountability to legislatures and voters demands reporting through recognized channels of authority. But even in small hospitals and those under voluntary control the trend is seen, though at a different historical pace.

We find, then, a medley of hospitals in the United States with different levels of medical staff organization (MSO) operating side-by-side. Rather than the simple dichotomy of "open-staff" and "closed-staff," the range of structure can be more realistically described along a continuum as follows: (I) very loosely structured; (II) loosely structured; (III) moderately structured; (IV) highly structured; and (V) very highly structured. What are the organizational elements that may be expected to place a hospital's staff of doctors in one or another of these categories?

A basic feature of any organization is its relative size. Thus, a group of physicians in a hospital must first of all be defined in terms of their numbers in relation to the size of the hospital (i.e., the bed capacity). The physicians' qualifications as to specialty or other educational background are relevant. Specialization tends to define not only technical ability but also the degree of rigor or discipline operative within the individual doctor himself, as well as in his relationship to the organization. The procedure through which the doctor passes in order to be appointed to the staff, and the technical boundaries within which he is allowed to work are other essential controlling factors.

The commitment of the various doctors to the work and mission of the hospital, as compared with other anchors in their lives (such as private offices or other institutions), is highly relevant. Then, the subdivision of the group into smaller groupings or departments is important. Beyond this, the establishment of committees of physicians for certain surveillance functions is a common instrument for social and professional controls of the organization. The conversion of policies into written rules and regulations is a sign of social order and permits a rule of law rather than of whim or prejudice. Permeating all these formal features of organization is bound to be a set of casual or informal relationships among the persons as individuals in the group, and these may, to some extent, either sustain or weaken the operation of the formal organizational system.

These basic features of medical staff organization (MSO) in a hospital can be categorized under seven main headings, as follows:

1. Composition of the staff
2. Appointment procedure
3. Commitment
4. Departmentalization
5. Control committees
6. Documentation
7. Informal dynamics

Within each of these elements of MSO, there may be a range of degrees of organizational structuring. They can vary from what may be epitomized as a maximum of individual autonomy through steps toward a maximum of social control. Moreover, there are subfeatures under each of these headings which contribute to the net position of the MSO in this range.

The components of these features or dimensions of MSO may now be examined a little more closely, with some explanation of our rationale for postulating a range of values from low to high and methods by which they may be measured.

1. *Composition of the staff.* A hospital which has no restrictions on the number or qualifications of physicians who may come and use its facilities would represent the low end of the MSO range; a hospital with severe restrictions of both types would stand at the high end. In terms of measurable units, these could be defined as:

a) *Number of different doctors in the "active" medical staff classification per 100 beds.* An intentionally lower ratio would generally indicate greater restrictiveness or higher organization.

b) *Percentage distribution of doctors among different categories of staff classification.* A higher percentage of the total in the "active" staff and a lower percentage in the "courtesy" staff would indicate higher organization.

c) *Specialty ratings.* A higher proportion of board-certified and board-eligible specialists, as against general practitioners, would indicate higher organization.

The central foundations of an organizational system are found in the process of appointment of members, their relative commitment to the framework, and their specialized division of labor (departmentalization), each of which features are subject to measurement.

2. *Appointment procedure.* The relative rigors of the path of entrance of a doctor to the hospital staff, and the mode of definition of his "privileges," once admitted, would indicate the degree of MSO structuring. Measurable elements within this feature would include:

a) *The selection process.* The degree of diligence required in the application process, the documentation of professional credentials, the elaborateness of review of applications, and a deliberate recruitment program for qualified staff members are among the factors involved in the selection process. More demanding procedures and higher selectivity would mean higher MSO.

b) *Granting of privileges.* More careful or restrictive policies, which attempt to match the individual doctor's qualifications with the privileges allowed him, would indicate higher MSO.

c) *Obligations.* Requirements of medical staff members to serve on committees, to attend meetings, to participate in intramural educational programs, to serve in clinics, and so on, are relevant. A greater range of obligations would mean higher structuring of the MSO.

3. *Commitment.* The relative dedication of physicians to the hospital concerned, as against other interests, would be a basic reflection of the degree of medical staff organization. If all the doctors on the staff have limited ties to the institution, being physically and professionally involved mainly elsewhere (e.g., in their private offices or at other hospitals), the degree of commitment would be low and the MSO would be at the low end of the range. On the other hand, engagement of all doctors full time in the hospital concerned would represent the high end of the MSO range. In between these extremes could be many gradations. In terms of measurable units, this basic feature of MSO can be defined as follows:

a) *Time-allotment or presence.* Of the total physician-hours theoretically available from the members of the medical staff, a higher percentage spent within the given hospital would reflect higher organization. Time-allotment is a complex measurement, for it is built from a sum of many individual doctor time-records which may show great variance. Within a medical staff, certain doctors may be full-time in the hospital (e.g., radiologists, pathologists, or anesthesiologists), while others devote very few hours per week. Thus, it is the aggregate percentage that would count, although it is composed of many different sets of individual percentages.

b) *Method of remuneration.* Private fee-for-service payment methods tend to be associated with maximum individual autonomy of the doctor, while full-time salaries usually reflect greater organizational commitment. In between these polar methods are many variations, such as a sharing of fee earnings between doctor and hospital (common in radiology and pathology) or part-time salaries. A higher use of the salary form of remuneration among staff doctors, therefore, would indicate higher MSO.

c) *Institutional affiliations.* The number of different hospitals at which staff members have medical appointments has a bearing on their degree of commitment to any one hospital, regardless of the time spent in each institution. In a sense, then, the number of institutional affiliations reflects the doctor's attitude or psychological commitment toward the hospital under consideration. A greater aggregate number suggests lesser relative dedication to the hospital concerned and would tend to weaken or lower the MSO.

d) *Contractual physicians.* A somewhat composite reflection of the above three measures of commitment, we believe, is the tendency of a hospital to have formal contracts with certain physicians. The extent of these "contractual physicians"—whether in supportive fields like pathology and radiology or in fields of primary patient care like medicine or surgery—seems to reflect in some degree the time-status, methods of remuneration, and institutional affiliations of the entire medical staff. Unlike these three features, it is easily measurable and may, therefore, serve as a practical indicator of over-all physician commitment in the hospital.[11] This has been discussed in chapter IV and will be explored further below.

4. *Departmentalization.* Different functions of many persons, directed toward a common goal, inevitably lead to subdivisions among them and a co-ordinating hierarchy of authority within and between them. Departmentalization is the skeletal structure of an organization; its complexity and rigidity in day-to-day work reflect the degree of structuring. As we will discuss below, the mere size of an organization has a bearing on its departmental structure, but for a given size there may still be a range from low to high values. One hospital of 100 beds may have no specialty departments, while another may divide these between medicine and surgery, and a third may have pediatrics and obstetrics as well. With adjustments made for the size of hospital, measurable elements of departmentalization would include:

a) *Bureaucracy.* A greater relative number of departments and subdivision within them would mean higher organization of the medical staff.

b) *Authority system.* A greater relative number of positions of leader-

---

[11] Milton I. Roemer and Max Shain, "Contractual Physicians in General Hospitals: A Pilot Study in New York State," *Hospitals* (1 May 1960): 38 ff.

ship and responsibility (e.g., chiefs of departments, assistant chiefs, sectional chiefs, secretaries, etc.) would mean higher MSO.

c) *Reporting and co-ordinating systems.* The formal channels and procedures of communication are relevant. Thus, more frequent meetings of departmental and sectional officials would imply greater MSO.

There are numerous control features of organization which develop pragmatically in order to fulfill needs of the basic structure or reinforce it. Where some of the basic features described above are weak, compensatory mechanisms assume greater importance. Thus, low commitment or weak departmentalization may be compensated for by an elaborate system of "horizontal" or interdepartmental committees. At the same time, a strong organizational framework may be further reinforced by committees, as well as by written documentation. Whether the purpose of these features of social control is compensatory or reinforcing, their net effect invariably is to strengthen the degree of medical staff organization.

5. *Control committees.* Certain forms of social control may cut across the lines of functional departments in medical staffs, as in other types of organization. A problem of drug dispensing may concern both the department of medicine and the department of surgery, so that a new channel of authority is required. This control is commonly provided through interdepartmental committees such as those for drugs, for tissue review (really surgical audits), for record surveillance and medical audits, for infection control, and so on. Within large departments there may also be internal committees with comparable monitoring functions. Medical staff committees help to establish standards and to review, regulate, and evaluate certain aspects of the staff member's performance. Elements of this feature of MSO which may be measured would include:

a) *Number.* A greater relative number of staff control committees (adjusted to size of hospital), with defined functions, would mean greater MSO.

b) *Scope of functions.* A wider span of authority for designated committees would mean higher MSO structuring. For example, a tissue committee might have greater or lesser powers of corrective action authorized with respect to its findings on unnecessary or inadequate surgical procedures.

c) *Diligence.* The frequency of committee meetings and the record of attendance would be relevant. More frequent meetings with conscientious attendance of its members would indicate higher MSO.

6. *Documentation.* Beyond the social control devices involved in committees, there may be written rules and regulations affecting the behavior of all members of a medical staff. Putting these policies in writing

implies a greater formality and objectivity in the functioning of an organization (see chapter VII). At the other end of the time-scale are written reports on past performance during a year or a month. Measurable elements of such documentation would include:

a) *Rules and regulations.* More explicit and detailed policies in written form, such as a constitution, bylaws, and manuals of procedure, would indicate higher MSO.[12]

b) *Formal reports.* Periodic written summaries of activities provide an opportunity for public review of past performance. A greater volume and thoroughness of these reports would mean higher MSO.

7. *Informal dynamics.* Finally, permeating the structure of every organization is a network of informal interpersonal relationships, and the medical staff of a hospital is no exception. There is a tendency to interpret this informal process as "anti-structure" because it frequently circumvents or ignores the formal authority system. Its impact, however, depends not on its informality, but on whether it weakens or strengthens the social controls of the formal organization. Informal channels may introduce flexibility and "safety valves" which maintain the viability of a formal organizational framework.[13] The elements of this feature of MSO are difficult to measure in the same way that formal features are measurable, but interviews with medical staff members and other hospital personnel may give an impression of their net import. Conclusions may be drawn in a particular MSO on the influence of informal dynamics, in terms of loosening or tightening the social controls of the organization.

With these seven sets of factors defining the degree of structuring of medical staff organization, it should be possible to characterize this aspect of any hospital. By so doing, the relationships between the medical staff organization and the output of the hospital in terms of patient service, research, education, and other functions can be explored.

It should be noted that the sponsorship of the hospital (government, voluntary nonprofit, or proprietary) is not strictly relevant to evaluation of the MSO. There is no theoretical reason why any form of sponsorship cannot be associated with any degree of MSO, even though we know that in practice government general hospitals are more likely to have highly structured staffs, voluntary hospitals moderately structured ones, and proprietary hospitals the most loosely structured staffs. There

---

[12] Roland C. Bower and Milton I. Roemer, "Medical Staff Organization in the Smaller Hospital," *Hospital Management,* Part I (September 1963): 46 ff.; Part II (October 1963): 56 ff.

[13] R. Dubin, *Human Relations in Administration* (Englewood Cliffs, N.J.: Prentice-Hall, 1951).

are, nevertheless, some small proprietary hospitals with highly organized medical staffs,[14] as well as some large government hospitals with minimal organization of their physicians. In examining the *relationship* between MSO and hospital performance, it may be necessary to make allowances for the effect of sponsorship on the goals of the institution. But this relationship should not be confused with the examination of the medical staff organization per se.

Size of hospital is another matter. As noted at several points above, a large bed capacity is bound to generate a higher degree of medical staff organization. For one thing, a large number of doctors tends to mean a wider range of medical specialties, which induces greater departmentalization and more need for co-ordination and other controls. But even if all doctors in a large hospital happened to be general practitioners, size alone would demand more organization to keep the system moving smoothly. If the effect of size is to be eliminated, so that the influence of medical staff organization by itself can be evaluated, then some size-adjustment must be made in the analysis. This is a difficult analytical problem that will be explored below.

AN MSO SCORING SYSTEM

The quantification of the seven above components into a net "score" for each type of MSO structure is not easy. It may be attempted, however, by assigning a weighting to each of the features of medical staff organization, and within these weightings to scale the values from low to high. As in any scoring system, the weights assigned to different components may be chosen according to some reasonable judgment on the degree to which each component contributes to the over-all phenomenon. Accordingly, a scoring system for the seven principal components of MSO, reviewed in the first part of this chapter, was developed as follows:

MSO feature	Weighting
Staff composition	10
Appointment procedure	10
Commitment	25
Departmentalization	20
Control committees	15
Documentation	10
Informal dynamics	10
Maximum score	100

[14] Jay W. Friedman and Tess Weiner, "A Small Proprietary Hospital Closes Its Doors," *Hospitals* (16 August 1966): 46–51.

Within each of these weightings the MSO feature may be scored along a five-level scale, and a composite score may be summated.

In this scoring schedule it may be noted that four of the elements are assigned 10 points each, but that three are assigned greater weights. The reasoning behind these decisions comes partly from the general literature of organization theory and partly from our field observations in ten case-study hospitals to be reported in subsequent chapters. "Commitment" is assigned the greatest weight (25 points) for reasons discussed below: we think it largely determines and interacts with all six other elements in MSO functioning. "Departmentalization" is assigned a weight of 20 points because of its importance in providing a basis for discipline and day-to-day surveillance in the operation of a complex organization. "Control committees" are assigned 15 points—less than departmentalization but more than the other four elements—because these can be an important compensatory mechanism in MSO structures that are otherwise relatively loose.

The four other elements of MSO, assigned 10 points each, are deemed more or less equally relevant to the structuring of the system. Conceivably, the "appointment procedure" is more decisive than the other three elements, but in as much as it is especially difficult to quantify with uniform criteria (among hospitals of different sponsorship—proprietary, voluntary, and government), we decided to assign it the standard 10 points. Regarding the 10 points assigned to "informal dynamics," our score is based essentially on an inverted calculation; that is, the highest level of informal dynamics would be scored 0, while the lowest level would be scored 10. Thus, 10 points could be earned only if the informal dynamics of a medical staff were of negligible proportions—a situation that was not found in any of our study hospitals.

With this scoring system for medical staff organization, we applied our best judgment to the data collected from the series of ten "anthropological" studies of hospitals, reported in subsequent chapters. While it is jumping ahead of the story, so to speak, it will be helpful to see the result of these estimates at this point, since they govern the sequence of the hospital accounts that will be presented. The estimated scores, therefore, are shown in Table 5, with each hospital identified by a symbol (*A* to *J*) and ranked in order of the over-all MSO score.

The subscores for each of the seven features of MSO were derived from a consideration of all the component factors on which measurements could be sought, as outlined in this chapter. Under "appointment procedure," for example, account was taken of three components—selection process, granting of privileges, and obligations. Whenever possible, numerical values were used and rank-ordering of the series was

TABLE 5. MEDICAL STAFF ORGANIZATION (MSO) IN TEN SELECTED HOSPITALS:
MSO SCORE BASED ON SCALING OF SEVEN FEATURES

MSO feature (Maximum score)	Hospital									
	A	B	C	D	E	F	G	H	I	J
Staff composition (10)	7	5	4	8	7	7	7	7	9	9
Appointments (10)	2	2	4	6	4	8	8	10	10	10
Commitment (25)	5	5	10	15	15	15	20	25	25	25
Departmentalization (20)	4	4	8	12	12	12	16	20	20	20
Control committees (15)	3	6	6	9	12	12	12	6	6	6
Documentation (10)	2	4	2	4	8	6	6	8	8	10
Informal dynamics (10)	2	2	2	2	2	2	2	4	4	4
Total MSO score (100)	25	28	36	56	60	62	71	80	82	84

done within each component to contribute to the derivation of a subscore. Thus, under "composition," numerical figures were available for
each of three components (active staff doctors per 100 beds, percentage
of total staff in the "active" category, and proportion of specialists) and
an average of their relative rankings was used to derive the subscores
shown in Table 5. Under "commitment," on the other hand, for three of
the four components (time allotment, method of remuneration, institutional affiliations, and contractual physicians) quantitative data were not
available and impressionistic estimates had to be made. Altogether,
there were nineteen components subsumed under the seven features of
MSO structuring, and either a numerical or impressionistic estimate was
made on each, in all ten hospitals. The nature of the information on
which these estimates were based will be more clear on reading of the
case-study chapters.

Because this over-all scoring approach is subject to debate—both
on grounds of the relative crudeness of some of our numerical estimates
and because of the various weightings assigned to the seven MSO features—we decided to explore also a separate single-factor score for MSO
structure. The obvious choice was the MSO item on which we had
already collected nationwide information: the engagement of contractual
physicians. In our general typology this was simply one out of four
components contributing to a subscore for "commitment," but our field
studies in the ten hospitals, as well as the national study, gave us the
hunch that it might serve not only as a good index of commitment but

also as a useful index of MSO structure as a whole. This, indeed, was the underlying hypothesis of the national survey of contractual physicians reported in the preceding chapter, and a more careful examination of the data from our ten study hospitals would permit us to test it.

The identification within a multi-faceted phenomenon of a single feature that would reasonably well reflect the whole phenomenon ought ideally to be based on statistical analysis, such as the stepwise multiple regression technique.[15] As mentioned, however, our quantitative sub-scores under MSO structure were too rough, and a series of ten cases was too small a number to justify such a sophisticated approach. An impressionistic selection of "commitment"—quantified through a count of contractual physicians—as a key indicator of total MSO structure seemed, therefore, a justified approach. Our reasons and methods of doing this will be discussed below.

COMMITMENT AS A KEY INDICATOR

The supposition that over-all MSO structure can be well reflected by the aggregate commitment of staff members to the hospital is drawn from various observations. The other six features of medical staff organization in our typology appear to be directly supportive of commitment, or else designed to compensate for low commitment, in order to achieve firm organizational controls. Commitment has a substantial influence on the staff composition, its basic organizational features (appointment procedures and departmentalization), its compensatory or reinforcing controls (committees and documentation), and its informal dynamics. If the doctor's commitment is low—which means, in effect, that his energies and loyalties are applied mainly elsewhere—then the organization will not have a great impact on his behavior. The force of social controls will be meager. If the commitment is high, then perforce the organization will largely determine the doctor's whole professional life, and his responsiveness to organizational mandates or social controls will be great.[16]

We have been led to this judgment also by observation of long-term historical trends in the relations of physicians to hospitals in America (see chapter II). It is suggested, furthermore, by a comparison of contemporary American hospitals with European hospitals (see chapter III), the latter being characterized by full-time salaried medical staffs

[15] See: Erving Goffman, "On the Characteristics of Total Institutions: The Inmate World," in D. R. Cressey (editor), *The Prison, Studies in Institutional Organization and Change* (New York: Holt, Rinehart and Winston, 1961).

[16] See: H. A. Simon, D. W. Smithburg, and V. A. Thompson, *Public Administration* (New York: Knopf, 1959).

and much more rigid structuring.[17] The paradigm of high commitment in the American scene may be found in a military hospital, where the total professional life of the doctor is inside the institution; there are few competing outside interests of significance. At the other extreme is a small proprietary hospital, where the commitment of most physicians who use it is minimal; the hospital is simply a place where they send their private patients, and it plays a very small part in their total professional lives. Between these two polar models are a range of commitment levels in diverse types of hospitals.

Measurement of Commitment. There are a number of ways that commitment can be conceptualized, as discussed earlier in this chapter, but only a few by which it may feasibly be measured. Perhaps at the heart of the concept is psychological dedication of the doctors to the institution being studied. But how can this be reliably measured? Attitudes can be solicited through questionnaire or interview, and psychological scaling done on the responses. But even if feasible among busy practicing doctors, the results would be subject to varying interpretations. Certain doctors might be emotionally devoted to a particular hospital from long association, yet only meagerly tied to it in their daily work. On the other hand, their emotional ties may be weak, while their work in the wards and clinics may sometimes be long and arduous. Ultimately, it is the performance within an organization that represents the commitment of its members.

But there are more objective attributes of commitment which can be used to describe the physical relationships of doctors to the medical staff organization. Four of these attributes, already described briefly, are: presence or time-allotment, number of other hospital affiliations, the method of remuneration, and use of contractual physicians. The number of affiliations and the methods of remuneration are fairly discrete elements, but their true significance is less clear than that of time-allotment. For example, the number of affiliations will indicate the potential dispersion of a physician's activities among a number of hospitals. In a sense, the fewer the affiliations the greater the psychological and physical dedication to each hospital. But this number by itself—unless it is only "one"—will not reveal the commitment to any single hospital. More detailed analysis of the number of admissions and the time spent in the several hospitals would be necessary.

There are other problems related to the method of remuneration. For example, a physician who receives no payment from the institution, depending entirely on private fees from patients, would generally be more loosely bound to an institution than a full-time salaried physician,

---

[17] Milton I. Roemer, "Influence of Hospitals on Medical Practice in Europe and America," *Hospitals* (1 November 1963): 61 ff.

but there might be significant exceptions. Some hospitals provide office space for private medical practice.[18] This arrangement places these physicians full-time in the hospital environs, allowing them to participate more fully in the medical staff organization. Even though they are paid entirely on a private fee-for-service basis, they become heavily committed to the hospital and its medical staff. On the other hand, some physicians may receive flat part-time salaries from a hospital for specific duties (e.g., reading electrocardiograms), but their time-allotment and commitment may be slight. Thus, while the method of remuneration, as we have defined it, may have some validity as an indicator of MSO commitment, it can be misleading.

As for time-allotment, it would appear to be a simple and direct indicator of medical staff commitment. Unfortunately, it is often the least identifiable factor among all those considered. Indeed, it is strange that —except for physicians on contract with the hospital—the time-allotments of private attending physicians are seldom known by either the hospital administration or the medical staff itself. Although they are the crucial persons in the patient-care system, few hospitals keep records of the number or duration of visits of doctors within the institution. Of course, such information would be theoretically obtainable through a time-clock study, but the mere suggestion of the use of such a research instrument by the average medical staff may precipitate a professional explosion. The independence of private physicians in general hospitals is jealously guarded, and even medical-social research would in all probability be viewed as a threat. Practically, therefore, a less direct form of measurement of MSO commitment had to be sought.

Contractual Physicians and Their Measurement. In the light of all of these qualifications, difficulties in interpretation, and inaccuracies or unavailability of precise data, there remains the fourth indicator of commitment mentioned above—the number of contractual physicians present in the hospital full-time or part-time. Data on this feature are relatively precise and available. In fact, it was possible to collect information on this feature in a survey of over 2,400 general hospitals throughout the United States, reported in chapter IV.[19]

Consideration of the dynamics of development of medical staffs suggests the rationale of regarding the number of contractual physicians in a hospital as a reasonable reflection or indicator of the over-all degree of structuring of its medical staff. If all hospital physicians are under contract to the institution, as in the typical federal government hospital, it is obvious that the bureaucratic structure is relatively firm.

[18] C. R. Rorem, *Physician's Private Offices at Hospitals* (Chicago: American Hospital Association [Monograph Series No. 5], 1959).

[19] Milton I. Roemer, "Contractual Physicians in General Hospitals: A National Survey," *Amer. J. Public Health*, 52:1453–64 (September 1962).

At the other extreme, the completely "open-staff" hospital has a manifestly loose structure. But when, in the latter type of hospital, one or a few contractual physicians are appointed, the existing framework of medical activity is noticeably strengthened. As relatively more such physicians are appointed, with ties to the institution, the over-all staff structure is further tightened. We know from frequent observations that there is usually resistance to such appointments by private medical practitioners, who see their autonomy and independence in the hospital thereby threatened. As still more contractual physicians are appointed, a stage is reached where the medical staff may become a highly structured system with firm internal controls.[20]

Thus, both logic and observation have led us to believe that the over-all MSO structuring of a hospital is well-reflected by the extent of its engagement of contractual physicians. This feature would seem to be a reasonable indicator of "commitment" which we believe operates as the heart of organizational strength. Numbers to define it are readily available. An important obstacle remains, however, if different hospitals are to be compared—the influence of hospital size. Quite aside from organizational tightness, a large hospital, with a large medical staff, is bound to have a greater number of contractual physicians than a small one. If a "score" for contractual physicians, as a measure of MSO structuring in different hospitals, is to be derived, therefore, it is necessary to make some appropriate correction or adjustment for hospital size.

The Contractual Physician Score, Size-adjusted. The first task is to determine the number of contractual physicians who are located in the hospital full-time or part-time. They may be paid by salary, percentage of departmental income, or even fee-for-service, as is often the practice with anesthesiologists and sometimes with pathologists and radiologists. The important factor is the existence of a written or oral agreement—a contract—designating mutual obligations between the physician and the hospital. To make a count, part-time physicians can be considered as one-third of full-time, so that a total number of "full-time equivalent" contractual physicians can be derived. All contractual physicians are included, whether they are engaged in direct clinical services to patients, in supportive specialties, in purely administrative roles, or in laboratory research or professional education. Tabulation of the full-time equivalent number of contractual physicians, as described, can be done with ease.

A critical problem, however, as mentioned above, is how to adjust this crude figure, or for that matter any other MSO variable, for hospital size. One method might simply be to divide the crude sums by the num-

20 C. F. Wilinsky, "Even the Medium-sized Hospital Should Have a Full-time Chief of Staff," *Hospitals*, 20:47 ff. (November 1946).

ber of hospital beds. Such a correction, however, assumes that the relationship between hospital size and other elements of MSO is merely
a direct linear one.

At an earlier stage of this research—the national survey of contractual physicians reported in chapter IV—we did not consider any
form of nonlinear correction for hospital size. We simply divided the
count of contractual physicians in a hospital by the number of beds. On
the other hand, our "count" of such physicians was not direct, but was
based upon a weighting of different specialty types and different remuneration methods, in accordance with their deviation from conventional patterns—the more unusual arrangements getting higher weights.
This approach probably had the effect of inflating the contractual physician "counts" in larger hospitals, where less-conventional patterns are
found, and this may have served as a subtle approach to nonlinearity
in deriving the "size-adjusted contractual physician score." Later in our
research, after the national contractual physician data had been analyzed
on this basis and after a number of hospital case studies had been done,
we set out to find a more appropriate adjustment of the contractual
physician score for hospital size. From many other social observations,
we have reason to believe that the relationship of bureaucratic structure to organizational size is probably not a simple linear one. A school
system with 20,000 pupils in it, for example, would not require an administrative structure two times as complex as one with 10,000 children.
A factory with 40,000 workers would not require ten times the administrative structure of one with 4,000 workers. The question is: What
mathematical function would make a proper correction for the apparent
nonlinearity of effect of size on the administrative complexity of an
organization?

Other investigations have faced this problem of the nonlinearity of
administrative structure in relation to the general growth of organizations. To organization theorists the question is usually epitomized in
terms of the expansion of "staff" in relation to "line" personnel.[21] In a
medical staff organization the contractual physicians may not be strictly
comparable to "staff" positions in a factory (since they also have "line"
or operational functions), but the analogy is still useful. Since we are
considering the number of contractual physicians as an indicator of organizational structuring, and since the problem is to adjust this number
in relation to the *size* of the organization (i.e., the number of beds in a
hospital), it seems reasonable to draw a rough analogy to industrial settings. Thus, we may assume that the number of contractual physicians

[21] A. W. Baker and R. C. Davis, *Ratios of Staff to Line Employees and Stages of
Differentiation of Staff Function* (Columbus, Ohio: Ohio State University [Mono-
graph No. 72], 1954).

will be related to the number of hospital beds, as the number of managerial personnel in a factory is related to the total number of employees.

On this basis, the problem is to decide which mathematical function may be applied to the number of hospital beds, in order to correct for the greater number of contractual physicians that may be found in a larger hospital, *irrespective* of the degree of structuring of the medical staff organization. Is there a mathematical "law of growth" of the size of an organization (i.e., number of hospital beds or number of factory workers) in relation to the growth of its administrative controls (i.e., contractual physicians or administrative staff positions)?

In the search for such a law, organization theorists have looked to physical or biological models. Mason Haire has found such models useful.[22] He points out, for example, that as an organism grows in size, its surface increases by a square power, while its mass increases by a cube power. This "square-cube" law influences the shape of larger animals, in comparison with smaller ones, because of the gravitation forces on greater mass (or weight). For another example, cellular growth in an organism occurs geometrically—that is 2 cells become 4, 4 become 8, 8 become 16, etc.—instead of arithmetically (2, 4, 6, 8, 10 . . .). Yet each control system in the body (brain, heart, lungs, intestine, etc.) does not grow in the same geometric proportions. Specialization of function occurs so that a heart weighing one pound pumps blood throughout the whole body of 150 pounds, and a brain of two pounds controls motor and sensory functions likewise. Moreover, the heart and brain of an adult are much smaller, in relation to total body size, than are those critical organs in the body of an infant.

Examining administrative structures in the light of this type of biological model, Haire reports data based on a series of industrial firms, as follows:

Size of firm (Number of employees)	Per cent of personnel in top and middle management
20– 50	13.6
50–100	10.5
100–200	5.9
Over 200	4.1

In other words, the relative growth of top managerial functions is less than the growth of operations (i.e., number of line workers) in a firm.

Without falling into the trap of reasoning by false analogy—either in the biological sphere or the industrial sphere—it would appear that increasing size of a medical staff in a hospital would probably not cause

[22] Mason Haire, "Biological Models and Empirical Histories of the Growth of Organizations," in Mason Haire (editor), *Modern Organization Theory* (New York: John Wiley, 1964), pp. 272–306.

a *proportionate* increase in its administrative structuring. It would follow that size-adjustment of our measure of structuring—the number of contractual physicians—should be achieved by dividing this crude number by something less than the linear increment of bed capacity. For example, the number of contractual physicians in a hospital of 1,000 beds, compared with the number in a hospital of 100 beds, should not be divided by 10 in order to adjust for size, but by some figure less than 10.

At this time, we have not been able to determine—nor to discover in the sociological literature—an empirically derived mathematical function by which to make this size-adjustment with scientific certainty. Organizational studies, in fact, suggest that the function may not be a constant one, but may vary with different orders of magnitude of a system.[23] On a trial-and-error basis, therefore, we examined two simple functions by which the count of contractual physicians could be corrected for the enlarging bed capacity of a series of hospitals, through a process "slower" than the simple linear ratios of the bed capacities. One such function would be the square root of the enlarging bed capacity; another would be its *logarithm*. By these adjustments, the number of contractual physicians in a 1,000–bed hospital, compared with a 100–bed hospital, for example, would be adjusted by a ratio of about 3:1 under the square root correction, by a ratio of 3:2 under the logarithmic correction, and by a ratio of 10:1 if the simple linear correction were applied. Thus, both nonlinear methods offer a correction much slower than the linear route, and this seems to coincide roughly with observations in biological systems and studies of industrial firms.

On the basis of this reasoning, we have derived a series of "size-adjusted contractual physician scores" on the same ten hospitals analyzed in Table 5, applying both the square root and logarithmic size corrections. The results are presented in Table 6, where the rank-ordering of the ten hospitals is based, as in Table 5, on their over-all MSO score.

It is evident from inspection of Table 6 that both types of size-adjusted contractual physician scores yield a ranking of the series of hospitals very closely parallel to the ranking of the total MSO scores. The correspondence is not perfect by either method, but it is slightly closer with the application of the logarithmic size-correction.

These findings tend to confirm our general supposition, posed earlier in this chapter, that the over-all structuring of a medical staff is well reflected by the degree of "commitment" to the hospital of its members, and the latter is reasonably measurable by a size-adjusted count of the contractual physicians. In spite of the relatively crude hospital size-correction used in our national survey of contractual physicians, this basic parallelism of measurements provides a linkage between the conclusions

---

[23] Amitai Etzioni, *Modern Organizations* (Englewood Cliffs, N.J.: Prentice-Hall, 1964).

TABLE 6. CONTRACTUAL PHYSICIANS AND SIZE-ADJUSTED CONTRACTUAL PHYSICIAN SCORES (CPS)
          IN TEN SELECTED HOSPITALS, RANKED BY THEIR TOTAL MSO-SCORE

MSO feature	Hospital									
	A	B	C	D	E	F	G	H	I	J
Total MSO score (See Table 5)	25	28	36	56	60	62	71	80	82	84
Number of contractual physicians	1.0	1.5	6.0	15.5	22.5	19.5	48.0	53.0	65.0	77.0
Number of beds	42	76	141	230	447	265	490	346	729	1500
CPS (square root size-correction)	0.15	0.17	0.51	1.02	1.06	1.20	2.17	2.85	2.41	1.99
CPS (logarithmic size-correction)	0.6	0.8	2.8	6.6	8.5	8.1	17.8	20.9	22.7	24.3

of the national survey and those of the "anthropological" case studies of ten hospitals to be presented in the subsequent chapters. In other words, derivation of a size-adjusted measurement of contractual physicians in a hospital—a relatively simple task in any hospital—seems to categorize the MSO pattern of that hospital in approximately (though not exactly) the same place on a scale of organizational structuring as a painstaking examination and quantification of all seven features and nineteen subfeatures of the over-all medical staff organization.

As a streamlined approach to quantification of MSO structuring in a general hospital, we believe that a count of the contractual physicians, adjusted by the logarithm of the number of beds, would provide reasonable measurements. We hope this may be useful in research on large numbers of hospitals, in which detailed field observations of the medical staff structure and operations are not feasible. In the ten "anthropological" case studies that follow, however, we have the benefit of relatively detailed field observations, so that the scaling of the medical staffs could be based on the quantification of all the component features of their over-all structure and function—that is, by means of the total MSO score, explained earlier.

In the chapters that follow, the typology for analysis of medical staff organization, offered in this chapter, will be applied. We will then be in a position to consider the association of MSO structure to the output of hospitals in terms of in-patient and out-patient care, professional education, research, and other types of community service. We do not thereby suggest that MSO structure is the only determinant of hospital performance, having reviewed in chapter I the many other influences at work. Our observations suggest, however, that it is an important intervening variable in the chain of determinants of a hospital's total program.

VI

A VOLUNTARY HOSPITAL WITH MODERATELY STRUCTURED MEDICAL STAFF ORGANIZATION

WITH THIS CHAPTER we begin the accounts of medical staff organization and hospital service programs in ten hospitals selected to demonstrate the range of MSO structuring conceptualized in the previous chapter. As explained in the Appendix on methodology, this "anthropological" phase of the research involved detailed exploration, through personal visits and extensive interviews of key informants, of the structure and activities of each of these hospitals.

THE SERIES OF TEN HOSPITALS

Lengthy case-study reports have been prepared on each hospital, but their full texts would make tedious reading. We have chosen, therefore, to present in this chapter a fairly complete account of one hospital in our series—a hospital at the mid-point of the MSO structuring range. In the following chapter we will present accounts of the medical staff patterns of the nine other hospitals in our series, along with brief comments on MSO relationships to the hospital programs. In the final chapters, we will be in a position to review the findings on both MSO and the many features of hospital performance "horizontally" across the series of ten hospitals, with derivation of any generalizations that seem warranted.

In the previous chapter the ten hospitals were identified by symbols, but now it may be helpful to the reader to attach names to them—fictitious names to be sure—so that one can understand how Pebble City Community Hospital, analyzed in this chapter, fits into the full spectrum. These identifications are as follows:

Symbol	Name of hospital	MSO level	Bed-size	MSO score
A	Kenter Hospital	I	42	25
B	Hillside Hospital	I	76	28
C	View Hospital	II	141	36
D	Midland Hospital	II	230	56
E	Pebble City Hospital	III	447	60
F	St. Martin's Hospital	III	265	62
G	Scopus Hospital	IV	490	71
H	Medical Group Hospital	V	346	80
I	Public Hospital	V	729	82
J	Veterans Hospital	V	1500	84

The five groupings of hospitals shown in the above list reflect the level of structuring of the medical staff organization, ranging from "very loosely structured" (Type I) to "very highly structured" (Type V), as previously explained. Pebble City Community Hospital is approximately at the middle of the range, with an MSO score of 60, according to our scheme of quantification. We designate it, therefore, as a general hospital with a *moderately structured medical staff organization*. Although it is approximately the median hospital in our small series, one must not conclude that it would represent the median in a random series of hospitals throughout the nation. General observation suggests that in the United States as a whole there are many more hospitals on the loosely structured side of this point than on the tightly structured side, so that the median for the nation would probably be more accurately represented by a hospital with an MSO score of 40 than of 60. Our purpose here, however, is to examine the central hospital in our conceptual range, rather than the "typical" hospital in the universe of facilities.

In this description of the Pebble City Community Hospital, we will first examine the social setting of the hospital and its over-all characteristics. Then we will analyze its medical staff organization (MSO) according to the seven features previously explained. Next we will describe the hospital's program under four headings: in-patient care, out-patient service, preventive and community service, and education and research. Finally, we will attempt to summarize the influence of the hospital's MSO on its general performance.

THE SETTING AND OVER-VIEW OF
PEBBLE CITY COMMUNITY HOSPITAL

Pebble City is a city of 400,000 population near to another even larger metropolis. It is itself the trading center of an area which includes more than one million people, although there is considerable interchange for employment and services with the neighboring metropolis. Two major university medical centers are less than twenty-five miles away, and two local colleges offer degrees in nursing. The hospital is located at the periphery of Pebble City but on the major arterials, so that it is accessible to and serves a larger population than that of the city itself.

Like many hospitals originating at the turn of the century, Pebble City Community Hospital (PCCH) was founded in 1907 by a group of physicians who purchased jointly a thirteen-room frame house for this purpose. Six years later, in 1913, the physician-owners built the first unit of a new building, and the final wing was completed in 1932. During the early 1930's the hospital supported a nursing school, but it was abandoned at the depth of the Depression when it became too expensive to operate. By 1937 the hospital was firmly established in the community, and it was converted from proprietary to nonprofit status. A city bond issue in 1956 provided funds for an entirely new building to be located on a larger site donated by the city, and two years later another successful bond drive for the purchase of equipment was completed. The current 447-bed hospital, constructed at a cost of nearly $11,000,000, was occupied in 1960.

Unlike some of the smaller and younger hospitals in this study, Pebble City Community Hospital has grown steadily throughout most of its history because of financial stability and wide community and professional support. As the median hospital in this study, mid-way between the very loosely and very highly structured medical staff organizations, it is described first and more fully than the other hospitals, so that they may be compared with it. It illustrates a large, modern, and dynamic general hospital with a moderately organized medical staff.

Physical Plant and Personnel. Pebble City Community Hospital combines the attractiveness of modern architecture with efficiency of functional design. Three wings, five-stories high, comprise the core of the building. The wings are connected at the lower levels by flat-top extensions of the building, which provide space for the various administrative departments and technical services. The hospital also has a four-story pathology laboratory, the largest such unit in a voluntary nonprofit hospital west of the Rocky Mountains. Just outside the emergency entrance is a heliport for reception of air-ambulance cases.

Spaciousness and good taste in interior decoration are evident everywhere in the hospital. The main waiting room, administrative offices, and conference rooms are carpeted, wood-panelled, and attractively furnished. Ten-foot-wide halls, Italian mosaic tile façades, permanent gray, fiberglass drapes against all windows to give uniform color outside—yet with interior drapes matching the motif of the individual rooms—and numerous tropical planters all lend a quiet and attractive atmosphere.

Each hospital bed has a control panel containing a telephone signal button, a radio, remote television dials, and controls for motor-driven bed adjustments. Instant contact with the nursing station is provided by an "intercom" system.

The hospital contains 447 beds and 65 bassinets, including a 44-bed pediatric unit, 54 obstetrical beds, a 28-bed psychiatric unit, and intensive care units with 20 medical and 6 surgical beds. There are 4 delivery rooms, 7 labor rooms, and 12 operating rooms. In addition to the extremely large pathology laboratory mentioned above, there are radio-isotope, cardio-pulmonary, and cardiovascular laboratories, and a large diagnostic and therapeutic radiology department. Electroencephalography, electrocardiography, and similar diagnostic services are provided through a separate "electrodiagnostic department." A complete rehabilitation department is housed in an attached building. The hospital operates its own laundry, with an output of 2,500,000 pounds a year or about 20 pounds per patient per day. The food service department serves an average of 584,000 meals a year, or 1,600 meals a day. The chapel, with one wall of beautifully designed modern stained-glass windows, has a seating capacity of 75, and daily services are held for patients or visitors. There is also an adjacent 26-unit apartment house for interns, residents, and their families.

A number of medical arts buildings, in which many of the physicians on the staff have private offices, are located nearby. In addition to the medical staff, the hospital has more than 800 employees, of whom about 400 are engaged in the professional care of patients and almost 100 in administrative and general tasks. PCCH has a ratio of 181.7 employees (full-time equivalents) per 100 beds or 224.3 per 100 patients (Table 7).

Finances. Eighty-six per cent of the nearly $9,000,000 annual hospital income is derived from payments by in-patients and slightly less than 10 per cent from the emergency service and out-patient department. More than half of the expenditures of the hospital are allocated to the professional care of patients, about 10 per cent to administrative and general costs, and about 40 per cent to dietary services, household and property maintenance, depreciation, and other items. In 1964 the total expense per patient-day was $53.54, with revenue of $55.75. In that year the hospital had a net surplus of more than half a million dollars.

The original cost of constructing the current hospital was $10,800,-000. These funds were obtained from the following sources:

City bond issue	$6,550,000
Individuals and organizations	2,500,000
Sale of the old hospital to the county	1,067,000
Ford Foundation grant	207,800
Federal Hill-Burton grant	467,000

TABLE 7. Pebble City Community Hospital: Salaried employees by category, number, and rate per 100 beds and 100 patients, 1964[a]

Category of employment	Number of employees (full-time equiv-alent—FTE)	Number of FTE per 100 beds	Number of FTE per 100 patients
Administrative and general	99	22.1	27.3
Dietary	81	18.1	22.4
Household and property	103	23.0	28.5
(Subtotal)	(283)	(63.2)	(78.2)
Nurses: R.N.	194	43.4	53.6
L.V.N.[b]	78	17.4	21.5
Aides, orderlies, clerks	128	28.6	35.4
(Subtotal)	(400)	(89.4)	(110.5)
Technicians and therapists	85	19.0	23.5
Physicians[c]	15	3.4	4.1
Residents	15	3.4	4.1
Interns	16	3.5	4.5
(Subtotal)	(46)	(10.3)	(12.7)
TOTAL	814	181.9	224.9

[a] Based on 447 beds and an average daily census of 362.

[b] Licensed Vocational Nurse [or L.P.N., Licensed Practical Nurse].

[c] Includes three PhD's. Only the director of medical education is paid a salary by the hospital; all others are contractual physicians on other schemes of remuneration.

In 1966 an 86-bed advanced-care unit for rehabilitation of semi-ambulatory patients was completed at a cost of $2,500,000.* Care in this unit is provided at 33 per cent lower per diem cost than that in the main hospital.

Since 1960, contributions from individuals and organizations have added $800,000 for equipment, services, and research. The professional staff itself contributed more than $1,000,000, and continues to make large contributions primarily for the purchase of new equipment. These contributions reflect the wide community support that the hospital enjoys.

Eligible Patient Population. The wide scope of services and facilities permit PCCH to admit patients with virtually any disease. The patient's ability to pay and the affiliation of his doctor with the medical staff are the only eligibility requirements. No one is refused emergency admission, however, although the limited funds available for care of indigent patients usually restricts them to relatively short-term care. After a brief period they are referred to the local government hospital, intended to serve the poor. Patients with active tuberculosis and communicable diseases may be admitted to the isolation unit temporarily, but they are also referred to public hospitals for long-term care. (Fur-

* The advanced-care unit raised the total number of beds to 533, but since it was not in full service at the time of the study, the older figure of 447 beds has been used for computations.

ther details on care for indigent patients are given in connection with out-patient services.)

Distribution of Administrative Power. Pebble City Community Hospital is a nonprofit corporation operated by a board of fifty trustees, appointed by the fifteen-member board of directors. The directors are themselves elected by the trustees from among their members. The trustees are generally representative of the community, with the largest number from consumers, but including certain members of the city government, such as the city health officer, one prominent local labor leader, and citizens active in community affairs. Six of the fifteen-members of the board of directors are physicians on the medical staff, who are elected by the trustees, rather than the staff. The chief and vice-chief of the medical staff are *ex officio* members of the board of directors, as is the hospital administrator.

The hospital administrator is employed by the board of directors. The present administrator has occupied this position for more than ten years. He holds a master's degree in business administration and prior to his employment by PCCH had been administrator of a large midwestern hospital. Far from being only a "business manager," he has been active in educational programs on hospital administration and has published numerous articles in professional and popular journals. His active leadership has contributed to the progressive developments in this hospital, but it has also been a cause of conflict with the medical staff, discussed below. Perhaps because of this conflict in interpretation of the appropriate functions of a community general hospital, the administrator is not an *ex officio* member of any medical staff committee, as is customary in many community hospitals. Administrative power is, in large measure, lodged in the office of this imaginative and dynamic director.

A joint conference or liaison committee, composed of nine physicians, eight directors, the administrator, and the assistant administrator, is designed to facilitate administrative decision-making, but this committee is not very active. It is less important than the fourteen-member medical executive committee, which shares much power with the hospital administrator.

MEDICAL STAFF ORGANIZATION

The structure and function of the medical staff may now be described according to the seven features outlined in chapter V.

Composition of the Staff. Only 150, or less than one-third, of the total staff of 477 physicians and ten dentists are in "active-staff" classifi-

TABLE 8. MEDICAL STAFF OF PEBBLE CITY COMMUNITY HOSPITAL: NUMBER OF PHYSICIANS BY SPECIALTY AND MEDICAL STAFF CLASSIFICATION, 1964

Specialty	Medical staff classification					
	Active	Associate	Consulting	Honorary	Residents	Interns
General practice	29	66		13		
Surgery						
General	24	31		5	1	
Cardiac-thoracic	2	5				
Gynecologic	4	6				
Orthopedic	10	14		1		
Neurologic	3	7	1			
Plastic	3	2				
Supportive specialists						
Anesthesiology	3	8				
Pathology	4	1			5	16
Radiology	2	5	1		1	
Other specialties						
Internal medicine	31	44		4	5	
Dentistry and oral surgery		10				
Dermatology	1	9				
Hematology, oncology			1	1		
Neurology		5				
Obstetrics–gynecology	13	37		1	2	
Ophthalmology	5	9		2		
Otorhinolaryngology (ENT)	3	6		2		
Pediatrics	6	19		1	1	
Physical medicine	1		1			
Psychiatry	1	9	1			
Public health		1				
Urology	4	5		1		
TOTAL	149	299	8	31	15	16

cation; almost two-thirds have "associate-staff" status (Table 8). Counting the total medical staff there are about 1.1 beds per doctor. The consulting staff is small, numbering only eight physicians. Within the active component of the staff there is a broad representation of the major medical and surgical specialties and some representation of virtually every subspecialty—supplemented further by specialists on the large associate staff. Of the active staff, 49 per cent are board-certified specialists and another 11 per cent are board-eligible.

Appointment Procedure. As for initial selection, any physician is eligible who has graduated from an approved medical school, is licensed to practice in the state, and has been engaged in practice within the geographic jurisdiction of the local medical society for at least six months. Membership in the medical society, however, is not required, although the physician must possess the necessary ethical qualifications.

Applications for staff membership, supported by personal and professional references, are reviewed by the credentials committee of the medical staff and by the department in which the physician seeks privileges. The departments require that the applicant be sponsored by a departmental staff member who is not associated professionally with the applicant. The medical executive committee then acts on the application; if approved, it goes to the board of directors, who make the final appointment.

A physician newly appointed to the staff is placed on probationary status for six months, or less if the physician admits enough patients to permit adequate observation of his work. During this period the candidate's sponsor is required to countersign all his charts, presumably after reviewing his work. After the probationary period, the physician is appointed to the associate staff for at least three years and then may apply for active status.

Regular professional privileges for doctors on the associate staff and the active staff are granted by the department or service to which they are assigned, with the approval of the credentials committee. This committee is supposed to review all credentials twice a year, but in practice it appears to be mainly interested in bed-utilization by active-staff doctors. Privileges are usually granted for specified categories of treatment, and qualified surgical specialists are allowed broad privileges within their specialties. General practitioners, however, are restricted in surgery to those specific procedures for which they have been approved. At present, three general levels of privileges are defined: (1) major; (2) intermediate; and (3) minor. The plan is to eliminate the intermediate category and to define major and minor privileges more explicitly in revised bylaws.

Emergency privileges may be granted to any licensed physician or dentist for care of a condition in which the life of a patient is in immediate danger. Temporary privileges may also be allowed at the discretion of the department head, the chief of staff, and the administrator, so long as the physician works under the direct supervision of the department head or his designee. In practice, temporary privileges are seldom granted.

In return for the privilege of using the hospital's facilities for the care of their private patients, members of the medical staff assume certain obligations, depending on the level of their staff classification. Members of the active staff are obliged by the bylaws to conduct the major portion of their hospital practice at PCCH and to participate in the daily affairs of the hospital. Because of this obligation some physicians prefer to remain as members of the associate staff even beyond the usual three-year period.

The obligation of the active staff to make use of PCCH for the majority of their patients is regarded as a reasonable method of assuring the necessary income to support the institution. The credentials committee periodically reviews each doctor's utilization of the hospital. Those physicians who admit too few patients are dropped from active-staff classification. In order to eliminate physicians with low utilization records from active- and even associate-staff status, a new "courtesy" classification is under consideration. This change would tend to provide a more realistic control over the number of doctors using the hospital in relation to bed capacity, since members of the active staff have priority in admitting patients when beds are in short supply.

In recognition of these preferential admitting privileges, active-staff physicians are expected to serve on committees, to attend general and departmental staff meetings, to assist in the teaching and out-patient clinic programs, and to staff the emergency room as necessary. Although there is no formal obligation on financial contributions to the hospital's construction programs, members of the medical staff have made sizable contributions for the purchase of new equipment, as mentioned. With continued medical staff involvement in fund-raising campaigns, the commitment of the contributors to the hospital is strengthened and their positions on the staff are consolidated.

Commitment. The amount of time that attending physicians spend in the hospital is determined by the number and kinds of their admissions and by their attendance at committee meetings or other medical staff functions. The active staff, comprising 31 per cent of the total staff, accounted for 86 per cent of all admissions and more than 75 per cent of the attendance at medical staff meetings in 1964.

With at least one admission a week and an average length of stay of 6.8 days, 90 per cent of the active staff may be assumed to visit the hospital at least daily. Many of the active physicians make rounds twice a day. On this basis, it is estimated that nine out of ten active-staff physicians spend an hour or more in the hospital each day. Obstetricians and surgeons are present, of course, more often and for longer periods, since a major portion of their professional activities requires use of the operating and delivery rooms, as well as follow-up visits to the bedside.

Most of the members of the total medical staff maintain affiliations with other hospitals also, but data could not be collected on these. As for members of the active staff, since they are expected to admit the majority of their cases to PCCH, it may be surmised that their affiliations elsewhere are few. It is common in the Pebble City area, however, for most physicians to have admitting privileges in from one to three secondary hospitals, other than the primary one used for most of their cases.

As for methods of remuneration for professional work, only the director of medical education is paid a direct salary by the hospital. Others (discussed below) have contractual arrangements with different remuneration plans, but the great majority of doctors receive fees from their private patients.

Among the contractual physicians, three of the pathologists are in partnership and contract with the hospital on a fee-sharing basis. They employ the fourth pathologist on salary. The three full-time radiologists also contract with the hospital, and receive 22 per cent of gross billings. They employ a part-time radiologist on a salary, but the hospital pays the nonmedical x-ray personnel and covers all overhead expenses of the radiology department. At the time of this study, the hospital acted as the billing agent for the pathologists and radiologists. The director of rehabilitation, a board-certified physiatrist, also contracts with the hospital for a percentage of departmental income, but this provides only part of his personal earnings. Billing for physical and occupational therapy within his department is done by the hospital, but he also bills patients directly for personal, as distinguished from supervisory, services.

The physicians who rotate assignments in the emergency service are paid on an hourly basis from pooled fees collected on their behalf by the hospital. These fees are in addition to the charges to emergency patients for the use of the hospital facilities. All other physicians on the staff of PCCH receive fees for services, including the anesthesiologists, billing their private patients directly.

In summary, at the time of this study Pebble City Community Hospital had the equivalent of 21.5 contractual physicians.* These include the four pathologists, three full-time and one part-time radiologist, a physiatrist, the equivalent of one emergency room physician, and the director of medical education. The eleven anesthesiologists are also full-time in the hospital, although their remuneration is by fee-for-service from patients rather than by contract with the hospital. The sixteen interns and fifteen residents are also full-time, but their commitment is obviously limited to the duration of their training programs, and they are not included in the total of 21.5 full-time equivalent physicians who are more or less fully committed to the hospital for the bulk of their professional activities. Since many of these physicians, however, also have private offices in nearby professional buildings, their commitment is not exclusive, as in government hospitals described in chapter VII.

Departmentalization. The bureaucratic structure of the medical staff in PCCH contains six major clinical departments and several supportive

---

* Three other full-time contractual physicians have since been added to the hospital's staff. They are a neurologist who heads the new "electrodiagnostic department," a specialist in radioisotope diagnosis and therapy, and a therapeutic radiologist.

services. The clinical departments consist of medicine, surgery, obstetrics and gynecology, pediatrics, general practice, and dentistry. The supportive services consist of anesthesiology, radiology (diagnostic and therapeutic), radioisotope therapy, pathology, physical medicine (rehabilitation), and electrodiagnoses (EEG, EGG, etc.).

The medical staff bylaws require that "each department, except dentistry, shall have as its head a certified specialist in the field concerned, except that in the department of general practice the department head shall be a member of the Academy of General Practice." Departmental chiefs are elected for one year by secret ballot of the department, but two-year terms of service are being instituted. The constant rotation of departmental chiefs has been recognized as a weakness in the medical staff organization, since tenure of one year is hardly sufficient to learn the administrative mechanisms, much less to influence them significantly. The hospital administrator, who now has substantial influence on hospital policy because of his long-term status, nevertheless, favors increasing the strength of the medical staff organization. He views longer tenure of departmental chiefs not as weakening his position, but as a step in the direction of more knowledgeable and responsible medical staff leadership.

Demands on departmental chiefs are minimal. They spend approximately three to six hours a week in departmental activities, such as committee meetings, supervision of the intern and resident training programs, and preparation of reports. Each department has its own executive committee and also a review committee, which audits medical records as a control on the quality of care. These committees are intended to fortify the authority of the departmental chiefs. Special review is made of all patient deaths occurring within a department. As mentioned, each department reviews the qualifications of new physicians seeking privileges in it, but the staff complement of the departments is controlled by the medical executive committee, which is responsible for the over-all size of the medical staff.

The interdepartmental hierarchy of the medical staff is headed by the chief of staff, assisted by the deputy chief and the secretary. These general officers are elected by the active staff for one year terms and may be re-elected for a second consecutive term, after which the chief of staff is ineligible for a period of two years. Both the chief and the deputy chief must be members of the executive committee at the time of their nomination and must have completed at least one full year of service on this committee. The intention of the staff, at the time of this study, was to extend the terms of these offices to three years, in order to strengthen their positions vis à vis the hospital administrator.

Co-ordination of departments is accomplished principally through the chief of staff and the medical executive committee. The chief attempts to attend most, if not all, departmental staff meetings, so that his responsibilities in this office require as much as thirty hours a week. The present chief, for example, works a sixty-hour week, spending about half of his time in medical staff administrative activities. According to the bylaws, the principal function of the chief of staff is "to report to the Executive Committee on matters affecting the welfare of hospital, patients, and staff and to give effect to committee decisions." The chief of staff is thus an agent of the medical executive committee, which by its very operation performs a co-ordinating function, since all heads of departments and supportive services are members. Other interdepartmental committees, essential to the communicating and co-ordinating processes, are discussed below.

The medical executive committee is the main governing body of the medical staff organization. It is composed of fourteen members, including the chief of staff as chairman, the immediate past chief of staff, the deputy chief, the heads of all departments, a representative of the technical services, the chairmen of the credentials and intern-resident committees, and two members at large. The elected members serve three-year overlapping terms. As mentioned, the hospital administrator is not an *ex officio* member, but may attend meetings on invitation.

While the executive committee has final authority over activities of the medical staff, subject to approval of the general staff, the internal affairs of each department are governed by its own head and administrative committee. The authority system is thus dispersed fairly broadly, with consequent lack of tight controls.

To achieve co-ordination, at each monthly meeting of the medical executive committee, the heads of departments and services and the chairmen of committees submit oral reports on their activities, which are summarized in the written minutes. Attendance of the chief of staff at most departmental and committee meetings is also part of the reporting and co-ordinating system within the medical staff organization. The minutes of the executive committee are accessible to the members of the board of directors and the hospital administrator. The physician-members of the board, including the chief of staff who is *ex officio*, also report on medical staff activities and problems at the monthly board meetings. Communication between the administrator and the chiefs and department heads is also achieved by informal conferences and conversations, as well as by the various formal meetings to which the administrator may be invited.

For the most part, the reporting system is identical with the co-ordination process. The medical staff is a relatively autonomous body, which is not required to submit public reports to account for its professional activities. In this sense, PCCH's staff resembles that of other more loosely structured medical staff patterns. What distinguishes PCCH, however, is the very highly developed reporting and co-ordinating systems of the hospital administration.

Control Committees. As a medical staff organization becomes more highly developed, the role of control committees seems to shift from compensating for a weak authority system to supplementing or reinforcing a strong one. The committee system at PCCH represents a midpoint between the compensatory and the reinforcing types of social control. The formal authority system is not very highly developed. The chief of staff and clinical department heads are voluntary part-time physicians, whose authority has been minimized by short periods of tenure. In contrast, the heads of the supportive services are full-time contractual physicians whose positions are consolidated by their permanence. The inter-departmental hierarchy, reviewed above, does not differ much from that found in more loosely structured MSO patterns. Within departments however, there has occurred a certain strengthening of the authority system through departmental executive committees, noted earlier.

Committees of the medical staff as a whole are of three kinds: (1) standing; (2) administrative; and (3) appointive.

1) The two standing committees—the liaison and the policy committees—have advisory functions only. The liaison or "joint conference committee" is composed of the chief of staff, the deputy chief, the secretary of the medical staff, the president, vice-president, and secretary of the board of directors, and the hospital administrator. It may be convened on the call of any two of its members. In practice this committee at PCCH is not very important, since the medical staff has direct access to the board of directors through its physician-members on the board, including the chief of staff. The policy committee consists of the chief of staff, the immediate past chief, and his five predecessors in office. This group is advisory to the medical executive committee. Like the liaison committee, it meets only on call and is not particularly concerned with the social control features under discussion here.

2) There are three administrative committees: the medical executive committee (discussed above), the credentials committee, and the intern-resident committee. The credentials committee consists of eleven members, two appointed by the heads of each clinical department, except dentistry, and one representing the supportive services. This committee meets monthly and, along with the executive committee, is considered one of the most powerful organs of the staff. It controls not only membership on the medical staff but also functional staff classifications. The intern-resident committee is made up of twelve members, ten appointed

by clinical department heads, one by the supportive service chiefs, and the director of medical education. Its functions are to supervise the educational program of the hospital, the recruitment of interns and residents, and over-all medical matters concerning house staff regulation and discipline. It meets at least monthly. Both the credentials and intern-resident committees are theoretically advisory to the medical executive committee, which is responsible for action on their recommendations.

3) More clearly identified with the compensatory control functions in the medical staff organization are the "appointive committees," with specific functions concerning the quality of medical care. There are some thirty such committees on the PCCH medical staff, including committees for the blood bank, disasters, emergency room, epidemiology study, fetal mortality, general practice, intensive care unit, library, medical audit, medical education, medical records, nursing staff, out-patient department, pharmacy, psychiatry, rehabilitation, surgical audit, therapeutic abortions, and other purposes. The bylaws of the medical staff state that these appointive committees "have less important functions" than do the standing or the administrative committees, but the appointive committees influence the decisions of the other committees. Moreover, the executive committee and the credentials committee are in a position to enforce recommendations proposed by the appointive committees on the work of individual doctors.

Perhaps the most important appointive committees, from the viewpoint of staff self-discipline, are the "audit committees." The medical department has its own "medical audit" committee and the surgical department its "surgical audit" committee for reviewing the quality of work of all staff members in these fields. In addition, there is the over-all tissue committee, which is intended to set general standards for surgical work. This committee, at the time of our inquiry, was doing a five-year review of selected operations (appendectomies, cholecystectomies, hysterectomies, etc.) in order to establish maximum acceptable frequencies for the surgical removal of nonpathological tissue.

In contrast to the standing and administrative committees, which are composed only of active medical staff members, the appointive committees may contain associate staff physicians. In fact, the committee participation of such doctors is an important factor in their advancement to active status. Since committee members are usually appointed for three-year overlapping terms, in contrast to the shorter terms of executive officers of the staff, the committees are better able to maintain some continuity of policy and performance.

The diligence with which the committees function is difficult to assess, but appears good. Most of the control committees meet at monthly intervals, and attendance records are said to be high, usually 90 per cent or better. Interviews with staff physicians indicated that committees are tending to exercise increased diligence and controls. Older well-established physicians seldom get more than a reprimand for unnecessary surgery, provided their patients survive, but as these physicians depart they will be replaced by younger men, more accustomed to some review and enforcement of standards, especially in surgery. The following excerpt from notes of an interview with a physician shows the efforts to strengthen the PCCH committee system:

Very few doctors are denied appointment. The main purpose of the Credentials Committee is to determine classification with respect to bed utilization—departments control privileges. The main issue is the competition for beds within and between departments. . . . The general practitioner is treated here better than at many hospitals, although the surgeons are pretty uppity as seems universal. They are granted privileges according to their demonstrated proficiency. Some of the more powerful doctors are treated more gingerly. For example, one surgeon, very active in medical politics and "important" in the hospital, was observed to have a long series of "unnecessary" operations. After much delay he was finally brought before the Credentials Committee—the other surgeons feeling that if they were controlled, why shouldn't he be also? Although he has improved, Dr. — thinks he will slip back and that they won't be doing much about it. His unnecessary operations included gastrectomies, hysterectomies, appendectomies, without the medical histories supporting the decision to operate. Every doctor has a record kept—and even this man continues to have close review of his cases—he is a "marked man" in this sense.

Documentation. The principal regulatory document of the medical staff organization is its constitution. Revised only three years earlier, it was again being rewritten at the time of this study. The main purposes of the new constitution will be to strengthen the authority in the executive positions of the staff and to incorporate more explicit rules and regulations concerning the duties, obligations, and privileges of all staff members. In the past, memoranda have been used to specify rules and procedures, and minutes of committee meetings have served as reference documents. Monthly newsletters are sent out to staff members to inform or remind them of changes in procedure. For the most part, however, rules, regulations, and procedures are passed on by word of mouth and customary practice.

Formal reports of the medical staff, as mentioned, consist mainly of recorded minutes based on oral reports presented at committee meetings. Statistical reports of the activities of departments and services are compiled by the hospital administration. These reports, although not the responsibility of the medical staff, reflect medical staff activities in considerable detail. In general, although the formal documents, reports, and manual prepared by the medical staff are meager, much emphasis is actually placed on written documents in the daily work of the doctors.

These documents have been produced mainly by the hospital administration, and are discussed later under "Hospital Programs."

Informal Dynamics. In any organization of ambitious men of diverse disciplines and goals, conflicts are bound to arise over personalities and issues. Pebble City Community Hospital is no exception. The basic conflict concerns the perceived function of the modern community hospital. Should it be primarily a private doctor's workshop or should it strive to become a comprehensive community medical center? For the most part, the medical staff wants PCCH to remain a "workshop" hospital, albeit a good one. It recognizes that certain concessions must be made to the idea of increased organization of hospital services, such as through the employment of a minimal core of full-time physicians in the key departments and services. But the medical staff does not view these developments as steps along the road toward a comprehensive medical center. Rather it contends that such a center should relate only to a university medical school, whereas the community hospital should be geared to the needs of solo private practitioners.

The Hospital Administrator contends that the tremendous complexity of modern medical care demands the establishment and co-ordination of all the specialty services in a service-oriented institution. Supported by the community, the hospital should constantly improve and expand its facilities and services. Not limited primarily to in-patient care, it should extend its functions to include comprehensive out-patient services, medical research, and educational programs. It should attempt to co-ordinate its activities with those of other hospitals and agencies, in order to prevent duplication and fill gaps in community service. Pursuing this concept, the Administrator recommended to the Board of Directors that the name of the hospital be changed to "Pebble City Medical Center," but the medical staff succeeded in having this proposal rejected. The medical staff argued that the words, "medical center," would be pretentious, and that they would presage future developments which it opposed.

This controversy permeates the entire relationship between the medical staff and the hospital administrator. While he is recognized as a "superb business manager" and an effective administrator, the staff resents his flamboyance. It irks the more conservative physicians to see PCCH represented as a modern, "space-age" hospital, when all they want is a good private facility.

The physicians also feel that the Administrator has a distinct advantage in dealing with the Board of Directors, many of whom are businessmen. They speak the same language, relying on the same kind of business criteria for making decisions. While the physicians may feel that the directors do not share their professional interests and values, it is significant that there has never been an instance in which the Board of Directors has overruled a firm recommendation of the medical staff.

The medical staff has other grievances. Whenever a problem arises, the physicians claim, the Hospital Administrator proposes a survey, which usually supports his position. The Administrator counters that medical objections relate essentially to personal inconveniences or to changes in established but inefficient procedures. Moreover, he tries to be co-operative in approving the purchase of new equipment, recommended by the doctors, provided it will add to efficiency and save labor. Some doctors are concerned that too much emphasis is placed on equipment and administrative personnel and not enough on such primary needs as an adequate nursing staff.

The medical staff acknowledges that much of the impetus for the hospital's progressive medical programs has come from the Administrator, even though they complain of his aggressiveness. The Administrator claims that what is really lacking on the staff is medical statesmanship—leadership from those elder physicians who can look beyond the narrow limits of their private practices to the technological and sociological demands of modern health service. According to him, there had been two such elder medical statesmen on the staff, but their recent deaths have left a void.

These remarks should not be construed as meaning massive dissatisfaction of the medical staff with the Administrator. Rather, they denote some of the major areas of conflict at PCCH, most of which are polarized between a progressive administrator and a more conservative medical staff. While the doctors object to the Administrator's emphasis on efficiency and his "medical center" philosophy, by and large they support most of his policies, although at a slower pace than he would like. For example, they generally support the medical education program, because they recognize that the training of interns and residents brings benefits for all the doctors if only to enable them to care for more patients. But to maintain accreditation for residencies requires enlarging the full-time medical staff. Certain highly specialized services also demand the presence of full-time doctors. The more successful these programs and services, the larger the full-time staff, the larger the hospital . . . and eventually one sees the "medical center." Thus, the physicians are not only in conflict with the Administrator over these issues but they are caught in some conflict among themselves; a number of them favor the medical center movement, thus forming a nucleus of support for the Administrator. The more conservative doctors appear to be fighting a rearguard and losing battle to preserve the privacy of their workshop.

These are some of the medical staff conflicts and inner turmoils of this large and attractive hospital which, to the outsider, conveys a sense of modern efficiency based on financial stability and professional harmony.

THE HOSPITAL PROGRAMS FOR IN-PATIENT CARE

Different patterns of medical staff organization are important in so far as they affect the quality of hospital service. If increasing degrees of structuring of the medical staff contribute to improved hospital programs, even if the extent of structuring is not the sole determinant, then analysis of these patterns is important and should be examined. Since Pebble City Community Hospital is the median hospital in this study—and a dynamic, growing hospital at that—it represents a good point of departure for comparing hospital performance in institutions of differing patterns of medical staff organization.

First, we shall examine some fourteen principal components of in-patient hospital care.

Admissions and Length-of-Stay. Admissions to this 447-bed hospital in 1964 totaled 18,295 patients, including 15,770 adults and 2,525 children, with an over-all average of about fifty patients each day. There were, in addition, 2,539 live births. The average daily census numbered 332 adults, 30 children, and 30 newborns. The average length of stay was 7.0 days for adults, 4.1 days for children, and 3.7 for newborns, for an over-all average of 6.8 days. Adult bed occupancy was 82 per cent and pediatrics 68 per cent, with an aggregate occupancy rate of 81 per cent. The corresponding figure for the nursery was 65 per cent. At a cost per patient day of $53.54, the cost per case averaged $364.07. (These figures do not include the recently opened advanced-care or subacute unit.)

Admission Procedure. In accordance with the usual pattern of admitting patients in "open-staff" hospitals, pre-admitting forms are available in private doctors' offices, to use for elective admissions. Generally, however, physicians reserve a bed by telephone, and the necessary information is obtained in the admitting office when the patient presents himself. Patients with limited financial means are usually referred to the county hospitals, but some exceptions are made at the request of the attending physician or occasionally at the insistence of individual patients.

About one-sixth of the 1,200 to 1,600 monthly emergency room patients are admitted as in-patients, some of whom are classified as medically indigent. The hospital also accepts a limited number of indigent cases with interest for teaching purposes. (Since this study was completed, the enactment of Medicare and Medicaid has meant that many patients formerly referred to government hospitals are now admitted to PCCH.)

The Department of Medicine. This department lists 31 active and 44 associate staff physicians. It has access to approximately one-fourth of the 447 hospital beds and maintains an occupancy rate of about 89 per cent. In 1964 the Department of Medicine accounted for 27.5 per cent of all hospital admissions. Average length-of-stay for adult medical patients in 1964 was 8.3 days. On the average, 3.6 different patients occupy each bed per month.

The relatively small size of the staff has not warranted its division into formal specialty subsections. The following major subspecialties, however, are represented in the department: cardiology, dermatology, endocrinology, gastroenterology, hematology, internal medicine, neurology, and pulmonary diseases. Privileges are not listed for internists, but are defined generally by their specialties. Informal consultations are required for the more seriously ill patients and for those patients whose condition worsens during the course of treatment. Diagnostic modalities from the laboratory, radiology department, and other supportive services are accessible and heavily used. Quality of care is reviewed periodically by the departmental medical audit committee.

The Department of Surgery. The following surgical specialties describe the range of services encompassed by this department: general surgery, cardiac-thoracic surgery, gynecologic surgery, ophthalmology, orthopedics, otorhinolaryngology, neurosurgery, plastic surgery, proctology, urology, and vascular surgery. There were 111 surgeons listed as active and associate members of the department in 1964, with the largest numbers in general surgery and orthopedic surgery.

The average daily patient load on the surgical service is about 140 patients, representing 38 per cent of all hospital admissions, or 43.8 per cent if gynecologic surgery is included. The average monthly turnover of each of the 150 beds assigned to this service is 3.7, maintaining an occupancy rate of about 90 per cent. In 1964, 8,500 operations were performed, a daily average of 24, excluding Sundays and holidays.

In view of the twelve operating rooms, the surgical workload seemed rather light. Two of the operating rooms, however, are reserved for cystoscopy, and three are specially fitted for eye and plastic surgery, orthopedic surgery, and neurosurgery. Eight operating rooms are scheduled for elective procedures between 7:30 A.M. and 3:30 P.M., Monday through Friday, and four rooms on Saturday. A room is always available around the clock for emergencies. The minimum requirements for an operating team in major surgery are the surgeon, an assistant surgeon, the anesthesiologist, one circulating nurse, and another nurse or "scrub" technician. Instead of a recovery room, a post-anesthesia service, integrated with the twenty-bed intensive care service, is under the direct supervision of the anesthesiologist. This unit is more fully equipped than the conventional recovery room.

The consultation rate for major surgery is approximately 15 per cent. Attending physicians are required to obtain consultations for such procedures as sterilization, therapeutic abortion, Caesarian section, and hysterectomy. Although consultations are basically the doctor's responsibility, the operating room supervisor maintains some surveillance over scheduled cases. Furthermore, the appropriate audit committee checks—after the fact—on the adequacy of the diagnosis, including necessary consultations.

While the bulk of surgery performed at PCCH is considered routine, the department has a cardiac surgery team which performs one or two open-heart operations per week. Several physicians questioned the desirability of allowing this procedure, on the ground that the relative infrequency of open-heart surgery here, as compared with university hospitals, might result in too high a mortality rate. Another objection was the high cost to the hospital of maintaining a cardiac surgery team, in spite of the prestige that such a service might bring to the institution.

The Department of Obstetrics and Gynecology. There are 13 active and 37 associate physicians on the staff of this department. Fifty-four obstetric and 38 gynecologic beds are assigned to it, including an isolation unit of 11 beds in private rooms. The average monthly turnover of new patients for each bed is only 3.2 for obstetrics and 7.1 for gynecology, producing occupancy rates of 37 and 116 per cent, respectively. (Noninfected gynecological cases are occasionally placed in obstetrical beds, accounting for the over-occupancy.) Thus, the average daily patient load is 20 for obstetrics and 44 for gynecology.

There are 46 bassinets divided among the 9 separate nurseries and also a post-delivery room, in which post-partum patients are placed for close observation of at least one hour. The occupancy rate of the nurseries dropped from 72 per cent in 1962 and 1963 to 65 per cent in 1964, and the 1965 rate was expected to be 55 per cent or less. Thus, obstetrics accounts for only about one-third of the activities of this department.

Prenatal classes, consisting of four sessions each, are offered three times a year under the sponsorship of the hospital. Both physicians and nurses give instruction in this program. Not a single maternal death has occurred in this hospital in the past five years. The neonatal mortality rate has been maintained at less than 20 per 1,000 live births. The Caesarian section rate has fluctuated between 5.7 and 8.0 per cent, more than half of which have been repeated Caesarians. Consultation is mandatory for any woman in labor over twenty-four hours.

The Department of Pediatrics. The medical staff consists of six active and nineteen associate staff pediatricians. In 1964 the number of children (under fifteen years of age) under treatment in the hospital averaged 30 per day, with an occupancy rate of 68 per cent for the 44 assigned beds. The monthly turnover per bed is about 4.5 patients.

Children are assigned to beds according to age, sex, and severity of illness. Parents, through the Public Relations Department, can arrange to tour the pediatric facilities with their child before an elective admission. Although parents are not encouraged to remain with their child overnight, cots will be provided for parents who wish to do so. Since they are not restricted to the formal visiting hours of 1 P.M. to 8 P.M. but can visit at any time during the day or evening, few parents feel the need to remain overnight.

A basic core of pediatric nurses is assigned permanently to the department, including the head nurse. A full-time "play-lady" is employed, whose sole responsibility is to keep the children occupied and entertained. As in other departments of the hospital, any untoward turn of events requires consultation. Even if the patient's attending physician is a board-certified pediatrician, consultation with another pediatrician may be required.

The Department of General Practice. The largest single department of PCCH is that of general practice, which lists twenty-nine active and sixty-six associate staff physicians. These general practitioners, by definition, cover the major fields of medicine and can admit patients with a variety of illnesses and conditions into all the major departments. They account for large numbers of obstetrical, gynecological, pediatric, medical, and surgical admissions, although the majority of total admissions is by specialists.

The privileges of general practitioners are more restricted in surgery than in the other departments. As mentioned, surgical specialists are granted privileges according to the customary scope of their specialties, but general practitioners are limited to those specific procedures in which they have demonstrated competence. Further controls over their performance are imposed by the rules—implicit and explicit—pertaining to consultations. Despite the over-all low consultation rate (15 per cent) in the hospital, according to one general practitioner, PCCH requires and obtains more consultations than any other comparable local institution. No data were available, however, on whether these consultations were in cases handled by general practitioners or by specialists.

The above clinical departments are supplemented by six organized supportive services which serve patients from all departments. These services are also set up as hospital departments associated with diagnosis (pathology and radiology), treatment (anesthesia, rehabilitation, and pharmacy), and record-keeping.

Pathology and Laboratories. The staff of this service includes 4 full-time pathologists, a full-time biochemist, and a part-time microbiologist. There are, in addition, 27 full-time and 5 part-time medical technologists, 14 laboratory technology trainees, 9 full-time and 2 part-time laboratory assistants, and 11 other employees, making a total staff of 56. The major services offered are in bacteriology, parasitology, tissue pathology, biochemistry, endocrinology, hematology, metabolism tests, microbiology, and virology.

Electrocardiography and electroencephalography are provided by a separate technical services unit. Bioassays are done by sending specimens to a private commercial laboratory. The blood bank is operated by the laboratory, under the supervision of the chief medical technologist; he is responsible to the pathologist who heads the transfusion service.

The full-time pathologists are under contract with the hospital to receive 15 per cent of the gross income of the department, with no additional pay for research or educational activities. The hospital purchases all equipment and supplies and pays the salaries of other laboratory personnel.

All tissues removed in surgery are examined visually by the pathologists and 75 per cent microscopically, the main exceptions being tonsils, hernial sacs, and veins. There is an unusual method of performing frozen sections. Most of the hospitals in this study have facilities just off the operating rooms which allow on-site examination of frozen tissue by a single pathologist. At PCCH, the tissues are brought to the laboratory where they are frozen-sectioned, and then examined by as many as three of the pathologists. A pathologist is also always available for direct consultation in the operating room. It is felt that in the fully equipped laboratory, better controls can be maintained over tissue examination techniques and that the judgment of several pathologists enhances the reliability of the findings. Mention should also be made of the relatively high percentage of deaths that are autopsied by this department—52 per cent.

Another unique feature of the laboratory is the use of microphones, attached to an automatic dictating system, for recording pathological reports while an examination is in process. These reports are then transcribed by clerks, thus reducing the work of professional personnel. The laboratory is also responsible for control of cross-infections in the hospital, averaging about 200 cultures per month. This surveillance requires a major share of the time of the bacteriologist.

Laboratory services are provided twenty-four hours a day for in-patient requirements and from 7 A.M. to 11 P.M. for out-patient services, the latter consisting mainly of special tests on ambulatory patients referred by private doctors. After hours there is always one pathologist and one pathology resident on call for emergencies.

Since PCCH contains such a highly developed diagnostic laboratory, it not only provides a full range of services for its own patients but it also serves as a reference laboratory for a nationwide research program—the National Blood Bank for study of unusual blood problems. It operates one of the two blood bank certification schools in the state. It has one of the principal virology laboratories in the metropolitan area. The department also conducts a school for medical technologists and a four-year pathology residency program (approved by the American Medical Association), with five of the six approved residencies currently filled.

The Tissue Committee mentioned earlier is, strictly speaking, a function of the medical staff organization, but its effectiveness depends upon the pathologists. Every surgical case has a special card listing the preoperative and postoperative diagnoses, which are then matched against the pathological diagnosis. On the average, the laboratory makes about fifty requests a year for additional information from the attending surgeons because of inadequate records or technical data. In the past five years, however, only two formal warnings or reprimands were issued to individual physicians for questionable performance, and only one physician failed to have his hospital appointment renewed as a result of the Tissue Committee's recommendation.

Despite the extensive examination of tissues, matching of clinical and pathological diagnoses, and review of records, the system of surgical controls was nevertheless described by one of the PCCH pathologists as "loose." Pathologists are perhaps reluctant to express critical judgments. One person interviewed commented that he knows of no pathologist who is "both competent and fearless."

Radiology. The radiology service is staffed by 4 radiologists (3 full-time and 1 part-time), 10 technologists, 1 technician, and 3 clerical personnel. There are also 9 radiological technology students and 1 radiology resident. The 4 radiologists also maintain a private group practice in a nearby professional building, although three of them are considered "full-time" in the hospital. The radiologists are under contract to receive 22 per cent of gross billings for their personal income, the hospital assuming all other salary, supply, and equipment expenses.

There are five diagnostic and three therapeutic x-ray units (including a 2-million volt maxitron), which permit both superficial and deep x-ray therapy, as well as diagnostic radiology. Radioisotope diagnostic studies and radium implant therapy are also available. Cinefluoroscopy (movies and televised tape recordings) is another feature of the service, used for both diagnostic and teaching purposes.

Normal hours of service are from 8 A.M. to 6 P.M., with twenty-four-hour coverage by a technician and a radiology resident. Radiological therapy is done by the radiologists, who also interpret all x-ray films, including those taken after hours when they are off-duty. A copy of the pathology, surgery, or autopsy report is automatically sent to this department for correlation with the radiological diagnosis. While this procedure is primarily intended for teaching purposes, it also serves to improve the quality of the service.

One of the chief complaints of radiologists—expressed here as elsewhere—is that other physicians tend to think of them as "technicians" rather than as medical consultants. Some physicians consult them for advice on what films and techniques should be employed, as well as on interpretation of films. Other physicians simply order standard films. Unless gross errors of judgment on the meaning of x-ray reports are discovered, the radiologists do not feel that they can insist on a consultation with the attending doctor. Thus, while the technical quality of the radiological service appears to be high, it is not being used as effectively as it might be, because of the independent style of work of most private physicians and the reluctance of the radiologists to impose controls.

Anesthesiology. The 11 anesthesiologists on the staff are virtually full-time, although they have no financial contract with the hospital. They are paid on a fee-for-service basis by the private patients, but must agree to serve also the nonpay clinic patients. While some patients are assigned on a rotating basis to the anesthesiologists, selections are usually made by the attending surgeons. The anesthesiologists, as mentioned, also provide postanesthesia care in the intensive care unit.

There is no particular hierarchy or administrative structure in the anesthesia service. Each anesthesiologist functions as an independent practitioner. From an organizational viewpoint, one physician stated that this department is "one of the weakest links. . . . The only time the anesthetists get together is when they oppose something."

Department of Rehabilitation. This department, part of the new "advanced care unit" described below, is responsible for physical therapy, occupational therapy, and medical social service. In addition to the full-time chief, who is a board-certified physiatrist, the staff includes 8 physical therapists (7 full-time and 1 part-time), 2 occupational therapists, a part-time speech pathologist, a part-time psychologist, and a full-time medical social service worker.

Occupational therapy is provided six days a week from 8 A.M. to 4:30 P.M. The physical therapy service is available for in-patients and out-patients from 8 A.M. to 9 P.M. Monday through Friday, but Saturday mornings are restricted to in-patient therapy and special out-patient cases. Hours are thus available in evenings and on Saturdays for patients who hold jobs and would lose income if they had to seek therapy during the day.

All therapists and other paramedical workers are paid by full-time salary, except the speech pathologist and therapist, who work on an hourly-rate contract ten to fifteen hours a week. The physiatrist is under contract to receive a percentage of departmental income, which provides about three-fourths of his personal earnings, the remainder coming from private fees. The hospital charges the patients for routine therapies and also for social service work, but the physiatrist bills separately for his own services. He does this not only to placate those physicians who object to full-time salaried physicians on hospital staffs but also because he feels that it preserves some degree of professional independence for himself in the hospital administrative structure.

Appointment of a full-time physiatrist as director of rehabilitation was the result of special efforts by the hospital administrator, supported by a few members of the medical staff. Although most of the private attending physicians did not object, they still seem to show little appreciation of the department, conceiving of it as merely providing a technical service—physical and occupational therapy. In response, the physiatrist has instituted weekly staff reviews of all in-patient cases receiving treatment in the department. About 2 per cent of out-patients receiving therapy are also reviewed, at the initiative of the therapists. Beyond this, no more formal systems of referral, case-finding or control over treatment modalities are being proposed. The physiatrist prefers to rely on education of the physicians by serving with them on case-review committees, including the interdepartmental rehabilitation committee, and by demonstrating his skills as a consultant and rehabilitation specialist.

The 86-bed advanced care unit is a separate rehabilitation facility attached to the main hospital by underground passage. It has 6 private and 40 semi-private rooms, all-electric beds, personal television, nurse–patient intercom, telephones for each patient, and showers in each room designed to accommodate wheelchair patients. There are three lounges with color television, writing areas, and other amenities. Meals are served in a central dining room and there is a pantry for refreshments. The central patio of the square building has benches and cement walkways, with radiant heating coils, which enable patients to sit outside in cool weather. The rehabilitation medicine services, covering 30,000 square feet, are located in this building. It contains complete equipment for physical therapy, occupational therapy, speech and hearing therapy, and an audiometric room for hearing diagnosis. There is also a physical therapy exercise area and a hydrotherapy area, including heated therapy pool, whirlpool agitators, hydraulic lifts for paraplegic patients, and a sauna bath.

A second-story "shell" was included in the construction of the advanced care unit, which could be completed to provide an additional eighty-six beds. The entire project, costing $2,500,000, was funded without government assistance. Its functional architecture, lively interior design, and exterior landscaping make the whole unit highly attractive.

Patients admitted to the main hospital, who are capable of responding positively to the rehabilitation program, are eligible for care, generally ranging from five days to a month, in the advanced care unit. A special admitting committee of the unit determines eligibility, most of the admissions being ambulatory patients suffering from post-coronary attacks, strokes, fractures, accidents, diabetes, and carcinomas. Acutely ill or very long-term patients, alcoholics, and mentally disturbed patients are excluded.

Except for direct referrals to the physiatrist-director of rehabilitation, patients in the advanced care unit are attended by their private physicians. Indeed, the physiatrist does not wish to control admissions or to supervise treatment in the unit. Although he is available for consultation, he feels that the attending physicians should be responsible for their own patients.

At the time of this study, the unit had been open for only six months and occupancy was about 50 per cent. (Experience elsewhere suggests that such units achieve full occupancy only after about eighteen months.) Most of the physicians are still not fully aware of the value of this type of patient care. While they refer an increasing number of patients simply for physical therapy, only a small portion of the staff refers patients for "advanced care." Even though occupancy is low, no formal case-finding program has been developed. The nurses in the main hospital, however, are beginning to identify patients who might benefit from rehabilitation services and to offer suggestions to their attending physicians.

The lesser cost of hospitalization in the advanced care unit, compared with the main hospital (33 per cent less), results mainly from reduction in professional nursing hours. The ultimate goal is 2.5 hours of nursing care per patient per day, as compared with 3.85 on the acute services, when maximum occupancy is attained. This lower rate is possible because almost all patients are ambulatory to some degree and capable of caring for many of their personal needs.

The Pharmacy Service. Twelve pharmacists, 2 stock clerks, and 1 clerical worker are employed in the pharmacy service. The central pharmacy, located on the first floor opposite a large waiting room, provides twenty-four-hour in-service to all departments. It is also open to the public. According to a publication describing the pharmacy, "for the first time in the history of the city, 350,000 people now have access to a qualified pharmacist at any hour of every day and night."

The many problems of dispensing and controlling medications in a 447-bed hospital, led the hospital administration to favor decentralized pharmacies on each floor, staffed by registered pharmacists from 8 A.M. to 8 P.M. Thus far, only one substation has been opened, but three others will soon be put into service.

The central pharmacy on the main floor, the storeroom in the basement, and the four decentralized substations on the nursing floors above are in a direct vertical line, connected by electrically operated supply elevators and an electronically guided pneumatic tube system. The effectiveness of decentralization, in which pharmacists rather than medication nurses dispense drugs at the substations, was demonstrated in a study of the care provided to about 500 patients in one nursing unit of the hospital. The majority of these were seriously ill patients, requiring extensive medication. In this total experience, only four medication order errors occurred, one charged to the pharmacist, the other three to nurses. Although the salary of a pharmacist is double that of a medication nurse, the hospital administration is convinced that the additional cost will be justified by a greatly improved quality of service and by increased efficiency.

Part of the efficiency is achieved by charging out total drug costs to the patient on discharge from the nursing unit, rather than billing for each item as it is dispensed. The floor nurses are able to devote more time to patient care at the bedside, rather than to the drug inventory. The physicians benefit from having a pharmacist on the floor with whom they may consult. Additional savings might be effected by use of a generic drug formulary, but the physicians at PCCH prefer to order by brand name, accepting no substitution of generic equivalents without their express permission.

Medical Records Department. The staff of this department numbers 16 persons, including 3 registered medical records librarians, 4 secretaries (3 full-time and 1 part-time), 9 clerks and typists. Charts are available in five minutes. After seven years the records are removed for storage with a commercial storage firm.

All records are reviewed before filing by one of the medical record librarians, except for records of normal deliveries and newborns, which are spot-checked. Incomplete or inadequate records are referred to the medical records committee for further action. If a doctor fails to complete his records, he is sent three notices at weekly intervals, after which he is given forty-eight hours to comply. At the end of this warning period, his name is placed on the "admitting list of delinquent doctors," which is sent to the medical records committee. If the doctor stays on this list for two weeks, he is then given ten more days, after which the credentials committee is notified and his association with the hospital can be terminated. This remarkable tolerance of unco-operative physicians is not peculiar to PCCH; it is observable in most of our study hospitals. Moreover, most doctors are co-operative, and most of the difficulties center in a few who eventually comply.

The Medical Records Department routinely prepares activity and occupancy reports, discharge analyses, infection reports (for the epidemiology committee), and census reports, copies of which are sent to the administrator. Case indices are kept according to disease, operation, and physician. Finally, the department receives emergency and out-patient department records after patients are dismissed from those services.

In addition to review of records by the Medical Records Department, the medical or surgical audit committee of each clinical department checks its records for completeness, signatures, progress notes, and the appropriateness or quality of treatment. This procedure is deemed more effective than review of both completeness of records and quality of treatment by a single records committee. It also places responsibility for maintaining proper records within each clinical department, which theoretically can enforce its own rules. Because of the reluctance of physicians to impose controls over their peers, compliance requires the joint efforts of the individual departmental audit committees, the Medical Records Department, and finally of the credentials and/or executive committees of the full medical staff.

The Nursing Department. Nearly half of the 400 members of the nursing staff at PCCH are registered nurses. The other half includes 78 licensed vocational (or licensed practical) nurses, 60 aides, 25 orderlies, 12 surgical technicians, and 43 ward clerks. Four RN's, two LVN's, and all the orderlies are males. The annual turnover of the nursing staff is about 45 per cent, with highest mobility among the RN's. Among the supervisory nursing staff, however, are many RN's who have been employed by the hospital for from twelve to twenty-five years.

In keeping with the orientation of the Administrator towards effective business management, each of the six floors has a "floor manager," a nurse who is responsible for budgetary and personnel needs on her floor. These managers report to the director of nursing, charged with coordination and administration of the nursing program. Clinical supervisors are under the direction of the floor managers. A "team system" of nursing care is used, although "case" and "functional systems" are adopted to meet the needs of special patients.

One of the unique features of the hospital is the nursing station, serving 100 beds, with a registered nurse on duty around the clock. Each station is located at the focal point of the three nursing wings on each floor. Beds are linked to the stations by call lights and intercoms. The main advantages of the large centralized stations are improved communication and co-ordination of nursing activities during the difficult staffing hours of evenings and weekends, which comprise about 70 percent of total time. According to the Administrator, four factors have been instrumental in compensating for the perennial shortage of night or even day nurses: (1) toilets in each patient's room; (2) electric beds; (3) the intercom system; and (4) the 100-bed centralized nursing stations.

The medical staff is less convinced about this policy. Many physicians feel that patients at the ends of the long wings do not receive sufficiently prompt attention. The Administrator contends that what the doctors really criticize is not the quality of nursing care—which is improved by more efficient organization of the RN's time—but the decrease in personal service to themselves. On the basis of the 3.85 hours of nursing care per patient per day, there would not appear to be a shortage of nursing attention. The minor dissatisfactions of some physicians with the nursing service are probably related mainly to the inevitable demands of complex organization in large hospitals.

The nursing department has many training programs, including a nurse's aide training program, an orientation program for new RN's, and an in-service training program for surgical technicians. On-going education is also a byproduct of frequent nursing team leader conferences and of review by the nursing audit committee of the quality of nursing records and care. A patient care committee, composed of representatives of the major clinical departments of the medical staff, the supportive services, the six floor managers, the director of nursing, and the hospital administrator, also reviews general patient-care policies and programs at its monthly meetings. Special cases may also be brought to the attention of this committee.

The Director of Nursing, supported by the Administrator, has provided much of the initiative for development of the highly organized nursing staff, the production of numerous written nursing care guides, the nursing audit committee, and the in-service training programs. At the time of this study, a computer system was being designed to transmit automatically doctor's orders, medication schedules, and chart recordings. The strong emphasis on modern management techniques undoubtedly contributes to the over-all efficiency of the nursing staff.

Some physicians complain that excessive automation interferes with communication between them and the nurses, with the result that their orders may not be followed, For example, the radiologist may issue an order to have a patient omit breakfast, and the patient arrives in the Radiology Department with a full stomach. The nursing staff attributes these occasional lapses to the shortage of nurses, which cannot be compensated for, no matter how efficiently the system may operate.

With respect to all in-patient services in PCCH, as in any general hospital, we have very few measures of the ultimate outcome of the care provided. The low neonatal and maternal mortality rates have been mentioned. Beyond these it may be mentioned that in 1964, when our study was conducted, there were 519 total deaths in the hospital, for a crude death rate in relation to admissions, of 3.3 per cent. If deaths within the first forty-eight hours are omitted—on the ground that these patients were "terminal" and could not have been saved (a questionable premise in current-day medicine)—the death rate declines to 2.3 per cent.

In chapter IX, we discuss the fallacies of using the crude hospital death rate as a measure of the quality of patient care, in the light of the varying mixtures of case severity coming to different hospitals. A method of adjusting this crude rate, to take account of the severity of illness in the patients admitted, has been devised. If this method is applied to the 1964 deaths in PCCH, the adjusted death rate becomes 2.1 per cent. In a later chapter we will see that this "severity-adjusted death rate" gives a lower, and therefore better, mortality record for PCCH than that in the four other hospitals in our series of ten that were judged to have less highly structured patterns of medical staff organization.

Having completed this review of the principal components of in-patient care in PCCH, we may now proceed to describe the operation of other services of the hospital. These involve a wider community role for purposes of ambulatory care, prevention, education, or research.

THE HOSPITAL PROGRAM—
ITS WIDER COMMUNITY ROLE

The Emergency Service. Throughout America the use of general hospitals for emergency medical care to ambulatory patients has been steadily rising over the last two decades. At PCCH, some forty to fifty patients seek service in the "emergency room" each day. Most of these cases, however, are not life-threatening conditions in which delayed action might be fatal. There are estimated to be about four or five such urgent cases per week, but the great majority are simply patients of any income group who come directly to the hospital because of a distressing symptom for which they cannot get quick help elsewhere. Most of these patients arrive between 3 P.M. and 10 P.M., and the workload increases on weekends when private physicians are less available.

A year prior to this study, the emergency service was staffed mainly by interns and residents who shared twenty-four hour duty. This house staff consulted by telephone with physicians assigned by the medical staff for on-call duty in the more serious cases. Since Pebble City Community Hospital provides emergency medical care for a large sector of the megalopolis, this loose system understandably had to be changed. In the past year, a group of twelve doctors on the medical staff was organized to provide systematic round-the-clock staffing of the emergency service. These physicians now take turns at being personally present in the emergency service for shifts ranging from four to twelve hours. There is the equivalent of one attending physician and one intern on duty at all times.

Prior to the establishment of the panel of twelve doctors, patients were usually charged a flat minimum fee of six dollars for use of the emergency service. Now they are charged a hospital fee, plus a physician's fee of at least eight dollars, both of which are billed and collected by the hospital. The physician's fees are pooled, and each doctor is paid an hourly rate out of this income. This arrangement has improved the medical staffing of the service, but it has also caused an increase in complaints by patients and many unpaid bills. The total cost of treatment in the emergency service may now exceed that of medical care in the office of a private physician.

The emergency room committee, a subcommittee of the surgery committee with representatives from the supportive services and other major specialties, is responsible for the conduct of the emergency service. It is currently auditing the waiting time for treatment, one of the principal complaints of patients; it plans to establish a review of records, so that the same principles of quality control can be applied to emergency out-patients as to in-patients. The committee has initiated a series of lectures by various specialists for education of the professional panel members on emergency treatment methods.

The hospital contracts with a number of private companies and governmental agencies in the locality to provide emergency medical treatment for their employees. Each company has a roster of physicians, all members of the PCCH medical staff, one of whom is called to care for the employee in the emergency room. Otherwise the emergency service doctor will render necessary treatment. The local County Emergency Aid Service also has a contract with the hospital for care to the injured, and the U.S. Public Health Service has a contract for emergency care of merchant seamen and other federal beneficiaries. Connected with PCCH is also a much-heralded helicopter emergency transport service, which is used about once a month. More significant is the location of the hospital near two major highways and other arterials for rapid transport by ground ambulance and private automobile.

The emergency service is functionally and architecturally integrated with the operating rooms, the intensive care units, and the radiology and laboratory services, all of which are located on the ground floor. The nonmedical personnel of the service consist of 7 RN's, 3 LVN's, 6 orderlies, 5 clerks, and 1 aide. The orderlies are assigned primarily to the orthopedic cast room located in the emergency service. Closed fracture reductions, out-patient minor surgery, and blood donations are handled by the service.

Of the 15,771 emergency service visits in 1964, there were 3,068 patients admitted to the hospital, representing about 16 per cent of total admissions for that year. Only those patients who are hospitalized receive follow-up care at the hospital. All other patients are referred to private physicians after receiving primary emergency treatment.

The Out-Patient Department. In contrast to the emergency service, available around the clock, there is an out-patient department, with scheduled sessions in seventeen specialty fields each week. The OPD, however, is much less active than the emergency service. In 1964, only 6,167 patient-visits were made to OPD clinics, although a much larger number of out-patient or ambulatory contacts were recorded for laboratory tests, radiological services, physical therapy, etc. Each session lasts about two hours. Of the approximately 120 patients seen each week, two-thirds are for prenatal, post-partum, and newborn care. Eligibility is confined to persons of low income, as determined by a means test. Patients are expected to make partial payments according to a sliding scale, the lowest charge being 50 cents a visit. Necessary drugs are also provided from the pharmacy on a sliding scale of charges. Patients are referred to the OPD by the city health department, private physicians, a few from the emergency service, and some come on their own initiative.

The large number of obstetrical cases seen in the OPD is explained by a formal contract between the hospital and the local health department. Expectant mothers are referred to the hospital for prenatal and later for post-partum care. In turn, city public health nurses are sometimes asked by the hospital to make home visits. Patients requiring home care are also referred to the Visiting Nurse Association, and contacts are made with a local adoption agency for placement of the newborns of unmarried mothers. Apart from these limited arrangements with voluntary and public agencies, there is no systematic method of assisting indigent and medically indigent patients. Since the only medical social service worker is attached to the Department of Rehabilitation, her professional service is not usually available to patients seeking care in the out-patient department.

The physician in charge of the out-patient department is the full-time director of medical education. Treatment is provided mainly by interns and residents, with some supervision by attending staff physicians, who donate their services. For the most part, OPD patient care is limited to short-term care of illnesses, in which special diagnostic workups are required. After a few weeks the diagnosis and summary of treatment are sent to the referring physician, who presumably will care for the patient in the future. Low-income patients with more serious illnesses requiring long-term care are referred to the local government hospital.

The services of the out-patient department of PCCH are clearly quite restricted, in consonance with the medical staff's emphasis on maintaining the traditional system of private medical practice. In the opinion of the medical staff and the administration, the main justification for the OPD is to provide "teaching material" for interns and residents. The consensus in the hospital is that private paying patients should not be taxed unknowingly to provide clinic care to the less fortunate. Therefore, the OPD program is meager and will probably remain so unless increasing pressures are exerted by the community.

Preventive Services. To some extent, description of the preventive services provided by a general hospital is a matter of viewpoint or definition. All in-patient and out-patient services are, in a sense, preventive if they forestall the occurrence of more serious illness.

More specifically preventive, however, are certain *routine* case-finding tests done on all patients, regardless of their diagnoses. At PCCH all in-patients routinely receive a urinalysis, a complete blood count, and a serological test for syphilis. Chest x-rays, however, are not routinely performed, although they are done on a large proportion of patients. Out-patients do not receive any routine tests, but only those specifically ordered.

In the pediatrics department, a child is occasionally given an immunization, but there is no systematic review of children to determine what immunizations may be lacking and necessary. This is left to each private physician. The prenatal classes and the maternal health clinics, conducted in co-operation with the local health department, have been mentioned.

Community health education is another preventive service offered by the hospital. A successful Health Information Forum is held four times a year, devoted to various medical subjects of popular interest. Speakers are drawn from the medical staff and as many as 700 people come to some of these sessions. The doctors were initially not enthusiastic about this program, but it has proved itself. After the success of the adult program, a series of talks on the health problems of adolescence has been started by the hospital, in co-operation with the local public school authorities.

As for its own personnel, the hospital practices preventive medicine by giving a pre-employment physical examination to everyone hired. Employees also receive free emergency or first-aid treatment of on-the-job injuries, after which they are referred to private physicians. This employee health program is supervised by the full-time director of medical education.

The Department of Public Relations. The public relations of the hospital are directed internally toward the personnel and patients, and externally toward the community at large. According to the brochure for new employees, "Public relations is responsible for strengthening of understanding and good will between the hospital and the community; for an employee information program, and the coordination of releases to public channels of information." This policy has resulted in the production of numerous excellent brochures, pamphlets, and guides which explain new hospital services, established programs and facilities, hospital bills, employee benefits, annual hospital service statistics, and hospital income and expenditures. Picture guide-books for children (and their parents), comic-book dramatizations of the helicopter emergency service, and reprints of articles from professional journals describe various departments and special features of the "space-age" hospital. Although the administration's flair for publicity on the hospital's modernity is sometimes irritating to conservative physicians, the public relations efforts are apparently successful in winning wide community recognition and financial support of the hospital.

Hospital Volunteers and Auxiliaries. Four separate organizations provide volunteer workers throughout the hospital: (1) The Volunteer Auxiliary, with about 450 members, provides admitting hostesses, operates the coffee cart for visitors in the waiting rooms and the craft cart for in-patients, delivers flowers and mail to patients, assists the "play-ladies" in the Pediatrics Department, and leads tours of the hospital for patients and visitors. Volunteers work 3-hour shifts at least once a week and are expected to contribute about 100 hours a year. Serving in the hospital each day are 30 to 35 volunteers, one of whom acts as "chairman of the day."

2) The Children's Memorial Auxiliary maintains the gift shop.

Through this and other fund-raising activities it contributes a minimum of $24,000 a year to the hospital. A special fund-raising project in 1965 resulted in a contribution of $7,000 for Rh-blood research. This auxiliary has about 200 participating members.

3) The 100-member Guild Auxiliary staffs and stocks the patients' library and also participates in some fund-raising activities.

4) The "Volunteens" number about 135 teenage girls and 15 boys, who work mainly on weekends during the school year and throughout the week during the summer months. Part of the rationale for maintaining this group is to introduce young people to health careers.

Co-ordination of the work of all the volunteers is the task of a full-time director of volunteer services who, in turn, is responsible to the director of public relations. Recognition of the contribution of the volunteers is reflected in the appointment of the presidents of several auxiliaries to the hospital's board of trustees.

Other Community Relationships and Activities. The hospital provides certain other community services. One of these has been the effort of the PCCH Hospital Administrator to co-ordinate some of the facilities and activities of several local hospitals, in spite of resistance both inside and outside of his own hospital. For example, when the new hospital was being constructed he suggested a combined laundry for PCCH and another city hospital that was being improved with funds from the same local bond issue that financed PCCH. The objective was to avoid unnecessary duplication of facilities; the location of the laundry was immaterial. The other hospital, however, insisted on having its own independent unit. Similarly, another hospital has an artificial kidney machine which could easily be shared by PCCH, since it is in use fewer than a dozen times a year. In this instance, the cardio-pulmonary laboratory and medical staff of PCCH insisted on having its own kidney machine. Recently the Administrator succeeded in activating a committee of representatives from the boards of trustees of the three major hospitals in the area to promote better co-ordination, including the sharing of special technical equipment.

One further aspect of the hospital community orientation is of interest. In the last year, PCCH accumulated a surplus of more than half a million dollars, which could be allocated in part to reserves or capital expenditures. The Administrator felt that those who created the surplus—the patients who paid their bills—should benefit from the efficiency of the hospital. He felt it would not be right to reduce hospital rates, which would give PCCH a competitive advantage over other hospitals. Since the surplus meant that the patients were being charged more than the actual cost of hospitalization, he was therefore entertaining the idea of refunding to each patient a pro-rata share of the excess earnings, much in the style of consumer co-operative dividends. These refunds would help patients faced with other medical expenses and also enhance the public image of the institution. The administrator recognized that this idea would be rejected by the Board of Trustees, but it is mentioned here to indicate the kind of community-oriented leadership provided in this hospital.

Several programs of education and research are carried out in the Pebble City Community Hospital.

Paramedical Education and Training Programs. The hospital participates in a variety of accredited teaching programs for radiological and laboratory technologists, pharmacy interns, dieticians, surgical technicians, student nurses (RN and LVN) and nurse's aides, physical therapists, and graduate student residents in hospital administration. It also conducts an accredited twelve-week course for hospital chaplains.

In-service training of its own staff consists of short-term programs for new employees and continual training in systems of "work simplification," for which manuals have been developed under the director of personnel training. These manuals range from detailed procedures and check-lists to "programmed" training guides.

The laboratory, radiology, and physical therapy training programs are under the general direction of the medical heads of these supportive service departments. All other paramedical programs, except nursing, are supervised and co-ordinated by the full-time director of training. In the nursing department there is a full-time instructor in charge of a month-long orientation program for new nursing personnel, as well as a continual program of in-service training for all nurses.

At various times, members of the medical staff have expressed interest in re-establishing the nursing school that was discontinued at PCCH in the 1930's. In the opinion of the administration, however, a nursing school would add to the cost of patient care and is properly the responsibility of the existing collegiate nursing schools nearby. The hospital now offers practical ward experience to those collegiate nursing students.

Medical Education. Pebble City Community Hospital is accredited by the American Medical Association for resident training in the following specialties: internal medicine, obstetrics–gynecology, pathology, pediatrics, radiology, general surgery, and general practice. The largest numbers of residents in 1965 were in medicine and pathology, and the general practice residency was vacant. In addition to the fifteen residents, there were also sixteen rotating interns.

The full-time director of medical education is responsible for the training of interns, and the heads of the several specialty departments assume responsibility for their respective residents. Selection of interns and residents and approval of teaching programs and policies are the main functions of the intern–resident committee, composed of representatives of the different teaching services. Part of the residency training takes place at two university hospitals in the area and at one of the public hospitals, where a radiology resident spends two of the required three years. In order to maintain accreditation for the internal medicine residency program, the hospital plans to employ another full-time physician.

Interns and residents are a mainstay of the emergency service, participating in the examination and treatment of most patients. The out-patient department functions largely as a clinical teaching unit, and out-patients who are hospitalized come largely under the care of residents, supervised by attending staff physicians.

The hospital supports a large medical library of more than 12,000 volumes and almost 800 journal subscriptions; it is staffed by two full-time medical librarians. At weekly journal club meetings the house staff reports on published clinical findings and research. The house staff and 25 to 50 per cent of the attending staff participate in weekly clinico-pathology and diagnostic radiology conferences, as well as in monthly surgical pathology conferences. Closed circuit medical television and audiotape programs are also presented for the house and attending staff physicians.

The attitude of the medical staff toward the medical and para-medical training programs is mixed. On the one hand, the staff favors anything that will improve nursing care, and therefore the physicians are willing to donate time to instruction of nurses. Training in medical terminology is given high priority in order to improve communications between physicians and all paramedical personnel. On the other hand, the physicians are not so enthusiastic about some of the training in "work efficiency" that seems to separate them further from direct contact with nurses. A few physicians are interested in patient education, but the majority are too busy in their private practices to participate.

Some physicians are also intent on minimizing the residency programs, but they are succeeding only in slowing their development. One of the more frequent complaints of attending physicians is that residents and interns over-prescribe diagnostic laboratory tests. The main concern is with the added costs for private in-patient care, but the attending physicians also feel that doctors in training should recognize that in later practice they will not be able to order all the tests recommended in medical school textbooks.

The present director of medical education has not had previous training or experience in this role. While he may prove an able ad-

ministrator, future development of the teaching programs will probably
depend largely on the pathologists, the radiologists, the physiatrist on
the full-time staff, and a few key members of the attending staff, supported by the hospital administration.

Medical Research. Medical and related hospital research at PCCH
is co-ordinated by a separate research council, formed in 1962 in place
of a research committee which had been inactive. Modest research projects were initiated through donations from patients and other citizens,
and, ultimately, funding was obtained through larger grants from governmental and private agencies. More than sixty-five research projects
covering a wide variety of subjects are currently in progress, with grant
or contract support of about $200,000 per year.

The research council is an independent corporation, governed by a
fifteen-member board, with equal representation from the hospital's
board of directors, the medical staff, and citizens from the community.
Voting privileges are restricted to the hospital directors, thus giving the
hospital board full control over policies. The full-time director of the
research council is its only salaried employee. The work of the council
is divided among five committees concerned with finance, project applications, research facilities, research review, and public information.
Twelve of the eighteen committee members are physicians, and each
committee includes representatives of the medical staff, the hospital
administration, and the board.

Initially, the attending staff showed little interest in development of
research at PCCH. Most of the impetus came from a few contractual
physicians, particularly from the directors of the pathology and cardio-
pulmonary laboratories. As seed money became available for the initiation of small projects, other members of the attending staff were stimulated to participate in clinical research. A small medical research
laboratory was then opened to permit animal studies. The remarkable
growth of the research program in the course of only three years presages
further expansion of animal and clinical research, as more members of
the attending staff become actively involved.

By far the largest research project to date is related to hospital administration rather than to clinical studies. Project DARE (Data Automation Research and Experimentation), financed jointly by the National
Institutes of Health and the International Business Machines Corporation, has expended more than $500,000 during the past three years
(although not all of this was for research). The results of this program, with installation of electronic equipment for processing doctor's
orders and related patient-care activities, will make Pebble City Community Hospital one of the most automated medical institutions in the
country.

MEDICAL STAFF ORGANIZATION IN RELATION TO
HOSPITAL PROGRAMS

Pebble City Community Hospital is a modern, 447-bed voluntary institution with a moderately structured medical staff organization. Generous community support has provided a good physical plant and the latest in technical equipment. Among its outstanding features are the 4-story pathology laboratory, the new 86-bed "advanced care" rehabilitation unit, the completely equipped radiology department, the decentralized pharmacy sub-stations, and the emergency service available to the entire community. Perhaps even more impressive is the air of progressive administration which spreads from the efficient business offices to the highly organized nursing and other supportive staffs.

At the administrative helm of PCCH is an energetic hospital administrator, who combines effective management with a flair for attracting community support. His advanced concepts of the role of a community hospital frequently bring him into conflict with the more conservative members of the medical staff. Under his leadership over the past ten years, PCCH has gradually become an embryonic "medical center." Ties have been developed with numerous outside agencies, and the functions of the hospital have expanded in the realm of ambulatory service, professional education, and research.

In contrast to the highly organized hospital administration, the medical staff organization has developed rather slowly. For most of its history, the one-year tenure of its officers limited their effectiveness. Prior to the current administrator's appointment, most medical staff committees were weak or even inactive. Under his prodding and with the support and assistance of a few key physicians, various committees were gradually activated. More strict review of surgery by the tissue committee, for example, resulted in a sharp drop in the number of non-pathological or normal tissue reports. The introduction of full-time supportive specialists in pathology and radiology also tightened controls, at least within these departments.

With the construction of the large pathology laboratory, many members of the medical staff began to worry about empire-building by the full-time physicians, although all firm policy positions taken by the medical staff have invariably prevailed in decisions of the board of directors. In order to protect the interests of the attending staff against the encroaching powers of the full-time staff and the administrator, the private physicians undertook to strengthen their own organization. They have become more active on committees and are currently moving to reinforce the positions of medical staff officers by extending their tenure to at least two years.

The essential question in this study concerns the influence of patterns of medical staff organization on hospital programs. Although many factors contribute to improved hospital programs, it is clear that the dramatic expansion in this hospital's facilities, services, and teaching and research programs has been associated with an increasingly structured staff. In order to obtain the benefits of advanced hospital technology, many members of the attending staff came to agree reluctantly to innovations stemming largely from the Administrator and a few key physicians. In the process of these developments in the hospital program, the medical staff has strengthened its own internal organization. Initially, this strengthening may have occurred to provide a counterforce to the administrator and the full-time contractual physicians. Subsequently, these measures were continued and extended to assure effective management, quality review, and other controls for the many supportive services, community programs, and the teaching and research activities.

Thus, a new pattern of medical staff organization is emerging along with the expanded hospital programs. A core of full-time contractual physicians has been appointed in several departments and to head special programs. They, in turn, exercise considerable influence on over-all hospital operations because of their full-time presence. Committees have been activated to monitor many activities of the medical staff. Tenure of medical staff officers is being extended. Attending physicians have organized themselves into a professional panel to staff the emergency service, with remuneration from pooled earnings on a per-hour rather than a fee-for-service basis. The former single office of director of medical education is being replaced by two full-time physicians.

The medical staff, recognizing the benefits to its own members of the expansion of hospital services, has moved with the tide of modern science. Although it is still "moderately" rather than "highly structured," it is nonetheless responding to these pressures by requiring more and more participation of its members in control committee activities, teaching programs, and the out-patient and emergency services. While this study has shown the initial reluctance of the medical staff to promote these developments, their implementation has, in the end, been associated with a heightened structuring of the medical staff organization and a more comprehensive community-oriented hospital program.

VII

NINE HOSPITALS ON THE SCALE OF
MEDICAL STAFF ORGANIZATION

HAVING REVIEWED IN some detail the structure and function of one hospital with a mid-range or moderately structured medical staff organization, we may now step back to get a broader view of the hospital landscape. In this chapter we will examine the MSO patterns and offer a few observations on their relationship to the hospital programs in a series of nine other general hospitals. Four of these have less-structured medical staff organization than does Pebble City Community Hospital, one is at about the same level, and four have MSO patterns more rigorous than does PCCH.

In rank order of their MSO scores, we will first discuss briefly the four hospitals at the loosely structured end of the range—Kenter, Hillside, View, and Midland Hospitals—followed by a slightly more detailed account of St. Martin's Hospital with its MSO score almost the same as that of PCCH. Then, more thorough accounts will be presented of circumstances in the four hospitals with more highly structured MSO patterns—Scopus, Medical Group, Public, and Veterans Hospitals. These fuller accounts are necessitated by the greater complexity of the medical staff structure and dynamics in these institutions.

KENTER HOSPITAL—VERY LOOSELY STRUCTURED MSO

Kenter Hospital is an attractive, modern structure which might easily be mistaken for a residential apartment. Although licensed by the state for fifty-three beds, only forty-two beds are in use. It is set back from the street on a small hill, surrounded by attractive middle-class homes and apartment houses. The interior of the one-story building is light, clean, and tastefully decorated. Most rooms are semi-private and contain two beds. The rooms are equipped for oxygen, and call-buttons connect to the nursing stations. The admitting desk, facing the main entrance, is next to the administrator's private office and in front of the combined business office and record room. The two hospital wings extend from this administrative area. A small laboratory is located in the basement, which also provides additional storage space for records and houses the power plant. Altogether the hospital is compact and efficiently designed for its purposes.

Background. The building was constructed in 1954 by a physician who was the sole owner until the hospital was purchased by a nonprofit medical corporation six years later. Two other small hospitals were some distance away, leaving Kenter Hospital in an advantageous position to attract patients. The new medical arts buildings nearby were bringing doctors to the community and its burgeoning population. In the ensuing years this trading center became one of the largest at the periphery of the metropolitan area.

The hospital's favored position, however, was short-lived. More beds were needed than Kenter provided, resulting in the opening nearby of a large voluntary nonprofit community hospital (225 beds). Thus Kenter Hospital's level of occupancy remained low and its profits did not match the expectations of the initial owner. In addition, many of the staff physicians could not get along with the owner-physician, even though he did not practice in the hospital. This factor, combined with the limited facilities of Kenter Hospital, led most local physicians to favor the larger community hospital, located only a few miles away. Kenter Hospital, therefore, came to be used as an "overflow" facility when beds were not available elsewhere. After a few years the original owner decided to sell out. A group of osteopathic physicians, denied privileges in most hospitals, offered to purchase the facility. However, the physicians in the nearby medical arts buildings disliked the prospect of a competing osteopathic hospital. Forty of them formed the Kenter Medical Foundation, a nonprofit corporation which obtained control of the facility in 1960. Legally, therefore, the Kenter Hospital changed from proprietary to voluntary nonprofit sponsorship. It was approved by the Joint Commission on Accreditation of Hospitals (JCAH) in 1956. It is almost exclusively a medical–surgical hospital, having no obstetrical service and receiving very few pediatric patients.

Medical Staff Organization. By our scheme of analysis, the MSO pattern at Kenter Hospital is "very loosely structured"—25 points in the scale of 100. Even so, a high proportion of its staff are specialists, located in the nearby medical arts buildings. One physician, the anesthesiologist, spends most of his professional hours in the hospital, and a radiologist is present half-time. Medical staff administrative and review functions, necessary to abide by the minimal standards for JCAH accreditation, are carried out mostly at breakfast or luncheon meetings.

The hospital administrator is the key executive in the hospital, acting on behalf of the Kenter Medical Foundation, whose members comprise the bulk of the active staff. Although not directly responsible for medical staff disciplinary and control mechanisms, his full-time presence in the hospital strengthens his authoritative and supervisory role. The chief of staff, department heads, medical executive committee, and the governing board of the hospital are dependent upon him for information on and co-ordination of the hospital's services. While responsible for fiscal solvency, he is also interested in maintaining the quality of care in order to encourage greater utilization of beds.

As at many small hospitals, the primary orientation of nearly all members of the medical staff is toward their private practices. The selection process for staff appointment is not very rigorous. The high proportion of board-certified and eligible specialists is related more to their preponderance in the nearby medical arts buildings than to medical staff policy. Unrestricted privileges are granted for treatment of medical cases, but some attempt is made to review and control surgical privileges according to specialty training and experience. Obligations to perform staff duties are minimal, although greater participation is sought by the administrator and by those few physicians who bear the major burden of committee work. The various control committees required for JCAH approval exist, but are not very active. The hospital thus provides a pleasant setting for the treatment of acutely ill medical and surgical patients, not requiring the special services of a larger community hospital.

MSO and the Hospital Programs. The services of Kenter Hospital are virtually limited to in-patient care of acutely ill surgical and medical cases. There is no maternity or pediatric service, no organized out-patient department, no systematic program of professional education or research. There is virtually no effort in the sphere of preventive or extramural community service. While there is a small emergency room, it is not regularly staffed and had only 104 patients in the year of study (1964). The surgical department for in-patients, on the other hand, is well-developed, with two major operating rooms and one minor one, in addition to a four-bed postoperative recovery room.

Although the majority of physicians on the staff are specialists, general practitioners are welcome and account for a sizable number of admissions. The staff performs the functions necessary to maintain approval of the Joint Commission on Accreditation of Hospitals. Communications and co-ordination between physicians and administration are very informal. Likewise the regulation and control of medical staff activities take place largely on an informal basis, supplemented by the required periodic review of medical records, laboratory tests, and tissue reports by the appropriate staff committees. The administrator is responsible for the supervision of hospital services and facilities, and provides liaison between the medical staff and the governing board of the sponsoring medical foundation.

The medical staff organization, while theoretically independent of the governing board, incorporates the board in its active membership. Thus, there is unity of purpose and policy between the major users of the hospital and its owners. The ownership group of physicians is not inclined to impose strict regulations on the medical staff so long as minimum standards are maintained. The goals of both medical staff and hospital are limited to the bed care of private patients in a setting which caters to personal comforts and needs. Although sponsorship changed from the proprietary ownership of a single physician to the nonprofit ownership of a group of physicians, the goals of Kenter Hospital remained substantially the same.

HILLSIDE HOSPITAL—VERY LOOSELY STRUCTURED MSO

Hillside Hospital is a proprietary institution of 76 beds (plus 17 bassinets) with a medical staff organization that must be considered "very loosely structured"—28 points on our scale. It is located in the "bedroom community" of suburban Hillside, twenty miles south of the metropolis.

Background. The hospital was founded in 1958 by two local businessmen and a physician, as a business venture. After a period of low occupancy and financial losses, it was bought out by another small corporation consisting of two physicians, two optometrists, and three businessmen. These seven men constitute the hospital's board of trustees, but the two physicians do not practice in the facility. By 1962 the operations of the hospital had improved to the level of gaining accreditation by the JCAH. The architectural design is "west coast commercial"—one-story, flat top, simple design, and pleasant landscaping. A central section of the building contains administrative offices, operating rooms, laboratories, and other technical service facilities, while the beds for medical–surgical, obstetrical, and pediatric patients are in three wings fanning out.

Medical Staff Organization. There are 103 physicians on the medical staff, but over half of these visit the hospital less than once a month. Thirty-six doctors comprise the active staff and about ten make heavy use of the hospital for their private patients. There are five part-time contractual physicians—two in pathology and three in radiology. Of the active physicians who admit patients (i.e., excluding the five contractual supportive specialists) only two are board-certified specialists, eight are board-eligible, and twenty-one are general practitioners.

The procedures for appointment and surgical privileges in Hillside Hospital are, theoretically, like those stipulated in JCAH standards. In practice, however, wide surgical and obstetrical privileges are granted to general practitioners on the basis of "demonstrated ability." Also, temporary privileges are rather freely granted, after a discussion between the applicant and the chief of staff. A doctor may also perform an operation not on his approved surgical privilege list, if he obtains concurrence from a consultant authorized to do this operation. The departmental structure is loose, with departmental chiefs elected annually from either specialists or general practitioners. Any disciplinary or control actions are taken by the medical executive committee of the entire staff, rather than at the departmental level. Aside from this committee, there is a medical audit committee, which theoretically combines the functions of a medical records committee, a tissue committee, and a transfusion committee. In the past five years only one doctor was removed from the staff as a result of review by this committee (yet, the pathologist stated the opinion that too many hysterectomies and other questionable operations were being performed).

Many of the physicians interviewed expressed the view that this small hospital was a sanctuary for them against governmental encroachments and for preserving their professional freedom. They enjoy the relatively easy-going MSO atmosphere which they would not expect to find in larger hospitals. Yet they see the necessity of somewhat tighter controls—while guarding the privileges of general practitioners—if only to maintain accreditation and ward off the long hand of government. Some of the pressures for tighter controls come from a few medical staff members, with appointments in other large highly reputable hospitals, who speak of Hillside's "poor reputation." There are various signs, therefore, pointing to a tighter MSO structuring in the years ahead.

MSO and the Hospital Programs. Hillside Hospital offers a wide range of in-patient services. Radiology, pathology, and anesthesiology services are adequately staffed and equipped for most routine functions. Surgical, obstetrical, and pediatric admissions predominate, with relatively few medical admissions or long-stay cases. An intensive care unit was being planned, but none existed at the time of our visit. Physical therapy is given by an outside private group of nonmedical therapists, on contract, but no physical medicine specialist is available. There is a full-time pharmacist, but no drug formulary is used.

Preventive services are limited to a monthly class on infant care for expectant mothers, conducted by a commercial dairy selling baby formulas. Nursing services are strong and appear to yield a high level of patient satisfaction. There is no organized out-patient department, although in the year of study 2,300 out-patient services, principally laboratory and x-ray procedures, were provided to private patients on the order of their personal physicians. Emergency services were also provided to 6,649 cases, but the medical staffing of this activity was beset with problems. Because the active staff was unwilling to cover this service, rotating "on call" arrangements had to be made with three newly arrived doctors, who could look upon this work as a source for attracting private patients. There is no social service in the hospital; an administrative assistant refers patients with social problems, such as unwed mothers, to social agencies. Aside from the monthly clinical staff conferences, there is no formal educational program at Hillside Hospital, nor any research.

The picture of medical staff organization and hospital performance in this small hospital, however, is not static. Pressures are brewing in the medical staff to convert from proprietary to voluntary nonprofit status, and the Administrator supports this desire. Both feel that such conversion would probably increase the resources of the hospital for improvement of in-patient care. In so far as expansion of the scope of hospital services is concerned, MSO influence tends to be negative. The main medical staff objective is to protect the private practices of the staff physicians by limiting services to in-patient care. Pressures from the community to increase the services of the emergency room are being resisted as much as possible. With respect to the quality of in-patient care, however, MSO influence is positive and increasing. The medical executive committee succeeded in expelling two physicians whose competence was questionable, one of whom had refused to co-operate with the audit committee. This act served notice on the entire staff that minimal standards of performance would be enforced. Although most of the physicians on the staff are relatively uninvolved in the hospital, as measured by time spent in the facility, the presence of a full-time radiologist and a nearly full-time pathologist injects a growing spirit of general surveillance in Hillside Hospital, as well as contributing to the quality of care directly.

VIEW HOSPITAL—LOOSELY STRUCTURED MSO

This is a 141-bed hospital under proprietary sponsorship, with a medical staff organization that we consider to be "loosely structured" (36 points in our scale). It is of special interest in our series because it illustrates certain inter-hospital dynamics—that is, the development of medical staff policies that are much influenced by the affiliation of a substantial portion of its doctors with the medical staff of another nearby community hospital of great prestige. Thus, it is a kind of informal satellite to the larger institution (Scopus Hospital—reviewed later in this series), with attributes that are partly a product of, and partly a reaction against, the policies of the larger hospital.

Background. Constructed in 1925, the hospital was originally planned to serve the patients of osteopathic physicians. In 1947 it was purchased by a nonpracticing doctor of medicine, who turned over policy determination to seven physicians on the staff of the nearby prestigious Scopus Hospital. In this postwar period, there was a great demand for hospital beds and a limited supply, so that occupancy rates were high. Later, as more hospitals were built, occupancy declined. In 1962 the hospital was sold again, therefore, to a corporation made up of fifty physicians who were its principal users.

Situated on top of a hill, View Hospital is attractive. In 1954 the ground floor, housing most supportive service facilities, was remodeled and in 1961 a top floor was added. At the time of our study (1964), major interior remodeling was being done, including the installation of a new four-bed intensive care unit, improvement of the surgical suites, and redesigning of the main entrance and parking areas. Plans had also been completed for a new 100-bed wing. Thus, View Hospital is obviously a dynamic institution. It has 292 hospital employees per 100 patients (1964)—higher than the national average for hospitals of this size.

Medical Staff Organization. The total medical staff of View Hospital is large, with 544 physicians having admitting privileges, and of these 138 are on the active staff. In the active staff, 38 per cent are board-certified specialists, but about an equal proportion are board-eligible, so that the great majority practice as specialists, rather than general practitioners. Selection procedures and assignment of privileges are similar to those detailed in the description of Pebble City Community Hospital. A record is kept of admissions by each active staff physician, and if they fall below a certain level he may be dropped to associate or courtesy staff status, with reduced priority in access to beds. Contractual physicians include a full-time radiologist and full-time pathologist (getting a share of departmental income) plus four anesthesiologists who are paid directly by patient fees. It is estimated that 95 per cent of the staff doctors have appointments at two or more other hospitals in the city. Departmentalization is relatively highly developed, with nine definable subdivisions (although some are called "departments," others "divisions," and others "sections"). The medical executive committee gives special strength to the hospital-based specialists, by including three of them, along with the hospital administrator, as *ex officio* members.

Control committees are relatively stronger at View Hospital than in the two hospitals reviewed above. There is a tissue committee, a mortality committee, two records committees (one for medical and the other for surgical cases), an infections committee, and a credentials committee, all of which meet regularly. A number of other committees (for the pharmacy, transfusions, sterilization, etc.) meet sporadically. Formal minutes of committee meetings suggest exceptional diligence for a hospital of this size. Unlike the situation in many proprietary hospitals, the doctors who are the principal users of View Hospital are not there for lack of qualification to serve in larger voluntary hospitals; they nearly all have such appointments, but use View Hospital for patients who cannot be promptly accommodated in the larger facilities. Moreover, the historic background of the hospital in the 1950's was marked by certain issues on civil rights, which has led to an unusual policy of racial integration on both medical and nonmedical staffs. This has led to disaffection from the hospital of certain white doctors and patients, combined with exceptional devotion by others.

MSO and the Hospital Programs. Because of this background inpatient care at View Hospital is characterized by a spirit of warmth, as well as by a wide range of basic technical services. Yet, remarkable caution is exercised to avoid treatment of complex surgical or medical cases which good judgment would refer to a larger hospital. Major traumatic cases, for example, are sent usually to the Scopus Hospital, and a deliberate decision was made to avoid open-heart surgery, even though a competent cardiac surgeon is on the staff. The laboratory is unusually well staffed, with 12.5 full-time (or equivalent) technical and auxiliary personnel, in addition to the pathologist. Likewise, for the radiology department, which offers radiation therapy as well as diagnosis. Physical therapy is not well developed, being provided through contract with an independent nonmedical therapist. The pharmacy is well-staffed with a full-time pharmacist and three other persons; a drug formulary has been established, but it is not regularly used. The medical staff pharmacy committee reviews the formulary periodically and makes policies on such matters as automatic "stop-orders" for certain drugs or reporting of drug reactions. The nursing service seems to be highly satisfactory, yielding very few criticisms from patients or doctors.

Educational activities are limited to clinical pathological conferences and tumor board meetings alternating each week; one Friday per month a special x-ray conference is conducted by the radiologist. Preventive services are lacking, except for routine laboratory tests, and there is no research. It must be recalled, however, that educational and research activities involve many of the View Hospital physicians through their appointments at nearby Scopus Hospital. The "satellite" character of View Hospital is largely confined to in-patient care.

The full-time radiologist and pathologist appear to exercise a great deal of influence on the diligence of the medical staff and, indeed, on all personnel in the hospital. Partly through their influence and partly because of the lack of a rigid departmental structure, informal dynamics in the medical staff are strong. Communication is high among physicians, hospital administrator, nurses, and others. In part, this spirit is encouraged deliberately, as a reaction against the relatively bureaucratic structure of Scopus Hospital, with which so many of the doctors are affiliated. The articulation with Scopus also justifies, to the medical staff of View Hospital, the lack of an out-patient service, rehabilitation program, social service, and the limited scope of educational activities. Yet, these deficiencies may result in less than adequate care for some patients. With the relatively loose medical staff organization, the leadership of the administrator, who has been in the job for eighteen years, has great importance in shaping the character of View Hospital's performance.

MIDLAND COMMUNITY HOSPITAL—
LOOSELY STRUCTURED MSO

This is a 230-bed hospital under voluntary nonprofit sponsorship, with a medical staff organization scored as 56 points out of 100. In our series we still considered this as "loosely structured," although it is noticeably more rigorous than that of the three hospitals analyzed above, and perhaps borders on the "moderately structured."

Background. Midland Community Hospital (MCH) was founded by a private physician in 1904, converted from a proprietary to a voluntary nonprofit facility in 1927 and expanded to its current size by several additions over the years (most recently in 1963). Unlike the environmental settings of the other hospitals reviewed so far, it is the only general hospital in the small town of Midland, which is thirty miles from the periphery of the metropolis. Its physical growth over the years has been supported mainly by donations from a few wealthy local benefactors. It differs also from the previously described hospitals by having an affiliated long-term care unit.

The hospital staff has 522 employees (full-time equivalents) for a ratio of 2.27 per bed or 3.16 per patient (1964). The patient composition is remarkably "white, middle-class," with only an estimated 10 per cent of admissions being Negro, Oriental, or Mexican-American. The board of directors of twenty-one persons is dominated by twelve local businessmen and three physician members. There is obviously an aspect of comfortable stability to the hospital, derived from robust financial support in a prosperous community, with virtually no "competitive" hospital nearby.

Medical Staff Organization. Differing also from the previous hospitals reviewed, the medical staff at MCH is relatively small, containing 137 physicians, of whom all but 24 are on the active staff. Sixty-eight per cent of the active staff doctors are qualified as specialists. The appointment procedure for new physicians involves review of applications by a credentials committee, whose membership is kept secret, and solicitation of letters of reference. Temporary privileges are rarely granted, and all new medical staff members serve not only on probation for six months (a common requirement under JCAH policies) but also as "junior members" for three years, unless they have full specialty board certification. Until senior staff status is achieved, consultation with senior staff members is required for all serious cases.

There are sixteen physicians who spend virtually full-time in the hospital, including not only the three common supportive specialties (pathology, radiology, and anesthesiology) but also one specialist in nuclear medicine, one part-time neurosurgeon, and a general practitioner on full-time emergency room service. Of the private attending physicians, fifteen are estimated to spend over twenty hours per week in the hospital, and seventy between ten and twenty hours. Unlike the other medical staffs so far reviewed, only about 10 per cent of the active staff members have appointments at other hospitals, so that the commitment level at MCH is relatively high.

There are ten departments, including one for "general practice." (The latter has no demarcated beds, but its members work in the other specialty departments.) Each departmental staff elects its chairman for a two-year period, but his authority is exercised lightly, according to the physicians interviewed. Departmental meetings are poorly attended and devoted mostly to such matters as considering patient complaints or discussing the credentials of new staff applicants. The real authority in the medical staff is exercised by the medical executive committee, made up of the several departmental chairmen and the elected officers of the total staff. Medical staff policies are implemented largely through the mediation of the hospital administrator and the director of nurses.

Control committees are numerous—there are twenty-six of them, but most meet only sporadically. Monthly meetings, suggesting greater diligence, are held by the tissue committee, general surgery committee, medical records committee, pediatrics committee, infections committee, and the laboratory and blood bank committee. A key informant remarked, however, that the committees do not function very well, and the work is usually done by one person on each. Medical staff bylaws are carefully drawn up at MCH—a forty-page booklet, continuously up-dated and given to every doctor.

Length of tenure makes a great deal of difference in the effectiveness of any office-holder in an organization, and on the MCH medical staff one of the important such persons is the elected secretary; the current secretary has been in this office for five years, and his predecessor held it for fifteen years. As an elected colleague, he exercises more influence, for example, than the contractual pathologist. The chief of pathology has also been at MCH many years, but he has come to be very contrite in giving tissue reports; he submits them without comment to the tissue committee, which may or may not act on questionable findings. The most serious problems in quality maintenance involved the older staff physicians, who are not easy to influence by the relatively loose MSO patterns in this hospital.

MSO and the Hospital Programs. Aside from the usual range of inpatient services at MCH, attention may be directed to certain hospital programs of special interest. The surgical suite is highly developed, with nine operating rooms, a recovery room of seventeen beds, and an intensive care unit of four beds. The twenty-two-bed pediatrics ward has an occupancy level of 73 per cent, which is higher than most such units. The pathology department is also very well staffed, with three full-time pathologists and an equivalent full-time staff of twenty-nine technicians. The laboratory space is unusually large and functionally designed. A very active blood bank and transfusion service is operated also. All surgical tissues are examined grossly and 90 per cent microscopically. The volume of laboratory examinations has been rising steadily— at the rate of 21 per cent annually over the last four years. The radiology department is likewise highly advanced, including not only the usual diagnostic service, but deep x-ray therapy, radium treatment, radioisotopes, and a cobalt therapy unit. The pharmacy is adequately staffed, but there is no drug formulary in use.

Physical therapy is another strong service in MCH, with a staff of ten therapists and aides, but no physical medicine specialist. This staff is not, however, employed by the hospital, but rather by an outside partnership of physical therapists which is paid 43 per cent of hospital collections for its services. A large volume of work is done by this department— 30,000 treatments in 1964, of which 80 per cent were for out-patients referred by private physicians. In a sense, the physical therapy service is a private concession operating within the hospital for ambulatory patients, but offering at the same time in-patient care.

Midland Community Hospital has on its staff four psychiatrists who may admit patients, but there is no organized psychiatric ward. The lo-

cal voluntary Mental Health Association has been requesting establishment of such a unit at the hospital, but action has not yet been taken.
Of special interest, however, is the long-term care unit associated with
MCH in an adjoining building. This contains thirty beds for aged and
chronically ill patients and offers strong nursing services.

The emergency service at MCH has been increasing rapidly, and in
1964 had 15,000 visits. To cope with the load, a full-time salaried physician was appointed to this duty for the daytime hours; for the night
hours members of the medical staff are called on a rotation basis, as
necessary. The emergency room physician does not, however, have admitting privileges and he must refer patients requiring in-patient care to an
active staff member. Out-patient services for physical therapy have been
mentioned, and similarly diagnostic x-ray or laboratory procedures may
be scheduled for private patients, but there is no organized out-patient
department for low-income patients. Twice a month, however, a cancer
follow-up clinic is held for examination of certain private patients discharged from the hospital. Except for routine blood and urine tests on
in-patients, there are no systematic preventive services. The local Visiting Nurse Association attempted recently to develop a program for continuing home care to patients discharged from MCH, but so few doctors made use of it that the idea was dropped.

Professional education is quite meager at MCH. There are no formal
medical training programs, except for the monthly medical staff meetings and audio-digest tape recordings on various clinical subjects. Practical experience is provided at the hospital for nurses and physical
therapists from a nearby college, but there are no schools for nursing or
other allied health personnel. There is no research.

Thus, the Midland Community Hospital, with its loosely structured
MSO (though at the high end of this level, with a 56-point score) has
well developed technical and supportive services for in-patients and is
unusual in its associated long-term care unit. Its extra-mural services,
however, consist of a reluctantly offered emergency service and a large
nonmedical physical therapy service for referral of private patients. Educational and research activities are weak. Protection of the business interests of medical practitioners seems to figure prominently in hospital
policy decisions, and the hospital's role is seen mainly as a "workshop" for
the doctor and his private patients.

ST. MARTIN'S HOSPITAL—
MODERATELY STRUCTURED MSO

Established in 1942 by an order of Catholic sisters (sponsoring thirteen hospitals in all), St. Martin's Hospital has 265 beds and a medical

staff organization that we scale as "moderately structured" (62 points). In the MSO scale it is at about the same level as Pebble City Community Hospital, whose story was detailed in the previous chapter.

Background. The hospital is located at the edge of the metropolis in a prosperous residential suburb, but not far from a depressed working class section. Land for the original facility of ninety beds was purchased by a group of physicians, who donated it to the sisterhood. Almost immediately the hospital was filled to capacity and expansion has been launched three times in its short twenty-five-year history. At the time of our study, construction was in process on another seven-story wing which would bring the capacity to 475 beds. The rapid physical growth, the dedicated efficiency of the sisterhood, and the qualifications of the medical staff give this voluntary hospital an aspect of proud strength.

As in most Catholic hospitals, administrative power is lodged in a board of directors composed entirely of sisters, and general policies are largely determined by the mother-house, which is located in another state. At the same time, there is smooth liaison with the medical staff, and an advisory "board of regents" brings to bear the judgment of leading citizens of the area and the bishop of the local diocese.

Medical Staff Organization.   The total medical staff of St. Martin's Hospital contains 475 physicians, but only 120 of these are on the active staff who admit the great majority of patients. Seventy-one per cent of the active staff are specialists, fully certified by their respective boards. Appointment procedures, through review by a credentials committee, are diligently carried out, with a usual requirement of six years—for courtesy and associate staffs—before active staff membership can be achieved. Professional privileges are based on specialty qualifications and surgery may be done only by qualified surgeons. In the nonsurgical departments privileges are controlled through mandatory consultations (at no charge to the patient) with senior specialists. Active and associate staff members are expected to attend at least 75 per cent of general and departmental staff meetings.

Time commitments of the private doctors on the medical staff are similar to those described in the Pebble City Community Hospital account. The majority of active and associate staff members have affiliations with two or three other hospitals. There is the equivalent of 19.5 full-time contractual physicians in the hospital, although the method of remuneration of the eight anesthesiologists is by fees from patients. The four radiologists and the chief pathologist have contracts based on a share of departmental income, but five other pathologists are hired by the chief on straight salaries. In addition, a specialist in internal medicine and a pediatrician are engaged on full-time salaries to staff out-patient and emergency services.

All clinical specialties are grouped under five departments—medicine, surgery, obstetrics, pediatrics, and general practice—the latter not accessible to any designated beds. Bureaucratic stability has been achieved in the clinical departments by a tendency toward long tenure of the elected departmental chiefs. The chief of medicine, for example, has held this position for fifteen years, although the staff is now planning a maximum of five-year terms for all departmental chiefs—longer, in any event, than the usual one or two year terms in the more loosely structured MSO patterns. The medical executive committee is strong and, in addition to departmental chiefs and generally elected officers, it contains *ex officio* the chief pathologist, chief radiologist, and the hospital administrator (the senior nursing sister). Thus, the voice of fully committed hospital personnel is well represented at the summit of medical staff authority.

Aside from committees in each of the clinical departments, there are about twenty committees of the medical staff concerned with various quality controls. It is noteworthy to see control committees on such subjects as the out-patient clinics, cardiology, inhalation therapy, neuropsychiatry, and radiation therapy. Meeting as frequently as every month are the tissue committee, education committee, general practice committee, library committee, records committee, and research committee. There is also a special "advisory committee" which counsels the board of directors on medical staff issues. The various committees—both in the departments and with staff-wide control functions—have a special importance at St. Martin's Hospital in the current period. They are seen not only as compensatory and reinforcing controls with respect to individual medical practitioners but also as a sort of countervailing force to the long-tenured departmental chiefs. While the latter positions have lent stability to the hospital, it is also felt by many doctors that they have engendered some favoritism in initial staff appointments, in access to hospital beds by certain physicians, and in appointments to various medical staff functions. Thus, there are definite incentives for staff members to serve diligently on various committees and to make their influence felt.

As for formal documentation, the St. Martin's Hospital medical staff distributes its written bylaws to all new members. More remarkable is a forty-page "Manual for Members of the Administration, Chief of Staff, Executive Committee, and Committee Chairmen." This instrument of MSO operations is designed to fortify the effectiveness of the whole medical staff organization and to reduce the influence of cliques and informal dynamics, which were said to formerly dominate this hospital.

MSO and the Hospital Programs. The high occupancy rate of 85 per cent at St. Martin's Hospital (1964), along with the major bed expansion under way, are evidence of the dynamism of this institution.

The surgical services are well developed, with six operating rooms in use from 7 A.M. to 11 P.M.—much later hours than found in most hospitals. There is a fifteen-bed recovery room and a seven-bed intensive care unit. The nursing management of the surgical operating suite is especially efficient; doctors have been suspended from the staff for rude behavior toward nursing personnel. When surgeons are observed to be performing poorly—a problem especially among older men—the surgical department committee can insist on a qualified assistant surgeon, even for operations done previously without intervention. The department of medicine is remarkable in one respect: it contains a unit of ten psychiatric beds. Patients may be admitted to these beds only by a psychiatrist or—if by an internist—with a psychiatric consultation. The obstetrical and pediatric departments are also well-staffed and operated. There is a special premature infant service attached to the pediatric ward, separate from the nursery for the newborn in the obstetrical service.

The pathology department is extremely well staffed and equipped. In addition to the six pathologists, there is a full-time medical microbiologist and a clinical chemist with Ph.D. degree, plus thirty full-time and eight part-time technical personnel. To encourage use of the laboratory, reduced rates are charged to patients for a "package" of several diagnostic or case-finding tests on blood specimens. A strong blood bank service is also operated by this department. The physical therapy service has four therapists and three aides, all employed directly by the hospital (instead of through an independent contractor).

Nursing services in St. Martin's, as at most Catholic hospitals, are particularly well-disciplined. Fully registered nurses comprise 65 per cent of the total nursing staff—a higher proportion than usually found in relation to vocational nurses and nurse aides. Catholic sisters are assigned to all supervisory positions. Nurses are encouraged to double-check prescription dosages and to observe the general diligence of attending physicians, with instructions to report questionable performance to the director of nurses; she, in turn, takes up problems with the medical staff officers.

In contrast to the four other hospitals with less structured medical staff organization reviewed so far in this chapter, St. Martin's Hospital has an organized out-patient department for persons of low income. This is over and above the emergency service to which anyone may come day or night. Clinic sessions are scheduled at regular hours in numerous specialized fields, such as dermatology, ophthalmology, gynecology, orthopedics, etc., and also general medicine and general surgery. Especially noteworthy is a psychiatric clinic, which treated 730 patients in 1965. A preventive orientation is reflected in an ante-natal (obstetrical) clinic, a well-baby clinic, and a glaucoma clinic stressing early detection of this eye disease. The two contractual physicians noted earlier (internist and pediatrician) constitute the core medical personnel of these clinics, but almost all members of the active and associate medical staffs are called upon to serve in them without remuneration; this is one of their obligations to the hospital in return for the professional privilege of treating private patients. The volume of out-patient services provided, however, is not very high—a total of 4,107 patients and 17,451 patient visits in 1965. During the daytime hours the emergency service is simply integrated with the scheduled clinics, but after hours emergencies are covered by engagement of medical and surgical residents from nearby teaching hospitals. These after-hour emergency visits numbered only 2,921 in 1965, perhaps because other large hospitals not far away receive the bulk of such calls. A full-time social worker is also attached to the out-patient department.

Another noteworthy community extra-mural service of St. Martin's Hospital is its Child Study Center. This is an extension of the hospital, financed by a private foundation and other donations, for ambulatory treatment and rehabilitation of retarded, emotionally disturbed, and physically handicapped children. It is headed by a full-time salaried psychiatrist and staffed with social workers, psychologists, teachers, and other rehabilitation personnel. Another facility contributing to the role of this general hospital as a "community health center" is the large, directly adjacent medical arts building in which many of the staff physicians have their private offices; this proximity doubtless increases the ties of these doctors to the hospital and their rapid availability to patients.

Certain preventively oriented out-patient clinic sessions have been mentioned. In addition, all new out-patients receive a routine chest x-ray, and children are checked for immunization status. In-patient laboratory routines include urinalysis, blood count, and serological tests for syphilis, but chest x-rays only on the attending doctor's order. Systematic health education of patients is not offered.

Educational activities, through the regular meetings of the medical staff, are like those at the Pebble City Community Hospital. There is no full-time director of medical education, however, although this idea has recently been considered. Residents from other larger hospitals sometimes come to spend a few months at St. Martin's in selected fields, like orthopedics or gynecology, but there is no regular residency or internship program. Practical experience is offered in the hospital for students of nursing, laboratory and x-ray technology, and vocational nursing, who are getting their basic education elsewhere. The relative weakness of the educational programs is attributed to the existence of other large university-affiliated hospitals not far away. A remarkably good medical library, with a full-time librarian, is in the hospital and doubtless contributes to staff education.

This account of five hospitals at the lower end of the spectrum of MSO structuring may be enough to show the similarities and also the differences from the situation detailed more fully in the previous chapter on the Pebble City Community Hospital. The characteristics of hospitals at the upper end of the MSO spectrum are more complicated, and their analysis will require more thorough accounts, which follow.

SCOPUS HOSPITAL—
HIGHLY STRUCTURED MSO

This section presents an analysis of Scopus Hospital—a general hospital of nearly 500 beds under voluntary nonprofit sponsorship, with a medical staff organization that is "highly structured." On our quantitative scale the MSO structure scores 71 points but, as we shall see, our scoring system probably fails to reflect adequately the degree of structuring by which Scopus is higher than that of the six other hospitals so far reviewed. The quantitative increment at this point in the spectrum of MSO patterns seems to yield a qualitative change in the basic nature of medical staff organization and the content of hospital performance associated with it.

The Setting of Scopus Hospital. Originating half a century ago in the heart of the metropolis, Scopus Hospital has grown from a twelve-bed wooden structure staffed by three doctors to one of the largest and most dynamic voluntary hospitals in the western United States. Recently in a national magazine it was rated by a jury of medical experts as one of the 25 "best hospitals" among the 7,000 in the nation. It enjoys similar acclaim in its own community because of the high qualifications of its medical staff, its extensive research program, and its dedication to a very wide range of medical services for the poor as well as the affluent. Built and developed largely through financial support from Jewish philanthropists and donors, Scopus is used and appreciated by patients of all faiths.

Classification of this hospital as having a highly structured MSO is influenced largely by its engagement of a basic skeleton staff of full-time salaried physicians in virtually every hospital department, supplemented by a large complement of residents and interns. Nevertheless, the great majority of doctors serving in the hospital are private practitioners and the great majority of patients are self-supporting.

The Scopus Hospital complex, spread over three city blocks, consists of a central eight-story building, a separate "clinic hospital," a modern rehabilitation center, and an adjacent research building. It has 490 beds (1964), of which 384 are in the main building and 106 in the "clinic" annex, plus about 50 bassinets in two nurseries (obstetrical and pediatric.) Thirty-five per cent of the beds (172) are in private rooms, the remainder being in semi-private accomodations containing two to five beds each. The separate four-story "clinic hospital" contains the out-patient department as well as the wards. Compared with the main building, this unit appears somewhat cramped and in need of renovation. New construction is awaiting decision on the larger question of a planned physical and administrative merger of Scopus Hospital with a sister-institution under similar Jewish community sponsorship.

Despite a sense of personnel shortage in most departments, Scopus has a relatively large staff. Including the full-time medical staff, there are 1,456 employees measured as "full-time equivalents." This amounts to 297 personnel per 100 beds or 383 per 100 patients—much above the national average.

The hospital operates on an annual budget of nearly $11,000,000. Eighty per cent of this comes from payments by patients (including insurance carriers or other third-party agencies), 17 per cent from voluntary contributions (including the Community Chest and the United Jewish Welfare Fund), and the balance from miscellaneous sources. These moneys sustain annually about 139,000 in-patient days, 115,000 out-patient visits, and numerous other services to be reviewed below.

In addition to private paying patients, certain indigent or medically indigent patients living in a designated geographic service area are admitted to the hospital. This area is defined by the charitable community agencies supporting these costs; at the time of our study, government funds (Medicare and Medicaid) were not yet available to pay for such welfare medical services in voluntary hospitals of this state. No religious or ethnic restrictions apply to these patients.

The administrative structure of Scopus Hospital is especially complex not only because of its size and rate of growth but also because of the recent decision, noted above, to merge with a sister-hospital six miles away. The united pair of hospitals is to be known as a "Medical Center," but Scopus is still physically separate and will be described here as a self-contained entity. The merger, it may simply be noted, was dictated by considerations of economy (especially for the sources of charitable funds) and the desire of the hospital sponsors to continuously upgrade the quality and range of services.

As might be expected, the execution of the merger of two large hospitals was marked by various controversies. The medical staffs were naturally involved, since two parallel but sovereign sets of clinical and supportive departments were to become merged into one. As a step toward this, a pattern of paired departmental and control committees —which would eventually coalesce—was being developed at the time of our study. Likewise, the boards of directors of both hospitals were combined, with appointment of various joint committees. The top hospital administrative officer, known as the executive director, was a truly unified authority over both merging hospitals, but below him other hospital administrative personnel were assigned to one hospital or the other. This top officer is a physician with long years of administrative experience, and the managerial heads of Scopus and its sister-hospital are both nonmedical hospital administrators.

Thus, while the two-hospital merger has complicated the lines of authority for the present, administrative power lies still in a board of directors. The executive director advises this board and, of course, carries out the policy decisions made by it. A large joint conference committee, advisory to the board, includes representatives of the medical staffs of both hospitals along with selected board members. Since Scopus Hospital is the older and larger of the two merging institutions, its voice is perhaps a little stronger in the duet that is being composed.

MEDICAL STAFF ORGANIZATION OF SCOPUS HOSPITAL

The structure and function of the medical staff of Scopus Hospital are especially complex, by reason of its combination of a large number of private physicians with a basic corps of salaried physicians attached primarily to the hospital organization.

Composition of the Staff. Excluding the "house staff" of 71 doctors-in-training (interns and residents), there are 909 physicians on the Scopus medical staff (1964). Medical staff classification is determined largely by length of tenure, but other factors also contribute. No less than six categories of medical staff members are differentiated:

1) The "courtesy staff" is essentially the lowest rung on the medical staff ladder. As the bylaws put it, "physicians of distinction whose major attachment is to some other hospital in the community," but who hope to make Scopus their major hospital affiliation, may apply for this status. New members remain on the courtesy staff for at least one year or until a vacancy occurs in higher grades. There are 170 physicians, or 18 per cent of the total staff, in this classification.

2) The next level is the "associate staff," in which doctors remain

usually for five years. This level contains 232 members or 25 per cent of the total medical staff. This classification carries important obligations to participate in hospital out-patient services.

3) The "active staff" is the central core of the medical staff, responsible for basic policies and their execution. It consists of 363 doctors or 40 per cent of the total. On the basis of seniority, it is further subdivided into three levels of "attending" physicians: (a) the "associate attending physicians" who must serve in this grade for five more years; (b) the "attending physicians" who carry the major responsibilities in committees, out-patient services, educational program, etc.; (c) the "senior attending physicians" who must have served at the previous level for at least six years or have reached sixty years of age. The latter doctors are relieved of out-patient department and other service responsibilities, but may be expected to serve in the bureaucratic structure of the medical staff.

4) The "emeritus staff" is composed of all active-staff physicians who have reached sixty-five years of age. They are relieved of all organizational responsibilities, but they may continue to admit private patients within the department to which they belong.

5) The "consulting staff" consists of a changing number and percentage (usually quite low—under 5 per cent) of doctors who are appointed because of special qualifications, without regard to age or tenure. They must be available for consultation on either indigent or private patients, and for instruction in various teaching programs. In return, they are granted privileges like those of the active staff for admission of private patients.

6) Finally, there are the contractual physicians, known as the "full-time staff." These doctors, while regarded as a special category of the over-all medical staff, are also granted a rank within the active staff at one of the three "attending physician" levels outlined above. More will be said of this important category of physician below.

It is obvious, then, that the over-all medical staff at Scopus Hospital is highly differentiated in its composition, quite aside from its functional features. About 90 per cent of total staff members (a higher proportion of the active staff) are qualified specialists—either board-eligible (one-third) or board-certified (two-thirds). Only some of the older doctors, who joined the staff before appointment policies became so rigorous, must be counted as general practitioners.

Appointment Procedures. Applications for medical staff membership are processed in a way similar to that described earlier for Pebble City Community Hospital. At Scopus, however, the most influential input to the decision comes from the department in which privileges are sought.

This departmental action, moreover, usually includes an interview by the full-time chief (see below), as well as by members of the active attending staff. While local private physicians ordinarily initiate applications themselves, it should be noted that appointment to the full-time contractual physician staff is usually based on an active search for available candidates from anywhere in the nation.

Promotions to higher staff classifications are based on a careful scoring system, in which points are given for years of service, work in the outpatient clinics, attendance at staff meetings, service on committees, teaching functions, and research accomplishments. In promotions, as in initial appointments, while annual reviews are made by a general medical staff committee, the principal influence comes from the governing committee of the doctor's department (see below).

Designation of professional privileges is based essentially on the doctor's specialty qualifications. Since all applicants must be specialists (either board-certified or eligible), there is not felt to be need for the explicit delineation of permissible procedures (especially surgical operations), which we have observed in hospitals of looser MSO structuring with many general practitioners on the staff. Since initial appointments are highly selective, subsequent freedoms are greater. The main exception to this policy is found in the department of medicine, where the older general practitioners have usually been assigned—doctors who joined the staff long before current specialty qualifications were imposed.

On rare occasions "temporary privileges" may be granted to an outside physician on recommendation of a departmental chief, while his application papers are being processed (the latter requiring one to three months). This is only done, however, for physicians of outstanding merit; it is convenient also for new full-time physicians whose appointments are primarily for research or educational purposes.

Because of its great prestige in the community, Scopus Hospital receives many more medical staff applications than it can accept. The limiting factor is the number of hospital beds to which a doctor's private patients can be admitted. Therefore, many qualified medical applicants must be turned away and asked to await retirement of the older doctors. Since beds are in short supply even for the current active-staff members, incentives are created for hard work to earn promotions which entitle the doctor to higher priority in gaining admission for his patients. This applies, of course, to elective cases, since emergencies are admitted on the basis of need and without regard to the doctor's status.

The obligations of medical staff appointment have been noted earlier. All active-staff and associate-staff members are expected to attend both business and scientific meetings. They are required to perform duties assigned in the out-patient clinics, to carry out teaching tasks, and to participate in the activities of their departments. On the younger physicians, who are in the "associate staff" or in "associate attending" rank of the active staff, falls the principal burden of out-patient services. On the higher levels of active staff and the full-time contractual physicians, rests the main responsibility for in-patient care of both private and indigent patients.

Commitment. Although the vast majority of medical staff members at Scopus Hospital are private practitioners, with their principal professional commitments elsewhere, the presence of a large staff of full-time contractual physicians has a major influence on the attitudes of all staff members. The obligations of medical staff appointment and the desire of most staff members to remain at Scopus and advance their rank lead them to devote more time and energy to the work at this hospital than we observed in other hospitals of looser MSO structuring. Although precise quantification of this judgment was not feasible, it was clearly our impression from numerous interviews and observations in the series of ten case studies.

Measured by time-allotments, the highest medical staff commitment, of course, is found in the staff of full-time contractual physicians. There are forty-two full-time plus twelve part-time physicians under a contractual relationship with the hospital, although their methods of remuneration differ. The anesthesiologists (twelve) receive fees from their patients, even though they spend virtually all their time in this hospital. The senior radiologists and pathologists are theoretically paid a percentage of departmental incomes, but in effect they receive basic salaries which are subject to certain adjustments for financial surpluses or deficits. Junior members of these departments start out on flat salaries and gradually acquire certain income-sharing rights. All the other contractual doctors receive straight salaries, and these include the all-important full-time chiefs of clinical departments, to be discussed below. Parallel with these staff members are the seventy-one interns and residents, not strictly on the medical staff, but obviously affecting the tone of all professional work in the hospital.

A kind of equilibrium in commitment to the hospital operates between the full-time staff and the active staff of private attending physicians. The very strength of the full-time staff induces the attending physicians to greater diligence in order to "protect their interests." Private doctors naturally see their primary goal as provision of good quality care to private in-patients; the other hospital functions of education, research, out-patient care, and general community service tend to take second place. For the contractual physicians the latter goals tend to have the higher priority. While these differences should not be exaggerated, certain conflicts inevitably occur; to guard the place of in-patient care, private members of the medical staff are actually induced to spend more time in organized hospital duties than would otherwise be likely.

Another aspect of commitment must be traced to the ethnic background of most medical staff members. About 75 per cent of the doctors are of Jewish faith and in the dynamics of medical practice in the metropolis—containing many other large hospitals with predominantly Christian medical staffs—a certain ethnic or cultural pride emerges. The result is a certain *esprit de corps* and an eagerness to enhance the community reputation of Scopus Hospital that strengthens the psychological commitment of its medical staff members. These attitudes also appear to spill over to members of the medical staff of other religious backgrounds.

Departmentalization. The bureaucratic structure of the Scopus medical staff is based on nine major departments. Two of these—internal medicine and surgery—are subdivided into eleven and fourteen sections respectively.

Each clinical department has two interlocking channels of authority, one emanating from an elected head and the other from an appointed head. The departmental chairman, vice-chairman, and secretary are chosen by vote of the active staff. Although their terms of office are theoretically for one year, they usually serve for three. As "clinical chiefs" (a term frequently used), these doctors tend to represent the private practitioners in the department. The chairmen preside over meetings, make appointments of staff members to serve in the clinics, and carry a general responsibility for the quality of work done by the doctors in the department.

Parallel with the elected clinical chairmen are the full-time heads or directors of the departments. They develop and administer the departmental budgets, take responsibility for teaching and research activities, and supervise the over-all care of both out-patients and in-patients who are indigent and not attached to a private doctor. Each full-time department director has an advisory committee, which he selects from the active staff with the approval of the elected clinical chief. This committee is important in maintaining cohesiveness between the private and the hospital-based contractual physicians. Advisory committee meetings are held frequently (usually every two weeks) to maintain good liaison. In addition, there are monthly meetings of the entire departmental staffs.

In the supportive departments—pathology, radiology, and rehabilitation—there is only one authority line, headed by the full-time director.

All of the full-time departmental directors are administratively responsible to a director of professional services, coming under the executive director of the entire hospital. Weekly meetings are held between this top-level medical administrator and the departmental directors, together with the elected departmental chairmen and the elected chief of staff of the entire medical staff. These formal meetings are obviously supplemented by day-to-day individual contacts among these medical men and by oral and written reports to the executive director. There are also channels of communication with the board of directors through the joint conference committee. The effect of all this participation of well-qualified physicians in the administration of medical staff functions is to reduce the role of the nonmedical hospital administrator at Scopus to the more clearly "business management" aspects of hospital affairs.

Corresponding to the hierarchy of the full-time medical staff, there is responsibility of the elected departmental chairmen to the medical executive committee of the over-all staff. This is composed of the elected chief of staff, a vice-chief, and secretary along with each of the elected departmental chairmen. At the meetings of this committee, the director of professional services is also in attendance to foster liaison in the other direction with the full-time staff.

The organization chart of these two parallel and interlocking lines of medical staff authority is obviously complex. Its viability depends on day-to-day interchanges and flexibility. The interdepartmental structure is intended to co-ordinate the different departments and to encourage initiation of new programs. The parallelism from bottom to top, between full-time and private staff members, provides plenty of opportunity for discussion of all problems and proposals, whether they emanate from the board of directors, the administrative staff, or the medical staff. Before any major innovations are implemented, some sort of consensus is usually achieved among these several entities.

Control Committees. Several medical staff committees in the interdepartmental hierarchy have been mentioned, and in addition there are numerous committees concerned with various technical aspects of staff performance. Altogether, some forty major committees operate in the medical staff organization of Scopus Hospital. The structure and function of five of them will be summarized.

The medical executive committee contains twenty-six voting members, all but six of whom must be of the rank of "senior attending" or "attending" physician on the active staff. They are elected by their departments for three-year staggered terms, and may be re-elected consecutively once. The full-time directors of supportive service departments (pathology, rehabilitation, etc.) are on this committee as full voting members, but other full-time medical personnel are on it *ex officio*, without voting rights. The latter include the full-time directors of clinical departments, the executive director and director of professional services of the whole hospital, and the director of the out-patient department. Nonvoting membership is also accorded to the former elected chief of staff and the chief of staff of the sister hospital being merged with Scopus. The elected chief of staff of the entire medical staff serves as chairman of the medical executive committee.

The medical executive committee has the widest scope of authority of any unit in the medical staff. It appoints members of the standing committees, and it receives and acts upon their recommendations. It supervises and enforces medical staff discipline and arbitrates disputes, although it delegates many functions to the departments. Since the private attending physicians of the active staff constitute the majority of the medical executive committee, their voice is obviously strong. Yet the various full-time medical staff members, voting and nonvoting, promote liaison and co-ordination.

Communication between the medical staff and the board of directors of Scopus Hospital is fostered by the joint conference committee. Since such a committee is required by JCAH accreditation, it is found in all the hospitals of our study series, but at Scopus it is especially active. This is evidently due to the unusually high level of interest of Scopus board members in new developments of medical science. It is also due to the current tasks involved in welding the two hospitals into the new "medical center."

The credentials committee reviews all proposed new medical staff appointments, after the qualifications of each applicant have been determined by the appropriate department. Last year, for example, half of the forty applicants for staff membership were rejected. The reasons related not only to the applicant's specialty qualifications or lack of them but also to the unavailability of beds for admitting private patients in various departments. Credentials committee recommendations are then passed on to the medical executive committee, where as few as four of the twenty-six votes can block favorable action. Formal appointment is then made by the board of directors, but if the board disagrees with the proposed appointment the case is referred to the joint conference committee for resolution.

The medical records committee is composed of twenty-five members representing the several departments, and also the nonmedical hospital administrator and director of nurses. At monthly breakfast meetings, the committee reviews records selected either by the departments (through the full-time director or the clinical chief) or the medical record office. All cases of postoperative infection, hysterectomy in women under forty-five years, neurosurgery, long-term medical cases (thirty days or over), and all deaths are automatically reviewed. This is intended to supplement review at the departmental level. Delinquency in completion of records by individual physicians is reported by the records office to the committee which, after suitable warnings, can curtail the doctor's admitting privileges until the records are completed.

The tissue committee at Scopus Hospital meets monthly to review surgical cases about which questions have been raised by the chief pathologist. In contrast to the other hospitals of lower MSO structuring in our series, this committee not only includes this full-time laboratory specialist but it is chaired by him. Sometimes cases are referred by the medical records committee. The common reasons for review include discrepancy between pre- and postoperative diagnoses, removal of normal uterus or appendix, or the performance of dubious kinds of operative procedures. A file of questionable cases is kept, classified by surgeon, and a few such cases attributable to one doctor may lead to a recommendation to terminate his privileges.

A few other committees at Scopus with unusual characteristics may be mentioned. There is a committee on size of staff which studies the optimal allocation of beds and clinic functions to various specialty departments. A committee on patient welfare and nursing is concerned with upgrading both doctor's and nurse's performance to meet patient needs. The pharmacy committee is very active, and is headed by a full-time internist who also holds an advanced degree in pharmacology. The out-patient department committee is headed by the full-time director of this department and contains a representative from each major department. There are also special committees on professional ethics, research, staff publications, and therapeutic abortions.

For reasons discussed earlier, physicians at Scopus Hospital generally take their committee responsibilities seriously. While sometimes committee procedures may tend to delay actions, their general effect is to buttress the medical staff discipline, which at this hospital is further strengthened by the corps of full-time contractual physicians.

Documentation. The strong formal organization of the medical staff at Scopus Hospital might lead one to expect a rich body of official documents. Actually these are relatively modest. There is an official medical staff constitution and bylaws, which outlines the structure of the departments and committees and the various grades of medical staff appointment. There are also rules and regulations within some departments, and various tables of organization are posted. The general impression from numerous interviews in the hospital, however, is that written rules are lacking or not well codified. The level of documentation is lower than that of the moderately structured MSO at Pebble City Community Hospital, and the Executive Director emphasizes that there is need for tightening up. Formal reports of staff and committee meetings, on the other hand, are more diligently made than in the other less structured MSO patterns.

Informal Dynamics. The great and rapid expansion of Scopus Hospital and its medical staff in previous years resulted in many informal strategies. There were cliques and pressures from socially prominent patients and doctors in the past. These have now been largely replaced, however, by equitable and formal policies. The frequent innovations, nevertheless, have created an atmosphere of crisis in Scopus Hospital at many times, with anxiety expressed by staff members who felt their positions threatened. This was especially associated with the rapid growth of the corps of full-time contractual physicians.

At the time of our study, the prominent issue was the two-hospital merger, and there were many concerns about the effects this would have on various individuals in the medical staff hierarchy. The merger process highlighted the whole question—always in the background—of Scopus Hospital's dedication to wider community functions (education, research, care of the indigent, etc.), as compared with private in-patient service. These issues were actively discussed both in committees and in the corridors.

The informal dynamics in any large organization are inevitably influenced by the attributes of its leaders. The most important figure in Scopus is its Executive Director, nationally recognized as an authority in hospital administration. He was recruited largely for the purpose of effecting the merger of the two hospitals, and his deliberate pursuit of this goal—despite the most careful strategy—has been disquieting to some staff members. He has approached the task by trying to strengthen the over-all medical staff organization and encouraging staff committees to think through the problems and arrive at solutions themselves.

Although some personality clashes are inevitable in any organization, the important trend in the Scopus MSO is the gradual enlargement in numbers and influence of the full-time staff. This very trend is stimulating greater diligence in the departmental and committee structure of the active staff of private physicians. Informal relationships seem to be strengthening, rather than weakening, the self-discipline of the doctors on the private-practice side of this equilibrium.

MSO and the Scopus Hospital Programs. Scopus Hospital illustrates very well the interplay between medical staff organization and a broad scope of hospital programs for in-patient care, out-patient service, professional education, other community service, and research.* This 500-bed voluntary general hospital has a highly structured MSO, achieved by a coalition between a central corps of full-time contractual physicians and a carefully selected, though large, staff of attending private practitioners. The commitment of the full-time staff is virtually complete, while that of the active attending staff is also relatively high, even though its members spend most of their time in private medical practice. The out-patient, the educational, and the research programs depend heavily on the private staff, although their supervision comes from the full-time staff.

The hospital is in the process of merging with a sister hospital to form a new "Medical Center." Although the two governing boards, hospital administrations, and medical staffs have already been merged administratively, Scopus Hospital at the time of this study was still identifiable as a separate institution. Its active programs in all sectors of modern hospital service will doubtless be expanded further when the new medical center comes into full operation.

Professional authority in the medical staff organization is exercised though a dynamic partnership between two hierarchies of full-time and of private physicians that are in liaison at the level of departments as well as at the top. Co-ordination between these two lines of authority is achieved through numerous committees and frequent meetings. Legitimation of the authority of the entire medical staff and establishment of over-all hospital policies are the responsibility of a board of directors implemented by an executive director who is an administratively sophisticated physician.

Over the years the MSO at Scopus Hospital has become increasingly structured. In its early days favoritism was shown to certain influential doctors and patrons. With the advances of medical science and the widening conception of the hospital's ideal role in community health service, greater adherence to formal rules and regulations has developed. Not all of these are firmly codified in written documents, but they operate nevertheless through oral communication, which is extensive. A great many control committees both within and across departments foster this.

The MSO structure has been tightened largely through the engagement of an increasing number and proportion of full-time contractual physicians. The outstanding professional competence of these doctors and their exclusive dedication to hospital objectives have led to a gradual enlargement of their role in all aspects of hospital activity. At the same time, the attending staff continues to exert its influence to protect

---

* The detailed content of these programs will be reflected in chapters IX and X, where comparative analyses of all hospital activities are offered across the series of ten institutions.

the primacy of private in-patient care. The very objective of protecting those interests has induced a higher level of diligence in the MSO structure by the private members of the medical staff. Thus, the total medical staff contributes to the hospital's high level of community service beyond the scope of in-patient care, and also to the enrichment of quality measures within the traditional role of bed care of the sick.

These changes are not without their tensions in the Scopus Hospital evolution. Debates continue on the relative allocation of money, time, and energies to medical education, research, out-patient and in-patient care of the poor, etc., in relation to private in-patient services. The decision to proceed with the development of a new and larger medical center, formed from the merger of two hospitals, is evidence of the ascendancy of the more socially oriented viewpoint and the decline in force of those physicians and board members holding to a more traditional approach. The highly and increasingly structured MSO at Scopus Hospital not only makes possible its broadly conceived hospital program but it gradually generates new ideas for further enrichment of that program.

MEDICAL GROUP HOSPITAL—VERY HIGHLY STRUCTURED MSO

This section describes a voluntary hospital of 346 beds with a medical staff organization intimately tied to a health insurance plan providing comprehensive medical care. The care is provided through a large group practice partnership, whose members constitute the medical staff of the associated hospital. Their commitment to the hospital, therefore, is almost complete and it results, in our scheme of analysis, in a very high MSO score (80 points). This relationship is expressed in the name of the institution: Medical Group Hospital.

The Social Setting of Medical Group Hospital. Medical Group Hospital (MGH) was established in 1953 in the center of the metropolis. The medical group (or "group practice") which was to staff the hospital was already organized to serve the members of a health insurance plan. The plan was about to undergo a major expansion of membership, which could only be done by construction of a hospital of its own.

The same health insurance plan was already operating three other hospitals in the state. Construction was financed from the resources of the larger plan, and the $3,000,000 building, opened in 1953, contained 224 beds. Within a few years, growth of the plan membership required enlargement of the hospital to its current size of 346 beds, and as this study was being conducted addition of another 100-bed wing was underway.

Medical Group Hospital is actually part of a network of facilities—

both hospitals and ambulatory care centers—that have been developed to serve the population of the rapidly growing health insurance plan. Starting in the early 1930's to serve certain industrial workers, the plan greatly expanded during World War II, and then after the war opened its membership to employed groups from other industries and occupations. From a wartime enrollment of 30,000, the plan membership grew to over 1,200,000. This growth of a medical care program tied to group medical practice, instead of providing free choice of private doctor (like the Blue Shield and commercial insurance plans), was met with much opposition from the private medical profession. For a period, membership in local and state medical societies (branches of the American Medical Association) was denied to doctors associated with the plan. With growth and success, however, the idea of "prepaid group practice," embodied in the plan, came to be reluctantly accepted by the medical societies.

The nationwide growth of private group medical practice,[1] the whole evolution of health insurance, and the evidence of economies possible in the combination of these two patterns has focused great national interest on the health plan of which MGH is a part. Our interest here, however, is on one hospital—its medical staff dynamics and hospital programs. The place of MGH in a "system" of institutions makes it different from the other autonomous general hospitals reviewed so far, because its internal program is heavily influenced by the policies of the system. Our analysis of this one hospital as a separate entity should be recognized, therefore, as somewhat of an abstraction, and the relationship of MGH to its parent system, and also to the national controversy on medical care organization, must be constantly kept in mind.

Although MGH is housed in a relatively new building, it appears more "modern" from the outside than from within. This impression results from the relatively crowded atmosphere, reinforced by the apparent emphasis on function at the expense of aesthetic values. The seven-story main hospital building is on the corner of a busy thoroughfare, close to two major city arterials. It is connected from the rear to a hospital annex which houses the orthopedic and obstetrical departments and various medical group offices and clinics. Across the street is the medical group administrative building, the out-patient pharmacy, and other clinics and doctors' offices. The pathology laboratory, radiology, and physical therapy departments, and in-patient pharmacy are located in the basement of the central hospital building. Considering the bed-capacity and activity of the hospital-medical group complex, the ground area covered is relatively small. Compactness has been achieved by high-rise construction and maximum utilization of interior space.

[1] U.S. Public Health Service, *Promoting the Group Practice of Medicine*, Report of the National Conference on Group Practice, October 19–21, 1967 (Washington, 1967).

In-patient rooms are somewhat less crowded, although beds are always at a premium. At present there are thirteen private rooms and five three-bed wards. All the other rooms contain two beds each. The beds are motorized, have access to a central oxygen supply, and are connected to the nursing station by call-lights and intercom.

Since many of the health personnel serve both hospital and medical group clinics, the number of employees assigned solely to hospital functions represents an understatement of the size of the hospital staff. Counting only those personnel carried on the hospital budget, there is a total of 183 employees per 100 beds or 197 per 100 patients. The relatively small difference between these two figures is accounted for by the high hospital occupancy rate of 93 per cent.

Most hospital employees are hired by the Personnel Department, which is part of Foundation Services, Inc., a separate organization established to perform administrative services for the health plan, the hospitals, and the medical groups. Thus, personnel can be hired and transferred easily within the entire system of which MGH is a part. There is uniformity of wages, fringe benefits, and working conditions, and a generally strong *esprit de corps* has been achieved. The majority of nonprofessional employees are members of labor unions.

Operating costs of MGH are met almost entirely from the insurance premiums of the health plan members. These premiums vary with the precise health insurance benefits of the enrollment group, and they may be paid fully by the individual, shared with his employer, or sometimes paid entirely by employers. Most of the "benefit packages" pay for 125 days of hospitalization per year, plus half the cost of the remaining 240 days, without "extra charges" for any elements of in-patient care (except for cost ceilings on drugs).

The health insurance plan, which must finance out-of-hospital services as well, contracts with MGH to meet its full costs on the basis of an annual budget. But the hospital has independent legal existence under an entity known as Foundation Hospitals, Inc. (which owns the other hospitals in the same network). A small proportion of patients— between 1 and 2 per cent of admissions—are not health plan members, and they provide a minor source of additional revenue to the hospital, as does the sale of out-patient drugs. Thus, the year may end with a financial surplus or deficit, as in any voluntary hospital. In 1965, for example, there was hospital income of $7,360,000 and a net surplus of $275,000.

Since the health insurance premiums must also cover the cost of all physician services, both inside and outside the hospital, there is an important interdependency between the allotment for the hospital and that for the physicians. A larger share going to one tends to mean a smaller share going to the other. Hence, the physicians have an interest in avoiding unnecessary hospital admissions or other wastages in hospital financing. This is achieved largely through the basic decision on hospital bed supply in the whole health plan system, which has been at a level of about 2.0 beds per 1,000 insured persons—considerably lower than prevails for the general population. With this limited bed supply in MGH, in relation to the population it serves, there are constant pressures for efficient use of the beds that are available. A small percentage of the health plan premium income is reserved for community service programs of the hospital, in addition to care of its own beneficiaries.

Unlike the other voluntary or proprietary hospitals in our study, MGH has a fairly well defined population to serve—the members of the associated health insurance plan. About 200,000 of these have access to MGH, although some may occasionally seek hospital care outside their plan. Likewise, an occasional noninsured patient may be admitted to MGH in an emergency or because of some special tie to one of the medical group doctors. Over 95 per cent of MGH patients, however, are members of the insurance plan, and they have been enrolled almost entirely through employed groups. These include industrial workers, government employees, university personnel, etc., almost all living within a thirty-mile radius of the hospital. A basic policy of the health plan is to enroll persons only from employed groups whose members are given a choice among various types of health insurance coverage. Thus, the individuals choosing this plan are not "captives," but have expressed their willingness to be served by MGH and the other facilities in the network.

There are no exclusions of medical benefits for treatment of pre-existing disorders. The hospital, however, does not accept patients with contagious diseases, including tuberculosis, for which government facilities are available. Industrial injury cases, financed under the workmen's compensation laws, are accepted, but the costs are then payable by the other insurance carrier. The ethnic composition of the plan membership, and hence the MGH patients, is quite diversified; it is estimated at about 14 per cent Negro, 21 per cent Oriental and Mexican-American, and 65 per cent "other white" persons. The aged are somewhat underrepresented, there being about 4 per cent of members over sixty-five years of age, compared with 9 per cent in the general population. After retirement from employment, aged persons can retain their membership as individuals and also belong to the plan under the national Medicare Law (through special financial arrangements with the government).

Because of the ties of MGH to the health insurance plan, the distribution of administrative power in the hospital is more complicated than in the sovereign hospitals previously described. There are actually four interlocking administrative entities in the entire system, to which we have already alluded and which may be summarized as: (1) the Foundation hospitals (including MGH and several others), (2) the Foundation medical groups, (3) the Foundation Health Insurance Plan, and (4) the Foundation Services (for personnel and other administrative functions). All four of these entities are repeated in various regions of the western states, where the program operates, and all of them are ultimately responsible to a single Foundation board of directors located in another city.

The operations of this entire system need only be briefly summarized, because our interest is in one sub-unit, the Medical Group Hospital. MGH is legally owned by Foundation Hospitals, Inc., which is a chartered nonprofit corporation. The Foundation Health Insurance Plan supports the hospital operating costs, by contract, as noted earlier, and the Foundation Services, Inc., performs various administrative functions. The Foundation Medical Group is legally a partnership, with the right to earn profits, and encompassing the doctors on the active staff of Medical Group Hospital.

MGH has a hospital administrator, who is responsible to a regional hospital administrator of the Foundation Hospitals, Inc. Thus, there is no board of directors within MGH, but only at the much higher level where the integrated Foundation board of directors co-ordinates all four entities in the system. The medical staff of MGH comes under a corresponding form of authority in the Foundation Medical Group, which as a partnership organization has a medical director. It is obvious that these parallel executives—the hospital administrator and the medical director—must work harmoniously together, since each is responsible vertically through a different line of authority. Co-ordination is achieved through almost daily contact, and also through meetings of the key executives from all four organizational entities four times a year. The top board of directors is involved only in major policy decisions on such matters as the construction of new hospitals, the general level of premiums and benefits in the health insurance plans, and the allocation of moneys between the hospitals and the medical groups.

The medical staff organization of MGH, as we shall see below, fulfills the requirements of the Joint Commission on Accreditation of Hospitals. Its basic authority structure, however, is dependent on the rules in the partnership of the Foundation Medical Group, which has its own officers and functions. The functions include the provision of general medical care, both inside and outside the hospital, and are therefore much broader than those of the typical medical staff.

MEDICAL STAFF ORGANIZATION OF MEDICAL GROUP HOSPITAL

Composition. The active medical staff of Medical Group Hospital consists of 214 physicians associated with the Foundation Medical Group partnership. All are on full-time or part-time salaries, as discussed below.

Another 85 physicians with the Medical Group are either general practitioners located at the hospital or physicians (either general practitioners or specialists) attached to eight satellite clinics, who are not, strictly speaking, on the hospital staff. The active staff physicians are located in offices within the hospital itself or in three clinic buildings adjacent to it. Their entire medical practice for both ambulatory and hospitalized patients is carried out from these locations.

All of the 214 active-staff physicians are qualified specialists—about two-thirds board-eligible and one-third board-certified. There are no associate staff or consultant staff physicians as such. There is a "courtesy staff" of 252 physicians, however, made up of specialists who are occasionally called for consultation, but their role in the hospital is minimal.

Appointment Procedure. Appointment to the active staff of the hospital involves engagement of the doctor in the Foundation Medical Group. This is usually done through a process beginning with interviews with the medical director of the group and the chief of the department in which the doctor will work. If the applicant is approved at these screening interviews he submits a formal application, including professional references. For work in the hospital, specialty board eligibility is required. The medical director, with the approval of the relevant departmental chief, can appoint new physicians directly, since the initial appointment does not involve partnership status. Recruitment is both passive and active; many doctors apply, but others are invited on the basis of nationwide tours of hospital training centers by the medical director and his assistant directors.

Once a physician is a member of the medical group, he must submit a formal application for appointment to the staff of the hospital, but this is obviously only a formality. His appointment is then legally finalized by action of the central board of directors of the whole network of Foundation hospitals. So long as the physician remains attached to the medical group his staff appointment is automatically renewed each year.

The Foundation Medical Group is cautious about inviting a physician into full partnership. He must serve as a salaried employee of the Group for three years and then be voted on favorably by 75 per cent of the partners. Once partnership status is achieved, a doctor may be removed by a majority vote of the partners, but this happens very rarely. There is a mandatory retirement age of sixty-five years, after which a physician may continue as an employee. Thus, both the selection and retention of members on the active medical staff of MGH are essentially functions of the Foundation Medical Group, which has separate legal existence as a partnership.

Although there is a credentials committee for control of professional privileges in the hospital, actual control is vested in the chiefs of the different departments. Full privileges are allowed within the scope of each specialty, and "limited privileges" may be given to a physician in fields outside his specialty. General practitioners in the out-patient clinics do not have admitting privileges, but they may occasionally be authorized to do minor surgery or normal obstetrics under the supervision of departmental specialists.

The Department of Surgery, which is most concerned with control of privileges, has two categories of surgeons: senior and associate. The senior surgeons are fully qualified in their specialties. The associate surgeons are completing the last two years of their residency training under the approved preceptor programs. Associates, therefore, do operations only under the direct supervision of senior surgeons on a rotating "buddy system." Upon completion of the period of supervised work, associate surgeons who remain in the program advance to senior status.

As for obligations to the hospital, the active-staff physicians are required to attend at least 50 per cent of business and scientific meetings, and all the meetings, unless excused, of the committees to which they are assigned. The requirement, noted in Scopus Hospital and some others, that active-staff members must work in out-patient clinics would have no meaning in MGH, since virtually all staff members serve also in the out-patient services of the Medical Group program.

Appointment to the MGH medical staff is ultimately based on a systematic consideration of the needs of the health insurance plan membership for doctors in certain specialties. A rough formula, applied by the medical group, stipulates one doctor per 1,000 insured persons or 100 doctors per 100,000 distributed among specialties as follows:

General practitioners	20
Internists	30
Pediatricians	15
Obstetrician–gynecologists	10
General surgeons	10
Orthopedists	2.5
Radiologists	2.5
Urologists	2
Otorhinolaryngologists	2
Ophthalmologists	2
Dermatologists	2
Pathologists	2
All doctors	100

The achievement of these ratios is not always possible; in 1965 the total was about 90 doctors per 100,000 and the mixture was not precisely as stipulated. The proportion of specialists on the hospital staff, however, is geared to an assessment of patient-care needs rather than to the specialty composition of the doctors who happen to apply to this particular hospital.

Commitment. Seventy-two per cent of the MGH active staff are full-time with the Foundation Medical Group, and the balance, while part-time, are on salaried appointments. The time commitment to the hospital, therefore, is high. Even when he is in his office treating ambulatory patients, the Medical Group doctor is not faced with divided loyalties involving his income; his earnings are not affected by the locale of his work.

Whether they are full partners or employees of the Foundation Medical Group, all hospital staff members are essentially "contractual" —but not with the hospital. Their contractual relationships are with the partnership which, in turn, has an over-all agreement to staff the hospital or, more accurately, to serve the hospital needs of members of the Foundation Health Insurance Plan. While there are obvious variations by specialty, it has been estimated that about 75 per cent of the total time of these physicians is spent in ambulatory medical care activities outside the hospital. Thus, calculation of the "contractual physicians" engaged in hospital work (see chapter IX) would require taking about 25 per cent of the 214 staff members, to yield a figure of 52.5 such physicians in MGH.

The employment status of Medical Group doctors who are not full partners, but are working within the partnership, may be full-time or part-time, and some may be paid simply on a per diem basis. The full-time employed doctors, furthermore, may be on the ladder of advancement toward partner status or they may be temporary; in the latter case, they do not acquire rights to longevity benefits, educational leave, etc. All "full-time" employees and partners, however, agree to participate in no medical practice outside the Foundation Medical Group. Of the total 299 doctors in the organization in 1965, 50 per cent were partners, 28 per cent were full-time employees, and 22 per cent were part-time employees.

The scheme of remuneration of these physicians is quite complicated. In addition to basic salaries, there are various supplementary awards based on length of tenure and, for partners, shares of the profits. There are numerous fringe benefits for retirement, vacations, life insurance, educational leave, malpractice insurance, etc. The basic salaries depend on specialty qualifications and are designed to be competitive with the net earnings of private practitioners in each field. Chiefs of departments also get salary supplements. The money for salaries is all derived from the insurance plan premiums, and it is important to realize that payments to doctors are not related to the specific units of services that each provides.

Regarding affiliations with other hospitals as a reflection of commitment, it is obvious that these are very few. Only some of the part-time employed doctors have such affiliations, but the partners and full-time employed doctors, constituting 78 per cent of the Foundation Medical Group, and a higher percentage of the hospital's active staff have no outside hospital ties.

Departmentalization. The departments of the MGH medical staff are identical with those of the Foundation Medical Group. There are thirteen major departments, and included within some of these are sections, numbering twelve. Each department is administered by a chief, and the larger ones have assistant chiefs. These positions are filled through appointment by the medical director, rather than through election, and the term of office is indefinite.

The departmental chiefs supervise the professional work in their departments, and they also assist the medical director in selection of new physicians, preparation of budgets, and planning of new services. They supervise the professional education programs. They investigate complaints from patients. The effectiveness of all departmental functions is obviously very much dependent on the leadership of the chiefs, and their tenure tends to be long. Departmental administrative meetings are held weekly.

The chiefs of departments confer frequently with the medical director on specific problems, and formal meetings of all the chiefs with the medical director are held monthly or bi-monthly. These persons constitute, in effect, the medical executive committee of the hospital staff, in terms of JCAH requirements, though it is evident that the scope of this committee is wider than in the average hospital. Co-ordination among departments is also achieved by memoranda, by communications of the hospital administrator, and by frequent personal contacts of doctors, nurses and administrators throughout the whole hospital.

Control Committees. In hospitals with more loosely structured medical staff organization, we have noted that numerous committees compensate for the weakness of an authority system at the departmental level. At MGH, where the departmental hierarchy is strong, the control committees count less. There are actually seventeen committees, but they are not considered very important because their functions are performed largely by the departmental framework. The traditional committees on medical records and tissue review meet monthly, but have few problems to tackle. Surveillance of physician performance in the hospital is a daily responsibility of the departmental chiefs. There is a patient care committee, however, which is regarded as important; it contains the hospital administrator and the director of nursing, along with the departmental chiefs. This committee copes with a wide range of technical problems—including infections, stop-orders on drugs, patient complaints, bed utilization etc.—that in other hospitals might be assigned to several separate committees.

Documentation. The medical staff of Medical Group Hospital has a constitution, bylaws, rules and regulations, in conformity with JCAH requirements, but they are simply part of the documentation of the Foundation Medical Group as a whole. The hospital staff, after all, differs from the medical group only in its provision for courtesy members and in the participation of residents in training (see below). The various departments also have their written rules, which vary from complete manuals to collections of memoranda. The full-time presence of virtually all active-staff members, however, leads to much reliance on oral communication.

Minutes are kept of important committee and departmental meetings and are circulated among medical staff officers and the hospital administration. Formal written reports do not come from the hospital staff, as such, but from the medical group and the health insurance plan. They are mainly statistical summaries on the volume of work being done and are used to support claims to the Foundation board of directors for expansion of staff or equipment, or modification of the scheme of payment by the health insurance plan to the medical group or to the hospital.

Informal Dynamics. Personal relationships among the members of the MGH medical staff appear to be congenial. They are not in competition with each other for access to hospital beds in the same way as doctors in private practice. Frictions may develop in connection with workloads, but these can usually be resolved by discussion between the parties involved.

Work in the Foundation Medical Group involves a built-in selection process, since physicians joining tend to remain only if they find the atmosphere of full-time, prepaid group practice agreeable. The principal stress comes from the pressure of work, which sometimes compels the physician to devote less time to patients than he would like. (The same pressures may be felt in private practice, but in the medical group adjustment to these pressures is not so clearly in the individual doctor's hands.) The pressures are associated not only with the steady growth of health insurance plan membership but also with rising rates of utilization generally. To adjust to the demands, additional physicians can be recruited, but this means a decline in average income of all the doctors, unless the over-all allotment of money from the health plan to the medical group can simultaneously be increased. Such an increase is possible only by (a) a relative reduction of the allotment to the hospital budget or (b) an increase in plan premiums. The latter might retard membership growth of the Foundation Plan, as a whole, in competition with other health insurance plans in the community.

Thus, there is a steady, if submerged, contention among the doctors, the hospital, and the health insurance plan. In spite of this, an equilibrium is attained in various ways. One is the use of a standard ratio of doctors to plan members of about one per 1,000, which has been generally agreed upon. Another is the broadly satisfactory financial awards paid to the doctors, earnings which they know depend on their own hard work. Another factor is the conviction, which grows in the doctors who stay in the medical group, that the basic concept of prepaid group practice is sound, even though it requires some compromises in their personal sovereignty. Those doctors who are not satisfied with these circumstances tend to leave the organization.

Since a major influence on the financial allocation to the hospital is the number of beds constructed, and since a frugal attitude toward this question means that more money will be available for medical salaries, there is little doubt that Foundation Medical Group doctors become adjusted to a relatively low rate of hospitalization of their patients. Here again, doctors who are dissatisfied with this restriction are likely to leave the medical group, but it is important to report that the great majority who remain for one or two years stay on to become permanent partners. The selection process, reviewed earlier, works effectively to weed out incompatible physicians, for whatever reason. As physicians approach retirement their competence may decline, but adjustments can be made through appropriate professional assignments in the hospital more readily than in a loosely structured MSO setting. The structure of the clinical departments, with so much authority vested in the chiefs, makes this feasible.

Prepaid group practice, like the Foundation Medical Group, tends to attract initially many different types of doctors. Those who stay and advance in the system, however, are probably the doctors who are satisfied with good, if not gigantic, incomes; who enjoy a professional setting where they are relieved from the business side of fee-for-service medical practice; who appreciate the free access to other medical colleagues without fear of "losing" the patient; and who generally are happy in a cooperative team environment.

Some of these physicians also have competence for and enjoy leadership roles. It is these men who come to be chiefs of the departments and to acquire other administrative responsibilities. Administrative tasks have multiplied as the health insurance plan has grown, so that there are many opportunities for "dominant personalities" to express themselves constructively through the formal structure—probably more in MGH than in less tightly structured institutions. In the latter, the strong individual may often exert his influence only through the informal dynamics of the system and thus cause various conflicts. At MGH the informal dynamics are generally supportive of the formal structure because of the process by which leadership positions are acquired and by which long-term membership on the medical staff evolves.

MSO and the Medical Group Hospital Program. The relationship between the medical staff organization and the content of the hospital program at Medical Group Hospital is probably more striking than in any of the other hospitals so far reviewed in this study. By strict legal definition, the MGH and the Foundation Medical Group are separate entities. Yet, each is almost entirely dependent upon the other so that, for all practical purposes, they can be viewed as two segments of a tripartite organization, the third segment being the sponsoring Foundation Health Plan. The physicians of the medical group are automatically members of the hospital's medical staff organization. Although there is also a large courtesy staff, these "outside" physicians play a very minor role in hospital activities. All members of the active medical staff are salaried physicians, 78 per cent of whom are full-time.

The medical staff organization of MGH is unusual not only because it is composed mostly of full-time salaried physicians but also because the population served by the medical group and the hospital are identical. Thus, the medical staff structure controls patient care both inside and outside of the hospital. The benefits of this control for both patients and physicians are reflected in the generally low rate of elective hospital admissions among the eligible population and the wide range of out-patient and in-patient services provided in the hospital, the associated medical group offices, and the satellite clinics.

The "very highly structured" designation of the MGH medical staff is due not only to the high level of commitment of its salaried staff. It is attributable also to the deliberate process of recruitment and selection of its members, the high proportion of qualified specialists, the day-to-day professional relationships and surveillance, and the substantial responsibility for quality standards exercised by departmental chiefs of long tenure. In the light of this authority system, it is noteworthy that the various control committees, which play a compensating disciplinary role in the more loosely structured MSO's, are of relatively minor importance at the MGH.

The departmental chiefs and, at the top, the medical director, supervise physician performance outside as well as inside the hospital. It is the total work of the physician that is evaluated when the medical group partners vote on whether he should be invited into the partnership after a three-year trial period. The closely knit organization permits economical, yet judicious, use of auxiliary personnel in many ways not seen in the ordinary hospital. Nurse-anesthetists give anesthesia under medical supervision, optometrists do most of the visual refractions, and much of the medical history-taking is done by nurses.

The greatest problem facing the Foundation Medical Group is the heavy demand for services due to the steady expansion of health plan membership and the increasing rate of utilization. Enlargement of the medical staff is continuously necessary, and this is not easy to achieve in the face of competing attractions of private medical practice. There are also financial dilemmas, because additional physicians may mean lower incomes for each, unless health insurance premiums can be raised (which creates other difficulties). The dynamics of the whole system, however, favor a frugal use of the hospital and maximum service on an outpatient basis.[2]

The health insurance mechanism lies at the base of most of the characteristics of the medical care program of which MGH is a part. Because it establishes eligibility for a defined population, it induces in the doctors and the hospital a sense of responsibility for their care. This responsibility, however, would probably not have been assumed through the wide range of ambulatory health services, the measures of quality promotion, the preventive services, the home care program, the regionalization benefits, the educational and research programs, etc., without the highly structured framework of the Foundation Medical Group. The professional consciousness evolving in the group, moreover, has created favorable attitudes toward medical innovations—e.g., home care programs, multiphasic screening, rehabilitation, etc.—which in loosely structured and individualistic medical staffs are often greeted with hostility. Pressures on the medical staff have also made it favorable to supporting administrative techniques which can increase efficiency without sacrificing quality.

Despite the large regional administrative structure of which MGH and its medical staff are a part, there is no question about the strength of the doctors. Not as individuals, it is true, but as a group they select their

[2] George S. Perrott, "Federal Employees Health Benefits Program: Utilization of Hospital Services," *Amer. J. Public Health*, 56:57–64 (January 1966).

own colleagues, supervise the paramedical staff, decide on hospital admissions, and control all the technical details of diagnosis and treatment. The size of the out-patient service has bred complaints from both patients and doctors, but it is noteworthy that within the hospital, patient satisfaction appears to be high. (A comparative study of state government employees, covered by different health insurance plans, showed a higher level of satisfaction in the Foundation Hospitals system than in other general hospitals.) Any impersonality that marks the out-patient care given by the Foundation Medical Group appears to be a function of the supply-and-demand disparity rather than the organizational structure as such.[3] In terms of the range of in-patient and extramural services and the various features of a hospital's wider community role, the MSO structure of Medical Group Hospital seems to yield an impressive record of performance.

PUBLIC HOSPITAL—VERY HIGHLY STRUCTURED MSO

This section describes a general hospital built, sponsored, and operated by a unit of local government. Dedicated mainly to serving the poor, it is financed almost wholly from public revenues. Public Hospital has 729 beds and, by our scheme of analysis, an MSO score of 82.

The Setting and Background of Public Hospital. The impressive modern structure that houses Public Hospital is an outgrowth of temporary facilities used for military purposes in World War II. At that time, the federal government had constructed about seventy-five barrack-type buildings on fifty acres of land, and after the war, in 1946, the local municipality purchased these to serve as a long-term care facility for the chronically ill. With rapid population growth, the city government decided that a new general hospital was needed on this site, and in the mid-1950's a bond issue for the purpose was approved by public vote. The current 729-bed hospital was completed in 1960, but many of the old frame barracks are still used for patients with chronic chest diseases or to accommodate the hospital's expanding research program.

The seven-story modern building stands in sharp contrast to the tawdry commercial buildings and low-cost wooden houses of this section of the metropolitan area. It is easily accessible by highway, although public transportation is not well developed. The reinforced concrete structure is fully air-conditioned. Attached to the main building are a two-story out-patient clinic structure and a large two-story laboratory. The cost of construction was nearly $12,000,000.

[3] Rashi Fein, *The Doctor Shortage: An Economic Diagnosis* (Washington: Brookings Institution, 1967).

The typical nursing unit contains fifty-six beds divided among rooms with four beds, two beds, or single beds; two of the four-bed rooms on each floor permit conversion to "intensive care units" if necessary. Each room has piped suction and oxygen, a toilet, and an audio visual nurse's call system by each bed. In the center of each hospital floor is a combination of service units, including a nurses' station, examination and treatment room, small laboratory, utility room, doctors' office, head nurse's office, pantry, storage space, and bathroom with showers.

In 1965 there were over 1,600 full-time employees in Public Hospital, including 236 full-time staff physicians and doctors-in-training. A substantial share of these personnel are for the out-patient service, but by the conventional ratios they amount to 223 employees per 100 beds or 291 per 100 in-patients.

Public Hospital, like hundreds of such local government facilities throughout the United States, was designed to serve the poor—either recipients of public assistance or other poor persons who are "medically indigent." With the impact, since 1966, of new national Medicare and Medicaid legislation and the easier access of poor persons to voluntary hospitals, the sharp line of eligibility for care in this type of hospital is changing, but at the time of our field study, Public Hospital was still restricted to service for the poor.[4]

State law charges local governments with the responsibility of caring for their indigent sick, authorizing the counties to levy the necessary taxes. The eligible patient must have legal residence in the state for three years and in the county for one year. There are other local government hospitals in the same metropolitan county, and the "catchment area" of Public Hospital is estimated to contain about 1,000,000 people. Except for emergency cases which are, of course, accepted from anywhere, patients using Public Hospital must reside in this area and meet the test of poverty.

Over 90 per cent of the operating costs of Public Hospital come from tax revenues—mainly from local government sources but partially from state and federal sources. The latter are payments on behalf of care to categorical public assistance recipients (families with dependent children, blind, etc.). Thus, although patients are expected to pay what they can afford and bills are actually sent to them (which may be payable in the future from life insurance benefits if the patient dies), hardly 10 per cent of the hospital income is derived from private or voluntary insurance payments.

The hospital operates on an annual budget which must be approved

[4] See for example: Commission on the Delivery of Health Services, *Community Health Services for New York City* (New York: Frederick A. Praeger, 1968). Also: Jan de Hartog, *The Hospital* (New York: Atheneum, 1964).

by the Municipal Council. In 1965 the approved budget was over $11,200,000. Eighty-one per cent of expenditures were for salaries, of which 15 per cent went to doctors, 29 per cent to nursing personnel, and 37 per cent to other hospital employees. This budget covers most of the educational expenses, which are considerable (see below), but the research program is supported by other special grants.

Since Public Hospital is owned and operated by the municipal government, general policies are laid down by the Municipal Council and implemented by a local official Department of Hospitals. Within the hospital, the top executive is the hospital administrator, who of course has various assistants. Medical services, however, come under the supervision of a full-time medical director, who likewise is aided by assistant medical directors. On the formal organizational chart, the medical director is subordinate to the hospital administrator, but in reality these two men work as a team. The medical director and his assistants are basically responsible for formulation and implementation of policies governing the work of the medical staff.

Thus, there is really a dual and co-ordinated authority system. The Municipal Department of Hospitals, as an arm of the Municipal Council, holds the ultimate authority and controls the purse strings, but day-to-day operating authority is delegated to the two top executives. There are bound to be some differences in emphasis and judgment between the hospital administrator, who must assure fiscal responsibility, and the medical director, who must face the demands of the doctors supervising patient care, but an equilibrium between these two viewpoints is maintained by their complete interdependency. On a day-to-day basis, the two men obviously influence each other, and there is enough leeway in decision-making within a stated budget, as we shall see, to permit innovation and creativity.

MEDICAL STAFF ORGANIZATION IN PUBLIC HOSPITAL

The medical staff structure of Public Hospital is especially complicated not only because of the hospital's size and its wide range of educational and other organized community services but because its government sponsorship has induced certain administrative devices to permit staff autonomy for certain purposes. A separate and legally incorporated "Medical Staff Association" accordingly plays a special role which will be discussed below.

Staff Composition. The total medical staff (1965) contains 452 doctors, divided between 65 full-time salaried physicians and an active attending staff of part-time doctors numbering 387. Unlike the voluntary Scopus Hospital which has a somewhat similar distribution, however, the latter doctors do not serve private patients in the hospital, although nearly all of them maintain private medical offices and have private patients in other hospitals. Eighty-seven per cent of the total staff are qualified as specialists. In addition, a substantial share of the medical service is rendered by a large house staff of 176 interns, residents, and fellows.

The core of the staff consists of the sixty-five doctors (including one dentist) on full-time salaries. There are three levels of positions: (a) chiefs of departments, (b) head physicians, and (c) "staff" physicians. The interns and residents are supervised by the head physicians who are in charge of the smaller sections into which the departments (ten of them —see below) are divided. All the full-time departmental chiefs are board-certified specialists, as are most of the section heads, the balance being board-eligible. Government regulations require also that the medical director must be a board-certified specialist, as well as having had at least three years of appropriate administrative experience.

The attending staff of 387 part-time doctors is entirely "active," with no "associate" or "courtesy" components, such as are found in most voluntary hospitals. It consists of (a) senior attending physicians; (b) attending physicians; and (c) consultants. Some of the older senior attending physicians are general practitioners, but all the younger doctors are at least specialty board-eligible. The consultants are all highly qualified specialists, most of whom are faculty members in the medical school with which Public Hospital is affiliated.

The "house staff" includes 127 residents broadly distributed across all the principal specialties. The 44 interns are predominantly on rotating schedules among several specialties. On each specialty service, the chief resident carries much responsibility for the work of the interns and junior residents, although they are all ultimately responsible to the full-time department chiefs.

Tying together the attending and full-time staffs and performing various MSO functions is a separate entity known as the Public Hospital Attending Staff Association. (Originally this body did not include the full-time salaried staff, as it now does, but the restrictive adjective "attending" is still retained in the title. This Association has its own constitution and bylaws, elected officers, and committees. The board of directors includes the officers plus, *ex officio*, the appointed medical director of the hospital, the hospital administrator, and the deans of the medical and dental schools in the affiliated university. Incorporated as a nonprofit organization, this body serves as a vehicle for receipt for medical fees on behalf of some patients from insurance carriers—fees not payable to the individual doctors under the law. Second, it can receive research and training grants from the federal government or other sources outside the bureaucratic structure of local government. All the funds of the

Attending Staff Association are used for educational and research purposes.

Appointment Procedure. For members of the full-time staff, the appointment procedure starts with application to the chief of the specialty department in which a doctor seeks a position. After interview, study of letters of reference, etc. the proposed appointment is reviewed by the credentials committee of the Attending Staff Association. From here it is sent, not to a hospital board of directors (since there is none), but to the Civil Service Commission of the municipal government, where the salary is determined and the appointment is finalized. Most of the full-time physicians are also appointed to "clinical professorships" in the affiliated medical school. All new appointments are probationary for six months, after which they are considered indefinite and terminable only for cause.

Part-time physicians on the attending staff apply for appointment through the credentials committee of the Staff Association. Approved applications are then referred to the medical director, who is authorized to finalize the appointment on behalf of the city government. These appointments are on an annual basis, with renewal dependent on the doctor's diligence in attending clinics, teaching rounds, and performing other duties. It is considered a valuable learning opportunity and evidence of professional merit for private physicians to hold appointments on the Public Hospital attending staff.

Professional privileges are granted at the department level by decision of the full-time chief. Since many of the new appointees to both full-time and attending staffs are former residents in the hospital, their abilities are well known. Control of privileges is based on the close day-to-day associations of the full-time and part-time staffs rather than on written definitions of professional scope.

Commitment. The staff composition implies the varying degrees of commitment to the hospital of its different types of members. The sixty-five full-time salaried or contractual physicians obviously have high commitment. Almost all their professional activity takes place within the hospital, with no diversions from private office practice or affiliation with other hospitals. Each year there is about a 12 per cent turnover in the full-time staff, and this is due mostly to movement of some physicians up the professional career ladder to full-time academic posts in medical schools. In fact, the opportunity for advancement from the Public Hospital full-time staff to regular university appointments is one of the attractions to meritorious young doctors and one of the reinforcements of the psychological commitment of the full-time staff.

Although the full-time medical staff members are not diverted by the demands of private practice, there are some points of conflict between patient-care duties and educational or research activities. Criticisms from the Municipal Council about "excessive" preoccupation with research led to a time-survey of one week's activities in 1965. It was found that the average full-time staff member worked 55 hours per week in the hospital, of which 6.2 hours or about 11 per cent of time, was spent specifically on research. The time spent on education was not analytically separable, since it is essentially part of the patient-care process. All these activities, in any event, are within the hospital arena and constitute an expression of commitment to the hospital's over-all goals.

The commitment of the attending staff, of course, is much lower. Most of these physicians are busy private practitioners who spend two to four hours per week, for six months a year, in the hospital. They participate in patient care both on the wards and in the out-patient clinics, but their role has declined as the size of the full-time staff and the house staff has increased. Perhaps the attending staff doctors have come to derive as much from the hospital in the way of learning as they contribute in the form of service; at the same time they contribute to the teaching of interns and residents through attendance of ward rounds, journal clubs, etc. The relative strength of the attending physicians in the MSO structure has been declining as the influence of the full-time staff has been rising.

Departmentalization. There are ten major departments of the medical staff, and the largest—such as medicine and surgery—have several sections. Within each department is a line of authority from chief down to intern; in the most highly developed ones the hierarchy is as follows: (1) chief of department; (2) head physician (for a section); (3) staff physician; (4) chief resident; (5) senior resident; (6) resident; and (7) intern. These ranks apply mainly to the full-time staff; it is at the third echelon of "staff physician" that the part-time attending staff members usually do their work.

The department chiefs have great authority. They are appointed only after clinical, teaching, and administrative skills have been well demonstrated. They are responsible for the assignment of duties to all staff members and supervision of all patient care. They also plan and supervise the whole educational program, and most are actively engaged also in medical research. Each department has its own administrative committee, meeting once to three times per week. These committees review cases, discuss general policies of patient care, and advise on teaching and research activities.

Interdepartmental co-ordination is achieved through the responsibility of the department chiefs to the medical director of the hospital via an assistant medical director. Problems of individual patient care are usually settled between the chief and the assistant medical director, and the medical director is only involved in major policy issues. Each week formal meetings are held between all the department chiefs, both medical directors, and the director of nursing. While relationships between the chiefs and the directors are not excessively formal, the lines of authority are clear. The directors, appointed as executives by the city government, are charged with enforcing government policies on care of the poor. Sometimes this requires written directives to a department chief, though ordinarily oral advice and discussion are adequate. It is only rarely that a department chief is subject to any disciplinary action for failing to abide by administrative policies. The give-and-take of "orders" tends to be more gracefully accepted in this type of highly structured MSO, where the team members are accustomed to working together, than in the more loosely structured medical staffs, where each physician tends to guard his autonomy.

The attending staff physicians participate only minimally in the formal departmental structure. They have an elected president of the Attending Staff Association, but he does not have the usual power of a chief of staff in a loosely structured MSO; the medical director at Public Hospital is more nearly equivalent to that role. The more senior attending physicians and consultants, however, can exercise certain informal influences on medical staff policies, as will be discussed below.

Control Committees. Aside from the administrative committees in each department, there are twenty-three committees in the medical staff, with functions which cut across the several departments. Because of the strength of the departmental structure, the committees in Public Hospital seem to be relatively less important than in more loosely structured MSO's, but they still perform several technical functions. Committee memberships are characterized by great stability for the chairmen and key members from the full-time staff, with rotation of members from the attending staff and also from the residents on the house staff. About half of the control committees meet at least once a month and the balance less frequently.

The most important committee has already been mentioned, in connection with interdepartmental co-ordination—the chiefs of staff committee which meets with the medical directors each week. It is roughly equivalent to the medical executive committee of the typical voluntary hospital, but it does not have the latter's ultimate power. Its responsibility is essentially to discuss problems with and advise the medical director, who must exercise the final executive authority in the medical staff. Obviously, however, this power is seldom exercised without the concurrence and support of the chiefs of staff committee.

The medical records committee meets monthly, and is composed of representatives of the main departments. Although each department is responsible for the completion of its own patients' charts, this committee reviews a sample of all discharged case records. It studies discrepancies between admission and discharge diagnoses, the length-of-stay, provision for follow-up care, and the recording of information that might have medico-legal significance. Problems noted are brought to the attention of the departments.

The therapeutics committee is considered relatively important because it is responsible for maintenance and revision of a drug formulary of generic products. Each active-staff doctor is given a copy of the formulary, which indexes drugs by their function as well as alphabetically and contains information on dosage, form of preparation, and brand-name equivalents. This committee also gives special attention to drug reactions. The chief pharmacist sits on the committee, along with department representatives.

A somewhat unusual function is carried out by the standardization committee which advises on the purchase of equipment and supplies. The objective is to prevent proliferation of items from competing manufacturers and to spend the limited allotments wisely. Ultimately, this committee advises the hospital administrator, who is responsible for all purchases.

It is of interest that the tissue committee is scheduled to meet only six times a year because surgical decisions are made largely on a team basis in the Department of Surgery. The committee is dominated by pathologists. A random check is made of all postoperative tissue reports, and certain procedures are occasionally subjected to special study. Only rarely are nonpathological tissues discovered, and disciplinary action has been advised only a few times.

The intern–resident committee has both advisory and disciplinary functions. It contains in its roster interns and residents, as well as full-time staff members. The committee establishes general rules of conduct for the house staff and also hears grievances. While formal disciplinary responsibilities rest with the medical director, the committee is the first level of review of problems and it advises him.

The research committee has a special role for the Attending Staff Association and is very active. Eight of its fifteen members are full-time departmental chiefs, and it contains also the hospital administrator and a full-time research administrator employed directly by the Staff Association. The importance of this committee is reflected by its having a formal written set of regulations and several subcommittees.

Documentation. All employees of Public Hospital, including the full-time medical staff, are subject to the regulations in the general Administrative Code of the municipal government. A copy of this document along with a special booklet on the conditions of employment within Public Hospital are distributed to all new employees.

Formal written rules and regulations are also issued in the hospital for each of the departments and services. With respect to the medical staff, the most important set of written rules is found in an orientation booklet prepared mainly for interns and residents. This 100-page document specifies house staff responsibilities, along with explanation of the programs and policies of such interdepartmental units as the dietary department, nursing department, medical records, the library, social service, and the volunteer program. Each major department and its rules are also described in this booklet.

The medical staff constitution and bylaws, consistent with JCAH requirements, are issued by the Public Hospital Attending Staff Association and given to each attending as well as full-time doctor. The research committee, as noted, also has its own special set of written regulations. Because of the accountability of the Public Hospital medical staff to a government agency outside the hospital walls, the rules of conduct are specified rather formally in published documents.

Informal Dynamics. As in almost any large organization, there are differences in the interests and goals of various participants in the work of Public Hospital. These differences revolve mainly around the triple demands of patient care, teaching, and research, which may partly reinforce each other but are also partly competitive.

From the hospital administration's viewpoint, the primary purpose of the hospital is patient care. The teaching program for interns and residents is intimately tied to this, but the linkage depends on supervision by the full-time staff. Some of these physicians, however, spend a great share of their time in the research laboratories, neglecting these supervisory functions. The part-time attending staff members, moreover, are sometimes more concerned with their own educational enrichment at the hospital than with their patient-care duties on the wards or in the clinics; the demands of their private practices may also lead them to cut corners on time spent in the hospital. The consultant staff members from the medical school may give disproportionate attention to the unusual cases of "teaching interest," to the neglect of other patients. The interns and residents may become so much focused on the technical details of diagnosis as to lose sight of the human needs of their patients.

These differences in viewpoint and priorities are bound to lead to some tensions in the day-to-day work at Public Hospital. These are not always dysfunctional, since it is the research and educational opportunities that attract the most competent doctors to the medical staff, both full-time and part-time, and the by-products of these interests certainly yield long-term improvements in the quality of patient care. But in the short run the immediate needs of patients may be neglected, and the municipal government, through its appointed hospital administrator, must be concerned about these. The most serious conflicts have concerned the time spent by full-time physicians on their nonclinical research in the laboratories and vivarium. Yet, the interns and residents have indicated in a formal opinion survey that they learn most about diagnosis and therapy from the teaching of the full-time doctors.

To some extent, conflicts are resolved by budgetary decisions which are made finally by the Municipal Council on advice of the hospital administrator and the city Department of Hospitals. Extra-mural grants support most of the research activities, in so far as special technicians, equipment, experimental animals, etc. are required. But the basic salaries of the full-time medical staff depend on the hospital budget, and the composition of that budget is influenced by the dynamic equilibrium among the several competing viewpoints. Within the administrative hierarchy the medical director plays a key role in achieving viable compromises on budget and program, which enable the institution to move ahead and give Public Hospital its special character.

MSO in Relation to Public Hospital Programs. The very highly structured medical staff organization at Public Hospital has obvious and important impacts on the nature of the hospital's programs in all spheres. The central corps of full-time salaried physicians and the large number of residents provide the bulk of the medical care and, since the environment is that of a teaching and research institution with continuous review by colleagues, the care is exceptionally thorough and comprehensive. Counting only the full-time staff and residents (not the attending part-time staff and interns), there is a ratio of one doctor to four patients in the departments of medicine and obstetrics–gynecology, and one to three in the department of surgery. Unlike conditions in the loosely structured MSO's, moreover, these doctors are in the hospital and available to face problems all through the working day.

The rate of consultations among specialists is high. While the officially recorded rate is 30 per cent, this doubtless understates the true interchange among doctors, which at numerous conferences and conversations does not always yield a written note on the patient's chart. The range of technical diagnostic and therapeutic services available is very wide, both on the wards and in the out-patient department. The OPD serves as a place for follow-up of patients after discharge, and social workers help to guide the patient to outside resources which can serve him. Specialized services include psychiatry and rehabilitation, with large full-time staffs, as well as the usual supportive disciplines.

It is doubtless the dedication of Public Hospital to the needs of the poor that, as in government hospitals throughout the nation, has led to the pattern of very highly structured MSO. The taxpayer's money must be spent with caution, and the costs are obviously higher under conventional fee-for-service patterns of medical remuneration. In return for his willingness to serve as a subject for teaching, the indigent patient (whether consciously or not) receives technical care of high quality; the comforts and amenities found in voluntary hospitals are probably fewer, however, because of budgetary restrictions on nursing and auxiliary staffs, food, etc.

The rich program of professional education and medical research is manifestly an outcome of the MSO structure. The opportunities for professional development that they provide attract to the hospital a corps of exceptionally diligent and alert doctors who would not come if their only duties were care of the sick. There is a continuous equilibrium between the demands made upon the medical staff for patient care, on the one hand, and for education and research on the other. The point of compromise between these forces varies with the characteristics of particular chiefs of the clinical departments and the varying pressures exerted by the top executives of the hospital—administrative and medical. Since competent full-time departmental chiefs are not easy to recruit —especially in the prevailing world of lucrative private medical practice in America—their wishes and priorities must be respected, and they inevitably acquire great power in running their departments. This fortifies the technical standards applied to patient care, as well as the emphasis given to education and research.

The teaching and research priorities inevitably result in a very high volume of diagnostic work. This may prove irritating for some seriously ill patients, but, on the other hand, it must be realized that patients are largely freed from any financial restrictions to getting all the diagnostic examinations they need. The lesser skills of young doctors-in-training, who do much of the treatment—including surgical operations—are compensated by the high qualifications of the medical team leaders, who supervise the total range of in-patient and out-patient service.

The patient-care deficiencies in Public Hospital can be traced more to the budgetary restrictions of a government, tax-supported institution than to the pattern of internal hospital or medical staff organization. Weaknesses in the sphere of preventive medicine relate to the total structure of municipal government, with its administrative separation of public health agencies and hospitals. The solution to these financial and administrative problems obviously requires social actions outside the walls of this or any other single hospital.

VETERANS HOSPITAL—VERY HIGHLY STRUCTURED MSO

Finally, we may examine a second government hospital, an institution with the highest score on the MSO scale in our full series—84 points. This is Veterans Hospital, with 1,500 beds owned and operated by the federal government of the United States. This sponsorship yields many features in common with but others different from Public Hospital, coming under the control of a local unit of government.

The Setting and Background of Veterans Hospital. Veterans Hospital is one of a network of federal government hospitals to serve the military veterans of several wars. This one is part of a complex of buildings, combining a mental hospital, a domiciliary institution, and a general medical and surgical facility—our focus being on the latter. The large scale of the over-all facility complex—600 acres of land, over 4,000 employees, and $30,000,000 annual operating budget—obviously influences the character of the general hospital.

Starting as a "home for disabled soldiers" in the later nineteenth century, Veterans Hospital was greatly expanded after World War I, as part of the nationwide program of the federal Veterans Bureau. During World War II, the whole network of veterans' hospitals was criticized for poor quality of medical care isolated from the "mainstream" of American medicine. In response, there occurred in 1946 a massive re-organization, including the development of medical staff affiliations with schools of medicine, and this policy shapes in large part the character of Veterans Hospital today.[5]

The 1,500-bed general hospital is housed in 4 interconnecting brick buildings 4 to 6 stories high. Most of the beds are in large open wards of 18 to 32 beds each, supplemented by some private and 2-bed rooms. The atmosphere is sanitary, orderly, but somewhat austere. There are 2,130 personnel for slightly under 1,400 patients, or a ratio of 155 staff per 100 patients. This noticeably lower ratio than characterizes the other hospitals in our series is explained by the special composition of the patient population, to be discussed below.

As defined by federal law, the patients served by the hospital must be military veterans (with certain exceptions). Top priority for admission goes to veterans with disabilities arising from military service, but admission is granted to veterans with other "nonservice-connected conditions" if (a) private care would cause financial hardship (by a very liberal means test) and (b) a bed is available. Thus, a majority of patients in Veterans Hospital (70 per cent in 1964) are men with a variety of diagnoses having no connection with military service. They tend to be largely men over forty-five years of age, of low income, and often without family ties.

The cost of operation, as well as original construction, of Veterans

[5] I. J. Cohen, "The Veterans Administration Medical Care Program," in *Medical Care: Social and Organizational Aspects* (Springfield, Ill.: Charles C Thomas, 1966), pp. 425–36.

Hospital is met almost entirely from federal tax funds. An annual budget is submitted by the hospital's medical director to the federal government, and funds are allocated on the basis of a formula based on the expected patient-load in the next year and the standard complement of staff and supplies required for that load. In 1964 the annual expense was about $13,500,000 for some 500,000 in-patient days of care and 27,000 out-patient visits. Of this sum, about $2,000,000 goes for the salaries of doctors.

Through its control of funds and technical standards, the medical department of the federal Veterans Administration in Washington, D.C., is the ultimate authority responsible for Veterans Hospital. As part of the post-World War II reorganization, however, much of the authority for the selection of medical staff members was delegated to local committees of medical school deans, in cities where such schools exist. At the hospital in our study this deans' committee represented three medical schools in the metropolitan area, and it contains various professors from these schools as well as the deans. The deans' committee is concerned not only with medical staff appointments but also with the supervision of various training programs.

Because Veterans Hospital is part of a complex of several local facilities, there is a veterans center director to whom the general hospital medical director reports. The hierarchical responsibility extends through a regional office to the federal Veterans Administration, but there is no local board of directors. As with the Medical Group Hospital in our series, ultimate ownership and control rests with an organization in a distant city.

MEDICAL STAFF ORGANIZATION IN VETERANS HOSPITAL

The basic MSO structure is similar to that in Public Hospital, except that there is no independent association of attending physicians. The overwhelming bulk of work and responsibility is carried by full-time salaried physicians.

Staff Composition. The total medical staff contains 290 doctors (1964), plus a house staff of 205 residents and interns. There is a corps of 61 full-time and 22 part-time salaried physicians (plus 5 full-time dentists), who constitute the "active staff," while the balance consists of 164 physicians on the "attending staff" and 43 on the "consulting staff."

Among the 83 active-staff members, 53 per cent are specialty board-certified and 30 per cent are board-eligible, but among the 61 of these doctors who are full-time, virtually 100 per cent have one of these specialty qualifications. It is these salaried doctors who, along with the interns and residents, provide nearly all the basic medical care to patients. The attending-staff doctors (paid $50 per session) attend ward rounds, review cases, and assist in the teaching program. They are essentially advisors to the active-staff members who carry the responsibility for patient care.

Appointment Procedure. The top executives of the medical staff— the medical director and assistant medical director—are appointed by the medical department of the federal Veterans Administration nationally. All other active staff members are appointed locally. Applications are first reviewed by the chief of department in the applicant's specialty, from whom they are referred to the professional standards board, which is equivalent to the credentials committee in most nongovernment hospitals. After this review the candidate must be approved by the deans' committee before finalization through federal Civil Service procedures. All initial appointments are probationary for six months. The most influential judgment in this process is that of the department chief, whose recommendation is usually accepted. Appointment on the active staff of full-time doctors carries the obligation of accepting no outside income from private patients.

The attending and consulting staff members are appointed through a similar series of steps. Consulting physicians are usually highly qualified professors from one of the affiliated medical schools. Attending-staff members are also expected to be well qualified, but the review of their applications is not so rigorous as that for active-staff members. These appointments are renewable annually.

Privileges of staff members are based simply on their specialty qualifications, without further elaboration. The department administration assures assignment of doctors to cases (surgical or other) on the basis of appropriate qualifications that have been confirmed by close working relationships. The work done by residents and interns, of course, is under continuous supervision of the active staff.

Commitment. The commitment of the sixty-one full-time salaried physicians on the active staff is obviously very high. Although they work theoretically a forty-hour week, these doctors seldom spend less than fifty hours a week in their combined duties of patient care, education, research, and some administrative functions. The part-time salaried physicians serve in the out-patient and emergency clinics, as well as in the scarcer specialties for which full-time persons are not needed (like urology, ophthalmology, or plastic surgery). The attending- and consulting-staff members typically visit the hospital one or two half-days per week, and their commitment is relatively slight. They value their connection with Veterans Hospital largely because of its educational benefits.

It should be noted, however, that the financial relationship of all of these doctors is essentially a contractual one with the hospital. None is paid privately by the patient, and even the attending- and consulting-staff members receive flat payments on the basis of time-allotments.

Their sense of obligation to the hospital organization, therefore, is likely to be greater than that felt in a loosely structured MSO by a private physician whose total financial reward comes from his patient.

Departmentalization. There are sixteen departments in the Veterans Hospital medical staff, representing all the usual specialties except pediatrics and obstetrics and gynecology. The patient composition eliminates the need for the latter fields. In each department there is a hierarchy of authority embodied in the active salaried staff and the house staff. Under the chief of department there is an assistant chief, followed by staff doctors, residents, and interns. The chiefs are appointed for indefinite periods, on the recommendation of the hospital's medical director and with the approval of the deans' committee. Their continued tenure is subject to periodic review.

The department chiefs and assistant chiefs carry heavy responsibilities. They supervise patient care as well as the teaching and research programs. They develop department budgets and play the major role in selection of staff. They must handle day-to-day problems of interpersonal relationships that arise. Weekly meetings of the departmental staffs are held to discuss all aspects of the hospital program. Interdepartmental co-ordination is the responsibility of the medical director and assistant medical director, fostered through weekly meetings with all the department chiefs. The consulting and attending staff physicians play a very little role in the administrative operations of the medical staff departments.

Control Committees. In order to maintain quality standards and to perform certain administrative functions in the educational and research programs, there are thirty-seven committees of the medical staff at Veterans Hospital. Some of these serve the other facilities at the Veterans Center as well as the general hospital. In contrast to more loosely structured MSO's, the committees at Veterans Hospital serve sometimes as back-up for full-time physicians who carry out the key functions; thus, the infections committee, which meets only four times a year, gives professional support to the antibiotics control officer, who exercises regular surveillance over the judicious use of these drugs. Some committees are designed to seek solutions to special problems; the length-of-hospital-stay committee, for example, studies and makes proposals for reducing the average stay, which tends to be relatively long in this hospital.

All committee chairmen and members are appointed annually by the medical director. In spite of the large number of committees, they do not meet frequently; only six of the thirty-seven meet as often as monthly, and several meet only on the call of the chairman, presumably when a problem arises.

The tissue committee, for example, has the usual functions but meets only three times a year. The chief of pathology reports to that committee any findings of nonpathological tissue removed surgically as well as cases where the pathological findings differ substantially from the preoperative diagnosis. Problem cases, which are rare, are brought to the attention of the responsible department chief.

The medical records committee meets monthly, but even so the principal supervision over records takes place on the wards, where the department staff officers review all charts before they are sent to the medical records librarian. The committee then reviews only a sample of charts for completeness. This committee works in liaison also with the medical care appraisal committee, which exercises a general surveillance over quality of care by noting disparity between discharge and admission diagnoses, unusually long durations of stay, or evidence of inappropriate therapy.

The pharmacy committee meets only four times a year, but a therapeutic agents committee working with it meets monthly to review new drugs for inclusion on the official formulary and to distribute recommendations on the use of new drugs. The pharmacy committee decides on general policies for drug stop-orders, detection of adverse drug reactions, etc.

Documentation. Detailed published rules and regulations for the medical staff as well as for the total hospital personnel are contained in a federal Veterans Administration manual. This is frequently revised by supplementary bulletins. The medical director is responsible for seeing that these rules and regulations are implemented, and he issues various memoranda and orders for this purpose. There are also numerous "manuals of procedure" and "training guides" within different departments. Thus, there are no separate "constitution" or "bylaws" of the medical staff in the usual sense, but the same purpose of influencing physician behavior to maintain quality standards is served by elaborate published documents of the over-all governing authority of the hospital.

Informal Dynamics. Because of its very highly structured pattern, the medical staff at Veterans Hospital probably attracts physicians who can accept the constraints of an organized framework.[6] The highly individualistic doctor is not likely to apply for this type of position, nor to remain in it for long if he does accept it. Still, ambitious men join the staff and express their drives through efforts to advance in the hierarchy and acquire greater control over the programs of patient care, education, and research.

[6] Gloria V. Engel, "The Effect of Bureaucracy on the Professional Autonomy of the Physician" (Ph.D. dissertation, University of California, Los Angeles, 1968).

Thus, competition develops, not so much between individuals as between departments, for access to the available funds, space, and personnel. Even within departments, cliques develop, and one set of internists or surgeons may vie with another. The relative stability of the full-time salaried medical staff at Veterans Hospital over the past decade, however, suggests that this competition has been more constructive than disruptive. The greatest difficulties in medical staff stability concern radiologists and pathologists—the types of specialists who are frequently on contractual arrangements with voluntary hospitals, where their earnings are usually much higher.

Acceptance of the authority of the medical director and the department chiefs contributes to a relatively low impact of informal dynamics in Veterans Hospital. Unlike the pattern in Public Hospital, under a local government body, or in the average voluntary hospital, the head of the medical staff is also the top executive officer of the entire hospital, representing its governing body (the Veterans Administration in Washington). There are not two lines of authority—one medical and the other administrative—which can clash. Decisions on the technical aspects of medical care are made within the departments, but the over-all administrative controls are still exercised by a physician. In so far as there are complaints, the blame can be shifted to a distant government bureau, which need not mar relationships between the medical staff physicians and the hospital's medical director.

MSO in Relation to Veterans Hospital Programs. The very highly structured medical staff pattern at Veterans Hospital is the logical approach of a federal government agency devoted to providing medical care for a special population. Since the costs are met almost entirely from general tax funds, maximum economy is sought. At the same time, quality standards are promoted through various mechanisms of professional review within the medical staff and above it, by means of administrative directives and a local deans' committee.

Unlike most voluntary general hospitals, and even the local government hospital reviewed earlier in this chapter, there is essentially one line of authority in Veterans Hospital instead of two. The head of the medical staff is a medical director, appointed by the federal agency, and he is also the top executive of the hospital as a whole. He is assisted, of course, by administrative personnel, but his authority stems from the sponsoring agency in Washington, and he exercises it through a hierarchy within the hospital composed mainly of administrative physicians. The various medical department chiefs are the key figures in implementing decisions.

The great bulk of medical work as well as the supervision of paramedical personnel is done by a core staff of full-time salaried physicians who are fully committed to the hospital, without competing private practices. Yet there are numerous connections with the "outside" medical profession through a staff of consultant and attending physicians and affiliation with a nearby medical school. A robust program of professional education and medical research serves to provide manpower (interns and residents) for many of the tasks of patient care, while at the same time stimulating all the medical and allied personnel to maintain good levels of performance. Within the whole hierarchy there is continuous communication and consultation. Individual decisions on technical matters have a wide range of freedom, within certain constraints such as those of specialty board certifications or the use of generic drug formularies.

Since the policy of the sponsoring federal agency is to encourage excellence through a strong education and research program, there is none of the conflict between this objective and that of patient care observed at the locally sponsored "Public Hospital." The emphasis on intellectual and creative work as well as the obvious necessity for teamwork attracts to the hospital physicians who are compatible with these requirements. Advancement of an individual within the system depends on demonstrated ability as a team member, flexibility in interpersonal relationships, and reliability in meeting the obligations of the system. The star performer who cannot work agreeably with others is not likely to stay for long. These conditions might lead to a placid mediocrity if it were not for the continuous influences from the national authority and the surveillance locally by the deans' committee and the consulting staff.

These circumstances make possible a program of in-patient care of wide scope and high technical quality. Critical review by committees of the American Medical Association some years ago judged the quality of service received in the Veterans Administration hospital system to be "the finest type of medical care in a country where medical science has reached its highest development."[7] The range of extra-mural and preventive health services is restricted by the legal entitlements of veterans, but within the scope permitted by law, Veterans Hospital provides remarkably comprehensive care for its beneficiaries. The long average stay of its patients is caused largely by a concern for the total recovery and rehabilitation of men who are typically handicapped in their family or community adjustment. The contributions of the hospital to the general education of doctors, and others, and to the advancement of medical knowledge through research are substantial.

[7] Roy E. Kracke, "Medical Care of Veterans," *J.A.M.A.*, 143:1321–31 (12 August 1950).

VIII

MEDICAL STAFF PATTERNS—
INTERHOSPITAL COMPARISONS

IN THE PREVIOUS two chapters we have examined "anthropologically," in some vertical depth, the medical staff organization in ten selected hospitals. Now we are in a position to examine "horizontally" across the series the nature of each of the components of MSO, and to search for meaningful comparisons of these components in different hospitals. Following this, in the next two chapters, we will be better able to consider the relationship of MSO patterns to the various features of hospital performance.

In chapter V, we proposed a typology for analysis of medical staff organization in hospitals according to seven features: (1) composition of the staff; (2) appointment procedure; (3) commitment; (4) departmentalization; (5) control committees; (6) documentation; and (7) informal dynamics. Within each of these features were several sub-items, and the theoretical basis for considering each of these was discussed. In the ten hospital case studies, this scheme of analysis was applied, and the hospitals were examined sequentially according to their rank in over-all MSO structuring—from very loosely to very highly structured.

Comparison of the components of MSO across the series of ten hospitals requires some degree of quantification. A great deal of data were collected in each hospital, and much of this has been presented in the previous chapters. Complete uniformity of definition and complete accuracy of reporting, however, were not always possible across our series of institutions. Our efforts at comparisons in the following pages, therefore, must be offered with great caution. They represent at best only a rough approximation of the relative characteristics of medical staff organization in different hospitals.

In a small series of cases, like this, the special circumstances of individual hospitals can exert a great influence on any search for quantitative relationships. These effects may be slightly reduced by grouping our series of ten hospitals into three levels of structuring, rather than the five levels used in chapter V. When this is done in the following pages we will use terminology as follows:

MSO types	Symbol	Terminology
Very loosely structured	I $\big\}$	"Permissive"
Loosely structured	II	
Moderately structured	III $\big\}$	"Medium"
Highly structured	IV	
Very highly structured	V	"Rigorous"

To remind the reader, the hospitals in our series corresponding to these MSO types were as follows:

Hospital	Bed-capacity	MSO score	Type
Kenter	42	25	I
Hillside	76	28	I
View	141	36	II
Midland	230	56	II
Pebble City	447	60	III
St. Martin's	265	62	III
Scopus	490	71	IV
Medical Group	346	80	V
Public	729	82	V
Veterans	1500	84	V

The MSO scores listed above, it will be recalled, were derived from a system of weighted values explained in chapter V. The detailed findings for each MSO feature, across the hospital series, will be discussed here.

COMPOSITION OF THE MEDICAL STAFF

The principal characteristic of a medical staff's composition is the degree of selectiveness or discrimination reflected in its membership. As explained in chapter V, this may be examined in terms of (a) its relative size, in proportion to the number of beds; (b) the proportion of qualified specialists; and (c) the proportion of total staff members who are in the "active" category.

Relative Size of Staff. To quantify this relationship so as to permit interhospital comparisons, the count of doctors was confined to an adjusted definition of the "active staff." This excludes the often large number of physicians on the courtesy or honorary staffs who are seldom in the hospital. On the other hand, we considered it necessary to take account of the house staff (interns and residents) and the consulting staff, since these doctors play an essential role in the daily work of the highly structured medical staff. Because the house staff and consultant doctors are not fully "active," however, and because "courtesy" members in all hospitals have been excluded entirely, only a fraction of these categories (75 per cent of house staff and 25 per cent of consultants) have been added into the figure for "active staff."

Through such calculations, adjusted figures for the active-staff members per 100 beds in our series were found as follows:

MSO type	Adjusted active staff per 100 beds	Range
Permissive (I – II)	87	(47–152)
Medium (III – IV)	60	(38–92)
Rigorous (V)	44	(20–72)

Thus, it appears that the relative size of the active staff decreases as the MSO patterns move from permissive to rigorous. Moreover, although there is much variation within each level, the range is narrower as MSO structure increases. From the case studies it was evident that the most permissive hospitals are eager to increase their active staffs as much as possible in order to maximize the demand for beds; their ratio of active staff to beds would be even higher if they could attract more doctors. The more rigorous hospitals, on the other hand, tend to have more applicants for staff membership than they can accept. Their ratios would be even lower, if we had not included a fraction of the house staff and consultants in the adjusted figures.

A relatively smaller number of active-staff members per 100 beds obviously permits greater controls over medical behavior. It should yield a more tightly-knit organization in which various forms of staff discipline are likely to be more effective.

Proportion of Specialists. Since hospitalization implies serious illness, one would expect the more rigorous MSO to be more demanding of specialty qualifications in its staff members. As a measure of this, we examined the percentage of doctors who were either certified by a specialty board or board-eligible (the latter meaning that they had undertaken all the necessary postgraduate studies, although not yet having passed the official examinations). It will be recalled that in the highly structured MSO's of the European countries, virtually all hospital physicians are qualified as specialists. Our findings were as follows:

MSO type	Specialists as percentage of active staff	Range
Permissive	68	(42–88)
Medium	81	(60–93)
Rigorous	87	(83–93)

It is evident that the proportion of specialists is reported to be high in all levels of hospitals in our series, although it is higher at the more rigorous end of the scale. The range of variation is also narrower at the upper end. There is some reason to suspect, moreover, that the reporting of specialty status is less accurate in the permissive hospitals, so that the above figures may understate the true differentials.

In metropolitan areas throughout the United States, the majority of doctors with hospital appointments are qualified as specialists, and the area of our investigation was evidently no exception. The rigorous hospitals in our series, moreover, are now virtually confining staff membership to specialists, and the existence of even a small minority of general practitioners on their staffs is usually due to "grandfather clauses," permitting the continued affiliation of doctors who joined years before. These hospitals, furthermore, make more of a distinction between full board-certification and board-eligibility than do the permissive hospitals; they usually stipulate that key positions, like departmental or committee chairmanships, go only to fully board-certified specialists. The permissive and some medium hospitals, on the other hand, still willingly accept general practitioners on the staff, even though their professional privileges may be somewhat restricted.

Proportion of "Active" Members in the Total Staff. Since active-staff membership entails certain obligations to the hospital, it implies greater group discipline than would characterize the medical staff as a whole with its many "courtesy" or "honorary" members. Hence, a higher proportion of the total staff in the "active" classification would mean higher MSO structuring. In this regard, our findings were as follows:

MSO type	Active staff as percentage of total staff	Range
Permissive	40	(26–84)
Medium	38	(26–47)
Rigorous	51	(46–59)

While roughly confirming our hypothesis, this particular measurement is probably not a wholly satisfactory reflection of the medical staff dynamics. In the permissive set of four hospitals, one—with 84 per cent of its total staff in the "active" category—simply places nearly all its doctors on the active staff in order to exact a certain loyalty from them; because of its size, location, and prestigious tradition it can do this, even though its general MSO structuring is permissive. Furthermore, if "total" staff were defined to include only physicians with admitting privileges (thus excluding consultants or out-patient service physicians), then the percentage figure for the rigorous hospitals in our series would be much higher than 51 per cent.

Thus, by these three relatively crude measures, the composition of the medical staffs in our series of ten hospitals suggests a higher level of discrimination in the more rigorous MSO structures. It should be realized, of course, that these simple ratios or percentages, reflecting staff composition, tell us nothing about the distribution of time or energy spent in the hospital among the various members of a hospital's medical staff. In the permissive hospitals a small share of the active-staff members usually do a large share of the medical work, while in the rigorous hospitals the workload tends to be more evenly spread. The meaning of staff composition as a component of MSO structuring, therefore, depends very much on the level of "commitment" to be examined below. Staff composition, in turn, is determined largely by the manner of appointment of doctors, which will be reviewed next.

APPOINTMENT PROCEDURES

As discussed in chapter V, the manner of entrance of doctors into a medical staff involves (a) a process of selection; (b) a method of granting professional privileges after affiliation; and (c) an assumption of obligations as a price for staff membership. With the data available from our ten case studies, it was very difficult to quantify these mechanisms, but their general nature in the different types of MSO structure may be described.

Selection Process. Theoretically, one would expect higher MSO structuring to be associated with more judicious review of applicants seeking to enter the organization and more demanding obligations after entrance.[1] The operation of these tendencies, however, is affected by the supply of physicians available and the existence of medical staff openings at particular times and places. Therefore, the relationship of selection process to the over-all MSO structuring may not be simple and direct.

In the four hospitals of permissive MSO structure (Types I and II),

[1] Richard W. Scott, *Formal Organization* (San Francisco: Chandler, 1962).

the entrance of doctors onto the medical staff is a relatively simple matter. Applicants come largely from the geographic area near the hospital and nearly all who apply are appointed. The availability of beds at the time is the major factor, in order that competition for access to a given supply of beds should not become too great. Specialty qualifications are not demanded. A procedure for review by the credentials committee of the medical staff may be in effect, but it is not very diligently carried out, and documentation of the applicant need not be thorough. The final appointment by the hospital board of directors is largely a rubber-stamping of the medical staff recommendations.

In the three hospitals of medium-MSO structure (Types III and IV), the review process on applicants is more demanding. The relative bed supply still plays a part, as it must, but the documentation expected of applicants (records of training, letters of reference, etc.) is more thorough and the credentials committee review more serious. Some few general practitioners may be admitted to the staff, but the preference is clearly for well-qualified specialists. The medical executive committee usually reviews applications as well as the credentials committee. In two of the three medium MSO hospitals, the chiefs of the relevant specialty departments also review applications and make recommendations based on a balance between the department's staff "needs" and the individual's qualifications.

The medium-MSO hospitals in our series, and perhaps in most communities, tend to be the most prestigious hospitals in their areas. They are, in a sense, the most highly structured of the "open-staff" general hospitals, catering largely to private patients and private practitioners. Thus, they attract the largest relative number of medical staff applicants, and this naturally permits them to be more selective in making appointments. These hospitals are also rapidly expanding their bed capacities, and when a new wing is open a sudden rise in bed supply invites many new applications to the medical staff, with consequent infusion of new blood. The desirability of staff membership in these hospitals permits imposition of greater obligations on new appointees, as will be discussed below.

Selection procedures in the rigorous-MSO hospitals are quite different. In the prevailing context of private medical practice in America, these hospitals with very highly structured-MSO patterns—built upon a "closed staff" of contractual physicians—are not flooded with applications. Yet their standards for selection are relatively high. Careful documentation is required and specialty qualifications are demanded. There may be review by a credentials committee, largely to satisfy JCAH requirements, but this is not the main step; the key recommendation is made by the full-time chief of department, in which the specialist would work, and sometimes there is a vote of the departmental administrative committee. Various periods of probation are necessary before an appointment becomes finalized. In two of the three rigorous-MSO hospitals in our series, a secondary review of candidates is made by an academic university committee, to assure high qualifications. Further approval may be needed by a government civil service body or (in Medical Group Hospital) by a final vote of the medical partnership.

Because of the relative sparsity of suitable candidates for appointment in the rigorous-MSO hospitals, recruitment of the staff becomes a more active process. Instead of simply waiting for local applicants, the hospital administration actively searches for good candidates, often on a nationwide basis. (This is in interesting contrast with the medical scene in Europe, where full-time salaried hospital positions are highly coveted and applications for them are abundant.) Advertisements of openings are published, and visits are made to medical training centers where young residents are about to complete their specialty qualifications. At this particular stage of development of the American medical profession, the proportion of doctors interested in full-time contractual employment in hospitals seems to be increasing, so that the reservoir of candidates for these appointments is enlarging and selectivity can steadily rise. The same dynamics applies to the appointment of contractual physicians even in the medium-MSO hospitals, and perhaps in some of the permissive ones, but in the rigorous-MSO hospitals, of course, the role of carefully appointed contractual physicians is far greater.

Professional Privileges. Following appointment to a medical staff, the physician is authorized to treat patients in the hospital, but there may be limitations on his right to handle certain types of cases or carry out certain procedures. In the ten hospitals of our series, the stipulation of privileges seems to be partially consistent with the over-all features of MSO structuring and partially compensatory to (and inconsistent with) other features of the pattern.

Thus, in the permissive-MSO hospitals, the appointment of general practitioners in the first place is associated with more or less careful stipulation of surgical operations that they are permitted to perform. A "surgical privilege control card" is maintained in the operating suite and enforced by the head nurse. Some permissive hospitals permit a doctor to perform certain operations only if a surgeon with "unlimited" privileges assists him. On the other hand, in spite of these compensatory safeguards, exceptions are readily made in some of these hospitals. A specific nonauthorized procedure may be permitted, if a consultation is obtained. Also, the hospital may grant "temporary privileges" to a physician not on the medical staff at all, with little formality.

In the medium-MSO hospitals, surgical privileges may also be spelled out for certain medical staff members, but this is considered exceptional. The great bulk of surgery is done by qualified specialists who have unlimited privileges in their fields; thus, no list of authorized procedures is maintained. The attitude toward "temporary privileges" is also more cautious. While these are granted under special circumstances (such as for medical substitutes during vacations or for highly qualified outside consultants), the qualifications of the temporary candidate are reviewed —usually by the department chief.

Paradoxically, it is the medium-MSO hospitals that in our study have "departments of general practice" more than the permissive ones. But this mechanism is intended to define and restrict general practice privileges more than to widen them. Through organization of such departments the work of general practitioners is more subject to surveillance, their in-patient functions are brought under the wing of various specialty departments, and other functions (such as out-patient services, teaching of nurses, etc.) can be more systematically assigned. Thus, the department of general practice is a device for exercising controls over general practitioners, in the face of pressures to eliminate them entirely from hospitals as MSO structuring increases.

The rigorous-MSO hospitals impose few if any formalities with respect to professional privileges. The same quality-control objective has been achieved by the requirement of specialty board qualifications for initial appointment to the staff, and by the day-to-day surveillance within the various departments. In surgery, the department chiefs routinely review the scheduling of all operations to be sure that the surgeon is qualified for the proposed procedure. Since the active staff is relatively small, the competence of individual surgeons is well known; where there are doubts, an assistant surgeon with known competence in the specific operation can be assigned. Moreover, the general pattern of surgical, as well as nonsurgical, services in these hospitals is characterized by teamwork; the qualifications of each individual physician are less critical, since they are buttressed by other members of the team.

Outside of surgery, the specification of privileges in the permissive hospitals is not well defined. The compensatory control conception is not found. Thus, serious "medical" cases may be treated by general practitioners or perhaps even surgical specialists, with consultations being left up to the individual doctor. In the medium-MSO hospitals consultations are more likely to be mandatory for certain conditions, such as initial Caesarian sections or very high fevers, and—with stronger departmental structures—these are more likely to be enforced. (In most hospitals, consultation on therapeutic abortions are customary or required by law.) In the rigorous-MSO hospitals, privileges are also not spelled out for non-surgical functions, but surveillance is simply left to the day-to-day teamwork within each department.

Our findings regarding appointments and privileges of doctors are roughly confirmed by another study of general hospitals, reported in 1962.[2] Walter J. McNerney and his colleagues studied a sample of thirty-three hospitals in Michigan, representing voluntary, government, and proprietary sponsorship. Classifying their series by hospital size—which probably corresponded roughly with our scale of MSO structuring—they found various methods of restricting a doctor's professional activities in 70 per cent of the large hospitals (500 beds or more), 47 per cent of the medium-sized hospitals (100 to 499 beds), and 26 per cent of the small hospitals (less than 100 beds). They did not probe the mechanisms of professional restriction, but they also found that it was mainly focused on surgical cases and seldom on medical cases.

Obligations. The third aspect of medical staff appointment procedures is the imposition of certain obligations as a condition of staff membership. These tend to be of two types, although they are interrelated: (a) obligations within the structure of the medical staff itself and (b) obligations in the implementation of various hospital programs. The first type includes such matters as service on medical staff committees, payment of dues, attendance of staff meetings, etc. The second type refers to such activities as service in out-patient clinics, giving consultations on in-patients (without necessarily being paid), and provision of education to paramedical personnel. Appointment to the medical staff always involves some degree of the first type of obligation, but may or may not require any assumption of the second type.

Among the permissive-MSO hospitals, the obligations of physicians are mainly of the first type—that is, participation in the medical staff structure itself. Even this, however, may not be done with much diligence. As for the second type of obligation, there are no organized out-patient services in these hospitals, and the staffing of the hospital emergency room is the usual extent of duties in this sphere. These tasks are usually assigned to the youngest physicians entering the staff, who are just starting to build a medical practice and can attract private patients from their emergency room work. In one of the permissive-MSO hospitals new staff members are expected to make personal donations to the hospital building fund.

In the medium-MSO hospitals the obligations of staff membership are much greater. In addition to medical staff mechanisms as such, the doctor assumes duties in the out-patient department and in the education of interns and residents, or both. The time devoted to medical staff

[2] Walter J. McNerney and Study Staff, *Hospital and Medical Economics* (Chicago: Hospital Research and Educational Trust, 1962), vol. II, pp. 1230–36.

committees concerned with quality controls is usually greater. In these hospitals the full-time contractual physicians naturally carry heavier obligations, because their professional lives are dedicated to service in the hospital.

In the rigorous-MSO hospitals, the nature of the doctor's obligation is of a different order of magnitude. Since the great bulk of the patient care in these institutions is given by contractual physicians, the obligations are simply part of all their daily work; they are not a "repayment" for the right to use the hospital for private patients and personal earnings. They are rather the central purpose of medical staff appointment and include a wide range of duties in the medical staff bureaucratic structure itself as well as in hospital programs of in-patient care, out-patient service, professional education, and medical research. Since the doctor is paid for all these activities, the obligations are clear and their fulfillment tends to be definite. Being in the hospital full-time, the contractual physician is not so hard-pressed in meeting his obligations. Moreover, he is in a good position to encourage the attending and other part-time physicians on the same staff to carry out their staff obligations with diligence.

COMMITMENT

Among the seven features by which medical staff organization has been conceptualized in this study, the greatest weight has been assigned to the aggregate "commitment" of staff members to the hospital. For reasons explained in chapter V, we weighted this factor with 25 points out of a total of 100. In the concept of commitment we include the doctor's dedication of efforts to the tasks involved in the mission of the hospital, as against other competing objectives in his professional life. These competing objectives might be a private medical practice, affiliation with another hospital, or indeed—within the same hospital—attention to certain privately paying patients to the exclusion of other hospital tasks.

We do not imply that 100 per cent commitment to a hospital is necessarily the "best" form of medical behavior at all times and places. Such commitment is, however, a measurement of the degree of structuring of the medical staff organization, and it is this that we are comparing in a series of hospitals. In back of commitment lie various factors of motivation and attitude.[3] We did not set out to probe these, however, because we were interested in the overt manifestations of commitment. It is these which contribute to a high or low degree of MSO structuring. No matter what physicians say or feel about a hospital, it is what they

---

[3] Saul W. Gellerman, *Motivation and Productivity* (New York: American Management Association, 1963).

actually do in it that contributes to its pattern of medical staff organization.

We consider the overt manifestations of commitment to be definable in three ways: (a) time-allocation or presence in the hospital, (b) method of remuneration, and (c) other institutional affiliations. To obtain aggregate or average figures on these three variables for the entire medical staff of any hospital would require collection of accurate data on the activities of each individual doctor. Our research resources did not permit such exacting data collection, but we did obtain a good many field impressions that suggest contrasts between hospitals. Moreover, we can make measurements on a fourth variable that we think reflects in some degree the other three—the hospital's engagement of contractual physicians. As explained in chapter V, this seems to yield a modest approach to quantification of the "commitment" embodied in a hospital's MSO structure.

Time-Allocation or Presence. The aggregate proportion of total physician-hours, spent within the hospital by members of a medical staff would reflect an important aspect of commitment. Obviously, some staff members spend more time than others and the frequency distributions in different MSO's undoubtedly vary. A national study in 1966 found that the median self-employed American physician spent sixty-four hours per week in professional work, of which fourteen hours were spent in hospitals.[4] But most physicians have more than one hospital affiliation, and we do not know from this study how much time was spent in individual institutions. Our study suggests a wide range of time allocations in relation to the MSO pattern.

In our hospital series, although we could not quantify it, we got the impression that the proportion of total potential professional time of the medical staff members spent in the permissive MSO hospitals (Types I and II) was very low. This would be attributable to many factors. There are relatively more doctors per 100 beds on the staffs of those hospitals, as noted earlier, so that the average amount of time per doctor spent in the hospital is bound to be less. Being less technically developed, the permissive hospitals tend to receive milder cases, requiring less medical time for their diagnosis and treatment. The fewer obligations of medical staff appointment in those hospitals demand less over-all time-investment from the doctor. Also, as we will see below, the smaller relative number of full-time contractual physicians in the permissive hospitals adds very little contribution to the aggregate time-commitment which might be calculated for the entire medical staff. No interns or residents,

4 Anon., "Time: How Doctors Spend It and Save It," *Med. Economics* (4 April 1966): 77–103.

furthermore, are on hand to compensate for the limited presence of private attending physicians. Thus, our impression in the permissive-MSO hospitals is that the average time-allotment in the doctor's total work-week is low, being composed mainly of visits to his own patients in the hospital at periodic intervals.

In the medium-MSO hospitals, the time-allotment of the average medical staff member within the hospital is higher. This would follow from the lower ratio of doctors to beds, the more serious types of cases, the greater range of medical staff obligations, and the higher proportion of full-time contractual physicians. In these hospitals the majority of active-staff members make visits to the hospital daily or nearly so, whether or not they have private patients on the wards. The communication with other doctors in the hospital corridors and staff rooms is a regular part of their professional lives.

In the rigorous-MSO hospitals, the time-allocation of the medical staff within the hospital obviously takes an upward leap, since so high a proportion of the staff is composed of full-time hospital-based physicians. This time-commitment is perhaps "diluted" by the presence of other attending or consulting physicians who visit the hospital only periodically, but even these visits are systematized according to a schedule of MSO obligations. Moreover, there are large staffs of interns and residents—young physicians who spend virtually all their time in the hospital. In a nutshell, the great bulk of patient care, as well as other hospital functions, is carried out by medical staff members who spend virtually all their time in the hospital. Even if allowance is made for the much smaller time investment of the visiting or part-time staffs, the time-commitment in these MSO's is very high.

Method of Remuneration. Financial ties between the doctor and the hospital are another aspect of medical staff commitment. The fee-for-service pattern of medical remuneration, of course, establishes a liaison between the doctor and his individual patient which may have important benefits. Nevertheless, it does little to fortify the doctor's sense of obligation to the hospital in which he is serving his patient. In so far as economic ties have an influence on behavior (and who can deny their relevance?), payment of the doctor by the hospital is bound to increase his commitment. It implies also a change of work incentives from strict and immediate monetary awards (fees for each item of service) to those found in an organized medical framework where peer evaluation and respect counts much more heavily.[5]

In the permissive-MSO hospitals of our series, fee-for-service economic

[5] Milton I. Roemer, "On Paying the Doctor and the Implications of Different Methods," *J. Health and Human Behavior*, 3:4–14 (Spring 1962).

relationships obviously predominate, and only a few medical staff members receive money from the hospital. These are confined to supportive specialists in radiology and pathology, with the exception of one emergency room physician (in one of the four hospitals in this set). The method of payment of the supportive specialists, furthermore, is a variant on the fee system, in that it depends on units of service provided rather than units of time. This is by an agreement between hospital and specialist to share the income from charges to patients for laboratory or x-ray services. The contractual physician on this payment method has a great deal of freedom from the authority of the hospital.

In the medium-MSO hospitals, while private fee-for-service relationships with patients still predominate, there emerges another pattern. Contractual sharing of department income is still also the method of remuneration for pathology and radiology services, but in all three hospitals of this set some physicians are engaged on a straight salary— not related to units of service. Some of these may be pathologists or radiologists engaged by the department chief and paid by him from contractual earnings. Others include emergency room physicians, a director of medical education, and a physical medicine specialist. Most important is the pattern in our single Type IV institution (Scopus Hospital), where all the principal clinical as well as supportive departments are headed by full-time physicians on straight salaries. Even though the great majority of medical staff members are paid fees by their patients, the small cadre of salaried physicians in this hospital has a large impact on the over-all level of staff commitment.[6]

In the rigorous-MSO hospitals, the salaried system of remuneration becomes the predominant one for the whole medical staff. Radiologists and pathologists are paid by salary, as well as the various clinical specialists working full-time in the hospital. Even the attending or consulting physicians who visit the hospital periodically are paid on a time-basis —that is, by session or part-time salary rather than by number of patients seen or units of service rendered. At one of the government hospitals, the part-time visiting physicians receive no payment at all, but accept the prestige and educational opportunities as adequate reward for their work. At Medical Group Hospital the level of salaries may be enhanced by bonuses at the year's end, but these are distributed to the collective staff members rather than being in proportion to the units of service rendered by each doctor. Thus, in the rigorous-MSO hospitals, the economic rewards to the physician are based on his commitment of time to the tasks of the institution rather than the volume of specific services rendered to individual patients.

[6] Victor Richards, "Full-time Service Chiefs," in C. Wesley Eisele (editor), *The Medical Staff in the Modern Hospital* (New York: McGraw-Hill, 1967), pp. 133–40.

Institutional Affiliations. This third reflection of medical staff commitment is the converse of the first one on time-allotments. The less time that is spent in a given hospital the more time is likely to be spent in others with which the physician has some affiliation.

While we were unable to collect hard statistical data, it was our impression from many interviews and conversations that virtually all physicians in the permissive-MSO hospitals had appointments on the medical staffs of other hospitals as well. These are deemed necessary to assure the doctor access to beds for his patients; if one hospital is filled he can turn to another. The patient's preferences must also be considered. The secondary hospital affiliations may be either on active or courtesy staffs. Our rough guess would be that among the members of the active staffs of the permissive-MSO hospitals in our series, the great majority have at least one other active-staff appointment at another hospital, plus at least one courtesy staff appointment at still another hospital. The reasons for these multiple affiliations in a metropolitan community may be understandable, but it is obvious that they must detract from the commitment of a physician to any one hospital. Even the contractual physicians doing pathology and radiology in the two smallest of the permissive hospitals are not fully committed to them, since they work also in other hospitals or independent laboratories.

Among the active medical staff members in the medium-MSO hospitals, secondary affiliations are also common, but they are more often limited to courtesy staffs. The demands of active-staff membership in these hospitals are too great to permit a secondary active-staff affiliation, except occasionally. Since active-staff membership in these hospitals is professionally coveted, physicians conserve their energies to fulfill the obligations. The contractual physicians in these hospitals are exclusively devoted to them.

In the rigorous-MSO hospitals, it is evident that the active staffs of full-time physicians limit themselves, nearly always, to the one affiliation. (Occasionally, a full-time staff member may have a courtesy or consulting appointment at another hospital, for educational or research purposes but not for the care of patients.) The various part-time attending, consulting, and courtesy staff members in these hospitals, of course, have their primary affiliations elsewhere, in so far as they serve private patients. But the level of commitment of the active staff is dominated by that of the full-time physicians whose affiliations are, with few exceptions, single.

Contractual Physicians. We can now examine the feature of commitment of a medical staff to the hospital, on which our data permit some quantification. As elaborated in chapter V, the proportion of medical staff members who work in the hospital under some contractual arrangement appears to reflect or run parallel with the over-all level of commitment of that hospital's medical staff.

Using the method of counting contractual physicians and adjusting for hospital size explained in chapter V, the "size-adjusted contractual physician scores" in the ten hospitals of our series are as follows:

Hospital	Bed capacity	Number of contractual physicians	Size-adjusted contractual physician score
Kenter	42	1.0	0.6
Hillside	76	1.5	0.8
View	141	6.0	2.8
Midland	230	15.5	6.6
Pebble City	447	22.5	8.5
St. Martin's	265	19.5	8.1
Scopus	490	48.0	17.8
Medical Group	346	53.0	23.9
Public	729	65.0	22.7
Veterans	1500	77.0	24.3

The above figures for contractual physicians include anesthesiologists because—in spite of their being paid fees by the patient—they have more or less-exclusive agreements to cover anesthetic requirements in the particular hospital. The figures do not, however, include interns or residents, which would tend to understate the index of commitment at the more rigorous end of the series. In the final two hospitals (Public and Veterans) there are large house staffs of doctors-in-training who do work that in other hospitals is done by medical staff physicians; if they were counted, the C.P. scores of the two government hospitals would be greatly increased.

To smooth out the various pecularities in our data and to show better the general relationship of contractual physicians to over-all medical staff organization in the hospital, the figures may be collapsed into three sets as follows:

MSO type	Size-adjusted C.P. score
Permissive (I and II)	2.9
Medium (III and IV)	11.6
Rigorous (V)	23.6

Thus, in the permissive hospitals, the contractual physicians are almost entirely confined to the supportive specialties of pathology and radiology. One should realize that even these fields do not necessarily require contractual physicians; a radiological department in a hospital could theoretically be attended by many different private radiologists, in the same sense that an operating room is used by numerous private surgeons. The problem, however, is that the radiologist and pathologist do not usually serve the patient directly, but are supportive to the diagnostic or treatment efforts of another physician who has primary responsibility for the patient. Thus, the medical staff itself usually seeks to achieve uniformity, order, and quality standards in these supportive services by having them covered through an agreement with one or more contractual physicians, thereby excluding others.

Once appointed, the contractual physician serves as a nucleus of the medical staff with high commitment to the hospital in terms of time, financial ties, and professional responsibility. But more than that, the presence of even a few contractual physicians adds a sense of self-discipline to the entire medical staff. A qualified physician is there to observe what all the other doctors are doing, and the departments of pathology or radiology are rather good vantage points for observation. This mechanism of "peer review" is operative even when the contractual physician is kept in a somewhat subordinate position on MSO control committees, as seems to happen in the permissive-MSO hospitals.

In the medium-MSO hospitals the higher proportion of contractual physicians means usually a strengthening of their role in pathology and radiology, as well as a widening of their influence to encompass other spheres, such as physical medicine, out-patient services, professional education, and—in the Type IV MSO (Scopus Hospital)—even the supervision of all clinical departments through full-time chiefs. Even in anesthesiology the stable and continuous presence of certain doctors in the operating room, month in and month out, probably enhances the sense of responsibility of the surgeons. Private attending physicians may show apprehension about the engagement of contractual physicians precisely because of the surveillance their presence implies, but in response they tend to tighten up their own mechanisms of MSO discipline. They become more diligent in the departmental structure, in the review committee, etc., if only to minimize the power of the full-time staff. Yet, with pressures from the community (for example, in the out-patient field), from JCAH accreditation, from the tough competition for interns and residents, from enlarging fields like rehabilitation medicine or psychiatry, there is no solution without appointment of more contractual physicians. Appointment of full-time directors of medical education and emergency room physicians in voluntary general hospitals with predominantly private attending medical staffs has become so common that national associations have been organized in both of these fields.[7]

In the rigorous-MSO hospitals the contractual physician becomes the dominant member of the medical staff. The private attending staff member is essentially a back-up man for special assistance. Both the administrative direction and the day-to-day tasks of in-patient care are performed mainly by contractual physicians, not to mention the functions of out-patient care, professional education, and research. The commitment of these medical staffs is obviously very high, since the hospital plays the dominant role in their professional lives.

The social status of contractual physicians in relation to the private practitioners on the medical staff obviously changes as their relative proportion in the total staff increases. When the contractual physician has a minority voice, as in the permissive and medium-MSO patterns, he may be looked upon by the majority as a "second-class citizen." These attitudes are obviously changing, but in the rigorous-MSO patterns the contractual physician clearly has the power and first-class status. The patients served by these staffs and these hospitals, it is true, tend to be categorically identified—they are indigent or veterans or members of a particular health insurance plan—and not drawn from the "open market" of American health service. In the American scene, the MSO pattern constituting high commitment to the hospital has been developed initially in organized medical care programs involving a clear social responsibility for defined populations. As hospitals acquire more socially organized and assigned responsibilities for wider sections of the population (for example, for the aged as under the Medicare Law) we may except that the fulfillment of those responsibilities will require increasing degrees of commitment from their medical staffs.[8]

DEPARTMENTALIZATION

The degree of structuring of a medical staff organization is reflected also in a fourth feature—its subdivision into smaller units which permits exercise of authority and controls with more specialized competence.[9] This is the degree of departmentalization which is regarded here as an aspect of the medical staff even though it is in large measure parallel with the departmentalization of the hospital service program also. Three features of MSO departmentalization, as they were observed in our series of

[7] George H. Reifenstein, "The Director of Medical Education," in *Hospital Chiefs of Staff: Relationships of Doctors and Hospitals* (St. Louis, Missouri: The Catholic Hospital Association, 1965), pp. 54–58.

[8] John J. Flanagan, "Implications for Hospitals," in *Hospital Chiefs of Staff*, op. cit., pp. 61–63.

[9] American Hospital Association, *Hospital Accreditation References* (Chicago: The Association, 1965), "Departmentalization," pp. 79–85.

ten hospitals, will be examined and compared: (a) the bureaucratic organization; (b) the formal departmental authority system; and (c) the interdepartmental co-ordinating system.

The size of a medical staff has an obvious influence on the degree of departmentalization. Some adjustment must be made for size if one wishes to quantify the process for comparative purposes, and this will be done. If greater departmentalization usually occurs in larger organizations, however, the influence of that process is none the less real because it can be ultimately attributed to size. As in so many social phenomena, there may be a chain of primary (or independent) and intervening variables necessary to "explain" a certain outcome; yet the last intervening variable is still operative.

Bureaucratic Organization. In general, a greater number of departments and subdivisions in the medical staff reflects a higher degree of MSO structuring. In our series these numbers, not surprisingly, vary almost directly in proportion to medical staff size. If we apply the logarithmic correction for size, explained in chapter V in connection with the "contractual physician score," however, we can derive an adjusted tabulation of departmental units in the ten hospitals. In the following table the "weighted units" are based simply on the sum of the "departments" plus half of the "sections." The "size-adjusted bureaucracy score" is this figure divided by the logarithm of the hospital bed capacity.

Hospital	MSO type	Number of departments	Number of sections	Weighted units	Size-adjusted bureaucracy score
Kenter	I	2	2	3.0	1.6
Hillside	I	3	3	4.5	2.4
View	II	6	3	7.5	3.5
Midland	II	5	6	8.0	3.4
St. Martin's	III	7	19	16.5	6.8
Pebble City	III	5	8	9.0	3.4
Scopus	IV	10	25	22.5	8.4
Medical Group	V	14	9	18.5	7.3
Public	V	12	34	29.0	10.1
Veterans	V	17	29	31.5	9.9

There are obvious differences in the detailed manner by which departments and sections are defined within various staffs, even of the same actual degree of complexity. To smooth out these irregularities the departmental bureaucracy scores for the three main groupings of hospitals may be averaged and show the following:

| | Bureaucracy |
MSO type	score
Permissive	2.8
Medium	6.2
Rigorous	9.7

Thus, even though the growth of bureaucratic structure is not simple and linear in our series of ten hospitals, it corresponds in general to the over-all tightness of MSO structuring, even when adjustments are made for hospital size. With the greater number of departmental units, authority over the behavior of doctors can presumably be exercised by colleagues or peers with greater sophistication in particular medical specialties and subspecialties.[10] The controls in a sub-unit of cardiology, for example, could be applied with more effectiveness than in a general department of internal medicine, covering cardiology along with all the other facets of this field.

Departmental Authority System. If the bureaucratic structure just described is the anatomy of departmentalization of the medical staff, the authority system is its physiology. How is authority exercised in the departmental units? What authority have departmental chiefs or other officers? Differences are found clearly among the three broad MSO types.

In the permissive-MSO hospitals, the chiefs of clinical departments are not very powerful figures. They are private practitioners, usually elected by the members of the department to hold the position for one year. While a chief may be re-elected once or twice, the tendency is to rotate the role—in large part an honorary one—among the more active and perhaps senior physicians. Responsibilities of the chief are few; they relate mainly to making recommendations on new staff appointments and delineations of professional privileges (especially in surgery), rather than supervising or controlling the actual work of doctors in patient care or any other sphere. Lengthy tenure as departmental chief is discouraged, to guard against acquisition of any real "power."[11] In so far as authority for enforcement of policies is necessary, it is exercised at a higher level than the department—usually by the medical executive committee. The supportive departments in these hospitals—radiology and pathology—are, of course, different in having contractual physicians in charge. These units, however, are not very strong in the dynam-

[10] Mary E. W. Goss, "Patterns of Bureaucracy among Hospital Staff Positions," in *The Hospital in Modern Society*, Eliot Friedson, editor (New York: Free Press of Glencoe, 1963), pp. 170–94.

[11] Anthony J. J. Rourke, "Medical Staff Organization," in *Hospital Chiefs of Staff*, op. cit., pp. 7–10.

ics of the MSO; their heads control a staff of technicians and paramedical personnel, but have very little influence on the behavior of other doctors.

The authority of the departmental chiefs in the medium-MSO hospitals is greater. In the Type III MSO's, the clinical departments are headed by private attending doctors, but there is a tendency to re-elect the same person for several years, so that he acquires some strength and self-assurance in the position. Being larger, the departments have periodic meetings of their members, and the chairing of such meetings helps to underscore the authority of the chief. Problems in patient care or in the relationships of doctors to nonmedical personnel in the hospital will be brought to the attention of the chief. In the Type IV MSO (Scopus Hospital), the clinical departmental chiefs have become full-time contractual physicians with heavy commitment to the hospital and long-term tenure. They exercise great authority over the care of indigent patients, both on the wards and in the out-patient department, as well as over the educational and research programs. They also exert an influence on professional standards applied in the care of private patients. Strangely enough (reflecting the evolutionary process in the Scopus MSO), there is also a parallel "department chairman" elected by the private attending physicians in each clinical department; he works closely with the full-time chief, and, while he is particularly concerned with protecting the interests of the private doctors, he exercises authority largely through his full-time colleague.

The supportive departments in these medium-MSO hospitals are all headed by contractual physicians who have greater general influence than their counterparts in the permissive hospitals. Such departments include not only radiology and pathology but also anesthesiology, physical medicine, and perhaps psychiatry. The chiefs of these departments have more important roles to play on medical staff control committees (see below). They are looked upon not only as upholders of professional standards but also sometimes as arbiters of difficulties that may arise between private medical staff members and the hospital administration.

In the rigorous-MSO hospitals the departmental authority system reaches its greatest strength. The chiefs of both clinical and supportive departments are all full-time contractual physicians, with authority that is clear and broad. They exercise surveillance over all activities in their departments, no distinction being made between service to private and indigent patients. Part-time attending physicians work explicitly under their direction. The positions are appointive, rather than elective, and they usually have long tenure. Many decisions are made at the departmental level, which in the more loosely structured MSO's would be left to the over-all medical executive committee. Because of the day-to-day supervision of professional work at this level, there is less importance attached to various control committees that cut across departments for disciplinary review. The educational and research functions of the departments add an *esprit de corps* to the fulfillment of their daily objectives.

Co-ordinating System. To achieve co-ordination among the various departments there must be channels of communication as well as decision-making with respect to issues involving more than one department. In hospitals of all degrees of MSO structuring, there is some mechanism of interdepartmental authority; in a sense, an equilibrium is achieved, under which weakness at the departmental level is compensated by greater strength at the interdepartmental level.

In the permissive-MSO hospitals, where the departmental framework is weak, greater authority is usually vested in the over-all medical executive committee. Most important decisions are referred to this committee, and disciplinary actions are enforced through it. In these hospitals, also, the hospital administration (as distinguished from the medical staff itself) plays a larger role in interdepartmental co-ordination. Since there are so few doctors deeply committed to the hospital, medical staff members from different departments communicate in part through the office of the hospital administrator. Of course, being of relatively small size, the medical staffs in these hospitals also communicate informally across departmental lines. Since the organized programs of the departments are not highly developed, however, the need for interdepartmental co-ordination is not great.

In the medium-MSO hospitals, while departmental structures are stronger, the medical executive committee also plays a major role in co-ordinating the departments. The hospital administration is likewise involved, and the administrator is often called upon to carry out tasks for the department chiefs. The increasing role of contractual physicians in these hospitals, especially the full-time department chiefs in Type IV, leads to their assumption of co-ordinating functions as well. The elected chief of the medical staff usually has considerable prestige in these hospitals, and as an individual he helps to co-ordinate the departments.

In the rigorous-MSO hospitals the medical executive committee or its equivalent plays a smaller role in interdepartmental co-ordination. Instead, the medical directors, to whom the full-time department chiefs report, are the major channel of co-ordination. The line of authority is clear, and there are frequent meetings of the department chiefs with the medical director to discuss problems and achieve co-ordination. Because these medical staff officials are heavily committed to the hospital and present in it all the time, there is less need to lean on the hospital administrator for MSO assistance; the role of the administrator is more clearly confined to managerial matters outside the medical staff prerogatives. At the top, the medical director, as head of the full-time staff, and the hospital administrator must work closely together, whichever of the two is the higher executive serving as agent of the hospital's governing authority.

CONTROL COMMITTEES

Cutting across the lines of authority operating within departments are a number of medical staff committees exercising social controls over specific aspects of physician performance. As noted in chapter V, these committee roles may be compensatory to a weak departmental structure or a low level of commitment of staff members. On the other hand, even if the basic MSO structure is strong, the control committees may act to reinforce it in specific ways. When there are very active departments, furthermore, specialized control committees may be set up within them.

A distinction should be made between MSO committees having administrative or executive functions and those having quality review or control functions in specific technical fields. The former would include the medical executive committee or the departmental staff committees. The latter would include such committees as those responsible for credentials (appointments and privileges), tissue review, pharmacy, medical records, infections, professional education, out-patient service, etc. As the JCAH points out, quality controls need not depend on a "committee" mechanism,[12] but this approach was found in all the hospitals of our study. In the smaller MSO's the administrative type of committee sometimes carries out tasks assigned to a quality control committee in larger hospitals. (An important control committee in most general hospitals today is the utilization review committee, prescribed under the national Medicare Law; since most of the data in this study, however, were collected before that law took effect in July 1966, this committee does not appear in our discussion.)

Analysis of the control committees in our series of ten hospitals is offered according to three attributes: (a) their relative number; (b) their scope of functions; and (c) their diligence. Since, as mentioned, the functional roles may vary in different-sized hospitals, our efforts at quantification take account of all organized committees of both administrative and control types. "Committees of the whole" are also included, in order to have comparability in measuring "diligence," as reflected by number of meetings per committee during the year. Thus, general meetings of

[12] Joint Commission on Accreditation of Hospitals, "Joint Commission Amends Medical Staff Function Standard," *Bull. JCAH*, no. 40 (December 1965).

the entire medical staff (including clinical-pathological conferences) are counted as committee activities.

Relative Number of Committees. The number of medical staff committees in our series, with logarithmic adjustment for size-of-hospital, are as follows:

Hospital	MSO type	Number of committees	Size-adjusted committee score
Kenter	I	13	8.0
Hillside	I	14	7.5
View	II	15	7.0
Midland	II	45	19.1
St. Martin's	III	33	13.6
Pebble City	III	43	16.2
Scopus	IV	52	19.3
Medical Group	V	23	9.1
Public	V	31	10.8
Veterans	V	37	11.6

In the collapsed grouping of hospital types, the relationship between MSO structure and relative number of committees becomes more clear. Unlike departmentalization or commitment, in which "scores," adjusted for size, were also computable, the strength of committees is not consistently related to MSO structure:

MSO type	Size-adjusted committee score
Permissive	10.4
Medium	16.5
Rigorous	11.1

Thus, it is the middle range of MSO structures that has the highest development of committees. It is in these hospitals that we see the maximum development of various control committees, as a compensatory adjustment to weaknesses in other organizational features. In the most rigorous MSO structures, the tighter operation of departments, with more highly committed staffs, evidently reduces the recognized need for control committees to about the same level, by a size-adjusted score, as in the very permissive hospitals.

Scope of Functions. The scope of activities of various control committees may be considered in terms of (a) functions within the basic committees and (b) functions assigned to special or unusual committees. The basic committees for quality control of physician performance are three, stipulated in the "Standards" of the Joint Commission on Accreditation of Hospitals (1964 edition): the credentials committee, the tissue committee, and the medical records committee.[13] Beyond these, are a variety of special committees that may be established for the control of pharmacy practices, infections, blood banks, radiation therapy, out-patient services, educational programs, research, long-term care, etc.[14]

The scope of functions of the "basic" committees tends to be modest in the permissive-MSO structures. With the dominance of the busy private practitioner in these hospitals, the responsibilities for credentials assessment, tissue studies, and records review are carried out with whatever thoroughness is deemed necessary to maintain JCAH accreditation. In the medium-MSO hospitals the duties of these three committees tend to be assumed with greater thoroughness. Disciplinary actions are recommended more seriously, with respect to physicians who fail to meet standards in surgical judgment or medical record completion. Contractual physicians play a more significant role on these committees, and help to tighten up their general impact. In the rigorous-MSO hospitals the three basic control committees operate, but with less thoroughness perhaps than at the medium-MSO level; the departmental structure, with full-time medical chiefs, performs many of their functions instead. With the departments being concerned about medical staff appointments and privileges, about surgical decisions and maintenance of patient records, there is less need for surveillance by control committees.

As for the scope of "special" control committees, the relationships to MSO structure appear to be different. In the permissive-MSO hospitals these committees are not well developed since the range of hospital programs is not wide. In the medium-MSO hospitals they acquire broader functions—both by reason of a great diversity of such committees and a greater scope of tasks within each. In the rigorous-MSO hospitals the scope of special committees does not decline (as for basic committees), but continues to grow wider in response to more elaborate hospital program requirements. Thus, for example, the pharmacy committee is active in the up-dating of a drug formulary or the detection of drug reactions; the research committee plays an enlarging and stimulating role; the out-patient department committee tackles problems in an expanding ambulatory health service. These special committees, in other words, perform technical review or standard-setting functions that cannot be done within individual departments, even when the latter are strong.

[13] American Hospital Association, *Hospital Accreditation References*, op. cit.
[14] Anthony J. J. Rourke, "Medical Staff Organization: Relating Committees to Functions," *Hospitals* (16 March 1967): 51–55.

Yet, the implementation of special committee decisions is facilitated by numerous full-time physicians on the staff.

Diligence. From these attributes of medical staff committees at the different levels of MSO structuring, it is evident that their diligence of operation does not necessarily run parallel to their quantitative strength, as reviewed above. If we attempt to judge "diligence" by the frequency of scheduled committee meetings and the record of attendance by committee members, the findings vary at the different MSO levels.

Calculations were made on the frequency of committee meetings held during the year, based on data from the ten hospital case studies. (Information on attendance by committee members was unfortunately too uneven to use.) Certain assumptions were necessary to achieve quantification; for example, committees scheduled to meet "as necessary" were deemed to have met once during the year. Averaging the number of meetings per committee per year in our three sets of hospitals yields the following:

MSO type	Number of meetings per committee per year
Permissive	6.7
Medium	8.7
Rigorous	14.9

Thus, it appears that, although the relative number of established committees was found to be greatest in the medium-MSO hospitals, the over-all diligence of the established committees—as reflected by number of meetings per committee per year—is greatest in the rigorous-MSO hospitals. This is probably influenced by the active record of the "special" control committees discussed above. It is also probably influenced by several interdepartmental committees in the rigorous-MSO hospitals, which meet frequently on the tasks of patient care, education, or research.

With respect to the general role of medical staff committees, the Michigan study referred to earlier offers an interesting finding which is relevant to our observations. Focusing on the tissue committee in the series of thirty-three general hospitals, it was found that committee review of surgical charts for "corrective purposes" was done in 46 per cent of the smallest hospitals (under 100 beds), 92 per cent of the medium-sized hospitals (100 to 499 beds), and down again to 63 per cent in the largest hospitals (500 beds or more).[15] Although these data, reflecting a

---

[15] Walter J. McNerney, *Hospital and Medical Economics,* op. cit., vol. II., p. 1234.

U-shaped curve, were not interpreted by the Michigan research staff, they would seem to be consistent with our finding of a more serious disciplinary role for control committees in hospitals of the middle range of MSO structure.

DOCUMENTATION

Somewhat like the control committees, the use of various written instruments of social control in a hospital may compensate for weaknesses in general MSO structure or operate to reinforce a firm structure. This documentation may be formalized in two ways: (a) rules and regulations intended to govern future behavior, and (b) reports summarizing past happenings.

Rules and Regulations. All the hospitals in our series were accredited by the Joint Commission on Accreditation of Hospitals, so that it is not surprising that relatively standardized "medical staff bylaws, rules, and regulations" should be in effect in all of them. The joint commission issues a model code for this purpose and, with various modifications, every accredited hospital tends to adopt it. Our judgment of the relative strength of documentation in a hospital, as a form of social control, is based on the presence and application of published materials beyond these model JCAH formulations as well as the degree of refinement within the bylaws themselves.

The bylaws, rules, and regulations of a medical staff define in writing the organizational structure of the medical staff, the election of various officers, categories of staff membership, procedures for appointment and professional privileges, requirements for review of patient care (through various committees), requirements for meetings, responsibilities for maintenance of quality in the care of both private and indigent patients (e.g., through mandatory consultations), and various other details governing the behavior of doctors in the hospital. In a word, they attempt to establish a formal democratic procedure by which the doctors work in a hospital according to an agreed-upon system rather than as sovereign individuals. At the same time, the bylaws establish the prerogatives of physicians, as distinguished from the governing board or hospital administration, for the immediate supervision of medical care. These documents must be approved by the governing authority of the hospital to acquire legal force. Such approval establishes, then, both the responsibilities and the rights of the medical staff.

In the permissive-MSO hospitals of our series there are written bylaws, rules, and regulations for the medical staff, based largely on the JCAH model. In one of the MSO Type I hospitals, there were rather detailed elaborations of certain medical staff committee functions, the objective of which appeared to be assurance of equal rights for general practitioners as compared to specialists. Revisions of the bylaws are made infrequently; in one hospital there had been no revision for nine years, in another for five years, and in a third there had been only five small changes made in the last thirteen years. One gets the impression that these documents are in existence mainly because of JCAH requirements, but they have little impact on physician behavior. They are referred to occasionally by the hospital administrator or the chief of staff, to help deal with problems posed by individual physicians.

In three of the four permissive-MSO hospitals the bylaws are not supplemented by any manuals of procedure on specific problems. In one, however, (Midland Hospital) there is a great deal of written material provided to medical staff members on certain features of patient care. A forty-page document, given to each physician, gives details on such matters as the content of medical records, the requirements for consultations, indications for culturing purulent wounds, and stop-orders for dangerous drugs. Moreover, there is a medical staff committee with the assigned task of continually reviewing and revising the formal documents. In this particular hospital the documentation is strikingly compensatory to the dynamics of an otherwise permissive over-all MSO structure.

In all the medium-MSO hospitals, the bylaws, rules, and regulations were under revision at the time of our study. The tenure and authority of department officers were being changed, and the obligations of staff members were being made more explicit. At one of these hospitals a forty-two page procedure manual had been developed for the use of members of the medical executive committee and the various control committees. At another, a number of "work-simplification manuals" had been developed by the hospital administrator for nonmedical personnel, but these were written with the assistance of doctors and perhaps indirectly influenced physician performance. Also, a lengthy procedure manual was provided to interns and residents and, while intended for their guidance, it was frequently consulted by medical staff members. In a third hospital of this set, there were extensive memoranda and posted notices on specialty qualifications required for staff membership and privileges, conditions for advancement in medical staff rank, obligations in the out-patient department, etc. There were also numerous "tables of organization" posted on the structure of various departments and the over-all hospital organization. Because this institution (Scopus Hospital) was in the process of merger with a sister hospital at the time of our study, new written rules and regulations for staff behavior within the future consolidated departments were being formulated, but had not yet been completed. The general flavor of formal documentation in these medium-MSO hospitals was one of relatively high activity and change, designed to sharpen self-discipline among members of the medical staff.

In the rigorous-MSO hospitals the formal documents governing the medical staff consist not only of the JCAH-required bylaws, rules, and regulations but also of other basic legal documents. In Medical Group Hospital the official partnership agreement and the appointment papers of each physician entering the Foundation Medical Group establish basic rights and obligations in detail. In the two government hospitals there are the official appointment papers of the sponsoring government agencies. The federal institution (Veterans Hospital) has two sets of regulations distributed to all appointees, full-time and part-time; one is issued by the national Veterans Administration specifying policies in the entire hospital system, and the other is issued by the local medical director for this particular hospital. There are also a variety of intradepartmental procedure manuals developed for the use of both the house staff and the active medical staff. All these written documents are rather frequently consulted and serve to reinforce the generally high level of MSO structure in these hospitals.

Formal Reports. Written reports of past events can exert a disciplinary influence on a medical staff by establishing accountability—exposing facts to public view not only by the medical staff itself but also by other observers. The possibility of inviting criticisms or other responses to formal reports may, in turn, influence future behavior. Almost all hospital administrations issue some type of periodic report of over-all hospital operations, but our focus here is on reports of the medical staff as such.

In the permissive-MSO hospitals formal reporting by the medical staff is minimal. In three of the four hospitals in this set it is limited essentially to the recorded minutes of meetings of the staff and some of its committees; in one of them there is an "annual report of the medical staff" issued as a supplement to the hospital administrator's annual report. In the medium-MSO hospitals, reports in the form of minutes of meetings tend to be more thoroughly executed. The hospital administration at one of the Type III hospitals (Pebble City) takes the initiative in producing frequent reports of medical staff activities. At Scopus Hospital, in addition to minutes, the medical staff issues a printed monthly bulletin which is widely distributed; this contains selected committee reports, articles by departmental chiefs, and various news items designed to strengthen the pride of the medical staff in its hospital. Among the rigorous-MSO hospitals there are numerous formal reports to the sponsoring agencies. Since the corps of full-time physicians are more closely integrated with the hospital administrations, however, these reports are not so distinguishable as coming from the medical staff. They constitute reports of the activities of various clinical and supportive departments, combining statistics on patients and services with discussion of problems in patient care, education, and research. Reports to the government agencies are important in establishing justification for future financial support of the whole hospital program.

Thus, while exact quantification was not feasible, our impression is that all forms of documentation—both rules and reports—tend to be greater as MSO structure increases. Although we conceive of documentation as a "compensatory or reinforcing" feature of medical staff organization, it does not follow the U-shaped curve found for the control committees, but is more or less linear in our series of ten hospitals. This is consistent with the findings of the substudy of bylaws in ninety-two hospitals reported elsewhere, in which more rigorous formal language was found to be associated with a more abundant hospital staff, a slightly lower proportion of surgery, an attraction of more difficult cases, a somewhat greater community orientation, and a generally higher qualitative level of hospital performance.[16] This is quite aside from the implementation of the written word in the daily actions of the medical staff.

INFORMAL DYNAMICS

A network of informal interpersonal relationships permeates the structure of every organization and, as noted in chapter V, it may operate theoretically to either weaken or strengthen the formal organizational structure.[17] Perhaps it is more accurate to say that the informal dynamics help every organization to survive by fostering flexibility, but the flexibility may have differing effects, depending on the degree of formal structuring of the organization. In medical staff organizations that are loosely structured the informal dynamics tend to make them even more *laissez faire* and to render the attainment of goals more difficult; in rigidly structured MSO's, on the other hand, the informal dynamics are functional and prevent internal conflicts that might crack the entire structure and impede the attainment of goals.

In our series of ten hospitals we found a very high level of informal dynamics in both the permissive and the medium-MSO institutions. In the permissive hospitals the private physician is the most powerful figure, and his influence as an individual is only slightly constrained by the

[16] Roland C. Bower and Milton I. Roemer, "Medical Staff Organization in the Smaller Hospital," *Hospital Management* (September 1963): 46–47 (part 1) and (October 1963): 56–58 (part 2).

[17] B. S. Georgopoulos and F. C. Mann, *The Community General Hospital* (New York: Macmillan, 1962).

formal policies of the medical staff. Certain physicians often exercise great personal influence, regardless of their positions in the formal structure.[18] With the generally smaller size of the medical staffs and the low commitment of their members to the hospital, decisions are commonly made though personal discussion, influenced only slightly by the formal rules and MSO procedures. A deliberate attempt may be made by the hospital administration and governing body to foster a personalized and nonauthoritarian atmosphere in the medical staff and the hospital as a whole.

In the medium-MSO hospitals the formal organization is, of course, stronger, but the predominance of the private doctor, with his main commitment elsewhere, leads to many stresses and strains within the MSO. The very trend toward tighter MSO structures in these hospitals accentuates those stresses. In such a churning situation the informal dynamics —the attempted strategy of some staff members to "beat the system"— are, therefore, very strong. With the staff being larger, the informal relationships and decision-making are done largely within departments rather than across departments, but still outside of the formal structural lines. The power of a few individual physicians may not be so great as in the permissive hospitals, but several cliques, sometimes competing, may operate to influence day-to-day decisions.

It is only in the rigorous-MSO hospitals, where full-time contractual physicians acquire the dominant voice, that the informal dynamics have a noticeably different impact. We judge them still to be moderately strong, but their principal effect is to lend flexibility to the MSO structure. They operate to lend a tone of voluntarism to the issuance of directives that are, in fact, based on a clear line of authority. Decisions are usually made after informal discussion among the parties involved, even though such discussion is not strictly required. The implementation of decisions, furthermore, is carried out through many informal exchanges occurring outside of the official channels. Doctors in positions of power within the formal structure have often acquired those positions through cultivation of effective personal relationships with their colleagues over the years. There are also some intrigues and subterfuges by which the medical staff in one department may gain its ends at the expense of the doctors in other departments. In these senses, informal staff dynamics, even in the rigorous-MSO hospitals, remain a moderately strong influence in the daily activities of the medical staff.

The concept of informal dynamics in medical staffs includes more than the process of decision-making in day-to-day patient care. It includes influences on the formulation of over-all hospital goals relevant to educa-

[18] Stanley H. King, *Perceptions of Illness and Medical Practice* (New York: Russell Sage Foundation, 1962), pp. 307–48.

tion, research, and extra-mural community service. As MSO structure increases, the primacy of the private physician in determining hospital programs gradually gives way to various broader social values. What the hospital can do for the doctor becomes less important than what the doctor can do for the hospital. In the process of evolution, through which all MSO structures are moving, there are various stresses and strains which maintain the informal dynamics at a high level, even while MSO structuring is becoming greater. Only in the most rigorous-MSO pattern, where the predominant voice in the medical staff is that of the full-time contractual physician, is there a slight reduction in the net impact of informal dynamics.

This completes our "horizontal" analysis of the seven features of medical staff organization in a series of ten general hospitals. Some of the features we have been able to quantify, but for many of the main features and subfeatures we have had to rely on impressionistic information obtained in the individual hospital case studies. Even where quantitative data are marshalled, we cannot be certain of their accuracy and meaning, because of differences in definition of certain items (e.g., "committees" or "departments" or "staff appointments" or "regulations") among the hospitals. For these reasons, we have kept the analysis intentionally on a very general level, grouping the ten hospitals into three broad sets of permissive-, medium-, and rigorous-MSO structures.

Yet, in chapter V, we offered a numerical scoring of the medical staff organization of each of the ten hospitals, based on a quantitative estimate of the strength of each of the seven MSO features within each hospital. At best, these scores were a series of working estimates to permit us to proceed with the presentation of the ten "anthropological" accounts in some systematic sequence. The figures were based on interpretation of our field observations after all ten hospitals had been investigated.

We must emphasize, however, that the numerical MSO scores represent only the roughest approximation, intended to establish a *sequence* among the hospitals rather than a firm scaling. At the extremes of the range we may feel assured of the differentiation, but along the continuum there may well be faulty judgment in the score and the precise placement of individual hospitals. Our purpose is served if these efforts to define the degree of structuring of medical staffs have enabled us to offer the general analysis in this chapter. We can now move to examination of the content of hospital service programs associated with the various levels of medical staff organization.

IX

IN-PATIENT HOSPITAL CARE IN RELATION
TO MEDICAL STAFF ORGANIZATION

HAVING REVIEWED IN the last chapter the range of patterns of medical staff organization in our series of ten general hospitals, we may now attempt to summarize the several features of hospital performance associated with those patterns. In chapter V it was hypothesized that a greater degree of organization of physicians in a hospital facilitates a richer scope of activities called for by modern medicine, both in its scientific and humanistic aspects. This was a rather sweeping hypothesis, and testing it requires subdivision and analysis of hospital activities into their many components. Descriptive accounts of the MSO patterns and some brief comments on the hospital programs associated with them have been presented in previous chapters. Here we summarize the data on the components of in-patient hospital care horizontally across the series.

This exploration does not imply an argument that medical staff organization is the sole determinant of hospital programs. In chapter I we reviewed the great variety of social, demographic, and scientific forces that are influencing the structure and function of modern hospitals. Those influences, in fact, also shape the nature of the medical staff itself. We do argue, however, that the character of the medical staff in a hospital is an important intervening variable in the complex of determinants of hospital performance. In many respects it mediates those influences as the final causative link in a chain of factors leading to specific hospital activities.

In-patient care still constitutes the principal function of the American hospital, in spite of the variety of other community functions that hospitals have also come to perform. These other functions will be reviewed in the next chapter. Our account will be mainly descriptive of the types and scope of services offered, in relation to MSO patterns, but at the end of the chapter certain limited data on the final outcomes of in-patient care will be offered.

233

Different hospitals, of course, have different programmatic goals. In large measure these are related to the hospital's size and sponsorship, and it may be argued that a small proprietary hospital, for example, should not be "judged" by criteria appropriate to the goals of a middle-sized voluntary nonprofit or a large government hospital.[1] In an integrated network or system of hospitals certain variations in goals and programs would certainly be reasonable; patients needing specific types of service would go to the appropriate unit in the system, and educational or research functions would be done where the circumstances are proper.

Unfortunately, we do not have such an integrated hospital system in the United States.[2] Most individual hospitals are quite autonomous, so that small peripheral facilities may be called upon to provide services that are only appropriate to large central ones. Moreover, certain hospitals, large or small, may not set for themselves goals important for community welfare and within their potentialities. There is no technical reason why hospitals of any size or sponsorship cannot provide effective out-patient services and offer sound preventive measures, as one sees in many other countries (the obstacles are not technical but social and philosophic). In the absence of a planned network of health facilities, furthermore, some hospitals are compelled by larger social forces to assume great responsibilities in certain spheres—such as care of the indigent or education of nurses—because other hospitals do not accept such responsibilities.

Our findings of association between medical staff organization and the various components of hospital performance should not necessarily lead to judgment that a particular hospital is "right" or "wrong" or that its program is "good" or "bad." Social, political, and professional influences are much too complex for such simplified conclusions. We do offer the findings as a statement of empirical associations between MSO and the elements of hospital performance. To the extent that any conclusions may be drawn from a small series of ten selected hospitals, we suggest that the hospital program characteristics described are meaningfully associated with, influenced by, and often facilitated through various patterns of structuring of the medical staff.

CLINICAL DEPARTMENTAL FUNCTIONS

The central in-patient care functions of a hospital involve the diagnosis and treatment of patients whose major illnesses are typically classi-

[1] James A. Hamilton, *Patterns of Hospital Ownership and Control* (Minneapolis: University of Minnesota Press, 1961).

[2] National Commission on Community Health Services, *Health Care Facilities: The Community Bridge to Effective Health Services* (Washington: Public Affairs Press, 1967).

fied by medical specialties. The findings in relation to MSO patterns may be briefly summarized in that way.

Medical and Surgical Services. In the basic in-patient medical and surgical services of the ten study-hospitals, the differences are substantially matters of degree in the availability of technical resources (personnel and equipment) and their use for diagnosis and treatment. All MSO types of hospital offer the fundamental services required by relatively simple and uncomplicated cases. Only for the more unusual and complex cases are there manifest differences in the resources and functions of the different types of hospitals.

The great majority of patients admitted to all the hospitals are adults in need of medical or surgical service (as distinguished from cases for obstetrics, pediatrics, or psychiatric care). There are differences, however, within the medical-surgical mixture. Among the permissive-MSO hospitals (Types I and II), in all four the proportion of surgical cases exceeds that of medical cases; in one Type I hospital the surgical case proportion is over three times as high as that for medical cases. The same predominance of surgical patients characterizes the medium-MSO hospitals. In the rigorous-MSO hospitals, however, this relationship changes; in two of these three hospitals (those under government sponsorship), the proportion of medical cases admitted exceeds that of surgical cases. These hospitals, more than the others, accept aged and chronic patients with nonsurgical disorders.

Certain routine admission laboratory tests on blood and urine are done on medical and surgical patients admitted to all the hospital types. Associated with the greater autonomy of physicians in the more loosely structured hospitals, however, is a lesser discipline in carrying out these tests on every patient. In the more highly structured hospitals, especially where there are interns and residents, the routine tests are more meticulously executed, and a wider range of laboratory procedures tends to be ordered on the patient. Both electrocardiography and electroencephalography are available in the full range of hospitals, but in the more highly structured ones these test findings are more apt to be interpreted by a fully qualified specialist.

Intensive care units are lacking in the two Type I hospitals of the permissive-MSO set, but they are present in the two Type II hospitals, as in all the other hospitals of the series. The sophistication of monitoring procedures in those units, however, tends to increase in the more structured hospitals. In the latter there is a greater likelihood of the intensive care units being used for medical as compared to surgical cases (especially coronary attacks).

The subdivision of the larger and more highly structured medical staffs into a greater number of departments, and also sections within them, naturally has implications for in-patient care. Under internal medicine, a section on endocrinology, for example, means that the nursing staff is likely to be better trained in coping with a diabetic patient admitted in critical acidosis. In surgery the differentiations are more striking. All the hospitals have well-equipped operating rooms for handling the common surgical conditions. Only in the medium- and rigorous-MSO hospitals, however, are there resources for open-heart surgery. Equipment for complex orthopedic surgery is also more elaborate in the more highly structured facilities. Neurological and brain surgery are offered only in the medium- and rigorous-MSO type hospitals. At the time of our study, kidney dialysis (using the artificial kidney machine) was available only in Veterans Hospital, the most highly structured hospital in the series.

Known contagious disease cases are excluded, as a matter of policy, from all the hospitals in our series except the two government institutions in the rigorous-MSO set. In the medium-MSO hospitals a patient discovered to have a contagious disease after admission is usually retained, under isolation precautions, but in the permissive-MSO hospitals, the case would usually be transferred to another hospital as quickly as possible.

The differing potentialities for dealing with difficult medical and surgical cases in the various types of hospitals are generally recognized by the physicians on their staffs. Thus, a patient requiring cardiac or brain surgery would not ordinarily be admitted to a permissive-MSO hospital. Likewise, cases of serious trauma—for example, major automobile accident victims—would usually be taken by an emergency ambulance to a medium- or rigorous-MSO hospital. Public Hospital, operated by a city government, is a resource frequently used by police and by ambulance agencies for serious accident victims. Thus, a certain amount of spontaneous "regionalization" applies to the use of hospitals, even without deliberate social planning.[3]

In so far as general practitioners have admitting privileges in a hospital, however, their selectivity among institutions is perhaps less careful; they have such privileges only in the permissive-MSO hospitals of our series, so that choice of a more highly structured hospital ordinarily would mean transfer of the patient to another doctor. This doubtless leads to some patients being admitted to permissive-MSO hospitals who properly should go to more rigorously structured institutions. A study of

[3] Milton I. Roemer and Robert C. Morris, "Hospital Regionalization in Perspective," *Public Health Reports*, 74:916–22 (October 1959).

hospital admissions made not long ago in a Canadian province documented this tendency.[4]

From our field observations in the series of ten hospitals, we got the impression that the rate of consultations on medical and surgical cases was higher in the more highly structured institutions. The presence in such hospitals of a greater proportion of full-time staff and the higher general commitment of active staff members facilitates such consultation, with or without cost to the patient. Unfortunately, reliable statistical data are not available to quantify this impression. In the four permissive-MSO hospitals, the hospital administrations reported "consultation rates" averaging about 25 per cent, which may or may not be accurate. In the rigorous-MSO hospitals, however, we are virtually certain that the rates are higher than this, since almost every patient is seen by two or more doctors; consultations are so commonplace, in fact, that the medical records departments do not tabulate them, so that comparable statistics are not at hand.

Services in Obstetrics and Gynecology. Among specific causes for hospital admission in the United States, childbirth is the most frequent. All but two of the hospitals (Kenter and Veterans) in our series operate maternity services. Gynecology services are available in the larger hospitals, while in the smaller ones this field tends to be part of the surgical department.

Maternity cases in the eight hospitals accepting them constitute between 10 and 25 per cent of the total admissions, being somewhat lower in the more permissive-MSO hospitals (14 per cent) and somewhat higher in the more rigorous ones (22 per cent). These differentials appear to be related to the social classes predominantly served by these hospitals—more middle-class families with lower birth rates in the former hospitals and more lower-class families with higher birth rates in the latter.

The obstetrical space and equipment for labor, delivery, and after-care conform to good modern standards in all the hospitals. All these units are separate from other areas of the hospital, to reduce the risk of cross-infection, as required in the state hospital licensure laws. The differences among these facilities are related essentially to their size— that is, more labor-room beds and delivery tables being found in the larger hospitals. In one of the medium-MSO hospitals, where the maternity beds have been occupied at a very low rate, noninfected gynecological cases are sometimes admitted to those beds.

---

4 Milton I. Roemer, "Is Surgery Safer in Larger Hospitals?", *Hospital Management* (January 1959): 35–37.

As to professional responsibility for maternity cases, however, there are differences. In the permissive-MSO hospitals, general practitioners are permitted to manage obstetrical cases with little, if any, surveillance. In two of the three medium-MSO hospitals (Pebble City and St. Martin's) general practitioners may also do deliveries, but the medical staff departmental structure imposes a greater degree of surveillance. In the two rigorous-MSO hospitals accepting maternity cases (Public and Medical Group), all deliveries are done by specialists in obstetrics and gynecology or by residents or interns under their immediate supervision.

Prenatal and post-partum care are not regarded as hospital functions in any of the permissive-MSO hospitals. These services are left entirely to private physicians. In all three of the medium-MSO hospitals, however some responsibilities are accepted in this sphere. One of the hospitals conducts prenatal classes for expectant mothers, and the other two operate prenatal and post-partum clinics for low-income patients. In the rigorous-MSO hospitals these ambulatory services associated with maternity are more developed. At Medical Group Hospital the mother is served by the same physician for all three obstetrical periods. At Public Hospital the jurisdictional divisions in the city government mean that health department clinics offer the pre- and post-childbirth care, while the hospital manages the delivery. (Liaison is maintained between the two agencies, although gaps occur.)

Nurseries for the newborn are maintained in all the hospitals with maternity service. In the larger medium- and rigorous-MSO hospitals, however, there are separate nurseries for infants suspected of having infections. There are also more fully developed services for the care of premature infants.[5] The relatively new conception of "rooming-in"— that is, having the newborn baby stay in a bassinet at the mother's bedside—is practiced only in one institution of our series, Medical Group Hospital of the rigorous-MSO level.

The rate of Caesarian sections, as a percentage of total deliveries in a hospital, is sometimes regarded as a reflection of the prudence exerted by doctors. In the permissive-MSO hospitals of our series those rates were 3.1 to 7.7 per cent, in the medium ones 5.7 to 11.0 per cent, and in the rigorous ones 3.9 to 5.8 per cent. It is difficult, however, to draw any conclusions from these data without knowing the composition of the maternity patients served. The one exceptionally high Caesarian figure of 11.0 per cent applied to Scopus Hospital, where it is very likely that the explanation lies in the tendency of that hospital to attract relatively difficult maternity cases because of the high qualifications of the obstetrical specialists on its staff.

[5] American Academy of Pediatrics, *Standards and Recommendations for Hospital Care of Newborn Infants* (Evanston, Illinois: The Academy, 1964).

Similar inferences may be drawn from data on fetal and neonatal deaths occurring on the maternity services of the three MSO sets of hospitals in our series. Examining the rates for these deaths (per 1,000 live births) at the eight hospitals handling childbirths, for the year 1964, we find the following:

		Deaths per 1,000 live births		
Hospital	MSO type	Fetal	Neonatal	Total newborn
Hillside	I	10	8	18
View	II	11	11	22
Midland	II	10	9	20
St. Martin's	III	8	10	18
Pebble City	III	15	15	29
Scopus	IV	10	15	25
Medical Group	V	9	12	21
Public	V	16	22	37

Averaging these death rates within each MSO set, we find the three permissive-MSO hospitals to have a combined newborn death rate of 20 per 1,000 live births, the medium-MSO hospitals 24 per 1,000, and the rigorous-MSO hospitals 29 per 1,000. A similar gradient applies to the averages of the fetal and neonatal death rates examined separately, although it is steeper for the neonatal deaths (due mainly to the exceptionally high rate in Public Hospital). Just as for the over-all hospital death rates discussed later in this chapter, however, these differentials undoubtedly reflect the level of risk of maternity patients coming to the several hospitals. We know, for example, that Public Hospital selectively serves low-income mothers, among whom prenatal care tends to be less adequate and the incidence of premature births higher.[6] Moreover, this hospital serves as a center for receiving premature babies from surrounding hospitals. Thus, it is not surprising that its neonatal death rate should be so high, and this cannot be taken as a reflection of poor obstetrical services.

Pediatric Services. All the hospitals in our series, except Veterans, admit children, but two of the four permissive-MSO hospitals do not have a special pediatric section; children are simply admitted to private medical or surgical rooms.

Among the seven hospitals with designated pediatric wards, there

[6] Welfare Council of Metropolitan Chicago, *Report of the Maternal, Infant, and Preschool Child Survey*, part I (Chicago: July 1965): 30.

are certain differences in facilities. In the small permissive-MSO hospitals, the wards are attractive but there are no designated "playrooms" for the children Also, there is no provision of beds or cots for the mothers who may want to stay overnight with their children at a critical stage of their illness. In the larger medium-MSO hospitals, the pediatric departments are better equipped and staffed; there is special play space and, in addition to the nursing staff, two of the three hospitals in this set employ a "play-lady" or "play-therapist" to help the children adjust to hospitalization. There is also provision of cots for mothers staying overnight. In the two rigorous-MSO hospitals with pediatric sections, there are also playrooms, but no provision is made for maternal overnight stays. At Medical Group Hospital the average pediatric stay is very short (3.9 days); the hospital policy is to send nurses from the local visiting nurses association to the homes of discharged children, when follow-up supervision is necessary. At Public Hospital the average pediatric stay is relatively long (8.8 days); a school teacher is on the staff to instruct children who are hospitalized for extended periods.

The qualifications of the physicians serving children are also somewhat different in the several types of hospitals. In all the hospitals, the great majority are indeed specialists in pediatrics, but in the permissive-MSO ones, general practitioners are allowed. In the medium and rigorous-MSO hospitals, pediatric responsibilities are substantially limited to pediatricians. In Scopus and in Public Hospital, the pediatric departments are especially advanced, with active programs of teaching and research. While the simpler pediatric cases are probably well served in all the hospitals of our series, more complex cases are likely to receive the care needed only in the medium- or rigorous-MSO hospitals. In the more structured medical staff organizations, there are physicians devoted even to subspecialties of pediatrics, and associated with them are nurses trained in highly specialized pediatric tasks.

Psychiatric Service. The policy of admitting mental patients to general hospitals has been rapidly increasing in recent years, especially as short stays with intensive treatment by drugs or other physico-chemical measures (shock therapy), as well as psychotherapy, has proved to be effective.[7] In the two more firmly structured of the four permissive-MSO hospitals, there are psychiatrists on the medical staff, but none of these four hospitals has a designated psychiatric service. In all six of the medium- and rigorous-MSO hospitals, however, there are organized units for psychiatric care.

[7] Phillip H. Person, P. L. Hurley, and R. H. Giesler, "Psychiatric Patients in General Hospitals," *Hospitals*, 40:64–68 (16 January 1966).

In the three medium-MSO hospitals there are designated wards for psychiatric patients—of 10, 21, and 28-bed capacities. In the MSO Type III hospitals (St. Martin's and Pebble City), there are private attending psychiatrists on the staff, while Type IV Scopus has a core-staff of four full-time psychiatrists, as well as another thirty attending private psychiatrists. There is also a strong supportive staff of psychiatric social workers at Scopus. In Pebble City Hospital the out-patient psychiatric service is weak, but in the other two hospitals of this set it is highly developed. Unlike other clinical departments of general hospitals, in psychiatry the in-patient service is regarded as an adjunct of the out-patient service, where a greater volume of care tends to be provided. (Out-patient services, in general, will be more fully discussed in the next chapter.) At the Type III hospitals any medical staff member may admit a patient with a mental diagnosis, after which psychiatric consultation is required. At Scopus, however, only a staff psychiatrist may admit psychiatric patients.

In all the rigorous-MSO hospitals psychiatric services are also formally organized, but their features are rather different. In Medical Group Hospital the bed occupancy for somatic disorders is so high that no beds are allotted in the building for psychiatric cases, but ten such beds are reserved for health plan members in another private hospital nearby. At Public Hospital there is a ward of twenty-five psychiatric beds, in which the average stay is relatively long for a non-mental institution, 50.5 days. At Veterans Hospital there are no psychiatric beds in the general hospital as such, but this is only because on the same grounds there is a large mental hospital to which patients are readily referred.

All three of these psychiatric units are served mainly by full-time psychiatrists and supportive staffs. All three are also associated with special out-patient psychiatric service programs. At Public Hospital, furthermore, there is a "day hospital" service for patients needing more extensive therapy than a clinic could provide, but still capable of living at home. At Medical Group Hospital the associated health insurance plan offers only limited psychiatric benefits to its members, so that the in-patient care is usually described as "psychosomatic medicine." At Veterans Hospital the same term is used, but for another reason—that is, the availability of "psychiatric" care in the mental hospital nearby.

While the psychiatric services offered in any of our series of general hospitals are doubtless meager in relation to the size of the problem in the population, they illustrate the generally higher level of development of relatively innovative health services that tends to be found in hospitals of greater MSO structuring.

SUPPORTIVE MEDICAL SERVICES

Supportive of in-patient (and also out-patient) care functions in the basic clinical fields just reviewed are a variety of special services requiring both medical and paramedical personnel. The scope and nature of four of these types of services in our series of ten hospitals may be summarized.

Anesthesia. As an essential adjunct of surgery, anesthesia service is offered in all general hospitals. The anesthesiologist, however, tends to have a different relationship to the hospital—in the great majority of institutions—than that of any other specialist. Like the pathologist or radiologist, he is, in effect, granted an exclusive concession for services in his specialty; unlike the laboratory specialists, he is seldom under a definite contract with the hospital, but—like the surgeon or other clinicians—is paid fees directly by the patient. He has greater independence from the hospital administration, therefore, than physicians in the other supportive specialties. Often he furnishes his own anesthetic equipment and supplies.

This is substantially the arrangement in both the permissive- and medium-MSO hospitals of our series. In all seven of these hospitals the equipment is good and the anesthesiologists are qualified specialists. They look after post-operative patients in the recovery room and may supervise inhalation therapy technicians. They work, however, as individual physicians rather than as a team. In the medium-MSO hospitals the range of anesthetic procedures offered tends to be wider than in the permissive ones—corresponding to the complexity of the surgery performed—but the principal distinction is simply the volume of anesthesia performed.

In the rigorous-MSO hospitals, the organization of anesthesia service is different. The anesthesiologists are mainly on full-time salaries, and the equipment is owned and maintained by the hospital. In Public and Veterans Hospitals there are large staffs of anesthesiology residents who do the bulk of the work, under supervision. In Medical Group Hospital there is a staff of sixteen nurse-anesthetists, working under the supervision of five anesthesiologists and serving the bulk of the cases; only the difficult or high-risk cases are handled by the medical specialists. Thus, in these three hospitals anesthesia service is given by a team of personnel. Anesthesia also has greater independence as a hospital department, rather than being—as in the less-structured hospitals—more or less dominated by the departments of surgery.

In so far as reported post-anesthetic deaths are a reflection of the quality of this service, in the year of our study not a single such death was reported in any of the ten hospitals. Perhaps such events are under-reported or attributed to other causes, but this accomplishment seems impressive. It is especially so for the larger rigorous-MSO hospitals, where the number of anesthesias administered is higher and the operative risks are often greater.

Radiology. Diagnostic radiological service is provided in all ten hospitals, and in all but the smallest it is supervised by full-time contractual radiologists. Radiation therapy is offered in all of the medium- and rigorous-MSO hospitals, but in only one of the four permissive hospitals.

The range of diagnostic x-ray procedures offered tends to increase with MSO structuring and hospital size. The more structured hospitals have more elaborate equipment and usually better trained technicians, capable of doing more sophisticated types of x-ray work. Moreover, the radiologist in the more structured hospitals tends to have greater freedom to use his own judgment on the precise form of x-ray studies or therapeutic regimes needed by the individual patient. In the less-structured hospitals he is usually expected to carry out the instructions of the primary physician, without discretion.

In the largest of the permissive-MSO hospitals (Midland), there is an unusually high development of radiological services, including radioactive isotopes and cobalt therapy. Among the medium-MSO hospitals the range of services at Pebble City and Scopus hospitals is very wide. Pebble City has a cinefluoroscopy unit providing televised fluoroscopic studies for teaching purposes, and also a two-million volt therapy machine. At Scopus Hospital diagnostic and therapeutic radiology are each separate departments with specialized staffs. The diagnostic radiologist customarily exercises great discretion in the type of x-ray films to be taken on each case. The radiation therapy department offers radium and cobalt therapy and operates as a highly developed "institute of nuclear medicine."

In the rigorous-MSO hospitals the diagnostic x-ray services are of the same wide range as at Scopus Hospital, and probably wider than at the other two medium-MSO hospitals. But the radiation therapy services are less well developed. At the time of our study neither Medical Group nor Veterans Hospital had a cobalt therapy unit, although both had such units planned for the near future. Public Hospital, however, had a comprehensive therapy program, including a six-megavolt linear accelerator; its full-time staff included a specialist in nuclear medicine and a radiation physicist.

Perhaps the remarkably high development of radiation therapy in the medium-MSO, compared with the rigorous-MSO, hospitals reflects the composition of their patient populations and the attitudes of their governing bodies. Radiation therapy is used largely for treatment of cancer, about which feelings are especially strong; upper middle class citizens in control of voluntary hospitals will spare no expense to acquire promptly the latest therapeutic equipment. In the hospitals serving lower income patients such equipment is also eventually acquired, but evidently somewhat later. On the diagnostic side, however, where a much greater volume of service is necessary in any hospital, the range of services offered corresponds closely to the level of MSO structuring of the hospital.

Pathology. The scope of pathology services seems to be more closely related to the MSO structure of hospitals than that of any of the other supportive medical functions.

In the two smallest (Type I) among the permissive-MSO hospitals, clinical laboratory services are quite limited. The common blood, urine, or stool tests are done, but almost any nonroutine examination requires sending the specimen to an outside laboratory. Both these hospitals are staffed only by part-time pathologists, who also conduct private laboratories to which most of the specimens for unusual tests are sent. Ordinary tissue examinations are done by the pathologists in the hospital, but if a frozen section examination is required at the time of surgery, prior arrangements must be made to assure the presence of the pathologist. Autopsies must be done in a mortuary, rather than at the hospital.

The other two permissive-MSO hospitals (Type II) have full-time pathologists and a wider range of services. Most biochemical tests can be done, but special examinations (like protein-bound iodine or electrophoresis) must be sent out to private laboratories. Tissue pathology is well handled and both laboratories supervise blood banks; at Midland Hospital a blood donor transfusion service is quite active.

The pathology departments of the medium-MSO hospitals are still more highly developed. In both Type III hospitals (St Martin's and Pebble City) virtually every hematological, biochemical, and bacteriological test required can be done. At St. Martin's, a "package" of biochemical tests is offered for a reduced flat fee, to encourage the ordering of routine case-finding procedures. One of the pathologists also participates actively in surgical operations, to contribute his judgment to the decision on the best surgical procedure to perform. At Pebble City, the pathology department includes a biochemist and a microbiologist as well as several pathologists, thirty-two medical technologists and twenty-two other employees. It serves as a reference center for unusual blood-typing problems and does virological studies. It also has an active teaching program for technologists and conducts research. At Scopus Hospital (Type IV), the physical facilities are less impressive than at Pebble City, but the range of specialized personnel is still wider. Its research program is especially strong, and the capabilities stimulated by it are applied to the regular laboratory service as part of patient care.

In the rigorous-MSO hospitals the pathology services are of about the same range as at Scopus Hospital, but the volume of laboratory work turned out is still greater. At Medical Group Hospital the high volume is due mainly to the requirements of the large ambulatory care program served by the same laboratory, as well as to this hospital's role as the central unit in a regional network of five institutions. Much automated equipment is used to cope with the vast demands. At Public Hospital the laboratory occupies a separate two-story building, with seven full-time pathologists, seven pathology residents, and over 100 technical and other employees. Its services include fluorescent antibody techniques, gas-chromatography, electron-microscopy, and other highly complex procedures. Veterans Hospital also has a great deal of automated equipment to cope with its large work load and enough work to accommodate twenty pathology residents. In this laboratory, bacteriological studies are done on all patients prior to instituting antibiotic therapy.

In all ten hospitals of the series, all or nearly all tissues removed at surgery are examined by a pathologist grossly and microscopically. The role of the pathologist on medical staff tissue committees differs, however. In the more loosely structured hospitals the pathologist is usually hesitant to play a very positive role, acting mainly as a consultant to the committee; in the more tightly structured hospitals the pathologist has a strong voice on the tissue committee and may be its chairman. He has greater independence and need not fear alienating doctors by strictly objective reporting of his findings.

The autopsy rate of a hospital has long been regarded as a reflection of the general diligence of its medical staff in probing its own possible failures, but it also reflects the performance of its pathology service.[8] The autopsy rates in our three MSO sets of hospitals were as follows:

MSO type	Autopsy rate (%)	Range (%)
Permissive	32	20 – 41
Medium	50	49 – 52
Rigorous	57	43 – 84

By this measure, professional diligence would seem to correspond to the level of MSO structuring. The pathological reports on autopsies, furthermore, tend to be done more thoroughly in the more highly structured hospitals, with teaching programs for interns and residents.

Physical Medicine and Rehabilitation. Physical therapy services are offered to some degree in all hospitals of the series except the most loosely

---

[8] J. E. Blumgren, "Success of Autopsy Program Rests on Organization and Planning," in *Hospital Trends and Developments 1940–1946*, edited by A. C. Bachmeyer and G. Hartman (New York: Commonwealth Fund, 1948), pp. 414–16.

structured one (Kenter). In none of the four permissive-MSO hospitals, however, is the physical medicine service sufficiently developed to warrant a full-time medical specialist in the field. In these hospitals physical therapists accept general orders from staff physicians, but are not supervised by a physiatrist.

In two of the three medium-MSO hospitals, full-time physiatrists are on the staff and the entire program is more highly developed. At Pebble City Hospital the department of rehabilitation includes occupational and speech therapy personnel as well as physical therapists; an eighty-six bed "advanced care" unit has been constructed for chronic patients with rehabilitation potential. At Scopus Hospital there is a full-fledged rehabilitation center, headed by a full-time physiatrist, along with a full-time orthopedist and a large staff of therapists of all types. While most of its services are rendered to out-patients referred by private physicians, the center also provides a full range of physical medicine and related services to in-patients.

The three rigorous-MSO hospitals also have well-developed services in physical medicine, with full-time physiatrists in charge. At Medical Group Hospital there are eight in-patient beds assigned to this field, so that it fills more than a "supportive" role. Three-fourths of the department's services go to out-patients, and there is close liaison with an organized "home care" program. Frequent conferences are held with other specialty departments, to educate physicians on the value of referrals for physical medicine service. At Public Hospital the program was only recently launched under a full-time physiatrist, but it is staffed with the full range of therapists; the most difficult cases, however, are referred to another hospital in the municipal system, where rehabilitation is the primary function. Veterans Hospital has the most advanced physical medicine and rehabilitation service of the ten hospitals in our series. All the supportive therapies are provided, as well as a program of manual arts and organized recreation. There is an extensive training program with four residents in physiatry and sixty students of physical or occupational therapy. The department is especially active in the "intermediate service" of the general hospital, where post-acute patients (mostly middle-aged males) are kept until they can return to active life or require transfer elsewhere.

There is a noticeable difference in the attitudes of doctors toward a rehabilitation service, shown in the three MSO-levels of hospital. In the permissive type the field is hardly regarded as a medical specialty, and physical therapists are used as auxiliaries whose functions are not deemed important enough to require medical supervision. In the medium-MSO hospitals physical medicine is appreciated as a medical specialty, but its role is regarded as rather secondary. No in-patient beds are assigned to it, and every in-patient or out-patient served by the program must be referred by his primary physician. In the rigorous-MSO hospitals the rehabilitation service is usually free to be more aggressive and independent. In addition to having assigned beds for their own patients, the staff may actively review other patients on the wards to determine if physical modalities would help, without awaiting referrals. The whole department has greater importance both for the medical staff and in the organizational structure of the hospital.

SUPPORTIVE PARAMEDICAL SERVICES

There are many supportive services in hospitals that are both provided and supervised by personnel other than physicians. All the business administration functions might be so considered as well as dietary services, the hospital laundry, housekeeping functions, etc. Here we will review, however, only two such in-patient services that may be considered subject to direct influence by the medical staff—the nursing services and the hospital pharmacy.

Nursing Services. No hospital function is more involved with the purely personal aspects of patient care than nursing.[9] Yet, as medical technology has advanced, the demands on the nurse to serve as an assistant to the doctor on technical aspects of diagnosis and treatment have steadily increased. Certain differences are discernible in the performance of nursing functions in these two spheres—the personal and the technical—within hospitals of different size and MSO characteristics.

In the permissive-MSO hospitals, the staffing of the nursing service tends to be generous. Counting all types of nursing personnel, these four hospitals have between 156 and 168 nurses (in full-time equivalents) per 100 patients. The mixtures among registered nurses (RN's), licensed vocational nurses (LVN's), and nurse aides or orderlies differs. Registered nurses hold the supervisory and critical positions in all the hospitals, but in one, LVN's are more numerous than aides, while in another the reverse holds. In terms of hours of nursing care available per patient per day, the permissive hospitals range from 4.6 to 5.6 hours—high figures. (These latter ratios, however, are somewhat influenced by the number of nurses assigned to intensive care units, since these nurse-hours are not always included in the former figures.) The nursing staff is also relatively stable, with annual turnover being under 10 per cent in three out of the four permissive hospitals.

The nursing complement of the medium-MSO hospitals is slightly lower than in the permissive ones. There are more nurses assigned to inten-

---

[9] Faye G. Abdellah, I. M. Beland, A. Martin, and R. V. Matheney, *Patient-centered Approaches to Nursing* (New York: Macmillan, 1964).

sive care units in these hospitals, and in the regular patient-care wards nursing services are available at a ratio of 3.9 to 4.7 hours per patient per day. Staff stability is lower, as commonly occurs in larger hospitals, with annual turnover rates ranging from 40 to 50 per cent.

In the rigorous-MSO hospitals there is a substantial decline in the nursing staff available to patients. At Veterans Hospital, where the average patient-stay is very long and the general level of care is much less intensive, the total nursing staff is only 43 per 100 patients, but even in the other two hospitals of this set (Medical Group and Public), the rates are only 103 and 117 per 100 patients. The time available per patient is only about 2.0 to 4.0 nursing hours per day. The turnover rate varies from 35 to 60 per cent per year.

These measurements of nursing service help to explain differences in their qualitative attributes and in the attitudes of patients in the different types of hospital. In the permissive-MSO hospitals, nursing time available on the wards is relatively high and, it must be recalled, these hospitals are smaller and tend to have fewer seriously ill patients. The patients are also from relatively affluent backgrounds, with virtually none being indigent. It is small wonder that the level of patient-satisfaction with nursing care is reported to be high in these hospitals, and, accordingly, the physicians have few complaints.[10] The atmosphere conveyed is warm and friendly.

In the larger medium-MSO hospitals there are not only fewer nurse-hours available per patient per day, but the demands on the nurse for technical services (e.g., giving and maintaining intravenous infusions or monitoring various forms of drainage apparatus) are greater. With more seriously ill patients, more copious observational notes are required on the charts, which takes time from the bedside. A greater proportion of nursing personnel is also required in the out-patient services. It is not surprising, therefore, that in these hospitals there seem to be more frequent complaints from both patients and doctors about the nursing service. There is said to be less "tender loving care," and the doctors frequently allege that the registered nurses spend too much time supervising other personnel and not enough time at the bedside.[11] Adjustment to these problems is attempted through more active programs of formal in-service training of nurses and allied personnel in the medium-MSO hospitals. There are also nursing team conferences, manuals on "work-simplification," and various other techniques (e.g., the "floor manager" at Pebble City Hospital) to improve nursing efficiency.

In the rigorous-MSO hospitals, where the nursing personnel are de-

10 A. M. Feyerherm, *Measures of Hospital Patient Care Loads* (Kansas State University [processed], December 1964).

11 Esther Lucile Brown, *Newer Dimensions of Patient Care* (New York: Russell Sage Foundation, 1965).

cidedly fewer, other dynamics come into play. The same diversion of registered nurses and even LVN's from bedside care to other tasks occurs, as in the medium-MSO hospitals, but the adjustments take another form. There is a great deal of in-service training, as in the medium-MSO institutions, and much use of nursing manuals and nursing team conferences, but the supervising and head nurses are in closer touch with physicians on the full-time medical staffs. They sit on various committees with the doctors, and communication is frequent and continuous by word-of-mouth. Accordingly, they need not write as copious notes on the charts. Moreover, interns and residents are always present, both for performing technical procedures and for writing progress notes. The patients, furthermore, being mainly of humbler social background, tend to be less demanding of personal attention.[12]

As a result of these factors, the rigorous-MSO hospitals manage to get along with a smaller relative complement of nurses. In contrast to both the other sets of hospitals, the nurses do not have to satisfy the wishes and habits of so many different private practitioners; there are fewer doctors per 100 patients, and medical care policies among them tend to be more nearly uniform. Thus, the MSO patterns exert a definite influence on the quantity and characteristics of the nursing services in our entire series of hospitals. The degree of structuring of the nursing services, as a whole, runs roughly parallel to that of the medical staff.

Pharmacy Service. The hospital pharmacist must maintain and dispense drugs on the orders of a physican, and the way this is done varies with the size and MSO pattern of the hospital. The distinctions relate mainly to the degree of responsibility allotted to the pharmacist, the use of drug formularies, and the general scope of functions of the hospital pharmacy service.[13] Pharmaceutical manufacturing has, of course, become a highly developed industry in the United States, with the great majority of its products being compounded and packaged in the factory—rather than at the pharmacist's counter—and advertised to doctors in a great many ways.[14] The drugs received by the hospital patient, nevertheless, still require the proper performance of the pharmacist as well as the nurse.

At all ten hospitals of our series, there is at least one full-time pharmacist. As a ratio of pharmacy personnel per 100 beds, therefore, the figure in the small permissive–MSO hospitals is relatively higher than in the large rigorous-MSO hospitals. The functions of the pharmacist in

---

[12] Milton I. Roemer and Louise M. Arnold, "How to Measure Patient-Centered Services," *Modern Hospital* (August 1962): 81–84.

[13] Charlotte Muller and R. Westheimer, "Formularies and Drug Standards in Metropolitan Hospitals," *Hospitals* (16 January 1966): 97–102.

[14] Milton I. Roemer, "Health Service Organization Changes—Impact on Drug Use and Distribution," *J. Amer. Pharmaceut. Assoc.*, NS8: 231–33, 242–46 (May 1968).

the permissive hospitals, however, are quite limited. Essentially, he dispenses prescriptions—nearly always brand-name products—ordered by the doctor. There are no drug formularies of generic products in use, and the pharmacist does not have the authority to substitute a less expensive generic equivalent for a brand-name product that has been prescribed. A very large variety of drugs must be kept in the inventory, to satisfy the prescribing preferences of different doctors. (The relatively high costs of this general policy are simply passed on to the patient in private charges.) Drugs are dispensed only for in-patients, not for out-patients.

In the medium-MSO hospitals the pharmacist plays a somewhat wider role. All three of the hospital pharmacies dispense drugs to out-patients as well as in-patients. At Pebble City Hospital, the pharmacy is open to the general public twenty-four hours a day. At the other two hospitals (St. Martin's and Scopus), the out-patient pharmacy service is intended for low-income patients using the out-patient department, and it employs a drug formulary of predominantly generic-name products. The in-patient service does not require use of a formulary at any of these three hospitals. In Scopus, however, for prescriptions to indigent in-patients, the pharmacist is authorized to substitute less expensive but equivalent generic drugs for brand-name products ordered by the doctor.

Being larger and more complex institutions, the medium-MSO hospitals permit delegation of certain pharmacy functions to nurses on the floors. Thus, bulk supplies of the more frequently used drugs are distributed to the nursing stations, from which they are dispensed to patients. The pharmacist is responsible for maintaining proper drug supplies at these stations, and for dispensing directly only the more unusual prescriptions sent to the pharmacy.

This delegation to nurses of dispensing functions—as well as the actual administration of drugs, which is always a nursing function—is believed by some to increase the problem of medication errors. At one of the medium-MSO hospitals (Pebble City), therefore, a system of four decentralized drug substations was set up, with staffing by pharmacists. Although this was a relatively costly innovation, a great reduction in the rate of medication errors was claimed. While we do not have data on medication errors in our series of hospitals, other studies have suggested that they tend to be higher in larger hospitals where—with more steps between pharmacy and patient—there is more chance for mistakes to occur.[15]

In the rigorous-MSO hospitals there is a substantial change in pharmacy functions. In all the other hospitals a good deal of the pharmacist's time is spent on billing patients for prescriptions and on various cost-accounting procedures. This is unnecessary in the three rigorous hospi-

---

[15] David Starkweather, *Organizational Performance of Different Sized Hospitals*, doctoral dissertation (Los Angeles: University of California, 1968).

tals, where hospital funds are derived in other ways. The time saved can be used in pharmaceutical activities designed to promote economy or quality. Thus, generic-name formularies are used for in-patients in all three hospitals. In the two government hospitals, they are quite strictly applied, while in Medical Group Hospital the formulary is somewhat loosely implemented; the pharmacist, however, has broad authorization to substitute generic equivalents for brand-name drugs that may be prescribed. Similar policies apply to prescription of out-patient drugs at both government hospitals, but not at Medical Group Hospital; here the out-patient pharmacy service is not a benefit of the health insurance plan and, since transactions are simply on a commercial basis, no formulary is applied.

In the interest of economy, both government hospital pharmacies manufacture many of their own intravenous solutions and certain other medications used in large quantity. As a quality control, Veterans Hospital has a unique program of antibiotics surveillance, operated by coordination of bacteriological findings in the laboratory with drug dispensing at the pharmacy. A pharmacy resident training program is also conducted here. In all three rigorous-MSO hospitals, the more frequently used drugs are distributed in bulk to the floor nurses, who do the dispensing.

It is apparent that more personnel than pharmacists are involved in the drug service of a hospital. The nurses on the wards not only administer the drugs and in the larger hospitals do much of the dispensing but they also are responsible for enforcing "stop-orders" on various dangerous medications, ordinarily stipulated by the pharmacy committee of the medical staff. The floor nurses are expected to review prescriptions for possible dosage errors that may have occurred because of illegible handwriting, careless dispensing, or for other reasons. They also are expected to report signs of possible drug reactions to the physician. The efficiency with which these functions are carried out obviously depends more on the organization of the nursing service than the pharmacy service in different hospitals. Disciplinary surveillance, however, can be provided both by the hospital pharmacist and the medical staff pharmacy or therapeutics committee.

SOME OUTCOMES OF IN-PATIENT CARE

Having reviewed the principal features of in-patient care, as they relate to medical staff organization patterns in our series of ten hospitals, what can now be said about the net effect of all these matters on the final outcome of the hospital service?

The great difficulties in measuring the qualitative outcome of patient care in various hospitals have been discussed elsewhere.[16] The ultimate measurement of hospital performance ought ideally to be made in terms of the rate of recovery of patients from their ailments or conversely in terms of their nonrecovery. Hospital reporting, however, of the course of patient morbidity—such as rates of postoperative complications or rates of "improvement" versus "nonimprovement"—is notoriously unreliable. The sharpest measure of the total nonrecovery of patients is the simple hospital mortality rate—that is, the deaths occurring during a year as a percentage of all hospital admissions that year. But such rates depend very much on the average severity of cases coming to a particular hospital, and this is determined by the population served by the hospital (its age-level, socio-economic status, etc.) as well as the specific diagnoses of patients admitted.

An alternative approach might be to conduct medical audits on a sample of patient records in various hospitals, with evaluation by an expert observer of the adequacy and soundness of the diagnosis and treatment carried out.[17] This method can adjust for the varying mixtures of cases of different gravity in various hospitals, but it is a very complex and costly process. The funds available for this research did not permit its use.

Mortality Measurements. For the reasons stated above, presentation of the *crude* death rates for our series of ten hospitals, as ultimate measures of their qualitative performance, would be totally misleading. We may, however, apply the methodology devised in our previously cited paper, by which adjustments can be made for variations in the patient-composition of different hospitals. To do this, we may start with a listing of the crude hospital death rates in our series of ten institutions which, for either 1964 or 1965, were as follows:

MSO type	Hospital	Crude death rate (per cent)
I	Kenter	3.1
I	Hillside	1.7
II	View	2.4
II	Midland	1.8
III	St. Martin's	1.6
III	Pebble City	3.3
IV	Scopus	2.9
V	Medical Group	2.9
V	Public	8.1
V	Veterans	5.7

[16] Milton I. Roemer, A. Taher Moustafa, and Carl E. Hopkins, "A Proposed Hospital Quality Index: Hospital Death Rates Adjusted for Case Severity," *Health Services Research,* 3:96–118 (Summer 1968).

[17] Leonard S. Rosenfeld, "Quality of Medical Care in Hospital," *Amer. J. Public Health,* 47:856–65 (July 1957).

The apparent tendency is for the crude hospital death rate to increase, in relation to the level of MSO structuring. The average for the four permissive-MSO hospitals is 2.25 per cent, for the three medium-MSO hospitals it is 2.60 per cent, and for the three rigorous-MSO hospitals it is 5.57 per cent.

It is obvious from our detailed case studies of the ten hospitals that these mortality differences must mainly reflect the characteristics of the patients coming to the three sets of hospitals, rather than the quality of service provided. We know that in the permissive-MSO hospitals, the patients are all self-supporting and usually affluent, and that their diagnoses are relatively uncomplicated. The somewhat higher death rate at Kenter Hospital (3.1 per cent) can be partly explained by the absence of a maternity service (where the risk of death is typically very low). In the medium-MSO hospitals the medical and surgical diagnoses tend to be more severe, and at Scopus there is a sizable proportion of indigent patients, among whom the risks are generally much higher. In the two out of three rigorous-MSO hospitals under government auspices, the patient population is of distinctly low socio-economic status, as well as containing a high proportion of aged persons; in addition, their diagnoses tend often to be complicated. These factors can readily explain the high crude death rates, in spite of the strong technological development in these hospitals; further confirmation is reflected by the much lower death rate in the third hospital of the rigorous-MSO set, Medical Group Hospital, where the patient population is predominantly from self-supporting families in the working years.

It has been customary to distinguish hospital deaths occurring within forty-eight hours from admission from those occurring later, on the ground that the former were largely hopeless and do not reflect a "failure" by the hospital. With modern potentialities of bold emergency care, this line of reasoning is probably no longer valid, but, in any event, the data on mortality so delineated were studied. It was found that in the series of ten hospitals, the under-forty-eight-hour deaths account for about 30 per cent of the total, ranging from 12 per cent in Veterans to 52 per cent in Medical Group Hospital. The residual deaths after forty-eight hours show no consistent differences in the rates among the three MSO sets of hospitals.

If the methodology developed in our cited paper, to adjust death rates for average case-severity, is applied to the ten hospitals in our series, the findings are of much interest. This approach considered the average length-of-stay as a practical over-all indicator of case-severity, especially when it was corrected, in turn, by the occupancy rate as a reflection of non-patient influences (pressure on beds, physician policies, etc.). It may also be noted that hospitals were compared better by excluding from the death rate denominator all maternity admissions and from the numerator all newborn deaths. Thus, the resultant figures for nonobstetrical deaths in 1964, calculated for the ten hospitals in our series are somewhat different from those listed earlier. Alongside these figures, shown below, are the hospital death rates adjusted for case-severity, according to the method outlined in our previously published study:

MSO type	Hospital	Crude death rate (nonobstetrical)	Severity-adjusted death rate
I	Kenter	3.1	4.71
I	Hillside	1.4	2.32
II	View	3.2	2.98
II	Midland	2.9	3.62
III	St. Martin's	2.4	0.97
III	Pebble City	2.9	2.12
IV	Scopus	3.8	1.45
V	Medical Group	3.1	1.63
V	Public	9.1	5.33
V	Veterans	5.0	-1.31

It is evident that the severity-adjustment tends to elevate the death rates in the more loosely MSO-structured hospitals and to reduce them in the more highly structured ones. (In the case of Veterans Hospital, with its extremely long average stay, the adjustment becomes so great as to convert the crude death rate of 5.0 per cent into an adjusted figure that has a negative value.)

Examining the severity-adjusted death rates for the three collapsed sets of hospitals, we find in the four permissive-MSO hospitals an average rate of 3.41 per cent, in the three medium-MSO hospitals a rate of 1.51 per cent, and in the three rigorous-MSO hospitals a rate of 1.88 per cent. Thus, the adjustment yields mortality rates that are higher in the most permissive-MSO hospitals and lower in the most rigorous ones. It will be recalled from our published paper, however, that the length-of-stay formula adjusts for only about 60 per cent, and not 100 per cent, of the misleading differentials in crude death rates. This may well explain why the adjusted deaths rates in the three sets of hospitals do not show a simple linear relationship and why the medium-MSO hospitals have a slightly lower adjusted death rate that the rigorous ones. On the other hand, it is quite possible that these differentials are, indeed, a valid reflection of the quality of in-patient care in the three sets of hospitals.

With the data at hand, we simply do not know, and solution of this problem must await further research.

If we compare, on the very simplest scale, the adjusted death rates in the four most permissive-MSO hospitals in our series with the other six of either medium- or rigorous-MSO structuring, then it is found that greater structuring of the medical staff is associated with a lower adjusted death rate of patients. On this basis, the loosely structured hospitals have an adjusted death rate among their patients of 3.41 per cent and the combined moderately and highly structured ones, 1.70 per cent. With all its simplifications and assumptions, this two-to-one relationship would seem to be a powerful finding, in support of the hypothesis that higher levels of medical staff organization are probably associated with higher quality of hospital performance.

Beyond this very generalized finding, we have no further direct evidence of the final "outcome" of in-patient care in the series of ten hospitals studied. One can point, however, to the interesting study of malpractice suits in a series of five California hospitals published in 1958, in which it was found that the three "high-suit hospitals" had greater deficiencies in their medical staff organization than the two "low-suit hospitals."[18] Malpractice suits, as a percentage of admissions, were regarded as a measure of extreme patient dissatisfaction. One can take note also of other studies, using the medical audit technique, in which higher rates of poorly managed cases were found in small proprietary hospitals—presumably with weak medical staff organization—than in large voluntary ones—with presumably stronger-MSO structures.[19] In this research, however, we are compelled to base our evaluation of the content and quality of in-patient care principally on the descriptive accounts of resources, policies, and practices in hospitals that have been summarized in this chapter.

Other Indices. A final word may be offered about the over-all resources devoted to all hospital functions in relation to MSO levels in our series of ten hospitals. Rough reflections of these resources would be (a) the over-all staffing per 100 patients served and (b) the over-all expenditures per patient-day. There are intricate problems of uniform definition for both of these measurements, which counsel great caution in interpreting them, but the data collected for our ten case-study hospitals were as follows:

[18] Richard H. Blum, *Hospitals and Patient Dissatisfaction: A Study of Factors Associated with Malpractice Rates in Hospitals* (San Francisco: California Medical Association, 1958), pp. 262–64.

[19] Columbia University School of Public Health and Administrative Medicine, *A Study of the Quality of Hospital Care Secured by a Sample of Teamster Family Members in New York City* (New York: The University, 1964).

MSO type	Hospital	Total personnel per 100 patients	Expenditure per patient-day
I	Kenter	369	$70.11
I	Hillside	381	78.00
II	View	292	67.96
II	Midland	316	68.52
III	St. Martin's	289	64.00
III	Pebble City	225	53.54
IV	Scopus	383	72.00
V	Medical Group	197	59.00
V	Public	291	45.52
V	Veterans	152	31.00

Because of the problems of definition and nonuniformity of inclusions and exclusions in both of these types of measurement, it is probably sounder to cluster the above figures into the three sets, as follows:

Simplified MSO type	Total personnel per 100 patients	Expenditure per patient-day
Permissive	315	$71.15
Medium	299	63.18
Rigorous	213	45.17

The trend of these figures might suggest a greater relative investment of resources in the less-structured hospitals, but one must keep in mind other possible explanations. As for staffing, the figures may mean that personnel are used extravagantly in the more permissive hospitals and efficiently in the more-structured hospitals. Support for this possibility is found in the average occupancy rates of the three sets of hospitals; from low to high structuring these rates in the year of study were 72, 81, and 88 per cent respectively. A higher occupancy rate usually means fuller use of the existing staff complement.

The lower expenditure per patient-day in the more highly structured hospitals would reflect, of course, the less abundant staffing, but it may also reflect lower salary levels, a personnel mixture with greater proportions of minimally trained workers, more frugal expenditures on supplies, and smaller capital outlays. In the three rigorous-MSO hospitals our observations suggest that all these factors are operative. As for the relatively high patient-day expenditure of the four permissive-MSO hospitals, the proprietary sponsorship of two of them must not be overlooked.

These relationships may seem to be somewhat at variance with national findings on the staffing and costs of general hospitals in relation to their size. We know that in our series, MSO structuring corresponds closely to hospital bed-capacity. Yet, for the nation as a whole, the American Hospital Association reports both staffing and expenditures in general, short-term, nonfederal hospitals to vary in the opposite direction from that implied above. In 1967 there were 232 personnel per 100 patients in 25 to 49-bed hospitals, increasing quite regularly to 288 per 100 patients in hospitals of 500 beds or more. The corresponding figures for "expense per patient-day" in 1967 were $42.19 in the small hospitals and up to $62.49 in the large ones.[20]

To explain this apparent discrepancy one must recall that our series of ten hospitals does not presume to be a random sample of the national hospital scene. All of our ten hospitals were accredited—one of them was a federal government hospital (excluded from the A.H.A. data)—and each of the ten was selected to illustrate a certain pattern of medical staff organization. Their bed-capacities, furthermore, are not exactly congruent with their degree of MSO structuring. Pricing policies in the western United States, moreover, where our study was conducted, may differ from those in other sections; a Massachusetts study, for example, found higher patient-day costs to go along with greater services, such as we see in the more structured but less costly hospitals.[21] Our resultant sample, therefore, is by no means parallel with the national distribution of hospitals. The characteristics of each of the ten hospitals, or of the three sets classified by MSO structuring, are claimed only to reflect conditions found in the deliberately selected cases—in accordance with the "anthropological" methodology explained in the Appendix.

These overall figures on hospital staffing and expenditures apply to the total hospital program, not solely to in-patient care of the sick. We must proceed now to examine "horizontally" the other functions of the institutions in our series—those identified with the wider community role of hospitals.

---

[20] American Hospital Association, *Hospitals: Guide Issue* (1 August 1968).

[21] Mary Lee Ingbar, *A Statistical Study of Differences in Hospital Costs: Cost Functions of 72 Massachusetts Community Hospitals* (Cambridge, Massachusetts: Harvard University [processed], 1965).

X

THE WIDER COMMUNITY ROLE OF HOSPITALS
IN RELATION TO MEDICAL STAFF
ORGANIZATION

BEYOND IN-PATIENT CARE of the seriously sick, the modern general hospital is ideally expected to serve many other functions. The nature of these functions, their historic origins, and their determination by many external social circumstances has been reviewed in previous chapters. Within the hospital its sponsorship obviously influences its goals and the range of its functions beyond bed care of the sick. A hospital's size also sets limits on its capability to fulfill various possible community roles.

Just as it affects the various components of in-patient care, however, the organization of the medical staff is an important intervening variable in the performance of the other hospital functions. MSO patterns can facilitate or inhibit the hospital's assumption of a wider community role. In this chapter we will review the elements of that role, in relation to MSO patterns in our series of ten hospitals. These will be summarized under five headings: (a) out-patient services; (b) preventive activities; (c) professional education; (d) medical research; and (e) other external relationships.

OUT-PATIENT SERVICES

Historically, hospitals offered out-patient services, like in-patient care, mainly for the poor. In the nineteenth century, however, when in-patient hospital care became commonplace for all social classes, out-patient services remained oriented to the low-income groups.[1] With respect to systematically organized out-patient services this is still largely true.[2] In recent years, however, general hospitals have come to be in-

---

[1] Michael M. Davis, *Dispensaries: Their Management and Development* (New York: Macmillan, 1918).

[2] E. R. Weinerman and W. A. Steiger, "Ambulatory Services in a Teaching Hospital, *J. Med. Education*, 39:1020–29 (November 1964).

creasingly used for emergency services by persons of all income groups—
that is, without reference to scheduled clinic sessions.[3] In addition,
ambulatory private patients of medical staff members are sometimes
seen in the hospital out-patient department for certain examinations
that cannot be done in the doctor's office.

Thus, there are three types of out-patient service that a hospital
may provide: organized out-patient clinics for the poor, emergency
services for anyone, and ambulatory private services. In some hospitals
these are administratively quite distinct, and statistics on the volume
of each type of service are kept separately. In other hospitals both the
organization and tabulation of these services overlap a great deal. We
can get a better picture of the wider community role of hospitals, however, by considering each of the three categories of service separately.

Organized Clinics. Scheduled out-patient department clinics for the
poor obviously require the time of doctors and, therefore, the with-
drawal of medical time from other activities, especially private practice.
It is no surprise, therefore, that none of the four permissive-MSO hospitals in our series operate such OPD clinics. Ambulatory private and
emergency services are offered, as we will discuss below, but the medical staffs of these hospitals, supported by their governing bodies, do not
regard the out-patient care of the poor as an appropriate function of
their particular hospitals. One slight exception is the provision at the
largest of the permissive hospitals (Midland) of a fortnightly "cancer
follow-up clinic" for patients discharged from the hospital. Although
these are virtually all private patients, no charges are made for the
examinations, which are intended to discover any possible recurrence
of the disease.

In all three medium-MSO hospitals, organized out-patient clinics
for low-income patients are offered, but the extent of their service differs. At the two Type III hospitals (Pebble City and St. Martin's), the
volume of services provided is relatively low; the maintenance of these
clinics is at a level suggesting a compromise between the reluctance of
the medical staff doctors, who regard OPD services as somewhat competitive with their private practices, and the desires of the hospital
management to offer a community service. At both of these hospitals
members of the active and associate medical staffs attend the clinics
without compensation, and at St. Martin's the Catholic religious order
in charge is especially insistent that doctors meet their obligations in
this respect. A special out-patient child study center for physically

---

[3] George S. Tyner, "The Emergency Room," in *Hospital Chief of Staff: Relationships of Doctors and Hospitals* (St. Louis, Missouri: The Catholic Hospital Association, 1965), pp. 63–64.

and mentally handicapped children is another feature of St. Martin's community orientation.

At the Type IV medium-MSO hospital (Scopus), out-patient services on an organized basis are well developed. There are 37 regularly scheduled OPD sessions in all the specialties, with about 60,000 visits per year—about four times the number of in-patient admissions. There are especially active out-patient programs in rehabilitation therapy and psychiatry. Medical staff membership carries an obligation to work designated hours in the clinics, but in addition there are eight full-time physicians and a full-time OPD medical director for this service. A special building is allotted for OPD services, which are generally recognized as a major function of Scopus Hospital.

In the rigorous-MSO hospitals organized out-patient services are still more highly developed and are closely integrated with the in-patient services. At Medical Group Hospital the ambulatory services are not oriented to the poor, since the hospital is part and parcel of a comprehensive health insurance plan whose members pay their own way. (Many of these families are, nevertheless, of quite limited income and without insurance might be considered eligible for OPD services in other hospitals.) Doctors on the medical staff of the hospital serve daily in the out-patient service facilities, equivalent to their "private offices," either within the hospital itself, in an adjacent building, or in a "satellite" clinic structure. The volume of services provided to ambulatory patients under these arrangements is far higher than under the conventional charitable concept of out-patient departments. There are no periodic "clinic sessions" in the usual sense, but in each specialized field there are designated quarters where patients are seen by appointment throughout the week.

At the two government hospitals, out-patient services are also highly developed as a basic and legally defined function. At Public Hospital there are 92 types of scheduled clinic sessions and 170,000 visits from eligible patients of low income per year. The Veterans Hospital out-patient services, however, are restricted by the federal definition of eligibility, which is limited to veterans having disabilities connected with military service; moreover, there is another separate out-patient clinic for such patients, more conveniently located in the center of the city. Most of the OPD services at both these government hospitals are provided by members of the full-time medical staffs or by interns and residents.

Ambulatory Private Services. At all the nongovernment hospitals in our series, private patients are sometimes individually scheduled for laboratory, x-ray, or other diagnostic procedures or for special therapies (such as physical medicine) in the out-patient department. Separate records are seldom kept on these cases, which are usually tabulated with "emergency services" (see below).

While we do not have exact data, the extent of this type of out-patient service in all the permissive-MSO hospitals seems to be small. There are private clinical laboratories, x-ray specialists, physical therapists, and other independent practitioners to whom the medical staff members conventionally send their patients. In the medium-MSO hospitals more of such private ambulatory services are provided, because the hospital has developed certain technical fields to a level not offered by private practitioners. These may be illustrated by the highly developed rehabilitation out-patient services at Pebble City and Scopus hospitals or the sophisticated radiological therapy services at the latter.

Among the rigorous-MSO hospitals, at the two government facilities, private out-patient services may not ordinarily be rendered. At Public Hospital low-income patients are charged small fees, according to a scale of ability-to-pay, but they are seen by the doctor-on-duty rather than a private physician. At Medical Group Hospital all the ambulatory services might, in a sense, be categorized as "private," but they have been discussed above since they are furnished by or at the request of physicians with full-time organizational connections rather than by private medical practitioners.

Emergency Services. These have been the most rapidly expanding out-patient services in recent years, and to some extent they are provided by all the hospitals in our series. To cope with the rising demand, medical staffs have been induced to organize coverage of the hospital emergency room more systematically than in the past, and thereby to increase the structuring of the medical staff itself. In the hospitals of more permissive-MSO patterns, however, there tends to be a reluctance to develop emergency services to an extent that might become too competitive with private practice—under the same apprehensions that have inhibited organized out-patient clinics for the poor in those hospitals.

There is also a kind of reciprocal relationship between the provision of scheduled OPD clinics and the demand for emergency services in a hospital. Where the organized clinic services are nonexistent or weak, emergency services come to fill the gap for low-income as well as other patients. Where organized OPD clinics are relatively strong, they fill a need even for certain "emergency" cases, and the volume of these may therefore be low. The geographic location of a hospital in relation to the homes of the poor and the location of other hospitals also has an influence on the volume of emergency services. The availability of private physicians in the local area to meet urgent medical needs is another obvious influence. Since emergency services are provided to persons of any income level, charges are ordinarily made by the hospital, and the administrative patterns for collecting and using this money differ among the MSO types of hospitals.

Among the four permissive-MSO hospitals, at two of them (Kenter and View) emergency services are offered at a minimum level. Patients coming to these hospitals in search of care are usually simply referred elsewhere. At one of the Type I hospitals (Hillside), however, a relatively active emergency service has been developed, with staffing by a rotating panel of three young physicians recently settled in the area. These doctors make charges to each patient, which they collect privately, and the hospital makes a separate charge for use of its facilities, nurses, etc. In order to reduce its "competitive" effect, emergency room policy requires referral to a private physician of all patients needing follow-up care; if the patient lacks a "family doctor," he may be referred to the private office of the emergency room panel doctor, who thereby builds up his practice. Some of the patients coming to the Hillside emergency room are brought by the ambulance of the county emergency aid system, with which the hospital has a contract for coverage of a defined district. The private orientation of this whole service, however, is underscored not only by the practice of levying two separate charges on each patient but also by a policy of referring elsewhere any indigent person who is not a truly urgent case.

At the fourth hospital in the permissive-MSO set (Midland), there is also a relatively large emergency service with a private practice orientation. Though originally attended by rotation of the younger members of the medical staff, the rising demand has led to engagement of two full-time contractual physicians. The fees they charge, in addition to hospital charges, are collected by the hospital, which guarantees them a minimum annual income. These physicians, however, are only "probationary" members of the medical staff and do not have admitting privileges; patients requiring hospital admission must be referred to a regular member of the active staff. As at Hillside Hospital, indigent patients whose conditions are not urgent are referred to a government hospital for attention; exceptions are made, however, for persons who claim they are not eligible for such public medical care by reason of nonresidency under the law.

Among the three medium-MSO hospitals, the emergency services have a private orientation, like that of the permissive hospitals, in one, but not in the other two. At one Type III hospital (Pebble City), the emergency room is served by a rotating panel of twelve members of the medical staff who assure twenty-four-hour coverage; there is also assistance from interns and residents. Patients are billed by the hospital both for hospital services and for physician fees; the latter, however, do not go to the individual doctor but are pooled into a fund, from which the panel members receive part-time salaries according to their hours of work. The organized medical staff has taken substantial responsibility for the whole service through a special emergency room committee, an educational program for local doctors on emergency treatment methods, and contracts with local industrial enterprises for emergency care of their employees. Although Pebble City Hospital has a moderately developed organized OPD for low-income persons, the volume of cases seen in the emergency service is more than twice as great.

At the other two medium-MSO hospitals (St. Martin's and Scopus), where organized clinics for the poor are more systematically sponsored, the emergency services are relatively less important. At St. Martin's, two full-time salaried physicians are employed to cover both the emergency room and much of the organized clinic program. The volume of demand for both these types of out-patient services, however, is reduced by the proximity of another large hospital with a highly developed OPD program. At Scopus, the services identified as "emergency" are relatively few, mainly because such patients tend to be seen in one of the regularly scheduled medical or surgical clinics that are held almost daily. In both these hospitals, while nonindigent emergency patients are billed for services, the hospital charges a single amount, and the "private-fee" aspect found in the less structured hospitals is absent.

In the three rigorous-MSO hospitals, emergency services are closely integrated with the organized out-patient programs and covered by the regular full-time medical staffs. Patients who are not eligible for care at the hospital (because they are not members of the health insurance plan or not indigent or not veterans) are charged for services, but the money collected simply becomes part of hospital earnings. At Medical Group Hospital the insurance plan members who come suddenly without prior appointments are seen at "walk-in clinics" staffed by regular full-time physicians; noninsured persons with a true emergency are seen in the same quarters. Of all ambulatory services in the health insurance plan, about 25 per cent are estimated to be "walk-in" cases. At Public Hospital twenty-four-hour coverage is provided by the full-time staff plus the interns and residents. The same applies to Veterans Hospital, where anyone—veteran or not—will be seen in a true emergency. Because of the well-developed organized out-patient clinics at all three rigorous hospitals, however, the emergency services are of relatively less importance; at Public Hospital they account for only 30 per cent of total OPD visits and at Veterans Hospital 7 per cent.

TABLE 9. OUT-PATIENT SERVICES IN TEN STUDY-HOSPITALS, BY MSO TYPE

MSO type	Hospital	Bed capacity	Organized clinic visits	Emergency visits	Total visits per bed
I	Kenter	42	—	104	2.5
I	Hillside	76	—	6,649	87
II	View	141	—	226	1.6
II	Midland	230	—	14,726	64
III	Pebble City	447	6,167	15,771	49
III	St. Martin's	265	4,107	2,921	27
IV	Scopus	490	59,773	2,004	126
V	Medical Group	346	720,000	—	2,080
V	Public	729	170,773	52,000	306
V	Veterans	1,500	27,450	2,080	20

This relatively detailed discussion of out-patient services of three types in our series of hospitals has been offered because, more than most hospital functions, this one seems to epitomize the degree of community orientation of an institution—its policies toward social needs beyond the care of private in-patients. Moreover, the extent of service to the poor in out-patient departments corresponds roughly to the level of in-patient care of the poor. The patterns of charges and remuneration to doctors reflect the relative strength of the voice of private medical practice in hospital policy formulation. The characteristics of the three components of out-patient services seem to be heavily influenced by the level of MSO structuring, but it is evident from the above discussion that other factors peculiar to each hospital also play a part.

Because of all the complexities, statistical data on out-patient services do not show any simple and consistent relationships to MSO patterns. In summary of the above discussion, however, we may give a tabulation of the limited data available at the time of our study for the year 1964–65 in Table 9.

Interpretation of the figures in Table 9, of course, requires reference to the text above and preferably the greater details presented in the hospital case studies of earlier chapters.

PREVENTIVE HEALTH SERVICES

The definition of preventive services in a hospital or elsewhere is not easy.[4] In a sense, any hospital activity designed to protect the individual against disease or to detect early a hidden disease has preventive implications. Despite much eloquent discussion about the broad role of the modern hospital, inclusive of prevention, our field studies

[4] Stanhope Bayne-Jones, "The Hospital as a Center of Preventive Medicine," *Annals of Internal Medicine*, 31:7 (1949).

actually found very little evidence of such services in hospitals of any level of MSO structuring.[5] Nevertheless, with a liberal interpretation of the meaning of prevention certain comparative findings emerge.

In the permissive-MSO hospitals the only preventive service that can be identified is the performance of certain routine laboratory tests on all patients admitted. Blood counts and urinalyses may point to some hidden disorder unrelated to the cause of admission. Even these tests, however, are not done with complete uniformity on all patients. Serological tests for syphilis are done when ordered by the physician but not routinely. The absence of organized out-patient clinics in these four hospitals reduces their opportunity to offer health education, and this is quite lacking. There is no systematized review of immunization status in pediatric patients; this is left to each individual physician.

In the medium-MSO hospitals somewhat greater orientation toward prevention is observed. At Pebble City Hospital, educational forums on selected health topics have been held at the hospital for adult and adolescent audiences. The hospital also provides quarters in which the local health department holds a prenatal clinic regularly. At St. Martin's Hospital the organized out-patient clinics offer preventive services, including chest x-rays on all new adult patients and necessary immunizations on all children. At Scopus Hospital the pediatric department reviews immunization status of all patients and lacking inoculations are given. Among the organized out-patient services for low-income patients, there is a well-baby clinic conducted by the hospital rather than the local health department. Women coming to the out-patient gynecology clinic receive vaginal cytology (Papanicolaou) examinations routinely. The routine blood and urine tests on all in-patients are carried out with greater uniformity in these three hospitals, and the wider capacities of their laboratories permit a generally greater variety of disease detection tests to be done.

In the rigorous-MSO hospitals prevention of disease is promoted in a greater number of ways. The health insurance plan with which Medical Group Hospital is affiliated has a fundamentally preventive orientation, in that its members are accessible to prompt ambulatory service for any symptom or for a periodic health check-up, without economic hurdles. All plan members also receive regular mailings of health educational literature. The organized ambulatory service includes routine well-baby examinations and immunizations in the pediatrics department, and in the obstetrics department prenatal examinations of every pregnant woman. Because of the highly developed laboratory

[5] Edwin L. Crosby, "Preventive Medicine as a Major Function of the Hospital: From the Viewpoint of Public Health," Proc. Eighth Int. Hosp. Cong. (London: International Hospital Federation, 1953).

facilities, a great many Papanicolaou smears are done on both in-patient and out-patient females. Educational classes are held by nurses
for diabetic patients and expectant mothers. On admission, of course, all
patients receive routine blood and urine examinations.

The two government hospitals are the most comprehensive of our
series in routine disease-detection procedures. In addition to the blood
counts and urinalyses, all in-patients of both hospitals receive chest
x-rays for detection of tuberculosis or other chest disorders. Many out-
patients also get chest x-rays, and serological tests for syphilis are commonly done. At Public Hospital there are health educational efforts
through posters and leaflets in the OPD. Well-baby and prenatal clinics,
however, are not held because these are regarded as a responsibility of
the health department—a sister agency under the same local government. Children in the pediatric wards are, nevertheless, checked for
immunization status and the necessary injections are given. At Veterans
Hospital the policy of comprehensive care for all veterans admitted
leads to prompt therapy of any condition discovered, quite aside from
the cause for admission.

The only other type of preventive program in many hospitals is
an occupational health service which may be offered for the hospital's
own employees This typically includes pre-employment examinations, necessary immunizations, and often periodic chest x-rays as well
as initial treatment of on-the-job illness or injury. Such personnel health
services tend to be better developed in the larger hospitals, where the
medical staff organization is more highly structured. It is of interest that
at one medium-MSO hospital (Pebble City), this service is the responsibility of the director of medical education, a full-time contractual physician qualified in internal medicine.

PROFESSIONAL EDUCATION

Hardly any hospital function is so dependent on the MSO pattern
as the education of professional personnel. Effective teaching usually
requires a large investment of time and energy from physicians, and this
is seldom available unless staff members have a heavy commitment to the
hospital. The educational activities in our series of hospitals may be
summarized in three categories: graduate medical training, continuing
or postgraduate education, and paramedical personnel training.

Graduate Medical Training. None of the four permissive-MSO hospitals have graduate training programs for interns or residents. Among
the medium-MSO hospitals there are approved internship and residency
programs in two of the three institutions. In one of the Type III hospitals (St. Martin's) there are no full-time doctors-in-training, but a few

residents come to the hospital part of the year for experience in selected fields (orthopedics or gynecology). This hospital has sought its own interns and residents, but has not been successful in competition with other nearby hospitals with well-developed teaching programs, in the face of a short national supply of medical graduates.

The other Type III hospital (Pebble City) has thirty-one interns and residents whose educational experience is supervised by a full-time director of medical education. In the Type IV hospital (Scopus) the graduate program is more highly developed. There are twenty interns and fifty-one residents, covering all the principal medical and surgical specialties. The program here is also supervised by a full-time director of medical education, and the bulk of the teaching is done by the full-time staff members in the various clinical departments. It may be noted that in 1965, directors of medical education were appointed in 914 hospitals throughout the nation—this being 62 per cent of the 1,474 hospitals with residencies approved by the American Medical Association.[6] In both Pebble City and Scopus, but especially at the latter, there are active schedules of clinical-pathological and other medical conferences, attended by both the house staff and the attending physicians.

In two of the three rigorous-MSO hospitals, the graduate training programs are still more highly developed. The exception is Medical Group Hospital, where the comprehensive full-time staff and the absence of indigent patients have obviated the usual basis for a large house staff; there are twenty-four residents but no interns. In the two government hospitals, the large indigent patient populations and relatively smaller full-time staffs, have set the conditions for extensive teaching programs. The 171 interns and residents at Public Hospital and the 205 at Veterans Hospital are heavily involved in the medical care of all the patients. While they are giving service, of course, they are also learning, and the teaching is done predominantly by members of the full-time staff. The learning process is not only through regular supervision of the intern's and resident's work but through a rich schedule of staff conferences within each department, ward rounds, and formal lectures.

A teaching program for interns and residents, of course, has implications beyond those of education. The very tasks of teaching are a challenge that keeps a medical staff on its toes, and this applies to the private attending as well as the full-time physicians. Our observations confirm those of others, however, that the most effective education of interns and residents comes from the full-time medical staff.[7] In spite of

---

[6] American Medical Association, "Physician-Hospital Relations," *J.A.M.A.*, 190:74–79 (5 October 1964).

[7] Melvin Seeman, J. W. Evans, and L. E. Rogers, "The Measurement of Stratification in Formal Organization," *Human Organization*, 19:96 (February 1960).

the time it takes from either full-time or attending staff, there can be no doubt that the quality of patient care in a hospital is uplifted by a graduate medical training program.

Continuing Medical Education. A hospital can serve also to provide postgraduate or continuing education for all the physicians on its staff, throughout their professional lives.[8] The extent of this, as of graduate training, varies strikingly with MSO patterns.

In the four permissive-MSO hospitals there are modest efforts at offering educational stimulation to the attending physicians, but their success has been limited. At one of them (Kenter) there is virtually no educational program aside from the business meetings of the medical staff. At the other three, there is a professional speaker scheduled at each of the monthly staff meetings. Two of the hospitals subscribe to a periodic closed-circuit television program on selected medical topics, but not many physicians view it. At only one of the four hospitals (View) are there scheduled clinical-pathological conferences, twice a month, to review cases. Attendance at educational sessions in these hospitals is seldom high, because of the numerous affiliations of the doctors with other hospitals and their limited time commitments in the permissive institutions.

Continuing education of physicians in the medium-MSO hospitals is more highly developed. At one of them (St. Martin's), there are regular clinical-pathological conferences, speakers at staff meetings, medical television, and various sessions held at the child study center, but the absence of a house staff and the nearness of a university hospital have inhibited greater activities. At the other two (Pebble City and Scopus), where the internship and residency programs are strong, continuing education for the entire medical staff is correspondingly active. At Pebble City there are weekly clinical-pathological conferences and monthly surgical-pathological conferences, in addition to frequent formal speakers, medical television, and a weekly journal club. At Scopus there are all these activities, plus a great many educational conferences and "teaching rounds" within the various departments. In both these hospitals the directors of medical education—while primarily intended for the house staff graduate training program—obviously provide many side-benefits for the attending medical staff.

In the rigorous-MSO hospitals, continuing educational activities are still more numerous and varied. At Medical Group Hospital the practices are especially interesting, since they do not constitute by-products of a house staff training program, the latter being relatively modest. Instead,

[8] Russell A. Nelson, "The Hospital and the Continuing Education of the Physician," in *Hospitals, Doctors, and the Public Interest*, John H. Knowles, editor (Cambridge: Harvard University Press, 1965), pp. 237–53.

education is built into the regular working schedule of the wholly full-time medical staff. One half-day each week is reserved for educational meetings, there are regular lectures and symposia, clinical-pathological conferences, etc. Each year one week of educational leave with pay (in addition to vacation time) is available to every doctor. In the two government hospitals, with their large house staff training programs, the tempo of clinical conferences, ward rounds, lectures, and departmental meetings is very high. The full-time staff members both teach and learn in these sessions, and most of the part-time physicians are attracted to work in Public or Veterans hospitals mainly because of the educational opportunities. The daily atmosphere of both these hospitals is permeated with an educational spirit, which is, of course, fortified by their ties to a school of medicine.

An educational resource for both the graduate and postgraduate programs in hospitals is the medical library. The number of books and journals, staffing, and budgetary allotments for the library tend to be distinctly greater in hospitals of higher MSO structuring.

Paramedical Personnel Training. Although the oldest form of paramedical personnel training in hospitals is preparation of registered nurses, none of the hospitals in our series operates such a school of nursing. This is doubtless related to the great development of nursing education in junior colleges and other institutions of higher education in the metropolitan region where our study was conducted. Instead of operating schools, several of the hospitals collaborate with such college programs, providing bedside experience for the student nurses. The hospitals may also offer training for other types of health workers.

Among the permissive-MSO hospitals, at the two Type I facilities, there are no training programs of any sort. At the Type II hospitals there is a small laboratory technician training program in View Hospital and in Midland Hospital a collaborative role is played in the training of vocational nurses, physical therapists, and inhalation therapists.

Both the medium and rigorous-MSO hospitals have quite highly developed training programs for a variety of paramedical personnel. These include laboratory and radiological technicians, dieticians, surgical technicians, physical therapists, nurse's aides, pharmacy interns, and even hospital chaplains. All of these hospitals collaborate with local colleges in training professional nurses and some of them in training vocational nurses. At St. Martin's Hospital (Type III), where graduate medical training is relatively weak, the medical staff has—perhaps to compensate for this—developed a relatively strong interest in training paramedical workers. On the other hand, the energies of full-time physicians in the rigorous-MSO hospitals are so heavily directed to the training of interns and residents, that they do not seem eager to expand into the paramedical fields. Nevertheless, there are active paramedical training programs in all of them. In the two government hospitals, there are substantial programs for training laboratory and x-ray technicians, associated with their large departments of pathology and radiology.

MEDICAL RESEARCH

Increasingly, hospitals have become places for medical research, but it appears to be confined to institutions with relatively highly structured MSO patterns. In none of the four permissive-MSO hospitals of our series is any research conducted.

Among the medium-MSO hospitals, research efforts are not significant at one of the Type III institutions (St. Martin's), except in its affiliated Child Study Center. As noted in the educational field, the proximity of other large academically oriented institutions (with which many of the medical staff members are also affiliated) has probably inhibited research aspirations here. At the other Type III hospital (Pebble City), there is a rapidly growing program of clinical investigation; with some sixty-five projects underway in the year of study, there was a full-time director of research in the hospital and an annual research budget (derived from extra-mural grants) of some $200,000. In the Type IV hospital (Scopus) medical research has attained a more remarkable level of development. Associated with the hospital is an impressive research institute, with a full-time staff of 65 persons, some 140 projects underway, and an annual research budget of about $750,000. The studies are not only in clinical medicine but include a great deal of animal experimentation (with a vivarium) and extensive laboratory investigation. The active medical staff is also much involved, with 125 doctors participating part-time in various research activities.

In two of the three rigorous-MSO hospitals, research is even more highly developed. At Medical Group Hospital the high preoccupation with medical care for health insurance plan members has necessarily reduced research opportunities, but even here some thirty studies are underway. At both government hospitals, research is regarded as a major hospital function. Almost the entire full-time medical staff and many of the visiting staff at Public Hospital are engaged in studies—both clinical and laboratory—which were supported by $1,300,000 from extra-mural grants in the year of study. In fact, the heavy research interests of the staff have caused administrative tensions in this municipal institution, whose sponsors naturally stress the primacy of patient care. At Veterans Hospital the annual research budget exceeded $2,500,-000 in the year of study, and 60 per cent of these funds came from the Veterans Administration itself. Thus, research is not dependent wholly on attracting extra-mural grants, but is regarded by the hospital sponsors as an integral part of the total program. Advancement of full-time physicians in the medical staff hierarchy is affected by their research output, and two-thirds of them are engaged in studies which absorb a good part of their time.

The relationship of research (like professional education) to MSO patterns is quite obvious. It takes physicians with a heavy commitment to the hospital, as against private clinical practice, to develop a research program. Thus, in a moderately structured hospital, like Pebble City, the initial research efforts came from the full-time pathologists and radiologists. When a program develops, personnel are hired (usually from special grants) exclusively for research purposes. Then physicians of other specialties become involved, and persons with advanced training in the basic sciences may be appointed to direct research projects. Animal quarters and special laboratories are added to the hospital to back up clinical investigation on the wards. As full-time salaried physicians become an increasingly important part of the medical staff, research opportunities play a major part in attracting well qualified men and women to these positions. Thus, research becomes less of an appendage on, and more of an integral part of, the hospital program. There is always the danger that research may become so dominant in the professional life of the doctor that patient care suffers, but the predominant effect seems to be one of enhancing the quality of medical service in hospitals.[9]

OTHER EXTERNAL HOSPITAL FUNCTIONS

Beyond the several aspects of a hospital's wider community role just reviewed, there are a variety of other ways that hospitals can extend their services. These may be summarized under four headings, in relation to medical staff patterns.

Medical Social Service. Orientation of hospitals to the social needs of patients in their total community setting requires personnel who can help people adjust to environmental problems. Social workers are trained to play this role and they do so through formal departments of social service.[10] Since environmental handicaps are greatest among the poor, social services are largely devoted to them.

In the permissive-MSO hospitals, with their virtual exclusion of indi-

[9] Sheldon King, "Medical Research Raises the Quality of Care," *Modern Hospital* (January 1960): 88.
[10] Celia R. Moss, "Social Service," in *Modern Concepts of Hospital Administration.* Joseph K. Owen, editor (Philadephia: W. B. Saunders Company, 1962), pp. 476–86.

gent patients (at the time of this study—before the Medicaid program), it is not surprising that no social service departments are found. Theoretically, the self-supporting patient is also sometimes in need of social work assistance, but up to now hospitals have seldom regarded provision of such assistance as their responsibility.

In the medium-MSO hospitals which provide some services for the poor—if only on an out-patient basis—social workers are engaged. At St. Martin's (Type III) there is one social worker in the out-patient department, but she has hardly any duties for in-patients and there is no separate department of social service. At the other Type III hospital (Pebble City), one social worker is attached to the department of rehabilitation, and her duties are fairly limited. At the Type IV hospital (Scopus), however, with both an in-patient and an out-patient service for indigent persons, there is a social service department with eight social workers, and three other psychiatric social workers are attached to the department of psychiatry. In Scopus Hospital, the social workers have the prerogative of reviewing all indigent cases for those in which they can potentially be helpful. This is in contrast to the two Type III hospitals, where social workers may only see patients on referral from a doctor. Steps are also being taken at Scopus to promote the use of social services for private patients, on referral.

In the rigorous-MSO hospitals, medical social services are still more developed. At Medical Group Hospital it is noteworthy that social workers function in a department of social medicine, and they serve any patient, in spite of none being indigent. They are chiefly concerned with making arrangements for post-hospital care of chronic cases, through family adjustments or referral to other agencies. At the two government hospitals, with large indigent or low-income patient populations, the social service departments are very strong, with twenty-four social workers at Public Hospital and eleven at Veterans. These staffs help to find gainful employment for discharged patients, offer general family counseling, make appropriate referrals to welfare departments for financial aid, and also assist in arranging long-term care for chronic patients. The latter is a particularly demanding task at Veterans Hospital, from which many aged veterans are transferred to nursing homes but still kept under surveillance by the social workers. In all three rigorous-MSO hospitals the social workers have freedom to seek out patients in need of their help, without awaiting medical referrals.

Volunteer Services. Another relationship between hospitals and the surrounding communities flows in the opposite direction, that is, from the community toward the hospital. Volunteers come into the hospital to help in various supportive tasks, such as the operation of gift shops, stocking and servicing book collections for patients, conducting tours of the hospital, soliciting blood donors, packaging bandages, or doing various personal chores for patients on the wards.[11]

Among the four permissive-MSO hospitals, in the two under proprietary sponsorship such volunteer services are quite lacking, and in a third they are quite weak. At Midland Hospital, however, there is an active volunteer service. Likewise, at both Type III hospitals the volunteer programs are strong. At these and also the Type IV hospital, the volunteer services include fund-raising by various "ladies auxiliaries." Even in the two government hospitals, although fund-raising plays no part, various patient-oriented volunteer activities are very well developed; at Veterans Hospital, through a network of organizational affiliations, as many as 2,000 volunteers are registered for some type of service. Only at Medical Group Hospital, with its philosophy of self-support through health insurance, is a volunteer program undeveloped.

Hand-in-hand with the volunteer services, most hospitals conduct a "public relations" program to win community support. In the large voluntary nonprofit hospitals (Pebble City and Scopus) there are full-time directors of public relations in the top management; their objectives include fund-raising as well as general projection of a favorable image of the hospital in the community. In the three rigorous-MSO hospitals the latter objective is also considered important enough to warrant engagement of full-time public relations personnel.

Organized Out-of-Hospital Care. As chronic disease has become more important in our aging population, some general hospitals have taken steps to organize services outside the hospital proper.[12]

At Midland Hospital in the permissive-MSO set, there is an adjoining building with thirty beds for long-term patients; this unit gives largely custodial care with little effort at rehabilitative therapy. At Pebble City Hospital there is an eighty-six-bed "advanced care unit" for chronic patients, with much more active rehabilitation services. In Veterans Hospital there is an "intermediate care unit," with a strong rehabilitative emphasis, and a "long-term care unit" for terminal patients.

Organized "home care" programs constitute a further extension of the general hospital's role.[13] Teams of medical, nursing, rehabilitative, social work, and other personnel visit the chronic patient in his own home. Not only are hospital beds thereby released for acute cases but more comfortable and reassuring surroundings are provided for the patient. None of the permissive-MSO hospitals have such a program, but

[11] Madolin E. Cannon, "Volunteer Services," in *Modern Concepts of Hospital Administration*, op. cit., pp. 502–20.

[12] American Hospital Association, *The Extended Care Unit in a General Hospital* (Chicago: The Association, 1966).

[13] David Littauer, I. J. Flance, and A. F. Wessen, *Home Care* (Chicago: American Hospital Association [Monograph No. 9], 1961).

a strong one has been developed at Scopus Hospital in the medium-MSO set. Headed by a full-time physician, this program has departmental status. While originally limited to indigent patients and financed through a special philanthropic grant, under "Medicare" this home-care program has been extended to private patients as well.

Among the three rigorous-MSO hospitals, two have home-care programs—Veterans and Medical Group Hospital. The former is limited to quiescent chronic patients who can be cared for in their own homes or in a private nursing home, and they are promptly readmitted to the hospital if there is a medical need. The Medical Group Hospital program is more diversified; about half of the home-care patients are in a terminal stage of illness, one-fourth are long-term chronic cases, and one-fourth are patients convalescing after an acute illness. With about 200 patients on its roster, this organized service releases a substantial number of beds in the hospital, where pressure for beds is high.

Thus, considering both long-term bed units and organized home-care programs, it is evident that more substantial developments are found in hospitals at higher levels of MSO structuring. Both these types of responses to the difficult problems of chronic illness are evidently more feasible where the medical staff has a relatively strong sense of responsibility to the hospital as a center for meeting community needs.

Regionalization. Finally, among external hospital functions, the formal relationships of a hospital to other community agencies or to other hospitals in a regional network should be noted. Every hospital, of course, has relationships with governmental and private agencies with respect to care of certain types of patients, such as industrial injury cases (workmen's compensation), patients coming under programs for crippled childrens or vocational rehabilitation, or other programs paying for hospital care.[14] (The Medicare and Medicaid programs have greatly increased these relationships since 1966.) Aside from formalized regional hospital systems, general hospitals have increasingly developed joint or shared services with each other for specific tasks, such as accounting, public relations, personnel training, certain laboratory and x-ray services, laundry operations, bulk purchasing, and blood banks.[15]

In our series, several hospitals by reason of their location have agreements with the county emergency aid program to receive accident cases by ambulance. All the hospitals with obstetrical services have arrangements with the county bureau of adoptions regarding infants born of unwed mothers. Aside from notifications of deaths and communicable diseases, which all hospitals send to the county health department, re-

14 Milton I. Roemer and M. H. McClanahan, "The Impact of Governmental Programs on Voluntary Hospitals," *Public Health Reports*, 72:537–44 (May 1960).

15 Mark S. Blumberg, *Shared Services for Hospitals* (Chicago: American Hospital Association, 1966).

lationships are sometimes maintained with a local public health agency for the operation of maternal and child health clinics. There are also liaisons with the local visiting nurse association regarding certain discharged patients, with the American Red Cross regarding blood for transfusions, and with other voluntary agencies. The maintenance of all these relationships depends very much on having hospital staff familiar with these resources and how to work with them. Such personnel, especially social workers, are better provided in the hospitals of higher MSO structuring, and in these hospitals various external relationships tend to be more well developed.

As for interhospital relationships, there are very few at the lower end of the MSO scale. Each of the four permissive-MSO hospitals is a sovereign entity. External restraints and influences are felt from the Joint Commission on Accreditation of Hospitals, the state department of public health (responsible for hospital licensure), and other such surveillance bodies discussed in chapter I. But in day-to-day management or even long-term policy-making, each of these hospitals is quite independent.

Among the medium-MSO hospitals, St. Martin's is owned and operated by a religious order, which sponsors also twelve other hospitals and many educational institutions. The Motherhouse establishes general policies of patient care and institutional management and plays an important part in the assignment of positions to religious Sisters. But the other hospitals of the order are in other parts of the country, and there is no interflow of services or patients among them in the usual sense of the term "regionalization."[16] Pebble City Hospital is fully independent. Its administrator has attempted to co-ordinate certain services (e.g., laundry operation and use of expensive medical equipment) with those of three other nearby hospitals, but with very little success. Scopus Hospital is likewise independent, although, at the time of our study, it was undergoing a merger with another general hospital about five miles away, under the same religious sponsorship. This process involved co-ordination of hospital activities of many types, but the eventual goal is physical unification into a large "medical center" at one location; geographically, therefore, the merger will actually reduce the regional relationships of the two institutions.

Among the three rigorous-MSO hospitals, the regionalization concept has much more operational meaning. Medical Group Hospital is one of five general hospitals sponsored by the same foundation in this geographic region. Not only are general policies established by the sponsoring body, but there are numerous operating relationships among the five hospitals, involving transfers of patients, medical consultations, pur-

---

[16] Leonard S. Rosenfeld and Henry B. Markover, *The Rochester Regional Hospital Council* (New York: Commonwealth Fund, 1956).

chasing of supplies, in-service training of personnel, public relations, etc. Medical Group Hospital is the largest of the network, with greater specialization of its medical staff, so that it receives complex cases referred from throughout the region. Also, in closer range around the hospital are eight satellite clinics, furnishing out-patient service to health insurance plan members more conveniently.

Public Hospital is also part of a network of five institutions in the metropolitan area under the same governmental body. All of these hospitals are devoted mainly to the care of the poor, and general policies are laid down by the municipal council. Two of the other hospitals are general in scope, covering different geographic sectors of the metropolis; the other two are specialized for care of long-term illness (including tuberculosis) and rehabilitation. Thus, patients are readily transferred between the units in this municipal network, and there is also a good deal of interchange of both administrative and technical personnel as well as bulk purchasing of supplies. On a broader geographic scale, Veterans Hospital is also part of a network of institutions sponsored by one federal agency. It receives complex cases transferred from other smaller general hospitals in the system, within a radius of about 200 miles. At the same location there is also a mental hospital and an institution for long-term custodial care, with which the general hospital has close working relationships.

Thus, certain advantages in the way of economies and quality promotion are enjoyed by the three rigorous-MSO hospitals, through regional relationships under common sponsorship. The value of such relationships has been underscored by national legislation enacted after data in this study were gathered; the national Public Health Service Act amendments of 1965, to promote "regional medical programs" (RMP) for improved services to patients with heart disease, cancer or stroke, helped to increase regional relationships among hospitals all over the country.[17] These RMP efforts are largely in the sphere of postgraduate education of physicians, and activities of this type have recently affected several of the hospitals in our study. The Medicare Law of 1965 has also come to increase the external relationships of hospitals by its requirement of "transfer agreements" between general hospitals and nursing homes (extended care facilities), as a condition of participation of the latter in the program.[18] The impact of these new laws will doubtless enhance the wider community role of hospitals of all types, even those of smaller size and lesser degrees of medical staff organization.

[17] Robert Q. Marston, "A Nation Starts a Program: Regional Medical Programs, 1965–1966," *J. Med. Education.* 42:17–27 (January 1967).

[18] Herman M. Somers and Anne R. Somers, *Medicare and the Hospitals: Issues and Prospects* (Washington: Brookings Institution, 1967).

XI

MEDICAL STAFF ORGANIZATION AND HOSPITAL PERFORMANCE: CONCLUSIONS AND IMPLICATIONS

WHAT DOES ALL this exploration of medical staff organization and hospital performance add up to? In this final chapter we will briefly summarize our findings from the several research approaches. Then we will offer our conclusions on an optimal policy for medical staff organization in hospitals within the current American setting. The implications of such an MSO policy in relation to several of the major current issues in medical care—quality promotion, costs, and planning—will then be explored. Finally, we will consider some major trends and prospects for the future.

SUMMARY OF FINDINGS

The relationships of patterns of medical staff organization to the program and output of hospitals have been investigated along several paths—sociological, historical, international comparisons, a national statistical survey, and "anthropological" case studies of ten institutions. The conclusions that may be drawn from any one of these approaches are not airtight, because the problem is very complex, and it has not been possible to exclude all the secondary variables from a cause-and-effect analysis. The combination of research approaches, however, offers us greater assurance. When findings all seem to point substantially in the same direction, the weaknesses of one type of observation are buttressed by the strengths of another.

From a sociological overview of the American scene, we observed that there are many current conflicts in the United States between doctors and hospitals, reflecting a steady broadening of the social role of hospitals in the face of a strong tradition of private entrepreneurial freedom among doctors. The determinants of that broadening hospital role

277

were found to arise from many sources: changes in the population and the spectrum of disease, advancements in science, extended social financing of health service, and general urban and cultural developments. Because of these widening responsibilities, a variety of external social controls over hospitals have emerged, from both voluntary and governmental sources. The responses of hospitals to these pressures and sanctions, however, are influenced by several internal characteristics, such as the sponsorship, size, and age of the institution. Thus, it was evident from a study of the literature of health services that many social and technical forces are shaping the character and direction of hospital programs. These forces also operate to shape the patterns of medical staff organization, which then serve as an intervening variable—a link in the chain of influences—contributing to the various components of hospital performance.

From literature study, we traced the historic development of the relationships of doctors to hospitals. We found that in the earliest days of the Old World some physicians were an integral part of hospital establishments; as the medical profession grew (with science, urbanization, etc.) there evolved a large class of doctors with no hospital ties and a smaller élite class attached to "closed-staff" hospitals. In America, however, the shorter hospital tradition and the rapid population growth and economic development led to much more extensive involvement of doctors in "open-staff" hospitals. As a result, disciplinary standards for medical work in hospitals were lax. As medical science advanced, a reaction set in among the leadership of the profession, and the "hospital standardization" movement arose. From this grew the Joint Commission on Accreditation of Hospitals, hospital licensure laws, and other social mechanisms promoting tightened organization of medical staffs. It was possible to trace the evolution of each of seven specific features of medical staff organization, identifiable today.

Further perspective on the American patterns of medical staff organization in hospitals was acquired from a study of practices in other countries. From both literature study and field observations, it was learned that the prevailing MSO patterns in other parts of the world are more highly structured than those found in the United States. These patterns are associated with greater social financing and stronger public controls over the entire system of medical care. Within MSO frameworks there were found to be certain significant contrasts, such as a lesser development of compensatory "control committees" in European hospitals, associated with a stronger basic departmental structure that provides day-to-day surveillance over medical performance.

Proceeding to the statistical survey approach, we studied the universe of American general hospitals (of fifty beds or more) with respect to a limited set of characteristics that might shed light on the relationship of MSO structure to hospital performance. As an indicator of the degree of medical staff structuring, we designed a "contractual physician score"; the parallelism of this with a more comprehensive measurement of MSO structuring was later confirmed by a series of hospital case studies. The level of contractual physician (CP) scores was then explored in relation to seven components of hospital performance: over-all performance, amplitude of staffing, diagnostic procedures, surgical facilities, other significant therapies, educational functions, and preventive and community service. Each of these components had several sub-items, totaling to twenty-six, and for twenty-two of these we found a clearly positive association with the CP score. Thus a firmer medical staff organization, as reflected by the CP score, was generally associated with a higher record for the great majority of specific features indicating effective hospital performance. Although the "contractual physician score" was inherently size-adjusted, the relationships were further explored by separate hospital size-groups, and the positive findings still prevailed. Positive relationships between CP score and the great majority of hospital performance features were also found to prevail within separate types of hospital sponsorship and the nine geographic regions of the nation.

The most laborious part of the research was the "anthropological" case studies. A series of ten hospitals in one geographic region were selected to illustrate a range of patterns of medical staff organization, along a five-step scale from "very loosely structured" to "very highly structured." Based on preliminary observations, a typology and scoring system were designed by which MSO structure could be quantified. The elements measured were: staff composition, appointment procedure, commitment, departmentalization, control committees, documentation, and informal dynamics. The ranking of the ten hospitals by the "total MSO score" was found to correspond closely to the earlier measurement of contractual physicians (modified by a more sophisticated adjustment for hospital size)—tending to provide a confirmatory linkage between our "anthropological" case-study findings and those of the nationwide survey of contractual physicians in hospitals.

Based on very detailed schedules for soliciting information, field investigations were made within the ten selected hospitals representing a range of MSO structuring. Data were gathered on the seven features of medical staff organization (involving a total of nineteen subfeatures) and on a wide variety of components of hospital programs. The latter were described under two major sets of functions: in-patient care and the wider community role of hospitals. In-patient hospital care was analyzed in terms of clinical departmental functions, supportive medical services, supportive paramedical services, and some outcome measures. The wider community role of hospitals was analyzed in terms of out-patient services, preventive health services, professional education, medical research, and other external relationships.

With respect to the detailed analysis of the seven features of medical staff organization, the gradient of structuring for each of the main features and nineteen subfeatures was generally but not wholly correlated with the ranking of the total MSO scores. The most consistent or linear gradients were observed for commitment and departmentalization. Slight irregularities, in spite of general linearity, applied to staff composition, appointment procedures, and documentation. The most striking deviance from the general trend of MSO features applied to the measure of control committees, which showed a curvilinear relationship; that is, the lowest subscores for control committees characterized both the most loosely structured and the most highly structured over-all MSO patterns, while the highest subscores characterized the mid-range medical staffs. This was a striking confirmation of our comparative observations in European hospitals, where a generally more rigorous pattern of MSO structuring is associated nevertheless with a weak development of control committees; it also supported our conceptualization of these as either compensatory or reinforcing mechanisms of formal staff organization. As for informal dynamics, our observations—which were admittedly crude —suggested an essentially flat plateau of considerable informal activity in all medical staffs except the most highly structured, where there occurs a slight drop in this feature.

Association of the total MSO scores in the series of ten case-study hospitals was explored with respect to each of the components of in-patient care and of wider community service. To permit some generalization in so small a series of hospitals, we collapsed them from five to three sets of institutions with permissive-MSO (4 hospitals), medium-MSO (3 hospitals), and rigorous-MSO (3 hospitals) structures. Wherever possible, quantitative data were used to describe the various performance features.

Among the components of in-patient care, the scope and technical development of most clinical departmental functions in all ten hospitals were found to be quite similar with respect to the medical needs of "routine" patients or cases of only mild or moderate severity. Differentials were noticeable, however, with respect to the hospital capacity to meet the needs of difficult or severely ill patients; for these, the range and richness of services were distinctly greater in the hospitals of higher MSO structuring. These observations apply mainly to medical, surgical, obstetrical, and gynecological services. For pediatric services there was a positive association of MSO structuring with performance, even for the care of the average patient. For psychiatric services the positive correlation is sharper, and this element of performance is available in significant form only in the more highly structured hospitals.

The "supportive medical services" in the ten study hospitals showed a consistently positive relationship in their scope and development to the level of MSO structuring. The differentials were perhaps least marked for anesthesia, moderate for radiology and pathology, and most marked for physical medicine and rehabilitation. The latter services were much more highly developed in the rigorous-MSO hospitals. The "supportive paramedical services," on the other hand, showed more diverse types of relationships. Pharmacy services were more systematized in the more highly structured hospitals. Nursing services, however, were most abundant in the less structured hospitals; with relatively larger nursing staffs and fewer technological demands made upon them, these hospitals are evidently capable of giving more "tender loving care" to in-patients.

The outcome measures available to evaluate hospital in-patient care were limited. Application of a formula developed separately for adjusting hospital death rates for case severity showed an adjusted mortality rate of 3.41 per cent in the most permissive-MSO hospitals, 1.51 per cent in the medium-MSO hospitals, and 1.88 per cent in the rigorous-MSO hospitals. In spite of this reflection of better performance in the more highly structured hospitals, their overall staffing and total expenditures per patient-day of care were found to be lower.

Among the various components of the hospital's wider community role, the correlations of their scope and development with the level of MSO structuring were even more strikingly and consistently positive. With respect to out-patient activities, there are certain reciprocal relationships between the volume of services in organized clinics and the output of "emergency rooms," but the tendency was clearly toward greater development in the more highly structured hospitals. Preventive health services were not very well developed in any of the ten hospitals of our series, but they were somewhat stronger in those with more rigorous-MSO patterns. For both professional education and medical research, the correlations with MSO structuring were strongly positive. In the permissive hospitals these activities were virtually nonexistent; in the medium-MSO hospitals they were moderately well developed; and in the rigorous ones they were highly developed. Other external relationships of the hospital (social services, home-care programs, regionalization, etc.) were also more developed and diversified as the level of MSO structuring increased.

In aggregate, the investigation along several paths points to a positive association between higher levels of medical staff structuring and the performance of a wider range of both in-patient services and activities in other spheres of community responsibility. The forces imposing an increasingly wider range of tasks on hospitals can be traced historically, can be observed in countries throughout the world, and can be seen all around us in contemporary America. The tightened structuring of medical staffs is, itself, a response to those forces, and it serves to facilitate the hospital's performance of the expected tasks.

These findings—except for the limited data on adjusted hospital death rates—furnish far from definitive "end-result" proof of the effects of different patterns of medical staff organization.[1] In the light of the multiple forces at play, however, these modest forms of measurement of the "outcome" of an organizational process have meaning as a guide to social policy decisions. It is not unreasonable to assume that various types of technical service, evolving in the world's centers of medical science, are more likely to save lives and reduce disability if they are systematically applied in a hospital than if they are not applied. In a word, our findings suggest that organization promotes technical excellence which, in turn, probably achieves better health care for people. But there are many subtleties to the organizational process and many anxieties about its application which call for discussion in the next section.

MEANING AND EFFECTS OF ORGANIZATION

Organization of individuals causes a restriction of their personal freedom in order to achieve certain social ends. Attainment of the long-term goal may yield greater freedoms—freedom from death, hunger, ignorance, or disease—but in the intervening process there are bound to be conflicts because of the short-term restrictions of personal freedom. In the health services these conflicts have been very prominent.

Organization and Individual Freedom. Almost every advancement in the organization of health services to better apply the discoveries of science has been met by social resistance.[2] From the debates over smallpox vaccination and the pasteurization of milk, we have progressed to controversies in the United States on the establishment of well-baby clinics, on voluntary health insurance plans, governmental subsidy of medical schools, up to the recent bitter political battles over the Medicare Law.[3] Within hospitals, we reviewed in chapter I the background of

[1] Sam Shapiro, "End Result Measurements of Quality of Medical Care," *Milbank Memorial Fund Quarterly*, 45:7–30 (April 1967).

[2] Bernhard J. Stern, *Society and Medical Progress* (Princeton: Princeton University Press, 1941), pp. 175–214.

[3] Selig Greenberg, *The Troubled Calling: Crisis in the Medical Establishment* (New York: Macmillian, 1965).

controversies over contractual physicians and the broader contentions about medical staff organization that these reflected.

In almost every hospital today, where the leadership is dynamic and innovations are being promoted, there is a substratum of tension between the hospital administration and the medical staff. Concerning three medium-sized voluntary general hospitals (180 to 240 beds) in the New England region that they studied in 1965, Arthur B. Moss and his colleagues write:

> We were disturbed by the recurring expressions of friction between the medical staff and the other two major units (Board of Trustees and Hospital Administrator) of the policy triangle. This friction appeared on the surface to be the result of differences in personalities, but closer examination revealed that there were some fundamental differences in the perceptions that doctors held with respect to their organizational functions and obligations. These differences have deep roots in the history of the medical profession.[4]

Similar observations were made by Temple Burling and his colleagues in their study of several general hospitals in New York State in 1955[5] and by Basil Georgopoulos and Floyd Mann in their study of Michigan hospitals in 1962.[6] Our study in California found these tensions to some degree in all ten hospitals. It is noteworthy that these studies were conducted in different sections of the United States, over a period of years, with similar observations of organizational tension.

In our series of hospitals the greatest contentions between medical staff and hospital administration seemed to characterize the institutions in the mid-range on the scale of medical staff organization. In the permissive-MSO hospitals, the behavioral values of the private medical practitioner are clearly dominant; there are few efforts at organizational innovation, and serious controversies seldom occur. In the rigorous-MSO hospitals, at the other pole, the organizational framework clearly predominates over medical individualism, but the doctors entering this arena have accepted its constraints, so that relationships are relatively peaceful. It is in the medium-MSO hospitals that numerous pressures for innovation tend to emanate from the board of directors or the hospital administrator, and the greatest resistance is encountered from the medical staff. The dialectics of social change are most active in this setting and the frictions are hottest. The price of *laissez faire* in a rapidly

---

[4] Arthur B. Moss, R. H. Guest, W. G. Broehl, Jr., and J. W. Hennessey, Jr., *Hospital Policy Decisions: Process and Action* (New York: G. P. Putman, 1966), pp. 318–19.

[5] Temple Burling, E. M. Lentz, and R. N. Wilson, *The Give and Take in Hospitals* (New York: G. P. Putman, 1956).

[6] Basil S. Georgopoulos and F. C. Mann, *The Community General Hospital* (New York: Macmillian, 1962).

changing society is conflict. It is significant that as noted in the Preface, selection of the sample of hospitals for our case studies was not easy, because several hospitals that we approached objected to being studied; all five hospitals that declined to participate had MSO patterns that we tentatively judged to be in the middle range. The reasons for non-participation invariably related to current contentions and sensitivities in hospital–doctor relationships.

Those who defend "individual freedom" have had a tendency to raise ugly specters of regimentation and oppression in the prospect of increased organization of medical services. In summarizing American Medical Association policies on physician–hospital relations over the last several decades, the AMA Council on Medical Service wrote in 1964:

Substitute an impersonal, machine-like coldness of corporate practice for the humane interest inherent in individual service and you destroy initiative and serve the public poorly, the House [of Delegates of the AMA] warned in 1930. In 1932 the House termed corporate profiteering from physician's services "absolutely destructive of that personal responsibility and relationship which is essential to the best interests of the patient."[7]

In this context "corporate profiteering" referred to any salaried appointment of a physician in a hospital. While AMA resistance to salaried medical practice, and the organizational policies associated with it, has been modified over the years, relative to the rising tempo of demands for such organization the resistance remains substantial.

Yet, the cumulative evidence all points to the positive benefits of medical care organization in terms of the output of the system. The weight of all the research reported in this book leans strongly in that direction. Rather striking confirmation of the benefits of more highly structured MSO patterns has come from a comparative study of hospital care in New York City, where patient's charts were audited by acknowledged professional experts. In several instances the work of certain specific doctors in two different types of hospital came under scrutiny; it was found that in the more highly structured hospital (voluntary versus proprietary sponsorship), the *same* doctor did higher quality work.[8] A California study in 1960 reported over 32,000 obstetrical deliveries in one general hospital with only one maternal death.[9] The remarkable point was that 51 per cent of the deliveries were done by general practi-

[7] American Medical Association, Council on Medical Service, *Physician-Hospital Relations*," *J.A.M.A.*, 190:74–79 (5 October 1964).

[8] Columbia University School of Public Health and Administrative Medicine, *A Study of the Quality of Hospital Care Secured by a Sample of Teamster Family Members in New York City* (New York: The University, 1964).

[9] S. G. Pillsbury, "32,465 Deliveries with Only One Mother's Death," *J.A.M.A.*, 174:2151–52 (24 December 1960).

tioners rather than specialists. This was a nonteaching hospital of 370 beds, with a staff of doctors who were deemed to be simply average in their qualifications. The achievement was attributed by the author to the operation of firm medical staff and hospital policies, such as mandatory consultation from an obstetrical specialist in any complicated case, administration of anesthesia by obstetrical interns (who were thereby also present to help in other ways if necessary), and availability of abundant blood from the Red Cross.

Thus, the consequences of social organization, in hospitals or anywhere else, must be judged largely by its effects on the behavior of the average person. The superior person may perform well under almost any circumstances, but society must cope, by definition, with a range of competences—high, low, and in-between. In the workaday world, organization is essential to uplift the performance of the inferior and the average person to higher levels. At the same time, the initiative and creativity of the superior individual should not be stifled. In our observations, the more highly structured MSO patterns did not discourage new ideas, but on the contrary stimulated them. In the hospitals with more highly structured medical staffs, moreover, the resources and channels for implementation of new ideas are more readily available.

The Optimal MSO Pattern. In the light of these effects of the organizational process and the realities of American society what can be said about the "best" or optimal pattern of medical staff organization in general hospitals to meet current needs? The answer, we believe, must be offered on two levels: within the walls of an average hospital and within a system of many hospitals in a geographic network.

Within the average hospital the soundest model for today, in our judgment, is represented by the "highly structured" MSO pattern—Type IV on our conceptual scale. The hallmark of this model, it will be recalled, is the salaried staff of full-time chiefs in all clinical and supportive departments of the hospital. These highly committed physicians set the tone for all medical staff activities, they supervise the application of quality standards, they offer education, conduct research, give consultations, and handle many administrative tasks. Yet, the majority of staff doctors are in medical practice out in the community, giving ambulatory care in the office and home. (While they are usually in private offices, they may also be in group practice clinics or local health centers.) Unlike the conditions in the more loosely structured MSO patterns (Types I, II, or III), the work of these attending doctors within the hospital is governed by firm policies. Their appointments are made with discretion, their daily actions are subject to department rules, and their ultimate performance receives periodic review.

Unlike the usual conditions in the Type V-MSO pattern ("very highly structured"), on the other hand, the active medical staff is not restricted to full-time salaried physicians. A distinctive class of "hospital doctors," separate from "community doctors," is not created. There is cross-fertilization between the two, to the benefit of both. The benefit is especially important for the community doctor, whose quality of work in everyday practice depends much on the educational stimulation received within the hospital. In the Type V-MSO pattern, moreover, there may sometimes develop some excessive rigidities, some slowness to change rules to meet changing needs. We did not actually find this problem to any significant degree in our Type V study hospitals; we were, in fact, impressed with the flexibility in these structures to tolerate deviation from the rules in particular circumstances. On the motivational level, moreover, a separate study in one of the Type V hospitals of our series found the organizational structure to be "moderately bureaucratic"—which was deemed more conducive to professional creativity than either a "highly bureaucratic" or a "nonbureaucratic" setting.[10] The hazards of excessive bureaucracy, however, while usually exaggerated, cannot be ignored altogether. Our rejection of the Type V pattern, nevertheless, is based not on such apprehensions, but on the great importance of strong ties between hospital medicine and medical service outside the hospital walls, embodied in the Type IV pattern.

This is not to imply that the specific Type IV hospital in our series of case studies (Scopus Hospital) is the perfect model for the future. As we saw in the text, there are various still unsolved problems. Tensions are sometimes high between the full-time and the attending doctors, and innovations in the development of various community-oriented programs meet resistance. But this pattern of medical staff organization, probably more than the other four patterns below and above it on the scale, is in active ferment. It is essentially a medical care pattern in transition, an administrative structure for medical service in the process of development. Its future prospects, we believe, are bright and they are important. Their applicability is not limited, furthermore, to large hospitals, like Scopus. In Hunterdon County, New Jersey, there has been developed an excellent small rural hospital (125 beds), with a core staff of full-time salaried departmental chiefs and numerous attending physicians from the entire local area; the arrangements fit our definition of a "highly structured" Type IV-MSO pattern.[11]

There is another factor in the American reality that must be con-

10 Gloria Engel, "The Effect of Bureaucracy on the Professional Autonomy of the Physician," (doctoral dissertation, Los Angeles: University of California, 1968).

11 Ray E. Trussell, *Hunterdan Medical Center: The Story of One Approach to Rural Medical Care* (Cambridge, Massachusetts: Harvard University Press, 1956).

sidered in formulating policies about the "best" or optimal-MSO pattern. In the prevailing environment of private medical practice, the attractions of salaried employment, in hospitals or elsewhere, are still relatively modest. The handicaps involve both status and earnings. As a result, some of the best qualified doctors may hesitate to undertake full-time hospital work. This is rapidly changing—especially as prestigious academic appointments on reasonable full-time salaries become more numerous—but the full-time hospital appointment in America still lacks the high rewards offered in Europe and on other continents. If present trends continue, this problem will disappear, and a future pattern of medical staff organization more rigorous than Type IV would suffer no handicaps in attracting the most competent doctors. For the moment, however, the Type IV pattern makes a sensible adjustment to prevailing attitudes in American medical practice.

The question about a "best" pattern, as noted above, must also be answered on a second level—that of a system of hospitals. Not every hospital in a region, state, or nation need perform all functions. Obviously, some hospitals should always have more highly developed responsibilities than others for teaching and research, as well as for special aspects of diagnosis and treatment. Elaborate cardiac surgery, for example, need not and should not be offered in every hospital. But this does not argue against the soundness of the Type IV-MSO pattern. Some forms of professional education should be carried out in every hospital; also some research, at least at the level of evaluating clinical performance. Preventive health services ought to be built into the scheme of every hospital, as well as a wide range of out-patient services. All these functions, including basic in-patient care, can be better performed, we are convinced, under the "highly structured" MSO pattern.

As for channelling patients to the facility most appropriate to their medical needs, this must depend on co-ordination among the hospitals in a region. It is reasonable to have a smaller scope of technical capacity in one hospital than another if, in fact, patients can be freely transferred among hospitals, or consultants across hospital lines are readily available. In the absence of such co-ordinated operations, some patients may be inadequately served in some hospitals. The solution to this problem, through regionalization, will be discussed below, but this would not reduce the need for a "highly structured" MSO pattern within every facility. On the contrary, the effective functioning of a regionalized scheme would call for relatively rigorous frameworks of medical organization in each hospital, so that all the parts in the system would mesh smoothly.

IMPLICATIONS OF MSO STRUCTURING IN
CURRENT MEDICAL CARE ISSUES

These findings and our judgments on an optimal pattern of medical staff organization in hospitals have various implications with respect to some of the pressing issues of contemporary medical care in the United States. Wider application of the highly structured pattern of medical staff organization could help to solve problems confronted in other spheres. Prominent among these issues are those of hospital costs, quality, and planning.

Hospital Costs. The rising costs of hospital care in recent years have approached the level of a national crisis. In the last ten years the costs of medical care to the average American family have risen much higher than have the total costs of living, and the differential is largely referrable to hospitalization. Between 1959 and 1968 the cost of a day of hospital care rose 122 per cent, while the aggregate cost of living (i.e., prices of all goods and services consumed by families) rose 20 per cent.[12] So critical is the issue that the federal government has been moved to hold a series of conferences to consider ways of stemming the tide of rising medical costs; among the proposals made, a search for more efficient methods of hospital operation always figures prominently.[13]

The components of hospital cost trends have been discussed fully elsewhere,[14] but what bearing do MSO patterns have upon them? Basic is the potential influence of medical staff patterns on the hospital utilization rate. There is plenty of evidence from European experience, and from observations in various prepaid medical care programs in the United States, that patients are hospitalized on a more discriminating basis, at lower rates, when the admitting decisions are made by hospital-based doctors. The more rigorous-MSO patterns foster such admission procedures; they enable a limited supply of hospital beds to be used with greater discretion and frugality than under conditions of private fee-for-service practice combined with loosely structured medical staffs.[15] Lower hospital admission rates do not, *per se*, reduce the cost of a day of hospital care, but they reduce the number of days used by the population, and hence the aggregate community costs of hospital care. These

---

[12] Anon., "The Plight of the U.S. Patient," *Time* (21 February 1969): 53–58.

[13] U.S. Department of Health, Education, and Welfare, *Report of the National Conference on Medical Costs* (Washington, 1967).

[14] Blue Cross Association, "Hospital Cost Trends," *Blue Cross Reports* (May–June 1967). Also: U.S. Department of Health, Education, and Welfare, *Report of the Secretary's Committee on Hospital Effectiveness* (Washington, 1968).

[15] U.S. National Advisory Commission on Health Manpower, *Report: Vol. II* (Washington: Government Printing Office, November 1967), pp. 206–28.

are expressible through hospital insurance premiums, which are quite visible to everyone.

Other MSO influences on hospital costs relate to hospital staffing with nurses and other paramedical personnel. We have noted how hospitals with more highly structured medical staffs, in our series of ten case studies, manage to operate with fewer nurses per 100 beds and with a lower total complement of personnel. This was strikingly corroborated by observations of the smaller total staff-to-patient ratios in European hospitals. With a small corps of hospital-based physicians, a more efficient medical care team can be developed than under circumstances where hospital personnel must learn to work with a wide diversity of visiting private physicians, each of whom has his own habits and demands. The lesser bulk of nurse's notes (which take time and, therefore, cost money) in the rigorous-MSO hospitals, compared with the permissive ones, is one small but interesting reflection of the economies involved.

Savings are also possible in the realm of drugs and supplies used under the more highly structured MSO patterns. Drug formularies, which save money, tend to be applied only in the more highly structured hospitals. Uniformity, and therefore lower inventory expense, is also more feasible with respect to the purchase of other hospital supplies.

The method of payment of contractual physicians also has a bearing on the total hospital costs that must be borne by patients. The frequent pattern, used in the more loosely structured medical staffs, of paying radiologists and pathologists by a percentage of departmental income tends nearly always to raise aggregate costs. When a flat salary is paid—even a high one—the earnings of the x-ray or laboratory department, beyond true production costs (erroneously called "profits" by some), can be applied to meet the operating expenses of other less lucrative hospital departments, thereby reducing the total per-diem cost figure. Even in the sphere of administrative expenses, the load on the hospital "business office" is lighter if physicians are paid by salary. Still other economies are possible through shared services between institutions, which, we have noted, are more readily developed in the hospitals with rigorous-MSO patterns.

These several possible implications of firm-MSO patterns for controlling hospital costs do not suggest a panacea. Many, if not most, factors contributing to cost increases are quite outside the influence of medical staff patterns. But the decisions of doctors still have a pervasive influence on medical care costs in general and hospitalization costs in particular. As pointed out in a vignette painted by the Secretary's (Health, Education, and Welfare) Advisory Committee on Hospital Effectiveness, a visitor from Mars would be hard-pressed to understand how a hospital administrator in America could control costs, when most physicians on the staff are not subject to his influence with regard to their decisions on patient care. "The arrangement," said the Martian, "must be impossible to manage . . . impossible—or very, very expensive."[16]

Quality of Hospital Care. The implications of MSO patterns with respect to current concerns about the quality of medical care are more obvious. Because of both professional leadership and public demands (not to mention the rising rate of malpractice suits), methods to maintain and promote a high quality of medical care in hospitals have aroused increasing national interest. Most of the research reported in this book explores the relationship between medical staff organization and the quality of care ultimately received by hospital patients, and the findings suggest that more highly structured MSO patterns tend to promote care of better quality.

A few specific implications of these findings for the current medical care scene may be mentioned. One concerns the level of standards applied by the Joint Commission on Accreditation of Hospitals. It will be recalled that all ten hospitals in our case-study series were accredited by the JCAH. Yet, the range of services offered and the practices employed in each of them suggested a very wide range of medical care quality. If the public is to be properly informed, and if the level of hospital performance is to be gradually upgraded, would there not be value in elevating accreditation standards? This might be done either by a general across-the-board elevation of requirements for accreditation, or by the use of a grading system. Hospitals might be graded A, B, or C— or even given numerical grades—in relation to a quantification of their merits. This would be helpful to both physicians and patients, but especially to patients who are now quite uninformed about the qualifications of an institution to which they entrust their lives. As in the immediate post-Flexner era of medical school approvals, which applied a grading system[17] (not to mention such programs as milk inspection by Health Departments), this policy would probably result in energetic efforts by all hospitals to attain "grade A" status.*

Another quality implication of our findings concerns the "conventional wisdom" about the advantages of "mainstream" medical care in the United States. Because of the impersonal connotations of public clinics and public hospitals in past decades, an understandable reaction has set in against segregated "charity medicine" for the poor. Everyone, it is

---

[16] Report of the Secretary's Committee on Hospital Effectiveness, op. cit., p. 20.

[17] Morris Fishbein (editor), *A History of the American Medical Association, 1847–1947* (Philadephia: W. B. Saunders, 1947).

* After this was written, steps were taken by the Joint Commission on Accreditation of Hospitals to upgrade its standards substantially.

argued, should have access to the mainstream of American medicine.[18] In the hospital sector this usually means voluntary and sometimes proprietary institutions, with relatively loosely structured MSO patterns. We have seen, however, that the quality of care in those hospitals may well be inferior to that in government hospitals with rigorous-MSO patterns. This is not to suggest that all public hospitals for the poor are superior, for we know that many suffer from serious under-financing, shortages of staff, and various bureaucratic deficiencies, resulting in impersonal or even inhumane treatment of indigent patients.[19] But it is important to realize that the deficiencies of these hospitals cannot be blamed on their patterns of medical staff organization. On the contrary, those patterns probably promote a relatively high quality of care on the technological level. Improvements on the humanistic level require stronger financing, to support more nurses and other personnel, as well as better quality food and supplies. Without the rigorous-MSO patterns in most of these public hospitals for the poor, the quality of medical service provided would undoubtedly decline. Improvements in the personal amenities of hospital care, which our society demands, require money and deliberate organizational efforts, no less than do technological advancements.

A final MSO implication relevant to the quality of hospital care concerns its measurement. Quantitative evaluation of medical care is very difficult, whether it is done in terms of final outcomes (health improvement of the patient) or of the medical process.[20] By either method, accurate records are essential for reliable judgments. As we have seen, diligent record-keeping is much more likely to occur under highly structured MSO patterns—quite aside from the organizational features that facilitate day-to-day peer review of performance. Continuous measurement and assessment of medical work is important not only because of considerations of administrative accountability—to hospital boards of directors, funding agencies, etc.—but more because of the value of incentives and motivation. Clear and visible evidence of the quality of performance is an important inducement to continuous self-improvement, and the diligent recording of the patient-care process necessary to furnish such evidence is much more feasible in the highly structured MSO patterns.

[18] Milton I. Roemer and Arnold I. Kisch, "Health, Poverty, and the Medical Mainstream," in *Power, Poverty, and Urban Policy*, W. Bloomberg and H. J. Schmandt, editors (Beverly Hills, California: Sage Publications, 1968), pp. 181–202.

[19] Commission on Delivery of Personal Health Services, *Comprehensive Community Health Services for New York City* (New York: City of New York, 1967). See also: Jan de Hartog, *The Hospital* (New York: Atheneum, 1964).

[20] Avedis Donabedian, "Promoting Quality through Evaluating the Process of Patient Care," *Medical Care*, 6:181–202 (May–June 1968).

Hospital Planning. A third current issue to which MSO patterns have relevance is the rising pressure for deliberate planning of hospital systems. Starting with the national Hospital Survey and Construction (Hill-Burton) Act of 1946—launched to assure accessibility of hospitals to rural populations—and stimulated now by the search for improved efficiency and economy, rational geographic planning of hospital construction has acquired high priority in the public debates about medical care.[21] The task has been to assure that hospitals are built with the capacity, location, and functions appropriate to the ecology and needs of the population. Many types of regional hospital planning councils have been established throughout the country, originally through private initiative and more recently with the inducement of federal grants (though their sponsorship remains voluntary). Many of these councils have become integrated with state bodies for comprehensive planning of health services.[22] The movement has been away from the sovereignty of individual hospitals toward regional systems of hospitals, in which services and patients flow freely, in order to achieve an optimal fit (both for quality and economy) of patient needs with health care resources.

Reasonable decisions on the sizes and sites for hospital construction are the first step toward achievement of effective hospital systems. Questions of architectural design governing the flow of services and communications within a building are also relevant.[23] But the ultimate challenge is the *operation* of a hospital system, and it is in this regard that the MSO pattern plays a critical role. The more highly structured MSO patterns are much more conducive to the implementation of the whole regionalization concept than the loosely structured ones. Referral of patients between institutions is not inhibited by entrepreneurial considerations. Consultant services between hospitals can be readily arranged. Joint programs in professional education, staff recruitment, or even quality review can be implemented. All the elements of teamwork necessary in a "hospital system" are difficult to achieve under the permissive-MSO patterns, while under the rigorous patterns they are achievable not only with greater speed but also with much less administrative struggle and friction.

In a regionally planned system of hospitals, with rigorous-MSO patterns in effect, there can also be greater efficiency in the use of expensive physician-time. Unorganized hospitals in metropolitan areas, show much

21 U.S. Health Services and Mental Health Administration, *Facts About the Hill-Burton Program July 1, 1947 to June 30, 1968* (Washington, 1968).

22 National Advisory Commission on Health Facilities, *A Report to the President* (Washington, 1968).

23 Anon., "Building for Tomorrow's Medicine," *Medical World News* (7 February 1969): 28–35.

wasted medical time in doctors traveling daily to two or three different hospitals where their patients may be distributed.[24] More rigorous patterns of medical staffing would result in attachment of each doctor to one hospital, with not only travel economies but with greater prospects of developing effective rapport and team relationships in that hospital. New court decisions in malpractice cases are giving further rationale to regionalized medical services; no longer are the standards of local "village medicine" considered satisfactory to define the legal expectations from a practitioner—but rather the standards achievable in a large geographic region.[25]

As noted earlier, differential capabilities in different hospitals may result in serious failures for certain patients under a *laissez faire* hospital culture. But under a regionally planned system it is quite reasonable for small peripheral facilities to have more modest resources than large centralized ones; patients and tasks can be sensibly matched with the facilities required or they can be readily transferred if necessary.

These are just a few of the current issues in American medical care, for which the patterns of medical staff organization in hospitals would seem to have relevance. Beyond the issues of rising costs, higher quality expectations, and rational area-wide planning, are the whole constellation of pressures demanding an ever-widening community role for the general hospital. This role is being demanded most insistently in the sphere of out-patient medical service, but it is also being expressed in the fields of home care of the chronically ill, liaison with extended care facilities, rehabilitation, psychiatric service, preventive medicine, education of all types of health personnel, and evaluative research.[26] Effective response to these demands would require a more highly structured MSO pattern to characterize the hospitals of the nation. Along with this are a number of important needs in other spheres of health service planning, which will be considered in the next and final section of this book.

TRENDS AND PROSPECTS

To estimate and design a wise course of action for the future, it is best to have an understanding of several current trends, and to assess the direction in which we are moving.

[24] Jerome W. Lubin, I. M. Reed, G. L. Worstell, and D. L. Drosness, "How Distance Affects Physician Activity," *Modern Hospital* (July 1966).

[25] William J. Curran, "Village Medicine vs. Regional Medical Programs: New Rules in Medical Malpractice," *Amer. J. Public Health*, 58:1753–54 (September 1968).

[26] Health Information Foundation, *The Impact of Changing Medical Practice on Hospital Administration*, Proceedings of the Sixth Annual National Symposium on Hospital Affairs (Chicago: University of Chicago, 1963).

Trends in MSO Patterns. With respect to patterns of medical staff organization itself, the movement is certainly toward higher levels of structuring. In the national universe of 7,000 hospitals, we cannot say how many institutions would be classifiable under each of the five levels of MSO structuring offered in this study, but the proportions coming under the higher levels are undoubtedly increasing. Strong evidence is seen in the rising proportion of doctors with full-time hospital appointments. Between 1963 and 1968, according to surveys of the American Medical Association, the number of physicians in full-time hospital practice in nonfederal institutions rose by 107 per cent, while the total number of physicians in the country increased by only 16 per cent.[27] These trend figures, moreover, excluded not only all contractual physicians in federal hospitals (such as the large Veterans Administration network) but also all in full-time university appointments, administrative posts, hospital-based research, and all interns and residents. Recalling our finding of parallelism between the "contractual physician score" in hospitals and the total MSO score (see chapter V), it is highly likely that the proportion of hospitals at the higher end of the range of MSO structuring must be rapidly increasing.

The method of remuneration of full-time hospital physicians—in so far as this reflects something about levels of MSO structuring—is also coming to be increasingly by straight salary. In 1964 a survey by *Medical Economics* magazine showed further progress of the payment patterns found in our 1959 study (see chapter IV). In that year, 50 per cent of contractual physicians were paid by flat salary, 7 per cent by salary plus other methods, and 43 per cent by other schemes. The 1964 data showed that nearly 75 per cent of full-time contractual physicians in nonfederal hospitals (the figure would doubtless be higher in federal institutions) were paid by salary only, and another 11 per cent by salary supplemented by other methods.[28] Inquiry about their personal attitudes, moreover, found that about 80 per cent of full-time hospital doctors intended to remain in this type of work, rather than shifting to private practice.

It is noteworthy that this apparent trend toward higher levels of MSO structuring cannot be attributed to any rising proportion of hospital beds coming under governmental sponsorship. Over the twenty-one year period from 1946 to 1967, the aggregate beds in all nonfederal (i.e., state and local) government general hospitals rose from 133,000 to 191,000 or by 44 per cent, while those in voluntary nonprofit general hospitals rose

---

[27] Reuben Barr, "Hospital Practice: Core of Tomorrow's Medicine," *Hospital Physician* (February 1969): 77–89.

[28] Arthur Owens, "Report on a Nationwide Survey of Full-time Hospital Staff Physicians," *Med. Economics* (25 January 1965): 73–89.

from 301,000 to 550,000 or by 82 per cent.[29] Thus, the trend toward increased MSO structuring evidently applies to private and public hospital settings alike.

We have suggested that the optimal-MSO pattern for meeting current health service needs is the "highly structured" Type IV model. While we do not have quantitative data on the point, the mounting discussion in hospital journals and conferences of "full-time chiefs of clinical services" and full-time "medical directors" suggests that this particular MSO model is on the rise.[30] The increasing number of full-time directors of medical education is further indirect evidence.[31] The many advertisements in medical journals for full-time hospital appointments in various clinical specialties give further reflection of the trends. The general growth in average size of hospitals—especially the multiplication of large urban medical centers—has further obvious bearing on the frequency distribution of the several MSO patterns.

Hospitals of the most rigorous Type V-MSO model may also be increasing, as a proportion of the total, but we are not so sure about this. The "very highly structured" hospitals, under federal government sponsorship, have not been expanding in recent years. Between 1946 and 1967 the aggregate beds in all federal hospitals actually declined from 236,000 to 175,000; while some of this decline was due to a closing down of long-term beds (mental and tuberculosis), the total number of admissions to these hospitals (predominantly for general illness) rose only about 6 per cent over these two decades, while in all nonfederal hospitals the rise in admissions was by over 95 per cent. The MSO-Type V hospitals, associated with railroad and other industrial establishments, have also evidently been declining.[32]

On the other hand, the hospital network of one large health insurance plan, under the Kaiser Foundation on the West Coast, has been rapidly expanding, and these hospitals apply the Type V-MSO model. Many university hospitals also apply this model, and these have obviously been expanding. Local government hospitals oriented to the poor do not seem to have declined, in spite of the impact of the Medicare and Medicaid laws facilitating care of the poor in voluntary hospitals; these public hospitals predominantly apply the Type V-MSO

[29] American Hospital Association, *Hospitals: Guide Issue* (1 August 1968): 448–49.

[30] Kenneth J. Williams, "Why a Medical Director," in *The Medical Staff in the Modern Hospital*, C. Wesley Eisele, editor (New York: McGraw-Hill, 1967), pp. 47–53. Also, in same volume, Donald C. Carner and R. D. Yaw, "Special Problems of Large Hospitals," pp. 277–89.

[31] M. C. Creditor, "How Full-time Chiefs Help Medical Staff Performance," *Modern Hospital* (August 1965): 136 ff. See also: Editorial "Full-time Chief for Every Department," *Hospital Physician* (September 1965): 53–67.

[32] James A. Hamilton, *Patterns of Hospital Ownership and Control* (Minneapolis: University of Minnesota Press. 1961). p. 131.

model, especially if they are affiliated with medical schools. The exceptional voluntary institutions with rigorous closed staffs of group practice doctors—like the Henry Ford Hospital in Detroit or the Mary Imogene Bassett Hospital in Cooperstown, New York—have not multiplied in number, but their capacities have been enlarged.

Determination of the real net rate of growth or even the current frequency distribution of each of the five MSO types of hospital in the United States as a whole would require further survey and analysis. Even without this, however, the evidence suggests that the predominant pattern is moving toward the higher end of the MSO scale. The movement would appear to be from Types I and II toward Types III and IV, but not so clearly toward Type V. This estimate would correspond to the emphasis in recent years on a social policy favoring "partnership" between the public and private sectors of health service, rather than an enlargement of separate government programs.[33] Public revenues are increasingly being used to finance health care provided in voluntary institutions, so that the latter are strengthened. It is in these voluntary facilities—obviously the predominant type of general hospitals in America —that the most important tightening of MSO patterns is apparently taking place.

Prospects for Financing Hospital Care. The rapidly rising proportion of hospital costs being met through social financing, discussed in chapter I, gives further insight into the prospects for the future. With voluntary health insurance now enrolling about 75 per cent of the national civilian population under age sixty-five, and with Medicare and Medicaid reaching approximately another 15 per cent, we have come to a time when hardly 10 per cent of the people lack protection against hospitalization costs.[34] Not that the financial protection is complete, for few health insurance policies give full benefits, but insurance and tax funds combined have eliminated most financial barriers to hospital care for nearly the whole population.

Under these circumstances, it is altogether likely that the balance of the population will be brought under some form of hospital cost protection before long. Since the enactment of Medicare in 1965, numerous proposals have been made to extend social insurance for hospital and medical services to the total population.[35] One approach has been to

[33] Paul G. Rogers, "The Partnership for Health Programs," *Amer. J. Public Health*, 58:1036–38 (June 1968).

[34] Health Insurance Institute, *1968 Source Book of Health Insurance Data* (New York: The Institute, 1968).

[35] Walter P. Reuther, *The Health Care Crisis: Where Do We Go From Here?*, Eighth Annual Bronfman Lecture to the American Public Health Association (Washington: Committee for National Health Insurance, 1968).

advocate extension of Medicare to another age group—children—as an intermediate step toward universal coverage. In our view, there might be greater wisdom in focusing the benefits initially on hospitalization (including physician services in the hospital), but extending coverage promptly to every adult and child. This was the path taken successfully by Canada and, with certain differences (like the greater use of general tax funds for hospital support), by Europe.

Various combinations of governmental and voluntary agency administration would be possible under a national social insurance program for hospital care. The existing Blue Cross and similar plans could act as "fiscal intermediaries," as they do now under Medicare. Alternatively, the law might simply require that everyone belong to an existing plan, as in the original nineteenth-century European legislation, with indigent persons enrolled at the expense of government agencies. Or the entire system might be simply administered by federal, state, and local public authorities. Whatever the mechanism, the important goal should be that everyone is covered for all or nearly all the costs of hospital care.

Such a nationwide program for financing hospital service would do much to enable hospitals to respond positively to all the increasing social demands being made upon them. Funds would be provided to support the necessary services, while at the same time pressures would undoubtedly rise for promoting economy and maintaining quality. The process of hospital certification, with its associated standards, developed under the Medicare Law, would probably be extended. Among other things, it is likely that more rigorous standards of medical staff organization would be demanded because of their relevance to promoting quality and economy.

Comprehensive medical care for everyone, with emphasis on prevention and early ambulatory service ought, of course, to be the goal of social policy. Enactment of a national hospital insurance program, however, would probably soon lead to expansion toward comprehensive benefits, as it did in Canada. This would follow, if only in the interests of economy—to eliminate incentives for unnecessary and costly hospitalization—not to mention the needs of patients. But choosing the path of universal hospitalization benefits as the next step toward a goal of comprehensive care, has the great advantages of prompt feasibility and substantial economic benefits for families (since hospital bills are the most serious and catastrophic of medical costs). Through the hospital system, moreover, more can be done to rationalize the over-all delivery of services, including ambulatory care, than through any other sector of the medical care complex.

Nationwide hospital insurance would also have important effects on hospital construction. Since the total rate of utilization, and therefore the total expenditures for hospital care, is strongly influenced by the supply of beds in an area, there would doubtless follow a system of governmental approval or franchising of all hospital construction and expansion. The type of hospital licensure law enacted in New York State in 1962 would probably be extended to the other states. It is altogether likely, furthermore, that public sanctions would develop to implement more *functional* systems of hospital regionalization than we now have.

Prospects for Regionalized Hospital Systems. With full social financing of hospital care, it would make sense for economic mechanisms to back up principles of quality maintenance. Thus, payment for certain procedures—for example, gastrectomies—could be authorized only in hospitals properly staffed and equipped to perform them. By the same logic, reimbursements made to hospitals doing complex work would be higher than to those doing simpler work. With such economic sanctions, the regional hospital systems recommended by various national commissions could be realistically achieved.[36]

In a properly regionalized system of hospitals, the sponsorship or ownership of particular institutions need not be affected. There would be no reason for the British pattern of nationalized hospitals, under public regional boards, to be emulated. If financial support came from social sources and standards were stipulated, the sponsorship or ownership of institutions could vary. It would cease to have the decisive importance it has today. In a regional network of hospitals, various facilities would simply be integrated and used in accordance with their size and technical capacities. Thus, a former federal hospital for veterans or a city government hospital for the poor would play a generalized role, equivalent to that of a church-supported or other voluntary general hospital. By the same token, all people would be served in facilities convenient to their place of residence and appropriate to their medical needs but not their social pedigree. "Eligibility" for a particular hospital's services would cease to have meaning.

Prospects in Hospital Management. Within the facility, current trends suggest a gradual tightening of all internal hospital administrative procedures in the decades ahead. We have spoken of the growing rigor of medical staff organization, but the same will doubtless apply to the nursing service, dietary service, business affairs, and all the facets of hospital administration. Hospital administrators are becoming better trained, and managerial techniques generally are becoming more automated and sophisticated. One state (Minnesota) now requires licensure

---

[36] National Advisory Commission on Health Facilities, op. cit.

of hospital administrators, and this pattern may be expected to spread. Indeed, the hospital may become a type of substate authority for surveillance over the work of various auxiliary health personnel, whose government licenses would be relatively broad in definition.[37]

With MSO patterns becoming more rigorous and hospital administration becoming more generally sophisticated, it is likely that the future holds a closer blending of these two channels of authority, which in most American hospitals have been all too separate. As has been incisively said of the administrative dynamics in a typical American hospital, "two lines of authority are one too many."[38] With doctors more fully integrated into the hospital organization, the controls over hospital costs and quality would become more effective and less abrasive.

As Somers and Somers have said, the pressure of Medicare and many other social measures is pushing all hospitals to extend their scope of services, to strengthen quality surveillance, and sharpen cost controls. "All medical staffs," they write, "will be required to assume closer identity with, and accountability to, the hospital."[39] The administrators of hospitals will be bound to acquire the breadth of viewpoint necessary to serve as the leaders of community centers for the delivery of all types of health service.

The Advancement to Community Health Centers. We have spoken of a struggle discernible in America between the conception of the hospital as a "doctor's workshop" and its potential role as a "community health center." There is enough contention between medical staffs and hospital administrations to keep reminding us of this controversy, but the weight of the evidence points to ascendency of the community health center concept and the likelihood of its greater importance in the years ahead.

The endless flow of developments in organized health services— through both legislation and private initiative—all have their impact in advancing the general hospital toward a community health center role. The Medicare and Medicaid programs are giving almost every hospital a function in serving the poor, even in states where such care was previously segregated in special public institutions. The regional medical programs (for heart disease, cancer, and stroke) are heightening the liaison of small hospitals with the large medical centers. Expanding government support for health manpower training is underwriting more edu-

[37] Edward H. Forgotson and Ruth Roemer, "Government Licensure and Voluntary Standards for Health Personnel and Facilities," *Medical Care*, 6:345–54 (September–October 1968).

[38] Harvey L. Smith, "Two Lines of Authority are One Too Many," *Modern Hospital* (March 1955): 59–64.

[39] Herman M. Somers and Anne R. Somers, *Medicare and the Hospitals: Issues and Prospects* (Washington: Brookings Institution, 1967), p. 284.

cational programs in hospitals, just as increased research grants are supporting more clinical and laboratory investigations. National mental health legislation is encouraging more psychiatric services in general hospitals, and extensions of the vocational rehabilitation program are broadening various rehabilitation activities in them. Comprehensive health planning agencies in each state, under the inducement of federal grants, are calling on hospitals to plan their futures with greater deliberation. With private group practice growing, more medical groups are seeking affiliation with hospitals. The demands of patients at emergency rooms are compelling more systematic arrangements for those services. Endless technological developments are raising expectations, and therefore norms, for the organization of intensive care units, laboratory and x-ray screening programs, and a widening scope of functions in all clinical departments.

Thus, the concept of the "community health center" has come to mean a locale for the delivery of all types of health service. In 1957 the World Health Organization defined this as "the role of hospitals in programs of community health protection,"[40] This role was defined as including in-patient and out-patient restorative service (including diagnosis, treatment, rehabilitation, emergency care, etc.), preventive service (including maternal and child health supervision, health education, communicable disease control, etc.), professional education, and medical and administrative research. It is the same broad role we speak of idealistically in the United States. Its implementation obviously depends on the patterns of internal administration and especially the organization of the medical staff.

While widening its functions along all the social channels reviewed, the hospital is also playing a steadily greater role in the professional life of the private physician. The American doctor is admitting to hospitals an increasing proportion of his patients. With the vast extension of hospital insurance, the average annual number of hospital admissions per doctor rose from 61.4 in 1940 to 111.5 in 1959.[41] This increasing use of hospitals is even greater in regions of lower doctor-population ratio, suggesting that the hospital is used to conserve the time of the busy practitioner.[42] Thus, the more that people increase their demands on doctors, and the busier doctors become, the more they both come in contact with hospitals—all of which enhances further the hospital's community impact.

[40] World Health Organization, *Role of Hospitals in Programmes of Community Health Protection*, First Report of the Expert Committee on Organization of Medical Care. Technical Report Series No. 122 (Geneva, 1957).

[41] American Medical Association, Council on Medical Service, "Physician-Hospital Relations," *J.A.M.A.*, 190:74–79 (5 October 1964).

[42] Milton I. Roemer, "Hospital Utilization and the Supply of Physicians," *J.A.M.A.*, 178:989–93 (9 December 1961).

There is another role sometimes implied in the term "community health center" that should be distinguished from that just described. It is the role of planning and co-ordinating all health services in a community or geographic area—services emanating from all the general and special hospitals, the local practitioners, the pharmacies, the welfare agencies, the health insurance or social security organizations, the voluntary health societies, the industrial health establishments, the schools, and all the other agencies involved in the delivery or financing of health care. This task belongs not to the hospital, but to the local public health agency.[43] Indeed, the future of health departments lies not in direct provision of health services, either preventive or curative, so much as in this planning and co-ordinating role, as well as standard-setting and surveillance over all health services in their geo-political jurisdictions. In carrying out this broad social role, the health department would have to work increasingly closely with hospitals, as jointly proposed (though with little achievement so far) twenty years ago by the American Hospital Association and the American Public Health Association.[44] If the health department is to fulfill such legal and organizational responsibilities in a county or region, it will have to depend on the effective performance of hospitals for the actual delivery of services.

From this research it is evident that advancement of the hospital toward the concept of a community center for delivery or provision of all types of health service will bear a reciprocal relationship to its medical staff organization. The widening community role will induce more rigorous MSO patterns, while such patterns will facilitate and even encourage hospitals to take on greater responsibilities. The stage of doctor-hospital interdependency has been reached, where, for the first time, the Director of the American Hospital Association could advocate that physicians should be made members of hospital boards of trustees, in order to participate—as informed citizens—in policy decisions.[45] The great diversity of MSO patterns we see in the United States today, ranging from very loosely to very highly structured models, is simply a reflection of the evolutionary process in a pluralistic culture, combining many streams of public and private activities. All the evidence, however, points to a steady movement of medical staff organization toward the more highly structured patterns which will best enable hospitals to perform effectively the functions expected of them by society.

[43] American Public Health Association, "The Organization of Medical Care and the Health of the Nation," *Amer. J. Public Health*, 54:147–52 (January 1964).

[44] American Hospital Association and American Public Health Association, "Co-ordination of Hospitals and Health Departments," *Amer. J. Public Health*, 38:700–7 (May 1948).

[45] Edwin L. Crosby, "The Physician's Place in Health Care Administration," *Hospitals* (1 August 1968): 47–49.

APPENDIX—METHODOLOGY

This study explores a problem in the social science field of complex organizations—specifically, the dynamics of organization of doctors in hospitals. From the viewpoint of medicine, it examines one aspect of health service delivery—the relationship of various patterns of medical staff organization to the output or performance of hospitals. A problem of this type is much more complicated by secondary variables than most research tasks in the natural sciences, where a narrowly definable factor can be isolated and examined at a laboratory bench or in the clinical wards of a hospital.

To cope with a question of such complexity, it was deemed necessary to approach it along several routes, using different feasible techniques. Broadly speaking, three separate research approaches were used, which may be epitomized as (a) scholastic; (b) statistical survey; and (c) "anthropological." Even though these three approaches are not entirely mutually exclusive, and more than one of them has sometimes been applied to certain sections of the study, it will be clearest to describe each approach separately.

THE SCHOLASTIC APPROACH

In this, as in other socio-medical research, much was learned simply by studying professional literature in the field—literature describing the observations of others. The historical phase of the study (chapter II) obviously depended on such scholastic review. Likewise, a certain portion of the international comparisons of medical staff organization (chapter III) was based on study of published reports. So also was the account in chapter I, on the social determinants of hospital programs in America. In 1960 when this study was started, however, there was only one book in the American literature specifically focused on the subject of medical staff organization in hospitals.[1] This book was devoted largely to a presentation and explanation of proposed standards on the structure and function of medical staffs; while the recommendations were based, of course, on the general experience of the author, the book contained no empirical data.

[1] Thomas R. Ponton, *The Medical Staff in the Hospital* (Second edition; Chicago: Physicians' Record Company, 1953). The first edition was published in 1939.

Since 1960 two additional books have appeared in the United States on the problems of medical staffs in hospitals. One, published in 1964, is—like the pioneer work—essentially an elucidation of proposed standards.[2] The other is a collection of forty-nine papers, presented at a conference, on numerous specific aspects of medical staff organization and related problems of graduate medical education in hospitals.[3] Of studies based on empirical observation, several books have been published in recent years on over-all hospital dynamics, although none has focused on medical staff operations.[4] In these studies, the medical staff has generally been considered as one of the three power centers in the American voluntary hospital—the other two being the board of directors and the hospital administrator—and light has been shed on the relationships among these three entities. The contributions of these works have been useful in our research.

In current scientific research—in the social sciences no less than the natural —there is a tendency to deprecate conclusions drawn from readings alone. The "armchair" philosopher is scoffingly compared to the empirical scientist. Nevertheless, the sophisticated scientist must draw upon the published observations of others and must relate these to his own observations. By piecing together findings from many sources, he may be able to establish significant new relationships previously missed. In the other two approaches of this research, explained below, the perspective provided by the scholastic approach has been a leavening influence.

THE STATISTICAL SURVEY

With limitation in research funds and staff, and with great complexity in the phenomena being studied, it is usually necessary to take short-cuts in the collection of data. One of the commonest is to identify certain limited characteristics of a phenomenon and to measure and tabulate these over a relatively large number of cases. Statistical correlations may then be explored. This is essentially the "survey technique" used in epidemiology, sociology, and other disciplines. In this study, the statistical survey technique was used in several connections, the most important being a nationwide survey of "contractual physicians" in general hospitals, the findings of which are reported in chapter IV. The strategy of this survey should be explained in some detail, keeping in mind the substantive issue on contractual physicians in hospitals, discussed in chapter I.

Rendering descriptions of administrative arrangements into quantitative terms is difficult enough, and finding numerical measures of the quality of

[2] Charles U. Letourneau, *The Hospital Medical Staff* (Chicago: Starling Publications, 1964).

[3] C. Wesley Eisele (editor), *The Medical Staff in the Modern Hospital* (New York: McGraw-Hill Book Company, 1967).

[4] See for example: B. S. Georgopoulos and F. C. Mann, *The Community General Hospital* (New York: Macmillan, 1962); also: Ivan Belknap and John Steinle, *The Community and Its Hospitals* (Syracuse: Syracuse University Press, 1963); also: Eliot Friedson (editor), *The Hospital in Modern Society* (Glencoe, Illinois: Free Press, 1963); also: Arthur B. Moss, W. G. Broehl, R. H. Guest, and J. H. Hennessey, *Hospital Policy Decisions: Process and Action* (New York: G. P. Putnam's Sons, 1966).

medical care is even harder. The performance of a "professional audit" within a single hospital is a long complex process, and our effort here was to characterize hundreds of hospitals. As in classical epidemiology, we decided to make a virtue of necessity and collect limited data from a relatively large number of cases, without deep probing of any particular case. We set out to determine the proportion of contractual physicians in general hospitals, and then to explore its relationship to various other hospital characteristics.[5]

Our first task, then, was to define the sample of hospitals we would examine. We decided on all general hospitals in the United States of a fifty-bed capacity or more. This size limitation permitted us to exclude almost half of the total of 6,040 general hospitals in the country at the time (excluding those for mental disease or tuberculosis, thereby making the data more manageable, while eliminating the small hospitals in which contractual physicians play little part anyway. This universe of 3,400 general hospitals, under all types of auspices, were then addressed with a letter and questionnaire. This was in the form of a table, containing 104 cells, in which the hospital administrator was asked to write the number of each type of physician engaged by his hospital for specified services. The structure of this questionnaire-table is given in Figure 1. (The numbers in the cells of this table will be explained below.) Through this relatively simple device, it was possible to obtain information on contractual physicians along three dimensions: (1) the specialty classification according to thirteen categories; (2) the method of remuneration analyzed into four categories; and (3) the time-status, whether full-time or part-time.

Hospitals in the United States are weary of receiving questionnaires from various sources. We paved the way for this national mailing by two steps. First we conducted a simple pilot study, by postcard-questionnaire in New York State. We published the numerical findings (not any correlations with hospital performance) in a national journal received by practically every hospital administration in the country.[6] Second, we wrote an advance letter to each of the forty-eight hospital associations in the continental United States, explaining our study and asking co-operation. Whether due to this preparation, the simplicity of the questionnaire, or simply the high level of interest in the subject of the study, our letters yielded responses from 2,850 general hospitals, or some 84 per cent of the universe. It was possible to keep the questionnaire simple because of the availability of much other data on general hospitals from the American Hospital Association. From its Annual Inventory, we were able to get information on numerous hospital characteristics, reflecting performance, which could be correlated with the findings on contractual physicians.[7]

The quantification of a hospital's policies and practices with respect to contractual physicians was not easy. It would be naïve to simply add up numbers

---

[5] An earlier report of this methodology was: Milton I. Roemer, "Medical Staff Organization in General Hospitals of the U.S.A., The Influence of Contractual Physicians," in *Epidemiology—Reports on Research and Teaching 1962*, J. Pemberton, editor (London: Oxford University Press, 1963).

[6] Milton I. Roemer and Max Shain, "Contractual Physicians in General Hospitals: A Pilot Study in New York State," *Hospitals* (1 May 1960): 38–43.

[7] American Hospital Association, *Hospitals: Guide Issue* (1 August 1960).

FIGURE 1.

Code _____

CORNELL UNIVERSITY

Graduate School of Business and Public Administration

SLOAN INSTITUTE OF HOSPITAL ADMINISTRATION

QUESTIONNAIRE on PHYSICIANS under "CONTRACT" with HOSPITALS

Instructions: If your hospital has an agreement or contract to pay one or more physicians for specified work, please record the *NUMBER* of such physicians in the box or boxes assigned to each specialty and for each method of remuneration, whether full-time or part-time. Please do *not* include interns or residents in training.

Physician's Specialty	Number of Specialists Whom Hospital Pays By:							
	Fixed Salary		Percentage of Departmental Income		Fee-for-Service Plan		Salary combined with other method	
	Full-Time	Part-Time	Full-Time	Part-Time	Full-Time	Part-Time	Full-Time	Part-Time
Pathology	3	1	2	1	1	0	2	1
Radiology	3	1	2	1	1	0	2	1
Anaesthesia	4	1	2	1	1	0	3	1
Physical Medicine	4	2	2	1	1	0	3	1
Medical Education	6	3	—	—	—	—	4	2
Administration	4	2	—	—	—	—	3	1
Medical Research	3	1	—	—	—	—	2	1
Internal Medicine (including medical specialties)	7	2	3	1	1	0	5	2
Surgery (including surgical specialties)	7	2	3	1	1	0	5	2
Obstetrics and Gynecology	7	2	3	1	1	0	5	2
Pediatrics	7	2	3	1	1	0	5	2
Psychiatry	5	2	2	1	1	0	4	2
Other Fields	3	1	2	1	1	0	2	1

Name of hospital _____ City and State _____

Date _____ Signed _____

Remarks (if any): _____

Kindly return this chart to CORNELL UNIVERSITY in the enclosed stamped envelope.

of such medical personnel, with different specialties, time-status, and methods of payment, without making allowance for the varying significance of each of these variables in the American scene. We coped with the problem by designing a scoring system, the theme of which was to give a specified weight to the content of each cell shown in Figure 1, ranging from 7 points down to 0. (These numerical weights are shown in the corner of each cell.) The weights were assigned according to an estimate of the contribution to systematic structuring of the medical staff, reflected by the type of personnel enumerated in each cell. Thus, a contractual physician in internal medicine or surgery was given greater weight than one in radiology or pathology, since the latter are commonplace and the former represent a much more daring approach to staff organization in the American scene. Likewise, a full-time salary method of remuneration was given greater weight than the other systems of payment, since it constitutes a more organized and less individualistic pattern. A whole chain of local negotiations and power relationships, involving physicians, hospital board members, and administrators, is implied in the decisions along the continuum of both the specialty and the remuneration method. Thus, the relationship of *changing* medical staff patterns to hospital performance could be more delicately measured.

But what about the absolute numbers of contractual physicians in any cell of our table, which would naturally be greater in larger-sized hospitals? Adjustments to hospital-size were made by simply dividing the weighted sum of contractual physicians in each hospital by the number of beds. The final scores, therefore, were intended to be comparable without distortion due to hospital-size. At a later stage of the research we came to realize that this form of simple, linear adjustment probably over-corrected for hospital size. For reasons explained in chapter V, it probably had the effect of weakening our own hypothesized relationship between the "contractual physician score" and measures of hospital performance. Accordingly, the findings reported in chapter IV are all the more impressive, since their computation down-graded excessively the contractual physician score of the larger-sized hospitals.

When the returns from the 2,850 hospitals were analyzed, it was found that certain modifications were necessary to yield reliable correlations. Regarding sponsorship, it was discovered that proprietary hospitals (relatively few in number) frequently misinterpreted our questionnaire and recorded *any* physicians with admission privileges as being "under contract." It was deemed best, therefore, to exclude these from the analysis. For another reason we decided to exclude hospitals of the Army and Navy—although Veteran's, Public Health Service, and other government general hospitals were included. The military hospitals were, of course, very high in their contractual physician scores, but frequently did not even participate in certain accreditation and approval programs (see below), by which the total series of hospitals were being evaluated.

Regarding the designation of specialists, certain other decisions had to be made. In a word, only fully trained physicians were included. Thus, interns and residents were excluded, as nurse-anesthetists, dentists, Ph.D's in any science, chiropodists, or other nonphysicians. Certain "ground rules" were followed on part-time physicians, counting each as one-third, except when the number was so large (in relation to the hospital's bed-size) as to suggest the plausibility of an even lesser fraction. Specialties like dermatology or urology, not specified in the original questionnaire, were assigned to other headings, such as medicine or surgery. Contractual physicians whose duty was simply to read electrocardiograms or metabolism tests were assigned the same weighting (usually part-time) as radiologists.

As for the methods of payment of specialists, several problems arose because of the variability and complexity of these arrangements in the American scene, and special analytical ground rules had to be applied. The definition of a contractual payment had to be broadened in many institutional settings to include remuneration from a third-party agency other than the hospital itself. This might be direct payment by a university, a government agency, or an independent medical clinic for work done in the hospital. The important point was that these physicians were paid by an organization and not by the individual patient, and they were working in an organized framework rather than as private entrepreneurs.

The next step in this survey analysis was also difficult—to classify hospitals by certain indices of the type or quality of care they give. To do this, data were obtained from the American Hospital Association on a series of characteristics reflecting performance. Though admittedly crude, this approach is perhaps as justified as the methods of classical epidemiology, in which a person is classified by his age, occupation, smoking habits, or marital status, when we know very well that numerous *other* variables are associated with each of these traits and may be responsible for causal relationships suggested. Thus, we considered seven sets of hospital performance characteristics and twenty-six specific activities or facilities, the rationales of which are discussed along with the statistical findings in chapter IV. Here it may simply be noted that no aggregate score on "performance" was computed, but each of the hospital features was separately related to the contractual physician scores.

Correlations among these two sets of data on our sample of 2,850 general hospitals—data on contractual physicians and on features of hospital performance—were then explored by ranking the series of hospitals sequentially according to their C.P. scores, and then dividing them into quartiles from low to high. In each quartile the percentage of hospitals with each of the twenty-six performance features (or for a few features, the mean rate or ratio) was calculated. The relationship could thus be determined between the level of C.P. score and the presence of various features associated with high-level performance.

This statistical survey of large number of hospitals, with regard to a small number of characteristics, yielded data for other analyses as well. One of these, on the detailed relationship of radiologists in hospitals, has been published separately.[8] Another separately published study, using a similar statistical survey approach, examined the relationship of medical staff bylaws, which were scored, to various performance indicators in ninety-two hospitals.[9]

Tangential to this research, we also set out to find a more ultimate measure

[8] Milton I. Roemer, "Radiologists and Hospitals—Survey Reflects Trends," *Your Radiologist* (Winter 1965): 5–10.

[9] Roland C. Bower and Milton I. Roemer, "Medical Staff Organization in the Smaller Hospital," *Hospital Management* (September 1963): 46–47 (part I) and (October 1963): 56–58 (part II).

of hospital performance, in terms of the final outcome of services to patients. The twenty-six measurements used in the contractual physician study are all *suggestive* of good quality care, but they do not tell us about the final rate of recovery of patients from their ailments. To tackle this problem, we set out to find a method of adjusting the crude death rate of hospitals (i.e., deaths as a percentage of admissions per year), so that proper account was taken of the varying severity of cases entering different institutions. This was done by collecting information on admissions, deaths, and other factors from thirty-three hospitals, and a formula was derived to compute *adjusted* death rates as an outcome measurement of the net quality of hospital performance. The paper reporting this study has also been published separately.[10]

THE "ANTHROPOLOGICAL" APPROACH—CASE STUDIES

The major approach of this research used a higher observational focus on a small series of hospitals. Because the number of variables affecting both medical staff organization and hospital performance are so great, we supplemented the statistical survey technique with a much more comprehensive examination of numerous variables in a manageably smaller number of cases.

Selection of the Hospitals. Thus, ten general hospitals were selected in which "anthropological" investigations were carried out. These hospitals were deliberately chosen to represent the full range of types of medical staff organizations, so that the relationship of MSO to hospital performance could be explored in detail. Because of the constraints of time and money, these intensive case studies were done on hospitals located in California, close to our university.

In contrast to the statistical survey approach, the case studies of a small series of hospitals permitted us to collect much detailed information in each hospital setting. The complexities of each medical staff and each hospital program could be examined in ways that simple "yes or no" answers from mailed questionnaires could never reveal. Field visits lasting several weeks in each hospital were carried out, interviews were conducted with dozens of key persons, and written data on hospital operations of all sorts were assembled. From these sources, it was possible to prepare detailed "anthropological" descriptions of each hospital studied.

The selection of ten general hospitals from the universe of 6,000 such facilities in the United States or about 600 in California posed some difficult methodological questions. First of all, our purpose was not to draw a picture of the universe through a random sample, but rather to analyze examples of specific types of hospitals. As in much anthropological research, we think the ten hospitals studied in depth can be defended as reasonable examples of the types of species we were seeking to describe and compare.[11]

[10] Milton I. Roemer, A. Taher Moustafa, and Carl E. Hopkins, "A Proposed Hospital Quality Index: Hospital Death Rates Adjusted for Case Severity," *Health Services Research*, 3:96–118 (Summer 1968).

[11] Barney G. Glaser and Anselm Strauss, *The Discovery of Grounded Theory: Strategies for Qualitative Research* (Chicago: Aldine Publishing Company, 1967), pp. 101–16.

Our entry to the task of selection of hospital "cases" was the working assumption, based on the contractual physician survey and other observations, that there is a range of degrees of medical staff structuring in hospitals. We considered medical staff organization to be definable along a scale from loosely structured or permissive to highly structured or rigorous, as elaborated in chapter V. To simplify the selection process we stipulated five levels along this scale, and we set out to find examples of two hospitals at each MSO level. In these, both the MSO and the features of hospital performance would be analyzed. It is important to recognize, however, that we did not permit any prior impressions of the level of hospital performance, as such, to influence our selection of the hospitals.

Los Angeles County, California, contained in 1963 about 170 general hospitals. Limited data on all of these were gathered from several sources: the Division of Hospitals of the California State Department of Public Health, the Hospital Council of Southern California, the Annual Inventory of the American Hospital Association, and the hospitals themselves. Applying the concept of MSO structuring, preliminary assignment of most of the hospitals was made to a place on this scale. This was done partly through our accumulated knowledge of the hospitals and partly through consultation with other impartial and knowledgeable observers. Inevitably, we selected hospitals of different sponsorships—not because we were studying sponsorship as such, but because it was quite obvious that sponsorship (governmental, voluntary nonprofit, or proprietary) influences the level of medical staff organization. Likewise, our selections inevitably resulted in a series of hospitals of different sizes.

It could be argued theoretically that a pure determination of the influence of MSO on hospital performance should attempt to hold constant in the series both hospital sponsorship and size, so that any cause-and-effect relationship could not be attributed to these two factors. The difficulty with this reasoning, as in so much of social science research, is that it would ignore the prevailing relationships of the real world. The fact is that higher-MSO structuring does tend to be associated with governmental sponsorship and large size, and looser-MSO structuring is usually found in voluntary and proprietary hospitals of small size. If one wishes to explore the effects of MSO structuring on hospital performance, therefore, one must realistically accept these background concomitant factors. By strictly logical inference, this approach inhibits firm conclusions, but it permits us to examine relationships between hospital performance and a "gestalt" of independent or causative variables, of which medical staff organization is clearly an intervening one. Moreover, we focused our attention on those aspects of hospital performance that may be plausibly and proximally related to the organization of doctors, even though sponsorship, size, or other background variables may also contribute to the outcome.[12]

With respect to one underlying characteristic, however, we did attempt to hold constant all the selections in our series of ten hospitals. We wished to be sure that our examples would not represent a qualitatively "good" example of

---

[12] Brian MacMahon, T. F. Pugh, and J. Ipsen, *Epidemiologic Methods* (Boston: Little Brown and Company, 1960); "The Web of Causation," pp. 18–21.

one MSO type of hospital and a "poor" example of another type. The most objective criterion for such judgment was the hospital's status with the Joint Commission on Accreditation of Hospitals; thus, we selected only hospitals with JCAH accreditation. Beyond this, we attempted to make sure, from discussions with several independent observers, that each of the ten hospitals had a general reputation of merit in its size and sponsorship class.

Needless to say, the final selection of a hospital for the detailed case studies depended on its willingness to participate in this research. To obtain the ten participating hospitals finally studied, we had to approach fifteen altogether. The five that refused did so generally because of current sensitivities about relationships between their medical staffs and the hospital administrative authorities; they feared having dirty linen washed in public. Thus, it can be said that all ten of the participating hospitals had relatively stable doctor–hospital relationships at the time of study. Moreover, if a hospital did not regard its own performance as relatively good, it would very likely have been unwilling to participate in the research. These elements of partial "self-selection," therefore, should not distort our small series of ten cases, but should actually heighten the comparability of the hospitals in the series.

We thus ended up with ten general hospitals of different sponsorships and sizes, but each presumably exemplifying good performance in its class. The salient differences, from our point of view, were in the structuring of the medical staffs. Although, as noted, our intention was to find two hospitals within each of five grades of MSO structuring, when more refined MSO quantification was done it turned out that one of the five grades (Type IV) contained only one hospital and another grade (Type V) contained three. Otherwise, there were two hospitals in each grade and, in any event, some representation of at least one hospital at all five grades of MSO structuring. Moreover, as will be evident in chapters VI and VII, the ten facilities in our series also represent the principal types of general hospital size and sponsorship found in the United States.

Data-gathering in Each Hospital. To collect information on (a) medical staff organization and (b) the features of hospital performance in these ten hospitals, two detailed research instruments were constructed. The first step was a very preliminary pre-test of a brief eight-page schedule of questions, applied in four general hospitals of upstate New York. Then, we developed two lengthy questionnaires on MSO and on hospital performance (about 100 pages each), based on consultation of several standard textbooks of hospital administration, other studies of medical staff organization, the data-collection schedule of the Joint Commission on Accreditation of Hospitals, and various other documents. Eventually, these were reduced to forty pages each, were pre-tested in two California hospitals, and finally were applied as the basis for interviews and other data-gathering in the ultimate series of ten hospitals.

It would be tedious to read a reproduction of the two data-collection schedules used. Some of the questions were quite specific, while others were open-ended. Some called for submission of official records and reports prepared by the hospital. The nature of the questions can be gathered from the material presented in the full case-study findings of chapter VI.

In the actual research a full "anthropological" account of 60 to 100 typed pages was prepared for each of the ten hospitals in the study, although only in chapter VI are the findings presented in relatively unabridged form. Only the main characteristics of the nine other case-study hospitals are summarized in chapter VII. In the subsequent three chapters, (VIII, IX and X) "horizontal" comparative analyses of the principal findings are offered on both MSO and hospital performance.

Before finalizing, a draft of each case-study report was resubmitted to the administrator of the hospital. Errors of fact were, of course, corrected, although occasionally and quite naturally there were some differences of opinion on the interpretation of certain points of information gathered from personnel other than the hospital administrator himself. In such circumstances, we had to use our best judgment on the true state of affairs. While we have attempted to assure confidentiality to each hospital, as well as to the individual respondents within a hospital, this may have been unachievable for certain hospitals of a singular type. Our viewpoint throughout, however, attempted to be neutral and yet sympathetic, seeking to understand and explain the circumstantial reasons for everything we found.

As explained in chapter I, the "output" of medical staff organization in hospitals is conceived as the "performance" of the institution in terms of several definable activities: (a) in-patient care; (b) out-patient service; (c) professional education; (d) medical research; and (e) preventive and community services. It may be noted that we have made little direct measurement of the rate of recovery of patients from their disorders—except for the limited data on death rates adjusted for case severity; nor have we examined the quality of patient care in our series of hospitals by the conventional "medical audit" techniques.[13] Our real goal in this research, however, is to understand the impact on the substantive hospital *program*, the scope of functions of a hospital that may be contributed by the scheme of work of its doctors. It is this meaning of "hospital performance" that we consider most salient in relation to variations in the patterns of medical staff organization.

While of much smaller proportions than the California hospital case studies, the comparative analysis of medical staff organization and hospital programs in certain European countries reported in chapter III was based also on "anthropological" field investigations. During the summers of 1960 and 1961, visits were made to two or three general hospitals in each of seven countries.[14] The selections of institutions were made by officials in each country's ministry of health, in response to the request for permission to visit a medium-size hospital more or less "typical" of the prevailing pattern in the country. In each hospital information was gathered by interview with the top medical and administrative officers. Further information was gathered from published reports and from discussions with officials in the ministry of health.

The weaknesses in our methodology throughout this study are only too evi-

---

[13] Leonard S. Rosenfeld, "Quality of Medical Care in Hospitals," *Amer. J. Public Health*, 47:856–65 (July 1957).

[14] Milton I. Roemer, "The Impact of Hospitals on the Practice of Medicine in Europe and America," *Hospitals* (1 November 1963): 61–66.

dent to the investigators themselves. All social research, however, is thorny, and we offer this study as at least an initial attempt to probe an aspect of health care organization that has assumed critical importance in recent years. We hope that the combination of research approaches—the scholastic, the statistical survey, and the "anthropological" design—may shed some light which any one of these approaches alone would have done with less assurance. We leave to other investigators the perfection of methodologies which will provide answers with greater certainty.[15]

[15] Edward A. Suchman, *Evaluative Research: Principles and Practice in Public Service and Social Action Program* (New York: Russell Sage Foundation, 1967).

INDEX

Abbe, L. M., 22n

Abdellah, F. G., 247n

Accreditation, 21. *See also* Joint Commission on Accreditation of Hospitals

ACS. *See* American College of Surgeons

Active staff, relative size and proportion of total staff, 204–6

Adair, F. E., 45n

Administrative power. *See* Informal dynamics

Administrator, conflicts of, 141–42; functions of, 145–46, 166, 175, 222–23; leadership of, 108, 113, 118–19, 137, 151, 186–87, 283; and quality of care, 131, 298–99. *See also* Conflicts; Informal dynamics; Issues; Medical director

Admission rates, and hospital cost, 288

Admission tests, 75, 235

Admissions, of Pebble City Community Hospital, 11, 120–21, 174, 182, 195; per doctor, 300

Adoptions, 274

Advanced care unit, 127–28, 246, 273

Affiliations, institutional, 215; of hospitals with medical schools, 74, 201; of medical staff, 89, 96, 111, 155, 179

Agnew, G. H., 7n

AMA. *See* American Medical Association

Ambulatory care, 47, 178, 238, 259–61, 263

American Academy of Pediatrics, 238n

American Academy of Political and Social Science, xiiin

American College of Physicians, 40

American College of Surgeons, and the hospital standardization movement, 35–41; and performance of hospitals, 71; surveillance by, 21; 35n

American Hospital Association, advocacy of physicians on hospital boards, 301;

conflict with AMA, 3; support of standards, 21, 38, 40; 7n, 9n, 10n, 40n, 81n, 85n, 218n, 225n, 257n, 273n, 295n, 301n, 304n

American Medical Association, attitude toward standardization movement, 38; evaluation of VA hospitals, 201; on hospital as center of medical care system, 85; opposition to prepaid group practice, 172; organization of, 34; policy on physician-hospital relationship, 2, 284; 2n, 267n, 284n, 300n

American Public Health Association, 301; 301n

Anesthesia, as a supportive medical service, 242–43

Anesthesiologist, as contractual physician, 216; influence on surgeons, 217; remuneration of, 126, 155, 164, 242. *See also* Nurse-anesthetist

Anesthesiology, department of, at Pebble City Community Hospital, 126; residents in government hospitals, 242

Appointment, to medical staff, 145, 147, 149, 152, 155, 162–64, 176–78, 188, 197; description of procedure, 88; obligations of, 210–11; privileges of, 208–10; purpose of, 44; relation to MSO score, 280; selection process of, 206–8

Apprenticeship, 34

Armstrong, G. E., 5n

Arnold, L. M., 249n

Audits. *See* Control committees; Medical audits

Australia, hospital authority patterns in, 50

Authority patterns, of hospitals, 49–54

Authority system, as a function of MSO, 89–90

Automation, of patient data, 140